Bush Pioneers and the Changed Face of Australia

Doug Morrissey

Connor Court Publishing

Bush Pioneers and the Changed Face of Australia

Doug Morrissey

Published in 2022 by Connor Court Publishing Pty Ltd

Copyright © Doug Morrissey 2022

All rights reserved. No part of this book may be reproduced or transmitted in any form or by any means, electronic or mechanical, including photo copying, recording or by any information storage and retrieval system, without prior permission in writing from the publisher.

Connor Court Publishing Pty Ltd
PO Box 7257
Redland Bay QLD 4165
sales@connorcourt.com
www.connorcourt.com

Printed in Australia

ISBN: 9781922815033

Cover image: JAMES ALFRED TURNER, Working For A Selector 1886.

Wikipedia Commons

Images in text used with permission.

Dedicated to the Bush Pioneers and the contribution they made to the prosperity and accomplishments of the nation.

Pioneers

They came of bold and roving stock that would not fixed abide; They were the sons of field and flock since e'er they learnt to ride; we may not hope to see such men in these degenerative years, as those explorers of the bush the brave old pioneers.

'Twas they who rode the trackless bush in heat and storm and drought; 'twas they who heard the master's word that called them further out; 'twas they who followed up the trail the mountain cattle made, and pressed across the mighty range where now their bones are laid.

But now the times are dull and slow, the brave old days are dead, when hardy bushmen started out and forced their way ahead, by tangled scrub and forest grim towards the unknown west, and spied the far-off promised land from off the range's crest.

Oh! ye that sleep in lonely graves by far off ridge and plain; we drink to you in silence now as Christmas comes again; to you who fought the wilderness through rough unsettled years — the founders of our nation's life, the brave old pioneers.

Andrew Barton (Banjo) Paterson

S T Gill Overlanders Circa 1865 National Museum of Australia

Contents

Acknowledgements   9
Foreword by John Howard former Prime Minister of Australia   11
Introduction   13

Part One: Gippsland Bush Pioneers   17
1   Growing up in the Strzelecki Ranges   18
2   Korumburra Pioneers   41
3   Coalminers, Crooks and Delinquents   61
4   Tambo Crossing and Warragul Pioneer Stories   71
5   Cobb and Co: A Gippsland Coach Journey 1873   83

Part Two: Irishmen, Pioneer Women and Anzacs   88
6   Irish Catholics, Daniel Mannix and Ireland   89
7   Priests, Nuns and Christian Brothers   105
8   Pioneer Women, Casterton and a Bush Lunatic   116
9   Anzacs Khaki Brave and Aussie True Blue   130

Part Three: Aborigines and the Colonial Frontier   142
10   Colonial Frontier Warfare   143
11   Aborigines and White Settlers   179
12   Cullin la Ringo, Hornet Bank and Faithfull Creek Massacres   197

Part Four: The Changed Face of Australia			212
13	Universities, Schools and the Demise of Australian History		213
14	Safe Schools, Gender Issues, Woke and Cancel Culture		233
15	Aborigines, Black Lives Matter: An era of Smoke and Mirrors		260
16	Migrants: Everyone was an Immigrant at Some Point		282
17	Climate Change, C02 and Renewables		295
18	A Sunburnt Country of Fire, Drought and Flooding Rain		324
19	It's as Simple as ABC — Australia Before China!		341
20	Quiet Australians and the Politically Correct Times in which We Live		354
Conclusion			266
Afterword			279
Bibliography of Recent Books			381
Index			385

Acknowledgements

My wife Joy acted as book editor and historical consultant her patient advice and literary skill made a difficult task easier. She has the common touch and reigned me in when needed and the book is better because of it. I thank former Prime Minister John Howard for writing a foreword to the book. Following in the footsteps of his father the late Bill Leak, Johannes Leak, has graciously allowed me to use his own and his father's satirical cartoons to illustrate the Changed Face of Australia section of the book.

Throughout the book there are extracts of poems, songs and stories written and composed by others. I acknowledge their copyright and thank the authors for their literary contributions which have made the book more entertaining and informative. The inspirational works of Henry Lawson, Andrew Banjo Paterson, Adam Lindsay Gordon, John O'Brien, C J Dennis and a host of others convey an intimate feeling of time and place that brings the past alive in a way most writers can only dream about. Their delightful word pictures are literary and poetical works of genius unsurpassed in the quest to recreate Australia's bygone days.

Gippsland Historian Patrick Morgan has been helpful in filling in the early history of the region. His books The *Settling of Gippsland: A Regional History* (1997) and *Shadow and Shine: An Anthology of Gippsland Literature* (1988) provided me with much insight and understanding of Gippsland settlers. Thank you, Patrick, for your wonderful books, the discerning history and deep love of Gippsland and its inhabitants.

I owe a special debt of gratitude to the late Dr John Hirst and Dr Inga Clendinnen, exceptional historians who taught me how to think critically and empathetically understand the past as it was daily lived and experienced. Both of them are solely missed in a time of academic submissiveness to fashionable social justice and political causes. In today's world the history of Australia's pioneers has been unfairly relegated to a dark 'racist' corner of the national curriculum. Studies in Aboriginal victimhood, migrant acclaim, gender diversity and post-colonial recrimination reign supreme. John and Inga had a broader and more penetrating view of history which was insightful and above all else humanist, fact-based and objective. I thank Professor Geoffrey Blainey and John Day for reading the manuscript and making valuable suggestions.

Jacinta Price and Warren Mundine are Indigenous Australians who view Australian history from a common sense, even-handed and truthful perspective. They are courageous, self-reliant individuals not afraid to speak up and call out the fraud of victimhood politics and symbolic tokenism wherever they encounter it. They are Indigenous leaders of distinction to be respected and admired by all Australians.

I write to preserve for everyday Australians a treasured pioneer past that is in danger of being erased from the national memory. It is an honour to acknowledge the pioneers. Like everybody they had their faults. However, they raised their children to be good citizens, respect others and to better themselves in mind and body. They passed onto the next generation a passionate love of Australia and a strong heritage of racial and cultural roots. These values led to self-awareness and bountiful nationhood. I write of an antipodean society that proudly remembered and valued its past as it optimistically looked forward towards a beckoning and bright future.

Foreword

Doug Morrissey has written a book which is in part social history and autobiographical. It is also systematic in its exposure of the false nostrums of much of today's anti-Western cult, which has gripped educational institutions and much of the media. His narrative of life within a rural community in South Gippsland reveals a legitimate pride in the pioneers of that and other parts of what we elsewhere in Australia call 'the bush'. Personal accounts graphically tell of those who struggled with and were ultimately overcome by recalling the horrors of wartime. They illustrate how anodyne is the description of Post Traumatic Stress Syndrome. They are moving stories.

Writing from the perspective of an Irish-Catholic family he puts his hand up for the decade of the fifties. Sectarianism was still very prevalent then, but these were also years of spreading prosperity and hope about the future, as Australia absorbed and successfully integrated hundreds of thousands of migrants under the rubric of assimilation. New arrivals embraced their adopted country, but there was always a place in the heart for the land of their birth. To many, the later however well-intentioned policy called multiculturalism, compromised that relatively simple approach. In the process Australia lost some of the unity of the 1950s.

As a splendid historian, Doug Morrissey is rightly appalled at the extent to which the proper instruction of students in even the rudiments of the actual story of Australia has been supplanted by a perverted doctrine, which is riddled with inaccuracies seemingly built on a hatred of who we are and where we came from. He highlights some of the absurdities. The enquiry, by an ABC journalist, of an expert chess player for a comment about the racial prejudice inherent in the white chess piece always leading off wins the prize.

Doug Morrisey has built an impressive defence of what our nation has achieved. This is all the more so because it is no misty-eyed version of our history. His flowing prose makes it very readable.

John Howard

Introduction

God bless America. God save the Queen. God defend New Zealand and Thank Christ for Australia!

Russell Crowe

The Australia of my childhood during the 1950s was a very different Australia from the country we live in today. It was a monoculture society, Christian in religion, priding itself on Aussie mateship, a fair go for all and predominantly Anglo/Celtic. Within the democratic consensus and perception of national identity, divisions existed between the working and middle classes, Catholics and Protestants, the Irish, English and Scots and an emerging post war European immigrant population. There was a sense of future prosperity and assimilation on the national agenda that today's politicians, with an emphasis on ethnic diversity and multiculturalism, tell us is still the goal of modern Australia.

In an era of Cold War politics, fear of communism and a general turning away from England towards America, unity not diversity was at the centre of Australian life. Prostitution was against the law. Homosexuality was morally shunned and illegal. Divorce required a courtroom trial of blame and shame. Abortion took place in backstreet venues. Equal pay for women and voting rights for all Aborigines were still to be achieved. Capital punishment was the law of the land for murder and heinous crime. In Victoria, due to a strong Protestant presence, gambling was illegal and six o'clock closing for pubs persisted until 1966. Censorship proclaimed what was considered acceptable behaviour and protected public morality. These things were taken for granted and were the community framework of everyday life. The British Empire was in decline, the Queen however was and still is our sovereign. The internet, emails and mobile phones were not yet the distracting focus of everybody's attention. It was not, as some reminisce and others criticise, a conservative golden age. Nor was it a time of social, political and cultural upheaval that the decade of the swinging 1960s was to usher in with a culturally unleashed vengeance.

My story is not about such things, at least not as issues leading to reform and change. I write of Australia as it was and as it perceived itself to be in a time now past. A nation, boundlessly optimistic, provincial in outlook and feeling its way in a world recovering from the trauma of two catastrophic wars and a global depression. There was trust and confidence in the nation and in ourselves as a Christian people with a manifest destiny to be achieved.

It is fashionable these days to talk of the 1950s as an era of cultural cringe and national stagnation. To those who lived through this period, especially as impressionable young children, there was no sense of cultural inferiority, no feeling of apathy or indecision. The world and society were there to be explored and understood, not to be ashamed of or complained about. The negative feelings instilled in today's young people who are told they should be embarrassed to be white and apologetic about the pioneering achievements of their ancestors was still in the future. It was a time of community hope and economic progress, where it was safe for children to walk to and from school, and play in the streets unsupervised until after dark. Front doors were rarely locked and neighbours knew and helped each other far better than they do today.

It was an Australia where the old country way of living was rapidly coming to an end. Within a decade it would be no more than a receding memory. For me it was the solid and steady world of childhood experience, neither questioned nor dwelt upon. A deep appreciation of the pioneers was embedded in the national psyche as something to be proud of. It is this vibrant, rural Australia I write of not as nostalgia or yearning for a long gone past, but as a series of vignettes recording the lives of everyday Australians who saw the world differently from the way we do today.

Introduction

The culture wars have turned a previously unified and patriotic Australia into a divided society of warring tribes. When allied with radical green politics and a global socialist agenda, the imported American term Woke, synonymous with political correctness, identity politics, climate change, cancel culture and virtue signalling, encompasses the Socialist/Green/Woke grouping referred to in the second half of book. The changed face of modern Australia is a place where free speech, traditional values, the nuclear family and the very idea of Christianity and western civilisation is under threat. Where being traditional and conservative in lifestyle and opinion is berated as inherently evil by the so-called progressive left, a political and cultural term that has lost all meaning in its totalitarian regression to doctrinaire communism.

The promised Woketopia of the radical left is a sterile, conformist and unimaginative future governed by mob recrimination, PC offence and authoritarian control. Where the uniqueness of the individual is undermined and a collectivist mediocrity extolled. This is a very poor substitute for the tried-and-true Aussie democracy, we are in danger of losing if this pernicious view prevails. Growing up in a socially and culturally stable Australia there was no hint of the woke instability to come. Australians knew who they were and supported one another despite racial, religious and political differences.

The information contained in the book comes from a multitude of sources. Published books, research monographs, newspaper and journal articles both online and hardcopy. Songs, poems, satirical cartoons, colonial government reports, personal memoirs, letters, historical society papers, census statistics and media interviews. Websites covering many issues relating to government, science, history, politics and family history have proven to be valuable sources of information. None of the information gathered from any source can be taken at face value. Everything has been checked and rechecked against validated knowledge to assess its accuracy and relevance.

Direct quotations from sources are rendered in italics and sometimes altered for greater clarity. If I were writing for a small academic audience, I would leave every quotation unaltered and adhere to scholarly strictures, but I am writing for a general audience. Occasionally sentences are joined together I correct grammar, punctuation and rectify spelling mistakes. I do not however alter the meaning of what a writer intends to convey to his audience. Reason and logic separate bogus invention from real world fact. The methodology and sources used throughout the book reject woke flights of fancy and political correctness in favour of expounding rationality and common sense.

Australia's pioneers have an extraordinary and revealing story to tell. An important story that needs to be told without white privilege and racist overtones obscuring their exceptional accomplishments. I seek to tell some of that story in the book for a generation of Australians in imminent danger of losing connection with the historical truth of their pioneer heritage. Today there is no one coherent national narrative acceptable to all. The pioneer past is denigrated by a noisy minority of political activists as something we should regret and be remorseful about to be maligned as inherently racist, genocidal and above all else deluded. The delusion is their own, as they seek to rob Australians of their pioneer past and national days of Aussie celebration. During my Gippsland childhood, I was acutely aware of the enduring and revered legacy of the pioneers, the hardships and the obstacles they faced with courage and perseverance and overcame against overwhelming odds. I thought then as I think now, they were remarkable men and women deserving of our respect and a truthful telling of their incredible story.

Part One

Gippsland Bush Pioneers

We Bushmen Know

We bushmen know what Henry (Lawson) means and understand his writing; for he expresses what we feel and does it without skiting. And we advise our only bard, and earnestly entreat him to heed not soulless city folks who can't or will not greet him.

They've never left the crowded street and haven't got a notion about the weird and solemn bush, the pathos and emotion. And 'Cockatoos' are far too dull to grasp a poet's saying; and think of nought but cows and pigs and where their hens are laying.

So why lament and get morose because those heartless tinkers can't understand the soulful songs so loved by men and thinkers. We bushmen know what Henry means and always feel delighted; when at the lonely western camps his poems they are recited.

Dick Steelman

1
Growing up in the Strzelecki Ranges

On easy grade and rubber tyre the tourist car goes through. They halt a moment and admire the farflung mountain view. The tourist folk would be amazed if they could get to know. They take the track Black Harry blazed 100 years ago.

A B Paterson

I grew up Australian, Irish and Catholic in the 1950s on a small dairy farm at Seaview along the Grand Ridge Road in the Strzelecki Ranges in South Gippsland, situated between the provincial towns of Korumburra and Warragul. I never saw the sea from the farm and as a child puzzled over why the district was called Seaview. Electricity was new to the neighbourhood and television a novelty that ran for only a few hours a day. The radio and newspapers brought entertainment and daily news of what was happening in the outside world. Farms were small with wooden houses usually painted white, outdoor toilets, occasional vegetable gardens, plenty of cows, some sheep, goats and other animals. The paddocks were covered with bracken ferns and in places swampy with clumps of thick reeds. Rabbit burrows multiplied and sometimes a wombat hole was to be found. Koalas sat in shady gumtrees and kookaburras laughed. Snakes thrived on Gippsland farms, district tales about reptile encounters were legendary.

The terrain was hilly and dangerous for tractor drivers traversing their properties. Joe an elderly returned serviceman and Gallipoli veteran, lost his life when his tractor overturned. He spent many hours pinned underneath before his crushed body was found. It was not for nothing that the grey Massey Ferguson (Fergie) tractor was known throughout rural Australia as the Widow Maker. The family was commiserated with by the neighbours, and the funeral and church service attended by the whole community. I was to have my own adventure with a grey tractor and clearly in my mind was old Joe's awful fate.

Our house, set in the side of a small hill, was painted green and white. It stood on timber foundations four feet high at the back door, which was reached by a succession of wooden steps and a porch. A row of mature pine trees separated the property from the road and acted as a windbreak. A long gravel drive led past the house to the dairy and a hayshed beyond. There were other small sheds, a chicken coop and a timber lean-to for the tractor and other farming equipment. The family's Ford V8 and Dad's old Indian motorcycle were left out in the weather to fend for themselves. Beyond the house paddock stretching down and along a wide gully, the rest of the property was roughly fenced, stony in parts and used as pastureland.

From the front bedroom window of the house an overgrown dam with a thick bulrush cover was visible. On hot summer nights, frogs could be heard croaking as they sought a mate. Snakes would slither around in the long grass. On one memorable occasion while playing among the tall pine trees, I encountered a large red-bellied black snake sunning itself and in no immediate hurry to depart. With mounting curiosity, I watched the reptile raise its flattened-out head with its red belly exposed preparing to strike. I turned and ran for the safety of the house.

My sister Mary and I use to play in the original settler's ramshackle hut, with its sawn timber boards and wooden shingles, warped and held together by a sturdy log frame. The inside walls were covered with calico sheets of fading printed flowers. The fireplace connected to a brick chimney had an iron swing grate with a large black kettle. It was dark, grimy and soiled with decades of smoke soot and ingrained dirt. The doorway and a single window were small, broken and open to the weather. A place of mystery and wonder it was easy to imagine the farmer and his wife were down the paddock and would soon return for supper. On one memorable occasion, we thought we saw and heard a ghost only to discover a grey and white barn owl in residence.

The hayshed some distance away, with its square bales of hay stacked close together in tightly knit rows 20 or 30 bales high, harboured a family of cats and kittens who would emerge at milking time for a milk can lid of fresh milk around which upwards of a dozen cats or more would congregate. Mary and I would try to capture and cuddle the kittens before they had time to escape back to the safety of their haybale hideout. The price we paid for our undertaking was claws, spitting and scratching, which left us with bleeding wounds and a stern parental rebuke to *leave those bloody cats alone!* Of course, we were back again next day to try our luck, with a similar result. Playing among freshly cut haybales seeking out fluffy kittens was a childhood pleasure without peer.

There was one animal escapade that Mary and I were never able to master and that was to corral and cuddle Min the goat and her seven kids. Like every goat, the troublesome Min and later her brood of kids ate everything in sight, escaped from wherever they were confined and did pretty much as they pleased. Fences and gates were no object to Min and her delinquent family, they charged straight through any weakness and we children believed they could even open gates. A lasting memory of Min and the kids is of helplessly watching them with their short tails raised in the air, running full pelt down the road to the safety of the bush beyond.

oooOOOooo

The memory of the past comes back to us in many ways. For some people it is visual and made compellingly real by competing images of colour and movement. The dreamlike imagery flooding in as jumbled bits and pieces of stories. The central aspect of memory comes to me as a vivid recollection of personal feeling associated with smell. The pervasive farmyard smell of freshly baled hay, half open bags of wheat and chaff, closely herded together cows and musty dairy odours. The freshly scrubbed smell of a cracked concrete floor washed and cleansed after every milking session. The kitchen smell of a freshly baked pie filling the senses with aromatic delight. The vivid recollection of summer fragrance, of flowering Grevillea and Callistemons, of frosty springtime mornings, of yellow scented wattles in bloom. Of icy winter fences, pristine white pastures, frozen hands and a chilled sharpness of breath. Of crinkly brown falling leaves decaying and scattered by soft autumn breezes. The menacing rawness and elemental power of an approaching storm.

My childhood memories are of natural rhythms and the invigorating smells of the Gippsland bush. Of carefree after school hours breathing in the scintillating bush aromas, of exploring and playing until darkness fell; inhabiting a magical spellbinding world of whimsical imagination. Where the physical realm intersected with fantasy and daydream. Real and steadfast for bush kids, the zest and zeal of country living. These were the good times permanently etched in childhood memory, freshly remembered today as yesterday.

Not everything was a good memory. There were also frightening times to be endured. One in particular, a ferocious night time thunder and lightning storm that uprooted trees, ripped up fences, tore down power poles and damaged houses and sheds. We could hear the roof of the diary unhinged and flapping in the wind, crashing up and down with a terrible force. The power went off, and it was a scary night sitting in a dim candle lit room with savage wind gales howling around the eaves, rain crashing in waves and heavy droplets against the window panes. The roof of the house rattling loudly, thumping under sustained attack, threatening to dislodge at any moment. Luckily, both the house and the diary roofs remained in place. The terror of this night of unbridled anguish and discomfort, was in some measure alleviated by Mum's toasted cheese sandwiches cooked on a small gas burner. A sublime experience in a moment of tense childhood anxiety.

Of lesser importance but worrying for a young boy was learning to ride a bike and later to drive a tractor. Riding a bike was a skill I mastered fairly quickly after several falls and a few minor cuts and bruises. Learning to drive our old Fergie tractor in hilly Gippsland country was another matter. With grating gears, poor brakes and a wide turning circle required, I was taught the basics of tractor driving and made aware of how dangerous it could be and remembered old Joe and his tragic accident. Only once after I had become proficient in handling a tractor, did I come close to overturning the machine with possible tragic consequences. I was carting haybales behind the tractor down the paddock for the cows. The steering locked on the edge of a rising slope and I was in trouble. I was sitting in the driver's seat in a dangerous situation. If the balance shifted to the left, in the words of a Slim Dusty song *It's over the edge and down the mountain side*. Luckily, I felt a slight correction in the steering wheel, which enabled me to return to safer ground. I said nothing to Mum and Dad, but was more cautious in future when approaching this hilly paddock.

oooOOOooo

The fondest memory I have of Strzelecki farm life is waking up on a crisp spring morning to the laughing sound of kookaburras and the warbling of magpies. It heralded the beginning of another day and was more important to the older generation of dairy farmers than alarm clocks and the radio. It signalled milking time was nigh. Our herd of milking cows numbered around 80 animals and each had a name and a distinct personality. Clarabelle, Gertie and Blaze come to mind. Blaze was a particularly cantankerous cow with a petulant will and testy stubbornness to match. In the milking yard when it came time to send Blaze into the dairy shed, we would stand and glare at each other, as Blaze deigned to decide whether or not she would allow me the privilege of herding her. On several occasions, I narrowly escaped a swift kick from her outstretched hindleg as she slowly and imperiously made her way to the stall to feed and be milked.

In calving season, we would average around 8 to 15 calves. When separated from their barely weened young calves, mother cows would call out for days. It was unsettling to lie in bed at night listening to the mournful bellowing. I remember the sadness I felt listening to plaintive moos echoing in the darkness, as I imagined the loneliness and confusion of young calves separated from their mothers. I buried my head deeper in the pillow and thought of other things.

Feeding calves with a bottle and rubber teat was a memorable childhood experience. My favourite was a Friesian bull calf named Blacky I raised by hand. At feed time, he used to follow me around the paddock butting his head against my stomach. As he grew older and more boisterous, I had to stay out of his way or risk being trampled. Mary would bottle feed her placid calf Cherry and all seemed right with the world. The calves were soon beyond our control and joined the herd or were sold off. I wept as a truck arrived one day and took away my Friesian friend to I know not where.

Twice a day at five in the morning and four in the afternoon, the small herd of heavily laden milking cows would make their way to the dairy stockyard to be milked and rewarded with wheat pollard and chaff. Winter was the worse time of all. The cows would arrive in the predawn light with frost on their backs and ice forming on their ears. Their breath would condense in the bitterly cold air and as they huddled together palls of steam would lightly rise from their bodies. I soon discovered that to get amongst the herd was smelly but warming. Nobody least of all bush children wore gloves on those cold winter days. I suffered from chilblains and the itching was exasperating. Later on, when I got my first pair of gloves, it was a luxury comparable to leaving boyhood's short pants behind for full-length grown-up trousers.

It was worse still to go about one's milking chores in a bitterly cold winter wind. I would crouch low in the stockyard using a cow's solid body as a temporary windbreak, while herding one or two into the dairy. The wind would howl, screech and relentlessly tear at the corrugated iron roof, unnerving the cows and making those being milked uncomfortable. One winter windstorm was so fierce during the night it tore half the roof from off the milking shed.

Shoes were never a childhood priority for country kids. At all times of the year, often in bare feet, it was my task as an eight-year-old to keep the milking stalls occupied. This meant encouraging cows to walk across a concrete floor to the empty stalls. It was not uncommon for a cow to resent being driven and on more than one occasion I was slapped in the face by a flickering tail and more seriously stepped upon by stamping hooves. So serious was one stomping on a bare foot that milking was suspended and I was rushed by car to Korumburra for medical attention. Luckily, I suffered no more than severe bruising and was back in the dairy stockyard a week later.

oooOOOooo

Country people in those days were prolific radio listeners. Television did not arrive in Australia until September 1956, just in time to live broadcast the Melbourne Olympic Games. At milking time in dairy sheds across the nation, families would listen to ABC news broadcasts and episodes of the long running bush serial Dad and Dave from Snake Gully. Radio was a source of news and entertainment and it was a practical way to keep the cows calm during milking. The most vivid memory I have of the daily round of milking each morning and afternoon, is hearing the stirring tones of the short majestic fanfare which preceded the ABC news bulletin. The newsreader had a plum in the mouth English accent which was typical of ABC presenters at the time.

The most famous song in rural Australia for more than two decades was Jack O'Hagan's The Road to Gundagai. It was the theme music that introduced another rambunctious episode of the adventures of Dad, Mum, Dave and Mabel. When the familiar strains were heard everybody would pay attention even the cows.

> *There's a track winding back to an old-fashioned shack along the Road to Gundagai. Where the blue gums are growin' and the Murrumbidgee's flowin' beneath the sunny sky. There my mother and daddy are waitin' for me and the pals of my childhood once more I shall see. Then no more will I roam when I'm headin' straight for home along the Road to Gundagai.*

Mucking out the diary after milking was the job I disliked more than any other. Cow pats and urine, steaming and slippery in combination were everywhere. It was not all bad, however; on a crisp winter's morning my toes would sink into the cow pats and warm my bare feet. Gumboots only later became required footwear in the dairy. The stockyard and concrete floor were hosed down and wooden handle rubber squidges mopped up the area ready for the next milking. The precious milk was channelled through a cream separator and stored in large metal cans with tightly sealed lids awaiting tanker pickup for delivery to the Co-Op Butter Factory.

The Korumburra Co-Op Butter Factory was a place of agribusiness smells and much activity, with milk tankers and transports coming and going all the time. I would occasionally visit the butter factory with my Dad Cecil whom everybody called 'Snowy' to pick up bags of wheat pollard and other farm supplies. On one of these journeys, I was given a guided tour of the butter factory and shown the tall metal tanks, in which milk was stored before being transferred to squat circular vats to be turned into large chunks of butter.

It was a wonderland to see the milk tankers come and go. I knew truckdriver Irish Mick and would sometimes help him at the dairy with our cans of milk. He was a wiry man, thin as a whippet, ruddy in the face with a bold military tattoo of an Australian flag emblazoned across his big fist. He had been a soldier in New Guinea during the war and was a man of very few words. His silence and melancholy demeanour spoke volumes of his wartime experience and he kept it shut away inside himself. Mick appreciated my help with the milk cans. On one occasion he gave me sixpence which made my day and later paid for a bag of lollies.

oooOOOooo

I grew up with a passionate love of animals and formed a strong emotional bond with all manner of wild and domesticated creatures. On my childhood travels through the bush, I would see and marvel at echidnas, wombats, kangaroos, koalas, kookaburras and magpies — my favourite bird. My love of magpies no doubt explains why I became a Collingwood football fan. There were many bush and farm animals big and small and I was fascinated by them all. I would ramble over bush hill and dale with Jack our brown Kelpie dog, and childhood was pleasant and carefree. Jack would meet his fate at the hands of an irate Italian neighbour who shot him for worrying his sheep. On that sad day the world changed for me and the wonder of childhood was lost forever.

Death is an ever-present reality for all of us. When I was five, I insisted on placing a small wooden cross on the makeshift grave of a baby chicken I found dead in the chicken coop. As I got older and was instructed in the use of a rifle, I would go rabbit hunting with Dad and never hit the target. Disappointed, Dad thought I was a hopeless shot and gave up. The truth is I deliberately aimed high so as not to shoot rabbits or anything else. I would not be the intentional cause of death to any creature and I kept my resolve to myself.

The ritual process of turning young boys into men was something fathers took seriously as a solemn duty in those days and it sometimes involved the killing of animals. At seven years of age, my father's understanding of this duty left me with a painful memory that haunts me still. Dad had taken me down the paddock to retrieve a lost sheep he said. The animal was found and without a word to me. Dad produced a sharp knife and instantly cut its throat. As the sheep lay dying, pouring out its lifeblood on the ground, I looked aghast at Dad who expressed no emotion. A few moments later the sheep was dead and Dad slit open the abdomen. He told me to reach inside and take out the heart and lungs to take home for the dog. He slung the carcass over his shoulder and with me carrying the still warm and bloody entrails, we set out for home. I said nothing but after this saw my father in an entirely different light. For me there was nothing manly or admirable in the slaughter of a poor animal.

A moment of great sadness all dairy farmers and their families experience is the day the abattoirs truck arrives to take away cows and calves. I saw tears in both of my parents' eyes as they helped to herd animals they had hand raised and milked, in some cases for several years. This was personal; each cow and calf had a name and now we would see them no more. As young children my sister Mary and I were told the cows and calves had gone on holiday. When we got older our tears added to the family discomfort as Bessie, Charlie and others made the fateful journey of no return.

When a travelling Rodeo arrived in Korumburra, my imagination was filled with cowboys and bucking broncos. I looked forward to attending and watching brave deeds performed. The reality was entirely different from what I expected. Horses were ruthlessly spurred till their sides were streaked in blood. Young calves were roughly brought to the ground by lassos. Bulls were cattle-prodded into angry response. When a bucking horse fell and broke a leg, the poor animal was shot on the spot. I had had enough and asked to be taken home. As a country boy, I grudgingly accepted the short life of farm animals as a commercial necessity, after all that is what dairy and beef farming is all about. Rodeo cruelty and senseless injury I could not abide; this was my first and last Rodeo.

oooOOOooo

One of the pleasures of a country childhood was the billy of full cream milk still warm and sweet tasting, brought to the house from the dairy after the morning milking. Mary and I poured it on our breakfast cereal and thought no more about it. Every time I open a plastic bottle of flavour-destroyed, pasteurised milk these days I remember that long-ago breakfast delight. On schooldays we would mount our pushbikes and ride to a small rural state school four miles distant. The road between Warragul and Korumburra was a twisting, turning and undulating delight. Bike rides to and from school were enjoyable with no fear of stranger-danger. We would race our neighbourhood friends on hilly roads largely devoid of cars and other traffic. Our racing mantra was the road belonged us and we made the most of it.

The kookaburra's laughing call brought a feeling of cheerfulness on bright summer mornings. The sun was golden in the sky, warm on our hands and faces. In winter heavily rugged up against the penetrating cold we peddled furiously to keep ourselves warm. Childhood days were filled with unfettered freedom as with our comrades we rode up and down the rambling Strzelecki hills. Occasionally someone would hit the gravel and slide into a fall. Grazed knees and pitted elbows were bike riding wounds proudly displayed. We would get a scolding from our parents and told to be more careful in our bike riding escapades. Nevertheless we would hit the road again with a reckless abandon the following morning.

During springtime and the magpie swooping season, we crouched down by the side of our pushbikes as we ran a gauntlet of aggressive magpies defending their nests. One bird in particular would wait for us to reach a certain spot before commencing the attack and flying from tree to tree with what seemed to us a spiteful vengeance. We became so frightened by the morning and afternoon assault Dad came out one day with his 22 rifle and fired a few shots. This had the desired effect of deterring the magpie from its vendetta assault, and luckily Dad was such a poor shot the irate bird escaped unharmed.

oooOOOooo

Mr Fielding the state school teacher always wore a tweed jacket with elbow patches, corduroy trousers and brown shoes. He was a pleasant, kindly, nondescript young man who clearly hankered to return to city life. For us children it was a time of wooden desks, hard wooden seats and colourful teacher stamps grading our work. Schoolyard games included cricket, football and marbles for the boys; rounders, netball and knuckles for the girls. Hide and seek, hopscotch and other such games were engaged in by everybody. Fights would sometimes occur, usually with a lot of pushing and shoving rather than actual physical injury taking place. However, fist to face contact was not uncommon. A blackeye was a battle wound to be admired and respected. A schoolyard code of honour was strictly observed with combatants shaking hands and leaving the battleground as ostensible friends when peace was restored. If the teacher became involved, it was detention, lines or worse.

Mr Fielding and his female assistant Miss Donavon presided over a classroom of thirty or more children divided into different classes. Miss Donavon taught the infants and lower grades at one end of the small wooden school building, with its large map of the world depicting the British Empire on which the sun never set marked in pink, and oversized letters of the alphabet with colourful pictures arrayed along the wall. A four-foot-high blackboard with a raised wooden platform in front ran the length of one wall for chalk and talk lessons. The older children were instructed by Mr Fielding whose voice was soft and reassuring as he taught English, arithmetic, history and geography.

Mr Fielding's history lessons were illustrated with colourful pictures and an occasional slideshow. The Aborigines, Convicts, Captain Cook and the Pioneers were topics he discussed. Mr Fielding's account of British Empire focused history stressed Christian ethics and the rule of English law. The benefit of white colonisation and the civilising nature of the British presence in Australia were taken for granted. Children were enthralled by stories of Australia's nomadic Aboriginal hunters and gatherers. We saw them as wonderfully different, not racially inferior human beings. We learnt the facts good and bad without the intolerant woke racism of today apportioning shame and blame. The British Empire's central role in abolishing the slave trade and the Magna Carta beginnings of England's democracy were taught to schoolchildren as the jewels in the crown of empire and the spread of western civilisation. The belittling of western civilisation and the vandalising of statues of Captain Cook and pioneer monuments we see today, would have been regarded by teachers and students alike as a national disgrace, perplexing and shameful.

During Mr Fielding English lessons, he introduced his older pupils to the wonderful world of Aussie poetry, to the lyrical works of Henry Lawson, Banjo Paterson and John O'Brien. A particular favourite of mine was Banjo Paterson's 1882 humorous story 'The Man from Ironbark'. An amusing 19th century tale of a visit gone wrong to a Sydney barber shop by an outback bushman with a long flowing beard. It is a style of Aussie bush humour no longer taught in today's schools devoted to accentuating victimhood, genocide and gender issues. Banjo Paterson's comedy masterpiece is presented here in its entirety.

It was the Man from Ironbark who struck the Sydney town; He wandered over street and park, he wandered up and down. He loitered here, he loitered there, till he was like to drop; Until at last in sheer despair he sought a barber's shop. ' 'Ere! shave my beard and whiskers off, I'll be a man of mark, I'll go and do the Sydney toff up home in Ironbark'.

The barber man was small and flash, as barbers mostly are; He wore a strike-your-fancy sash, he smoked a huge cigar; He was a humourist of note and keen at repartee, He laid the odds and kept a 'tote', whatever that may be, And when he saw our friend arrive, he whispered, 'Here's a lark! Just watch me catch him all alive, this Man from Ironbark'.

There were some gilded youths that sat along the barber's wall. Their eyes were dull, their heads were flat, they had no brains at all; To them the barber passed the wink, his dexter eyelid shut, 'I'll make this bloomin' yokel think his bloomin' throat is cut'. And as he soaped and rubbed it in, he made a rude remark: 'I s'pose the flats is pretty green up there in Ironbark'.

A grunt was all the reply he got; he shaved the bushman's chin; Then made the water boiling hot and dipped the razor in. He raised his hand, his brow grew black, he paused awhile to gloat, Then slashed the red-hot razor-back across his victim's throat. Upon the newly-shaven skin it made a livid mark — No doubt it fairly took him in — the Man from Ironbark.

He fetched a wild up-country yell might wake the dead to hear; And though his throat, he knew full well, was cut from ear to ear. He struggled gamely to his feet, and faced the murd'rous foe: 'You've done for me! you dog, I'm beat! one hit before I go! 'I only wish I had a knife, you blessed murdering shark! 'But you'll remember all your life the Man from Ironbark.'

He lifted up his hairy paw, with one tremendous clout He landed on the barber's jaw, and knocked the barber out. He set to work with nail and tooth, he made the place a wreck; He grabbed the nearest gilded youth, and tried to break his neck. And all the while his throat he held to save his vital spark, And 'Murder! Bloody Murder!' yelled the Man from Ironbark.

A peeler man (policeman) *who heard the din came in to see the show; He tried to run the bushman in, but he refused to go. And when at last the barber spoke, and said 'Twas all in fun — 'Twas just a little harmless joke, a trifle overdone'. 'A joke!' he cried, 'By George, that's fine; a lively sort of lark; 'I'd like to catch that murdering swine some night in Ironbark'.*

And now while round the shearing floor the list'ning shearers gape, He tells the story o'er and o'er, and brags of his escape. 'Them barber chaps what keeps a tote, By George, I've had enough, 'One tried to cut my bloomin' throat, but thank the Lord it's tough.' And whether he's believed or no, there's one thing to remark, That flowing beards are all the go way up in Ironbark.

oooOOOooo

At Monday morning school assembly, we would gather around the school flagpole, place our hands over our hearts and swear the oath of allegiance. *I love God and my country. I honour the flag. I cheerfully obey my parents, teachers and the law.* The national anthem 'God Save the Queen' was sung without much enthusiasm given that it was Monday morning and a long school week beckoned. Those of us without a good singing voice such as myself would silently mouth the words to avoid ridicule from our classmates. The flag was saluted and we would march to the classroom for lessons to begin. At larger regional schools such as Saint Joseph's primary school Korumburra, which Mary and I would later attend, marching was considered a perfected art. Arms would be swung high and legs raised and lowered in time to stirring march music broadcast over a loudspeaker. The teacher's approval was eagerly sought by the younger students. They exaggerated every movement. It must have looked a ridiculous sight, as scores of primary schoolchildren swaggered and strutted towards their classrooms to strident military marches. I remember these occasions well every time I hear a brass band playing marching music.

On Friday afternoons there was a choice between sports and craft activities. Cricket and football matches were hotly contested events with lots of shouting and commotion. It was a pleasure to be outdoors away from schoolbooks, blackboards and teacher's dirty looks. In the wet weather cane weaving was the only option available for boys. My basket making skills were not good. The baskets I made always came out lopsided and weird looking. Mum was being kind when she praised the cane basket shambles I brought home.

Once a week nature walks at Mr Fielding's school were a get-out-of the-classroom adventure. My favourite nature walk took place after a springtime shower of rain with the refreshingly scented smells of the bush. I still remember the mossy green stony rises, the myriad of colourful flowering plants, the large ball golden wattles and the leafy canopy of tall gumtrees gently dripping with globular droplets of rainwater. I remember walking across bracken fern-filled paddocks, spotting wildlife and enjoying being outdoors. Koalas, kangaroos and echidnas were our favourite bush animals and an unexpected sighting was a highlight to be treasured. The teachers were consulted and suitable specimens of native flora were collected for classroom discussion. A good find would bring praise and approval from Mr Fielding and his teacher's aide Miss Donavon. Children being children, someone always managed to get lost or to hurt themselves involving a hurried search, a hastily applied band-aid and generally brought an end to our weekly bushland excursion.

Gippsland's giant earthworms (Megascolides Australis), between a metre and 3 metres long, would sometimes be encountered on these nature study excursions. These impressive creatures, resembling a snake without the danger of aggressive attack and being poisoned, lived their entire life underground. During a particularly wet winter with heavy rainfall, they would come to the surface to escape drowning in the sodden soil. Korumburra the Aboriginal word for 'Maggot' is thought to refer to Gippsland's giant earthworms. When as a five-year-old I saw one for the first time it was a fascinating and a frightening experience.

oooOOOooo

Children in those far-off days were generally Roman Catholics or Protestants. Religious instruction took place at regular intervals in country state schools. A priest or parson would arrive to deliver the denomination's Christian message. Children of the opposite religious persuasion would eagerly file out of the classroom for a period of playground fun, envied and resented by those left behind to learn their prayers and recite the catechism. Of course, when it was the turn of exuberant Catholics to experience the unrestrained freedom of the schoolyard, we always made sure to make as much noise and commotion under the window sill of religious instruction as we warily thought we could get away with.

Dad owned an old Indian motorcycle with a metal sidecar sporting a small Pyrex glass windshield. As we grew older and were in spiritual need of more sustained Catholic religious instruction — Dad wearing thick goggles and a leather helmet, would drive us to Saint Joseph's Catholic primary school in Korumburra each morning and make a return journey in the afternoon. The sidecar was small and cramped. I would position myself inside and Mary would climb in and sit between my legs as we uncomfortably travelled to and from school. Arguments would erupt over the restricted space and Dad would intervene to restore order. On frosty mornings, it was exciting and invigorating to hear the droning roar of the engine and feel the wind take one's breath away. When it rained, a black tarpaulin roof was buttoned down across the sidecar making it steamy, foggy and claustrophobic. Dad weathered the rain as best he could in his heavy khaki army coat.

After school on hot summer days a treat was sometimes in store, an orange or lemon icy pole and a sought-after bottle of Korumburra-produced Joe's Soft Drink. Juggling these childhood delights in a cramped motorcycle sidecar was not an easy matter, particularly when Dad was in a hurry to get home to commence milking. The sidecar had even less room when a load of shopping was added. Consequently, the grumbling and shoving inside the confined space escalated exponentially. Eventually the old Indian motorcycle gave up the ghost and journeys to school became a more sedate and comfortable affair by car or school bus.

Occasionally, an upcoming event of some importance would be brought to the attention of the district's schoolchildren. Princess Alexandra, a minor member of the English Royal Family, visited Australia in 1959. She was to tour Gippsland following a route that would take her directly past our school. For weeks we were taught England's history and the strong connection to Australia. We made flags of both countries and signs welcoming the princess. When the great day arrived, we lined up along the roadside in front of the school eagerly awaiting a glimpse of a real princess. A car was heard in the distance and soon came racing past with the princess dressed in a tiara and totally oblivious to our presence. Some of the girls cried. When later I told Mum of the rapid drive-by, she sourly remarked *Typical Royal Family!* My family and many others in the district with an Irish heritage and republican sympathies, followed the troubles in Northern Ireland closely and had little fondness or respect for the Royal Family.

oooOOOooo

Snakes were never far from most people's minds in Gippsland. Children were warned from an early age concerning the deadly danger these reptiles posed. I saw snakes on a regular basis and the encounter was always chilling. Children and adults died from snakebite; caution was therefore of paramount importance. A *Great Southern Advocate* newspaper report from March 1893, describes the disturbing nature of trying to save a Gippsland snakebite victim's life before antivenene treatment was available:

> *A fatal case of snake poisoning at Korumburra has been quite sufficient to terrify the bravest of hearts. Every remedy was tried, the forearm and arm were ligatured, the wound was scarified, liberal portions of brandy were supplied, strychnine was injected and the patient was kept walking about. When he became worse, hypodermic injections of ammonia and sulphuric ether were resorted to. Transfusion of a saline solution was tried; artificial respiration was prolonged for many hours; a warm enema of*

egg and brandy was given and as a final effort galvanism was efficiently employed. But alas! To no effect and our young friend setting out on life with bright prospects before him was removed from those who loved him.

Another snakebite incident dubbed 'The Strange case of Snakebite Mirboo North' occurred on the 9th of February 1919:

A curious case of snakebite occurred at Budgeree on Wednesday. A man named Edward Feutrill was lying on his bed, when a snake fell from the rafters of the hut and bit him twice on his hand. The man was taken to Boolarra, but died soon after arrival. The *Traralgon Record* on 8th of December 1908 recounted a case of snakebite in a rather jovial fashion. *Archie Bridges was bitten on the leg by a snake on Monday, 30th of November. Bridges was camping in a tent with some mates at Narracan, and while in the act of dressing in the morning he stood upon the reptile which instantly bit him. He was brought to Traralgon and attended to by Dr Smithwick and is now out of danger. Bridges is a well-known resident and is the possessor of a wooden leg. Referring to the matter Bridges says he would not have minded had the snake bitten the wooden leg, but to get his only sound leg attacked in that way was something beyond a joke.*

However, it is a dual case of Gippsland snakebite that reveals the true terror of being bitten by the slithering reptiles and the horror of 19th century medical remedies applied. The *South Bourke and Mornington Journal* on the 14th of October 1891 carried the following harrowing newspaper account of snakebite survival:

Few of those who witnessed the terrible and protracted struggle between medical skill and the slow, painful, and almost fatal effects from a black snake bite will ever forget the horror which the case inspired. To see a strong, robust man, stricken down in such a terrible manner, and to have to acknowledge that one was utterly incapable of rendering the poor fellow any assistance, was almost maddening. But thanks to the indomitable exertions of Drs Moore and Smith, the struggle ended in a victory for medicine, and a gratifying proof that the venom of the bite, if ably treated, may be stayed even at the 11th hour.

The facts of the case referred to are as follows: on Monday week last, a man named John Hourigan, who resides in Dandenong, and who follows the calling of Inspector of pumps on the Gippsland Railway, received a bite on the hand from a black snake whilst oiling the plunger of the pump at the Pakenham railway station. The effects of the bite was nullified through Hourigan scarifying and sucking the wound, and the result was only a slight drowsiness. On Friday morning, however, whilst Hourigan was again oiling the plunger, he was bitten on the same hand, presumably by the same snake, the fangs penetrating so far that Hourigan had to pull the snake off with his left hand. He hurried to the Pakenham railway station where Mr Ryan, the stationmaster, put two ligaments on — one on the wrist and the other on the elbow, and sent the man to Berwick.

Dr James attended to him there, and after injecting strychnine, sent him to Dr Moore at Dandenong, where the sufferer arrived at 1:30 pm. The poor fellow was taken to the dispensary, being then in a state of stupor and prostration. However, after the injection of 1/30th of a grain of strychnine and keeping Hourigan walking up and down the street between two strong men, a slight improvement took place. At 2.10 pm Hourigan became worse, and another 30th of a gram of strychnine and 20 minims of ammonia were injected, and brandy was also given him. This revived him for a time, but about 3.30 pm he collapsed again — it was feared for the last time. A similar dose of strychnine and ammonia livened him up, however, and he was walked up and down till 4.30 pm, when he gave way completely, and was carried to the dispensary in a terrible condition.

He was quite black in the face, and his figure appeared to have shrunk to half its original size. Ether was injected, but in vain, and as a last resource a galvanic battery was applied to the nape of the neck at the apex of the heart, with the effect of galvanising the apparently dead man into life. Owing to congestion of the brain, Dr Moore opened a temporal vein, but the blood was so thick that cupping had to be adopted, by which 4 ounces of blood was taken away. From this Hourigan gradually recovered and is now quite well. The battery treatment was continued till 2 o'clock next morning, Drs Moore and Smith remaining with the patient till 7am.

oooOOOooo

Every Gippsland family has a distressing tale to tell of an encounter with one or more snakes. In our family, it was Mum's washing machine skirmish with a red bellied, four-foot-long black snake, said by the locals to be on a par with a Henry Lawson snake story. On the back porch of our Seaview house stood a centre loading Bendix washing machine. Mum would keep the dirty washing in a cane basket on the floor next to the porch door. She would load the washing machine by scooping up an armful of clothes and add soap powder through a receptacle opening located on the top. On this occasion with the machine in operation, a red bellied black snake could be seen tumbling and turning with each rotation. Suddenly the head of the snake could be seen attempting to escape through the receptacle opening. Quick as a flash, Mum slammed the lid closed and began pouring boiling water down the chute. When the machine was opened the body of a large snake was pulled out. The reptile had slithered up the back stairs of the porch and settled down in the cane washing basket. Mum was not bitten in the handling, which everybody regarded as something of a miracle.

On another occasion, Dad was bitten by a tiger snake down the paddock while tending to the cows. Ashen grey and walking with a dog chain tourniquet wrapped around his left leg Dad appeared at the kitchen door and announced he had been bitten. He roughly cut open the wound, applied 'Condy's Crystals' an antidote used at the time and went to bed refusing to see a doctor. He spent a restless night sweating profusely and tossing and turning. There must have been minimal venom associated with the snakebite as next morning he was back milking the cows at 5am as if nothing had happened. Dad put his miracle recovery from snakebite down to an inherited immunity from a colourful Morrissey ancestor by the name of 'Snakes' Morrissey.

Dad would tell stories of being related to James Snakes Morrissey an early 20th century snake charmer, who travelled the pubs and fairgrounds with a bagful of snakes entertaining the crowds wherever he went. He claimed to have been bitten 52 times by the venomous reptiles and developed a cure for snakebite patented as 'Morrissey's

Snakebite Antidote guaranteed to cure'. New South Wales newspaper the *Clarence and Richmond Examiner* quoting a Melbourne newspaper wrote on the 26 October 1907:

> *James Morrissey the snake charmer again fell into the hands of the police last week at Prahran, where he was arrested on a charge of drunkenness. Morrissey, as usual had a bag of snakes with him, and the constable deemed it expedient not to lay hands on his prisoner. By constant coaxing he induced Morrissey still holding fast to his bag of reptiles, to follow him to the watchhouse. A large crowd of people also followed Morrissey, and it needed no more than an extra lurch on Morrissey's part to make the crowd scatter. He was sentenced to 14 days imprisonment. Some hours prior to his arrest Morrissey was in a hotel in Malvern inviting all and sundry to kiss his snakes, which invitation was declined.*

There are two versions of James Morrissey's death; one he died painfully from a puff adder bite, the other he passed away peacefully in a Sydney nursing home.

Whether or not the Morrisseys were in fact related to the dodgy snake charmer remains a mystery. Dad believed there was a family connection and that it had saved his life when dairy farming in Gippsland. Many years later while visiting the Commonwealth Scientific and Industrial Research Organisation (CSIRO), I found out that Snakes Morrissey was a name fondly remembered for his ability to milk snakes for their venom in the 1930s as part of a CSIRO's antivenene research program. Maybe this was the snake handling Morrissey Dad remembered and wrongly assumed was James Morrissey? Maybe they were the same person? As a very young child, I remember being taken to an old terrace house in South Melbourne belonging to a Snake Wrangler who had boxes of snakes in the shed outside. It was a scary experience watching writhing snakes emerge from their hiding place to be lovingly handled and fed.

oooOOOooo

Dad's side of the family, the Morrisseys, were city dwellers, not farmers, spending their time in and around the inner-city suburbs of Melbourne and Sydney. My grandfather Stanley was an Anzac; I never knew him.

My grandmother Ethel Gladys was a petite woman overly indulgent of her wayward children. She looked every inch the fairytale grandma and, in my memory, I see her plainly as if it was yesterday. As a young child I remember visiting her with my parents when she was living in South Melbourne in a converted stable with one of her many daughters. I thought it strange that somebody would live in a stable and asked her *where do you keep the horses?*

Morrissey family history is confused and leads in many directions. My mother's relatives, the respectable Murrays and Byrnes to be discussed later, were the offspring of free immigrant Irish settlers proud of the fact there was no convict taint to stain the family name. The same could not be said about the Morrissey clan who had past and present run-ins with the law. There was bygone and ongoing criminal shame in the Morrissey family. In Mum's respectable Irish relative's eyes, there was also the blemish of English heritage to be endured as well.

Tracing the Morrissey lineage back to its convict roots, George Green and Ann Doran emerge as convict ancestors. George was born in Staffordshire, England in 1808. He was a farm labourer who engaged in crime rather than pursue an honest living. In 1827 George was convicted of housebreaking, sentenced to life imprisonment and transported to Australia. He had two previous convictions and was considered an habitual criminal. He arrived in Australia aboard the convict ship *Bussorah Merchant* and landed at Sydney Cove on 26 July 1828. George's convict record sheet describes him as 5'4" in height, fair complexion, brown hair and blue eyes. He had distinctive tattoos on both hands. *On his left-hand blue rings on the first and third fingers with five dots on the left arm; a figure 3 on the right hand and a blue ring on the middle finger of the same hand.* The significance of these tattoos has been lost in time, but they may have been gang tattoos.

On the 12 November 1838, George married Ann Doran in Goulburn New South Wales. Ann was an Irish lass born in County Longford in 1814. In March 1833, she was convicted of stealing a handkerchief and sentenced to seven years transportation. Ann had an earlier conviction and served three months in gaol. She arrived in Australia aboard the convict ship *Andromeda*. When released from convict servitude, George and Ann settled at Bombowlee near Tumut in New South Wales and raised a family of six children. There is a suspicion that George and Ann were connected to horse and cattle stealing in the district. There is a further suspicion they may have disposed of stolen horses and cattle through Ned Kelly's relatives the Quinn's intercolonial livestock stealing ring. Whether there is any truth to the Ned Kelly connection remains a mystery.

Mum's Byrne relatives had their own Ned Kelly story to relate. It was said that Ned's bushranging lieutenant Joe Byrne was related to my Byrne relatives in Ireland. As far as I can tell there is no truth to the tale. The broader question to be answered is why Joe Byrne a notorious bushranger was claimed as a Byrne relative by respectable people, who had no truck with criminals and ne're do wells during their law-abiding lifetimes? The power of associative myth is strong and no doubt played into the bogus story of a Byrne family connection.

oooOOOooo

Living on a farm occasionally there would be a muffled knock at the backdoor. When the door was open a swagman dressed in rough bush clothes with his swag lying at his feet would enquire *Could you spare some food Missus?* It was never a good idea to refuse such a request, the consequences could be a broken fence, a burnt haystack or worse. Not all swagmen were ne'er-do-wells to be regarded with caution and fear. Many were returned servicemen unable to settle back into civilian life, humping their bluey seeking work and solace wherever they could find it. There is a Korumburra story of Pat the Irishman travelling the wallaby track, *when he began to feel the pangs of hunger and on coming up to a farmhouse, and knocking at the door, and with a serious look on his face said 'God bless your Cows, Ma'am, would you give me a drink of water?'* Pat was not turned away with a drink of water. He was given a sumptuous meal by a bemused farmer's wife, who appreciated the Irish blarney politeness of the swagman's backdoor approach.

Mum answered these swagman requests with kindness, and no doubt with a certain amount of trepidation given the Bushy Daniel's story I will relate later, filling the swagman's tuckerbag with vegetables, meat and even a homemade cake. Most were quiet, retiring men down on their luck and would spend the night nearby without incident. A neighbour who took exception to an occasional swagman camping on his property and drove them off at gunpoint, woke in the middle of the night to find his dairy ablaze. The police were called but the culprit was long gone. Mum and Dad were more accommodating and never experienced theft or loss when a swagman called. What became of these itinerant swagmen wandering the countryside alone and in all kinds of weather intrigues me still.

In his classic poem *The Swagman* (1921) C J Dennis wrote of an earlier generation of wandering swagmen. *He was old and he was spare; his bushy whiskers and his hair were all fussed up and very grey. He said he'd come a long, long way and had a long, long way to go. Each boot was broken at the toe, and he'd a swag upon his back. His billy can, as black as black, was just the thing for making tea at picnics, so it seemed to me. I sometimes think when I'm a man, I'll get a good black billy can and hang some corks around my hat, and lead a jolly life like that.*

Overall, it was a laid-back country childhood, rustic, sequestered and comfortably safe among the cows and farmyard animals. An idyllic bush upbringing, just beginning to be impacted by a burgeoning post-war city sophistication. The loss would be great and barely noticed at the time as we raced eagerly forward to a future dominated by mass consumerism and unprecedented economic growth no longer hard-fought on the Merino sheep's back. The loss would be all the greater with the passing into history of the last of an older generation of Australians, who with determination and sturdiness pioneered the land and gave us the prosperous way of life we take for granted today.

2

Korumburra Pioneers

The sunrays dance a merry jig on grass and bracken brown, and right and left and left and right, the magpies piped in sheer delight as over Creekside flat in height — We drove the cattle home.

Roderic Quinn

The Gippsland Forest was a dark and brooding place for pioneers. Historian Patrick Morgan describes the primeval Gippsland Forest cover thus: *The forest* (selectors) *encountered on their blocks was dense and dominant. Over 200 feet high, it consisted of three layers or strata. The undergrowth was of ferns, sword grass, wire grass, fallen logs, musk, dogwood and sassafras. Above the bare stems of the saplings was the second layer, the thick scrub tops of the medium-sized trees like the blackwoods. The third layer was the giant trees, mountain ash called blackbutt which towered above — one is listed in the Guinness book of records as the world's largest tree. All this was bound together with twisted, matted ropes of supplejack and creepers. Burning off one type of scrub often produced another type. So dense and tall was the forest, no neighbours' properties could be seen, nor any idea gained of local topography. The rainfall was higher than today, and a constant wet, damp drizzle or mist existed in the forest.*

The giant Mountain Grey Gum (Eucalyptus Cypellocarpa*)* native to the Gippsland Rainforest, was so massive in height and girth that pioneers would sometimes set up home or stable horses inside the hollowed-out stump. There are photographs of several men standing inside such a tree, the circumference of which could measure 20 metres or more. Legendary splitters tales speak of monster gumtrees reaching 121 metres in height. When felled in the Strzelecki Ranges in the 1880s, the 'Cornthwaite Tree' was measured at a whopping 114 metres. One pioneer settler said *clearing the land was a fearful task. There were 400 to 500 saplings to the acre and bracken ferns 10 feet high.* Gippsland's pioneers cleverly used a domino style technique of felling, to remove the tree canopy and dense forest undergrowth from their farms. Trees were individually notched and from a ridge higher up, a large tree was felled crashing into those down below. The logs were burnt where they lay, adding a rich layer of charcoal fertiliser to the soil. It was slow and tedious work that continued for the lifetime of the original selector — *It almost drags the heart out of a man to get the country clear* — and was passed onto his descendants to complete.

Clearing the land of these giant gumtrees and bracken ferns was no mean feat, timber milling was carried out in the Korumburra area for many decades. Commercial timber milling plants were spread throughout the region in the early days employing scores of expert axemen. Skill with the axe was a much-admired quality and a major drawcard then and now at country shows throughout Australia. The United Australasian Axemen's Association drew hundreds of entries each year from as far away as New Zealand and Canada for its annual woodchopping championships. Korumburra axemen would always give a good account of themselves at such public demonstrations and we would enthusiastically cheer from the sidelines.

oooOOOooo

For Korumburra pioneers faced with the daunting task of clearing the land, the Strzelecki Ranges named after Polish explorer Count Paul Strzelecki with towering gumtrees and matted groves of ferns would have seemed visceral, primeval and overpowering in natural beauty. The filtered daylight of the tangled bush undergrowth beneath the giant tree canopy was a leafy setting where the shaded sun shone only in streamed ringlets to the ground. The pervasive darkness, silence and stillness of the night time bush except for the cries and movements of animals, was an unperturbed place apart where the cacophony of modern noise and artificial light was still to come. This primordial landscape must have filled those working alone or in small groups in the bush with a dread and foreboding, dampening the spirit and adding to the arduous pioneer undertaking of establishing a cleared, fenced and viable farm. It turned them inward looking, but also drove them on in equal measure.

In taming the Australian bush, Gippsland's pioneer settlers were half a world away from village and city life in the old country, where for countless generations their families had travelled no more than a few miles from their ancestral homes. The traditional boundary of their physical and social world was narrow, predictable and regimented. The vastness of the Australian bush and the trials and tribulations of pioneer life were new to them. The distance and loneliness must have seemed overwhelming; fear and exhilaration combined together on the razor edge of a newfound colonial lifestyle.

In this feathery fern tree, cool shadow world hidden away from human eyes lived the elusive Lyrebird. The Lyrebird is nature's greatest mimic of all manner of bush sounds, including the plaintive call of dingoes, kookaburras and koalas. They have been recorded mimicking the human voice, crying babies, gunshots, chainsaws, car alarms and even the ring tone on mobile phones. During mating season, male Lyrebirds fan out their long-feathered tails in magnificent courtship display. Early Gippsland settlers marvelled at the Lyrebird's ringing call and elegant bush dance.

> *By channels of coolness the echoes are calling, and down the dim gorges I hear the creek falling; It lives in the mountain, where moss and the sedges touch with their beauty the banks and the ledges: Through breaks of the cedar and sycamore bowers struggles the light that is love to the flowers, and softer than slumber, and sweeter than singing, the notes of the bellbirds are running and ringing.*

Biologist Dr Anastasia Dalziell from the Australian National University writes:

> *like humans, male Lyrebirds have different dance movements to go with different songs. Male Lyrebirds sing four different song types, matching each with a unique set of movements and delivering song and dance types in a predictable sequence. While singing a song a male Lyrebird typically steps sidewise with his tail spread over his head like a veil; but when he sings* (another) *song he narrows his tail so it resembles a mohawk, flaps his wings, and performs little jumps and bobs. The Lyrebirds' dance*

movements are a voluntary embellishment to their singing; in other words, they can and do sing without dancing. Sometimes they also make mistakes in their dancing, an observation that suggests that dancing is challenging for the birds, just as it is for us humans.

The Gippsland Forest was noted for its celebrated Lyrebirds.

Towards the ends of the summers of 1875 and 1877, I visited some virgin forest country that was being thrown open for selection at Neerim, about twenty miles northward of what is now the flourishing district of Warragul. (Imagine) three great forests rolled into one. Firstly, thickly studded elegant fern trees entwined with various parasitical creepers, forming fairy like bowers carpeted with a ground scrub of innumerable ferns; secondly, trees of medium height, such as sassafras, musk, pittosporum, native hazel, blackwood and other acacias, etc.; and thirdly, towering above all a great forest of gigantic eucalypts. Within, and under the triple shades of these leafy solitudes, is the true home of the wonderful Menura (Lyrebird), commonly but erroneously called a pheasant by the selectors.

William Johnstone in *The Land of the Lyre Bird* (1920) wrote of arriving in the Gippsland Forest with his parents in the 1870s to take up a selection of land near Poowong.

After a few days we started off one morning to visit our selection, about 2 miles further on. We followed a survey line running in the direction we wished to go. Through the dense forest we pushed our way — we walked along logs, climbed over logs, crept under logs, crawled through logs, but seldom or never did our feet touch the ground. At last, we came to an enormous log. Oh, what a monster! and father said that on the other side of that big log lay our selection. Anxious to view the promised land, we made a desperate effort and clambered on top and had a look, and what do you think we saw? Why more logs. Were we downhearted? No! Eager for the fray, we slid down off the log and swung our axes, and in less than an hour our first tree came crashing down, and the battle had begun.

Ernest Emerson, a relative of celebrated American poet Ralph Waldo Emerson, lived for a time in Gippsland. He wrote lyrical poetry describing Gippsland's springtime mountain beauty. Here is some of what he wrote:

The silver wattles, brave with golden glory, bend to the singing waters of Gippsland Mountain creeks. The trickle of water slips noisily down the gully. Beneath the tree ferns, coral ferns wave light green fronds. Lower down the oak leaved bracken spreads batlike wings above the sleepy maiden hair. Bend low through the tangled scrub, tread softly between the orchids. The yellow wrens and the bluecaps sing; other birds are carolling — the white backed magpie and the butcher bird; and up in the towering gums, black cockatoos screech noisily welcoming the rising sun. The glistening creek throws back from its crystal water, the reflected splendour of bloom laden wattles. The sun climbs up; the valley grows heavy with shadow.

oooOOOooo

The Gippsland Forest occupied 1.2 million acres of fertile ground, with mountainous terrain in some parts reaching a height of 2,000 feet and steep gullies as deep 400 feet. Before the primeval tree cover was removed the annual rainfall was in excess of 50 inches. In 1887, the Victorian Minister for Lands John Lamont Dow, felt a twinge of ecological regret that *the magnificent blue gum ridges throughout south Gippsland have been alienated from the Crown, every acre of this land has now passed into the hands of private selectors.* Gippsland was renowned for its spring and winter downpours, which sometimes would go on for days. English poet Henry Wadsworth Longfellow could have been writing about a gloomy, rainy Gippsland day, when in 1842 he penned the following short poem.

The day is cold and dark and dreary; it rains and the wind is never weary. At every gust the dead leaves fall; and the day is dark and dreary.

In winter the ground was a swampy mess, a quagmire of rotting vegetation and deep mudholes that made farming and travelling difficult. As Ned Kelly said in his famous Jerilderie Letter (1879) the slippery north east mud *would bog a duck.* It was the same, only more so for Gippsland. Rainwater would cascade off sloping hills in rapidly flowing rivulets and flood the valleys. The rivers and creeks would overflow causing animal deaths, property destruction and the loss of human life. In July 1949, a newspaper banner headline read:

> 'The Worst Gippsland Floods for 26 years'. *One life has been lost and there has been heavy stock losses and property damage. Many homes have been isolated and residents cut off. They will receive food by boat tomorrow. Because of the washaways, roads have been blocked and telephone services dislocated.*

As a Gippsland child during the 1950s, I saw dams, creeks and rivers overflow for weeks on end. Sometimes, the journey to school would be called off, because of flooded culverts and water flowing over low-lying bridges. Children expressed an unconcealed delight when the parental message was announced *No School Today!* Other childhood flood experiences were not so welcomed or pleasant. I helped Dad with the aid of a tractor and chain to pull bogged and exhausted cows from out of slimy mudholes and the mushy edges of dams, as rain pelted down in sheets and my gumboots stuck firm in the soft and spongy ground. The physical helplessness and pleading fear in the eyes of trapped cows I loved has never left me. I remember the not always successful rescues as if they occurred yesterday.

Pioneer families living in rough bark huts suffered terribly during long winter days and gloomy nights, in which rain fell in torrents drenching man and beast alike. The cold, damp wintery months of drizzling rain with moist dank mist all around was the source of colds and pneumonia, brought on by never really dry clothes and inadequate shelter. As 19th century Gippsland cemeteries attest, deaths from influenza and other winter ailments among adults and children were common.

> *Let me slumber in the hollow where the wattle blossoms wave with never stone or rail to fence my bed. Should the sturdy station children pull the bush flowers on my grave, I may chance to hear them romping overhead.*

Gippsland tracks and roads in winter became deep boggy ditches of slimy mudholes. Small corduroy logs were laid crossways along the worst stretches, making for a bumpy and uncomfortable coach journey. In 1872, the *Herald* newspaper reported on a treacherous section of

Gippsland coach road colloquially known as the 'Gluepot':

It is not an unusual thing for leading (coach) *horses to go suddenly down into mud pits, and to be seriously injured by the* (coach) *polls and the coach itself coming into sharp contact with them before they can struggle to their feet. It is an established rule now for the passengers to be asked by the coachmen to walk a bit* — *meaning weary miles with mud up to their knees and bitterness in their hearts.*

oooOOOooo

Coping with the towering Gippsland Forest and the sheer hard work needed to clear a homestead paddock, engendered stamina and introspective reflection in Gippsland's pioneer settlers. The inward focus was on farming and family life. The rhythm of the seasons and rising and setting of the sun determined the settler's daytime tasks. Nobody ventured outdoors after dark, unless it was absolutely necessary to do so. The dictum early to bed and early to rise governed the daily life of selector families sequestered on their farms.

Journalist and novelist Mary Grant Bruce, herself a Gippslander, wrote *on many of these little farms one day is the same as another, week in, week out. Sometimes Sunday makes a break, but very often there is no church near enough for people with cows to milk and young children to tend. There are many mothers who leave the farms* (only) *half a dozen times in the year. The weeks and months go by quickly, for time flies and people are busy packing as much work as possible into the waking hours of each day; and nobody expects anything but work.* The work ethic was strong among Gippsland's earliest pioneers, who had a proud Victorian image of themselves as respectable, religious and law-abiding people battling the immensity of Mother Nature.

Gippsland Historian Patrick Morgan sees a clannish provincialism and strong suspicion of outsiders. He writes of *the development of specifically Gippsland families, that is, large groups of relatives forming a very strong group at the local level. Distances were short and relatives often lived within visiting distance. So, clans or tribes based on race, religion and relationship grew up, and this was the basis of the Gippsland community essentially a private network of stationery cousinage groups with strong roots, who conducted their business by* means of an extended gossip circuit. The struggle wasn't acquiring a block from grasping squatters, but clearing it once you had secured a selection. The task of felling, burning and clearing giant mountain ash in dense fern gullies, and then preventing the forest growing back, exhausted a settler, consumed his whole life. Mud, rain and poor transport systems meant a lifetime of backbreaking tasks. Pioneering continued (in Gippsland) up till the 1940s.

A Gippsland pioneer said he took up land and built a house, *to enjoy the glorious privilege of being independent. The home is surely, and ought to be, a place where one feels there is rest when weary and peace from the world's strife. My first abode was indeed humble enough for anyone. It measured about 18 x 14 feet, was built of logs and thatched with bark. It was where my ideas were centred, where I could work and do as I liked. There was fencing, yards and sheds to build, enough to keep me in constant employment and I did not get many holidays.*

Pioneering the land was tough in the hills and valleys of the Strzelecki Ranges. The lofty South Gippsland Mountain Range became known far and wide as the 'Heartbreak Hills'. As witnessed below Henry Lawson wrote poignantly of the trials and tribulations of those teetering on the cusp of being beaten. The lot of pioneer women was particularly challenging.

> *Now up and down the siding brown the great black crows are flyin'; and down below the spur, I know, another milker's dyin'. The crops have withered from the ground, the tank's clay bed is glarin'; but from my heart no tear nor sound for I have gone past carin'.*
>
> *Through childbirth, sickness, hurt, and blight, and nervousness an' scarin'; through being left alone at night, I've got to be past carin'. Our first child took in days like these, a cruel week in dyin'. All day upon her father's knee or on my poor breast lyin'. The tears we shed, the prayers we said were awful wild despairin'! I've pulled three through and buried two since then and I'm past carin'.*
>
> *'Twas ten years first, then came the worst, all for a dusty clearin'; I thought, I thought my heart would burst when first my man went shearin'. He's drovin' in the great north west, I don't know how*

he's farin'; for I, the one that loved him best have grown to be past carin'.

My eyes are dry, I cannot cry, I've got no heart for breakin'; but where it was in days gone by, a dull and empty achin'. My last boy ran away from me, I know my temper's wearin'; but now I only wish to be beyond all signs of carin'.

Some gave up the constant worry and seasonal strife. They left the land to begin anew elsewhere. Others despite the many obstacles and setbacks encountered, stubbornly persevered and eventually won through.

oooOOOooo

It is a modern-day furphy to suggest that the pioneers were environmental vandals with little concern for the ecological damage they caused. Pioneers had a 19th century vision of land management, which involved clearing the land of wilderness, scrub and trees to establish an old world portrayal of farming. Primeval nature was something they both admired and feared in equal measure but in order to survive the natural world had to be tamed and a farming and community structure imposed. With today's ecological hindsight, it is easy to condemn those whose only environmental sin was to follow the practical dictates of their time. By the 1950s Gippsland farms were cleared, fenced and the pioneer achievement spoken of with pride and affection.

As pioneer land settlement got under way, Gippsland was described as teeming with dry timber inviting disaster. *There were three layers rising 100 and 200 feet, in some instances higher, carrying leafy branches and combustible tinder dry bark. Blackwoods, hazel and wattles grew in profusion. Musks, tree ferns, sawgrass and a tangle of fallen timber lay in all directions.* The forest was logged and the fallen timber burnt. A clearing was made around a settler's house with trees cut down and logs left lying on the ground in flammable disarray. When weather conditions were deemed right these dried out woodpiles would be set alight. In 1897 and again in the following year Gippsland was ravaged by out-of-control bushfires, fuelled in part by the pioneers' land clearing woodpiles which burned for months until extinguished by heavy rains, which in turn brought winter and spring flooding.

In January 1898, newspapers reported on a serious bushfire at Korumburra:

> *Bushfires have been raging in the vicinity of the township during the past two or three days. From the township bushfires are seen raging fiercely, some of the roads are impassable. A strong wind is blowing which makes the task of the fire brigade all the more arduous. Along Whitelaw's track the road is entirely blocked and rumours are afloat that several selectors have been burnt out. At McDonald's track on the Strzelecki Ranges, Mr Faulkner of Seaview had a very narrow escape. Although he managed to save his homestead, he lost several acres of crop and a mile of fencing. Unless rain comes soon, there is no knowing where the bushfires will end.*

During dry summer months hot northerly winds, searing heat and sultry weather conditions:

> *created a chaos of conflagration from which terrified people would have no means of escape other than in a cultivated paddock or a waterhole. The livestock would be trapped and incinerated. Around Korumburra, there were families which sought refuge in wells and saved their lives by standing up to their necks in water. Men fainted from the scorching heat while saturating blankets with water to protect women and children huddled together. A nervous mother sent her four young children into Korumburra with an anxious message. If you please, Mother says will you take care of us tonight? She expects to be burnt out before morning.*

Henry Lawson wrote of the ravages of bushfire on the lives of the pioneers in an iconic poem, titled 'The Bush Fire' published in *When I Was King and Other Verses* (1905). Here is some of what he wrote.

> *On the runs to the west of the dingo scrub, there was drought and ruin and death; and the sandstorm came from the dread north east with the blast of a furnace-breath. Till at last one day at the fierce sunrise, a boundary-rider woke, and saw in the place of the distant haze a curtain of light blue smoke.*
>
> *It roars for days in the hopeless scrub and across where the ground seems bare, with a cackle and hiss, like the hissing of snakes, the fire is travelling there. Till at last, exhausted by sleeplessness and*

the terrible toil and heat, — the squatter is crying 'My God! the Wool!' and the farmer 'My God! the Wheat!'

A pioneer settler of the Korumburra district describes his labour-intensive battle to re-establish himself on the land after an interval away earning wages and the subsequent devastation caused by bushfire:

> In September 1893, I again began working the land. There was now about 200 acres of grass, with what I had just sown, although some of the old clearing had grown up with hazel and other scrub. This I set to work to clear and burn first of all. Then I built a log house and afterwards added a skillion on each side. At first, I grazed cattle and sheep and aimed at getting some cow's and go in for dairying. Little by little, I managed to get together a small dairy herd. Then the great bushfire came in 1898. We turned out 22 cows in the morning and next morning there were not more than 12 alive, and out of 430 sheep only a few over 200 were left and hence were marketed immediately. The remaining cattle, I managed to keep alive on a few acres of maize until there was grass again. All the buildings and fences were burned and considerable labour was required to replace these and more to cut down the undergrowth that sprung up after the fire.

The bushfires, droughts and floods I experienced as a child, although property and life destroying, were not of the same magnitude or devastation as earlier or later environmental disasters. The ground was parched and cracked in drought years. In winter the paddocks would flood and become boggy with the old Fergie tractor sinking to its axles in the slimy mud. In the bushfire season, I watched anxiously as fire and smoke came ever closer and breathed a sigh of relief when the wind direction changed. Along with the rest of the family, I cried when I heard of farmers forced to shoot their animals following disasters because they were injured or starving in the paddocks. Rebuilding, restocking and replanting crops after bushfire and flood damage was a reoccurring pattern of farming life that touched everyone. No one spoke of climate change or climate catastrophe in those days. Weather, heat and cold, were variable cyclical events, sometimes mild, sometimes extreme. Following the bad times always came bountiful crops and thriving livestock. It was the natural order of things acknowledged and accepted by all farmers.

oooOOOooo

In April 1880 under the banner headline 'Farming in Gippsland', the *Australasian* newspaper wrote of the difficulty and uncertainty of the pioneer farmer's life:

> *People living on the plains have no conception of the hardships which the early pioneers of thick forest country have to put up with; but it seems a healthy life, and most of them appear much attached to their pretty but rude homes, and do not seem to wish to leave them for more populous and settled districts. At Poowong a colony of Danes have taken up much of the country and are spoken of as hardworking and very frugal people. They have had a hard time of it this year, poor fellows. They expected to be able to sell about 60 head of cattle, but just when they were half fit for sale the caterpillars came and ate up all the grass; the cattle were turned out, and it is very unlikely that all of them will ever again be recovered.*

With the Gippsland Forest trees ringbarked, laboriously felled by axe and burnt, the backbreaking work of ploughing the ground and sowing a crop began:

> *After debris from the fire has been cleared off, the land, if intended for growing grain, is at once ploughed or rather the surface is scratched over. But the more usual and apparently the best course, is at first to sow a crop of English grass. After three or four years, the roots of the stumps still standing begin to decay and either fall by themselves or are made to do so with the help of the axe. Subsequently, attended by considerable labour and expense, comes the grubbing of the large trees and second burning process. Which as the trunks are an enormous size and cannot be moved together, have each to be destroyed separately and perhaps from their great length, ignited in 20 or 30 different places. Then another clearing of the land has to take place to remove what has been left unconsumed by the fire.*

> *The standard crops of the district must for some years, however, be chiefly confined to potatoes and oats. There appears to be no natural grass seed in the land, and if cleared and left fallow nothing but scrub or weeds grow up. A hand to mouth system of*

> *farming is at present being carried on by a great number of the poorer selectors. The farm of Mr Percy Smith is situated on what is known as McLeod's track about 2 miles from Warragul, and consists of 60 to 70 acres which have been planted with potatoes. An early crop taken from a part of this land, turned out a failure and is now being used to feed stock of all kinds. Mr Smith has had his share of troubles this year first caterpillars swarmed over the ground, destroying much of the English grass and also attacking the oats. Immediately after this came the grasshoppers, taking almost all that the caterpillars had left, and now the place is inundated with an army of crickets who devour every green thing that comes their way. The farm is enclosed with a chock and log fence.*

Not all Gippsland farming was predicated on doom and gloom.

> *Mr John Rogers, of Brandy Creek, one of the pioneers of the district, has English grass on 600 acres, and makes cheese and butter largely, milking about 80 cows. He was one of the first to prove that the (dairy) industry would pay in this place and commenced operations about seven or eight years ago. Mr Owen Mulhare was an early settler and owns a fine block of about 300 acres. He is reported to have done remarkably well out of his potatoes last year, and will have the produce of 20 acres to dispose of this year. In the parish of Neerim, 14 miles north of Warragul, past Brandy Creek, is some of the best land in the district. Mr Algie, who comes with a good reputation as a first-class farmer from the neighbourhood of Sunbury, has purchased Mr Archibald Sherrard's property at this place and breeds some grand livestock. Mr Barr of Berwick has a large establishment for the production of cheese and butter.*

The pioneering life was not for the fainthearted or those without courage, determination and the stamina to persevere. Problems faced by pioneer men and women were numerous, ongoing and at times soul destroying. Self-reliance and the undaunted ability to adapt to changing circumstance, went hand in hand with strength of character and a stubborn passion to win through. The hardship left behind in the old country fuelled an ardent and steadfast desire to succeed in the new.

oooOOOooo

In selection days, when dense bush scrub was all around, children were sent off to school with a small bell attached to their clothes in case they became lost in the bush. Before fences were erected the same thing happened to wandering cattle. Children would sometimes become disoriented and lost. Search parties were hurriedly formed by anxious parents and neighbours to scour the bush to find the absent youngsters. The literary tale of children's bush survival was often melodramatic and heroic.

> *Three long and weary days and nights, Jim lay in helplessness. Though faint for food he would not eat, but gave it all to Bess. He was only a rough, bush youngster, and hunger is hard to bear, but Jim preferred to starve out right than eat her scanty fair.*

The reality was more dramatic and survival accounts more inspirational than fictional stories of lost children.

> *Clara Harriet Crosbie was twelve years old when she went missing in the bush near Yellingbo in the Yarra Valley in May 1885. 'The child had been sent on a visit to a neighbour about a mile from her mother's house', reported the Argus, but 'as a town-bred girl, of warm affections and quick impulses she resolved to find her way home, although she did not know the way'. Faced with the perilous wilds, Clara took shelter in the hollow of a tree for three weeks, crawling to a nearby creek to drink and trying to cooee her way to safety. Her cries for help were eventually heard — by chance — by two men named Cowan and Smith while they were in the vicinity searching for horses. A low sound, 'like a young blackbird's whistle', had caught the acute ear of the two experienced bushmen and they followed the 'wailing note borne softly on the breeze' to its source. With the return of each low and piercing cooee, the men at last caught sight of the little girl, frail and woebegone. 'The little creature was tottering towards us, in her ulster, without shoes or stockings on, but quite sensible', they recounted.*

The establishment of schools in country districts was often a contentious issue with patience disturbed and tempers bristling. In July 1893, the *Great Southern Advocate* newspaper reflected community frustration at the appalling condition of the Korumburra State School.

The Korumburra school is positively disgraceful. A large unsightly barn like structure perched on top of a hill, unlined, without a fireplace or classrooms, serves as a school building during the day. At night it may be let out for any purpose. In the morning the teacher has found it in such a filthy, disgusting state, that the health officer reported it was 'altogether unfit for occupation as a school'. It appears said the health officer, the building had been used the night before for an exhibition of wrestling and no attempt had been made to clean or ventilated it before the children assembled. The floor was thickly covered with mud, mixed with saliva and chewed tobacco.

At the neighbouring school of Bena, it was said *the children during the hot weather, after being cooped up in a small room, had to be carried out in fainting fits. The District Inspector's attention was directed to the fact, but no alteration was forthcoming to remedy this state of affairs.* Everyone was greatly angered by the Korumburra school situation. The local Member of Parliament was approached and asked to raise the matter with the Minister for Education. *The draughty building with rain dripping down upon the children at work, no fireplace during severe winter days, and everything pointing to an amount of misery to be endured by children scarcely conceivable under the present administration of the Education Act* (is intolerable). *Cases of sickness among the children arising from the insanitary state of the building have been brought to the attention of the medical gentlemen at Korumburra. In at least one particular instance, they have forbidden the attendance of the child at school until the termination of the winter months.* The scandalous situation was finally resolved but not without further community agitation.

oooOOOooo

British Empire Day although still observed in the 1950s was beginning to lose the community significance accorded it in earlier times. The older imperial sense of Britishness fêted in 'The Children's Song' (1906) by Rudyard Kipling had become passé. *Land of our birth, our faith, our pride, for whose dear sake our fathers died; Oh, motherland, we pledge to thee head, heart and hand through the years to be!* Although respect for Britain and the British Empire remained strong. Since January 1901, Australia expressed a federated consensus of national identity. *Unsevered still, the tie that knits earth's greatest land with thee; The brightest gem in England's crown — Australia fair and free.*

Schools in particular were a principal focus of British Empire Day activities. On 28 May 1914, two months to the day before World War 1 commenced, the *Great Southern Advocate* reported.

> *The Korumburra State School celebrated Empire Day in an enthusiastic and loyal manner. A program of patriotic songs and recitations was excellently rendered by the children after which speeches were delivered. The respective speakers impressed upon the children the lesson that to maintain the integrity and greatness of Empire everything depended upon them. Each child was the recipient of a bag of lollies and they were also given a half holiday in the afternoon. At night the children were given a free picture show in the Mechanics Institute. A picnic was held at the Strzelecki state school, there being a very large gathering of children, parents and residents. Races and games were taken part in and all thoroughly enjoyed themselves.*

On 8 March 1925 *the* (Victorian) *Minister of Education visited schools at Creswick, Kingston and Clunes and attended a patriotic demonstration at Creswick in the evening. Under a program prepared by the Education Department the Union Jack and Australian flags were saluted by the children who also sang appropriate songs. Short lessons in British history and geography were given by the teaching staff.* Empire Day ceased to be celebrated as a public event in 1958.

Australia Day was and still is observed on 26 January each year. The day's celebration was about the arrival of the British in Australia and the colonial settlement that followed. Peaceable occupation not invasion nor genocide was the proclaimed goal of the colonisers. It was an observance of British and Christian values transported abroad to a fledgling pioneer setting. Australians of Irish heritage celebrated Australia's foundation day along with their Scots, English and Welsh counterparts. Nobody was celebrating the dispossession of the country's Indigenous inhabitants. It was a day of national pride for the whole nation not national shame. The Aboriginal voice was not yet heard and there were dark periods of history not yet acknowledged. Yet, white settlement had taken place and its pioneer achievements were everywhere to be seen.

On 18 January 1950, the *Melbourne Herald* carried the following article. 'Big Australia Day Celebrations urged 161 years since Phillip came'. *Everyone should fly a flag the Secretary of the Australia Day Council said today. He quoted from the first public speech made in Australia by Australia's first Governor Arthur Phillip on 26 January 1788. 'I do not doubt but that this country will prove the most valuable acquisition Britain ever made. We have come here today to take possession of this fifth great continental division of the earth on behalf of the British people. How grand is the prospect which lies before this youthful nation'.* This accorded with the history I was taught in school and Australian flags were flown to honour the occasion.

oooOOOooo

The national curriculum in those days was taught through a standardised series of Australian School Readers and the School Paper Magazine. History, geography, spelling, poetry recitation, good citizenship, short stories, composition, comprehension and extracts from great works of literature were showcased in an engaging format designed to appeal to children. There were evocative lithograph pictures depicting children participating in all manner of bush adventures, some carefree others tragic. Captions such as *They Stopped, and Cooeed, and Shouted, Glad hearted and Free, Beneath a Silk Smooth Gum* and one illustrating the drama of a child lost in the bush *How the Child was Found*. Stories by Charles Dickens, Hans Christian Anderson and even William Shakespeare were to be found in the Victorian Reader series. The Ugly Duckling was a particular favourite read by children as a morality tale of exclusion.

Some stories taught in school remained etched in the memory well into adulthood. 'The Hobyahs', a Scottish fairy story in its original format, was first published in 1930 in the Second Book of Victorian School Readers. It is a haunting folktale with mythic power to frighten children. Mum remembered the scary story from her own schooldays in the Western District. After hearing the tale, my sister Mary sought solace in the parental bed for several nights, too afraid to close her eyes.

She was convinced the Hobyahs were hiding among the reeds in the dam near the house and would come and take her away.

Once there was an old man and his old wife who lived in a house made of stalks. At the bottom of their garden was a reedy marsh. Hobyahs lived in a hidden house in the reeds. The old man had a little dog named Dingo and one night the Hobyahs came Creep, Creep, Creeping through the reeds crying 'Hobyah! Hobyah! Hobyah! Tear down the stalks, eat up the Old Man and Woman!' But little dog Dingo barked so loud the Hobyahs ran off. The old man said 'Little dog Dingo barks so loud I cannot sleep. If I live till morning, I will cut off his tail'. Next morning the old man cut off little dog Dingo's tail.

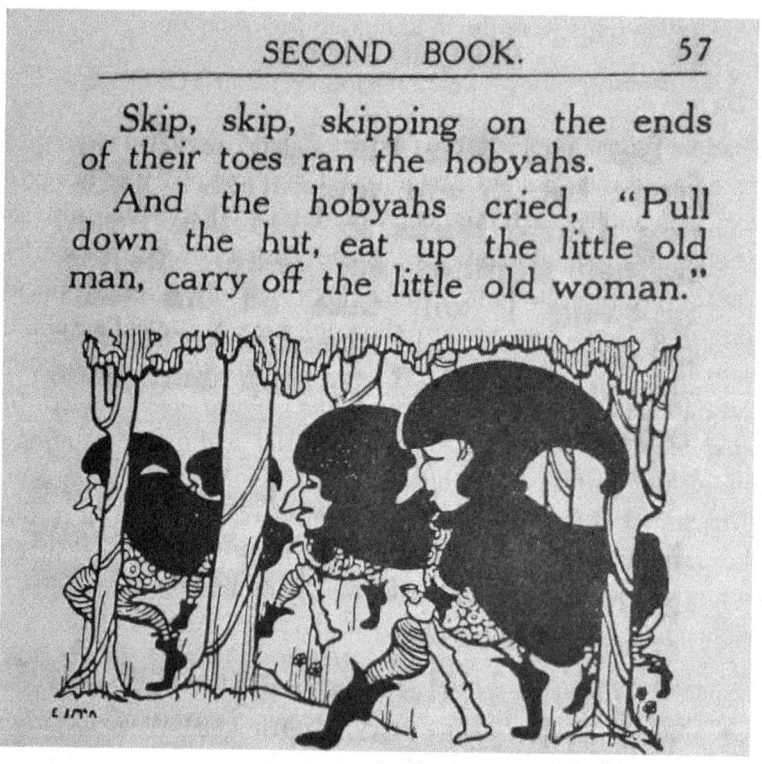

Second Book Victorian School Reader (1930)

Over several verses the old man gradually dismembers little dog Dingo for his raucous night-time barking. The Hobyahs abduct the old woman and little dog Dingo lays scattered about in dissected pieces.

> *The old man regretted what he had done to little dog Dingo and he sewed him back together again. He then got little dog Dingo to lead him to the Hobyah's home and rescued his wife from the sack while the Hobyahs slept. That evening the Hobyahs took down the sack. They poked it many times and then opened it expecting to eat the old woman. When they opened the sack, little dog Dingo jumped out and ate them all up and that's the reason there are no Hobyahs today.*

Education Departments in each state developed their own version of classroom readers and school paper magazines. The Victorian School Reader series contained eight books which were studied by students at different grade levels. The School Paper magazine was a monthly supplement with a circulation of 211,670 copies, which added topics of current interest to the curriculum as they occurred. The February 1954 edition had on its cover a map of Australia with a Crown and a stylised ER beneath. Four cherubim with flowing ribbons and trumpets heralded the first visit of Queen Elizabeth to Australian shores. To this day, Queen Elizabeth is the only ruling British monarch to come to Australia.

The John and Betty book for primary schoolchildren was introduced in 1951. Colourfully illustrated with full page pictures of John, Betty, Scottie the dog and Fluff the cat, the text was simple and easy to read: *This is John. This is Betty. Scottie can run. Scottie can run to John. Fluff can run. Fluff can run to Betty.* The primary school reader defined gender roles for boys and girls. In these politically correct, gender denying obsessed times, it is no longer considered a desirable reading aid. For those of us who grew up with the John and Betty book, we remember it affectionately as a stimulating introduction to a wider world of reading.

The triumphs and tribulations of the bush pioneers were ever present in the school curriculum. The first page of the Victorian Education Department's 5th Grade Reader printed in 1927, and still a classroom textbook when I attended primary and secondary school in the 1950s, contains a memorable poem by Frank Hudson simply titled 'Pioneers'.

> *We are the old world people ours were the hearts to dare; But our youth is spent and our backs are bent and the snow is in our hair. Back in the early fifties, dim through the mists of years; by the bush grown strand of a wild strange land we entered — the pioneers.*

> *Our axes rang in the woodlands where the gaudy bush birds flew; and we turned the loam of our newfound home where the eucalyptus grew. Housed in the rough log shanty, camped in the leaking tent; from sea to view of the mountains blue where the eager diggers went. We wrought with a will unceasing; we moulded and fashioned and planned. We fought with the black and we blazed the track that ye might inherit the land.*

> *There are your shops and churches, your cities of stucco and smoke; and the swift trains fly where the wildcat's cry o'er the sad bush silence broke. Take now the fruit of our labour, nourish and guard it with care. For our youth is spent and our backs are bent and the snow is in our hair.*

Those of us with snow in our hair today remember school readers with appreciation, nostalgia and affection. They instilled a lifelong love of literature and brought the Australian bush and pioneer spirit alive, without sledgehammer identity and gender politics and a belittling sense of white guilt etched on every page. We were impressionable young children. The wonderful stories allowed our childhood imaginations to soar and many of us remember and can recite them still.

3

Coalminers, Crooks and Delinquents

At dawn, we would feel the breeze that stirred the boughs of the sleeping trees. And brought a breath of fragrance rare that comes and goes in the scented air.

A B Paterson

Korumburra, originally named Coal Creek was a town central to my family's perspective of Gippsland community life. We would sometimes visit Warragul (meaning 'Wild Dog' in Aboriginal dialect) 20.5 miles (33 kms) away. The township of Korumburra occupied land on what was previously the heavily timbered Wild Cattle Pastoral Run established in 1846. Cattle freely roamed the bush in wild herds, until rounded up and taken to market towns by station drovers, the bush equals of the famed men from Snowy River. The squatting era in Gippsland was short compared to other districts and soon gave way to farmers, coalminers and others. Selectors began to arrive in Gippsland from the mid-1870s onwards. The forest landscape began to change radically as they began to clear and fence the land.

When coal was discovered at Coal Creek in the 1870s, the newly established township of Korumburra became an important centre of coal production. Between 1893 and 1962, 2,000,000 tons of coal were extracted from the ground. In the early days of coal extraction, the method was indeed primitive. *The entrance was not more than 2 feet high. A man, clad only in trousers, was lying on his side — there was no room to either stand or sit — chipping away with his pick at the wall of coal. The dungeon was lit by the man's tiny coffeepot lamp, giving the* scene a *Rembrandtesque effect. The tiny cell, the big muscular, naked, recumbent digger, the gleam from the jutting points of coal in the wall and on the ground, all made a picture I shall never forget. I shudder at the sight of this fine big fellow lying on his side, eight hours a day in his little dungeon, far down below the glorious light, digging, digging, chipping, chopping day after day, week after week, to earn his bread.*

In 1907 Korumburra's Coalminers went on strike over wages and the consequences were devastating for many. A Letter to the Editor in the New South Wales newspaper *The Worker* signed with the pseudonym 'Jack Hardgraft' gave a harrowing eyewitness account of the failed strike and its union busting aftermath:

> *Eight or nine years ago a man in search of work couldn't have struck a likelier spot than Korumburra. The Coal Creek, Outtrim and Jumbunna mines were in full swing. The man who could fire a charge or swing a pick was sure of a start. He was certain of making good wages. The Union was flourishing. Every man was a Unionist; every man was working; and the purchasing power of the South Gippsland Coalminers gladdened the heart of the small shopkeeper, the large shopkeeper and the fat publican. Then came the strike.*
>
> *The Korumburra men made one of the most gallant fights recorded in the industrial history of the state. The miners sacrificed their homes, sticks of furniture, and their last shilling in the cause, and only let go their hold when they were literally starved out. If ever anything shone out brighter than the heroism of the Korumburra strikers, it was the militant spirit of their wives. It was in the last days of the strike, half a dozen young women, the oldest not more than 25 years, laid hands on a pair of scabs. They ducked and half drowned the Judases in a cold green quagmire and then chased them up the road that led to the Coal Creek mine. It was a sight to fill a defeated striker's heart with savage joy.*
>
> *A few weeks ago, the writer returned to the coal mines. A change had come over the spirit of the place. It was a crime to talk Unionism. There is no Union now. The miners are paid whatever the miner owners like. The men have got to take the company's coal tally, whether they like it or not. This much I know. I grafted*

my soul out for a fortnight for a fiver. The same amount of labour would have brought me £10 in the old days. I bought an axe and took on a bit of bush work at six bob a day. Take it from me, if the miners have to keep up the volume of work expected of them for 12 months, there will be a rise in the price of coffins not accounted for by the tariff.

oooOOOooo

Antonio Radovick, a Croatian immigrant dubbed The Father of Korumburra was formerly the proprietor of the Exford Hotel in Russell Street Melbourne, which he ran with his wife for 20 years before relocating to Korumburra. Radovick was a man with considerable wealth and great enthusiasm for the pioneer township. Radovick's Korumburra Hotel which cost an astonishing £7,000 was granted a liquor license in December 1889 by Magistrates Francis Augustus Hare and Charles Hope Nicolson, both formerly senior policemen involved in the hunt and capture of Ned Kelly.

The Korumburra Hotel opened in February 1890 and from the outset was considered the jewel in the crown of Korumburra community life

> *The building consists of two storeys and has a frontage to the main street directly opposite the railway station. It contains about 50 rooms lined and floored with pine throughout. The bar is roomy, the fittings excellent and the cellar is unusually large. A billiards room adjoins the bar. The dining room is furnished with mirrors, handsome chandeliers and venetian chairs. The kitchen is provided with every convenience. Then there is the bar parlour, commercial room, private parlour and dining room all elaborately furnished with pianos and mirrors. Access to the second floor is obtained by means of a massive staircase and it leads to a roomy landing. Each room is carpeted and furnished luxuriously with spring mattresses and every article for the comfort of visitors. Stables, buggy sheds, etc., occupy yard space adjacent to the main building and complete without doubt the most handsome and commodious hotel in South Gippsland.*

People came from near and far to experience the luxury and lavish entertainment of the grand hotel. With mingling crowds of people came community law and order problems. A 'Rambling Correspondent' commenting on the coming of the railway to Korumburra, described the rowdy disruption to town life caused by railway navvies and sly grog shanty keepers.

I made the acquaintance of Constable Foley who, to be sure, I had no difficulty in discovering was a generous son of the Emerald Isle. Foley was to my mind the right man in the right place, as during the last 12 months he had experienced some rough times amongst the navvies and shanty keepers. His last encounter with one of the latter he informed me, nearly resulted in consequences of a serious nature. A female shanty keeper who did not relish seeing one of her patrons arrested, came to the rescue and applied with telling effect a billet of wood to the constable's head which fortunately his helmet saved.

A more serious incident occurred when railway navvy David Riley, as the result of a heated card game dispute, killed his adversary John Donnelly in a bareknuckle street fight. *Both men stripped to the waist and surrounded by about 150 persons the fight commenced. Riley struck Donnelly a severe blow behind the right ear which caused him to stagger and fall to his knees. He then fell backwards, his second threw some water over his face thinking he was only knocked out, but Donnelly never spoke again and had breathed his last.* Riley and two others who had helped in the fight were arrested and charged with manslaughter. The three men were acquitted; the court determined that what took place was not done in malice.

In July 1891, just 18 months after opening his splendid hotel, Radovick was honoured with a testimonial dinner and presented with a handsomely framed and illuminated address by Korumburra notables. *We have very great pleasure in expressing our appreciation of the enterprise and spirited public action displayed by you on so many occasions. We cannot fail to observe the large amount of energy you have bought to bear on every movement calculated for the good of our town. The zeal with which you carry out whatever you have undertaken, and that neither time nor money have been spared in furtherance of every necessary movement for promoting the advancement of Korumburra.* Today a Korumburra street bears Radovick's name.

oooOOOooo

Stock theft was a perennial problem in country districts. In pioneering days, livestock thieves like Ned Kelly and his lawbreaking relatives, would steal their neighbours horses and cattle, drive them across the border into New South Wales and sell the animals to the highest bidder. If there was a danger of the law catching up with Ned's gang of thieves, they would cut the throats of the animals, burn the carcasses and dispose of them down an abandoned mine shaft or secluded bend of a river. Ned and his larrikin mates were brutal self-interested men, with no concern for their victims or humane treatment of the horses and cattle they stole.

Occasionally an alert would go out that stock thieves were operating in the Korumburra/Warragul districts. Fences were cut in the night and next morning horses, cattle or sheep would be missing. The police would investigate, but the criminals had already moved on and only rarely were they caught. Farmers who had spent many years building up dairy and breeding herds with pedigree animals were greatly annoyed by these thefts. Once the pioneering horse and buggy era was over it was more likely that a farmer's car, truck and machinery would be stolen. Thieves risked ferocious farm dogs and an angry farmer's shotgun in their dishonest quest for stolen goods. Sometimes at night we would hear a shotgun blast in the distance, and wonder whether it was someone out hunting or a warning shot that there were thieves about.

Neighbours would sometimes commit crime against another farmer's livestock. In January 1915, the *Great Southern Advocate* carried an article titled 'Blacktrackers Good Work at Korumburra.'

> *Mr Leslie Wilson reported to police that one of his sheep had been found dead on the road. Mr Wilson also stated he had missed other sheep during the past month. An investigation by police found the sheep had been killed by having its head smashed. Apart from a few footmarks near the dead animal, no other clue could be obtained. Senior Constable Bartley decided to get the blacktrackers up. Two of them, in charge of Constable Downes and Detective Bell, arrived by Saturday night's train. On Sunday morning, the trackers traced the footprints through a paddock to a neighbour's stockyard, where a youth named Herbert Christian Jensen, 18 years of age, was questioned by the police. He said*

he had killed the sheep because it had been trespassing on his father's property. Jensen will be proceeded against by summons on a charge of having feloniously, unlawfully and maliciously killed sheep.

When brought before the Korumburra Bench, Jensen's defence lawyer in mitigation of the crime, said *Jensen was merely putting these sheep out of his father's property and used too much force on one sheep and killed it.* Jensen struck the animal with a wooden paling and left it to die on the road. No mention was made of other occasions when farmer Wilson's sheep went missing and were never found. The case was withdrawn. Jensen, who his lawyer said was *of irreproachable character and spoken well of by everybody,* was ordered to pay all costs. One can assume that tensions between the warring neighbours remained high and unappeased.

Organised criminal gangs targeted Korumburra and Warragul shops and business premises. In September 1950, the Melbourne *Argus* reported 'Thieves busy again in Korumburra'. *A well organised gang of shop breakers is believed to be responsible for the thefts of goods worth £5,550 from various Korumburra stores in less than a year. They have always worked so silently that the thefts have not been noticed until daybreak. The latest occurred early yesterday when stock in the Bronwyn frock salon worth more than £2,000 was stolen. It was the second raid on the shop in four months. In the first thieves took goods valued at £500. Warragul detectives and Korumburra police are investigating.*

Between January and July 1950, Victoria Police blamed two mobile criminal gangs for stealing clothing worth £40,000 in a series of state wide burglaries masterminded by fences. *Police are being hampered in their investigations, because the thieves are using stolen cars with false number plates. The cars are abandoned after each robbery. The stolen goods reach the market through clever 'fences' who are the brains behind the gang. Thefts from factories and shops have become so prevalent in the past three months that police throughout Victoria have been asked to coordinate their investigations with Russell Street detectives. Police say shop breaking increases during the winter, when thieves take advantage of dark nights and deserted streets.*

Delinquency among the young riled law-abiding adults. In January 1921, the *West Gippsland Gazette* published an angry letter under the heading 'Boy Thieves' from an irate Warragul resident identifying himself as 'A Victim'.

> *Is it not time that the boy thieves of Warragul receive a check? Their depredations are becoming unbearable. Day after day petty thefts are going on. Fruit, vegetables, flowers (roots and all), eggs, wire netting, bags, bottles, wood; everything indeed, that can be unobtrusively carried off by these young gaolbirds in embryo is sneak-thieved. If they are detected by a man, they scatter and go for their lives; if by a woman, they defy her and use disgusting language. This little band of boys about six in number, hunt in couples before folks are astir in the morning and on moonless nights. They are well known to the police who have warned them and their parents time and time again. If left to themselves these lads will most certainly grow into dangerous rogues.*

oooOOOooo

In April 1892, the *Great Southern Advocate* newspaper described a concert disturbance caused it reported by the 'uncouth behaviour of Korumburra larrikins'. *The unpropitious state of the weather on Friday night last, did not prevent a very fair audience attending at the Mechanics Hall to listen to one of the grandest concerts held in the district for some time. Rain began to come down in torrents, just about the hour when many would be starting from home, and the elements continued in dull and damp mood for the rest of the evening and night. Yet notwithstanding this serious drawback, many came from a long distance to enjoy the musical and Terpsichorean pleasures of the evening.*

Songs performed included 'Come back to Erin', 'Erin my Heart beats for thee', 'Terrence's farewell to Kathleen' and 'It was a Dream'. Mr Lightbody followed with a comic song in character 'Off to Ireland' and fairly convulsed the audience. He was recalled and responded with an Irish jig. The Irishness and Catholicism of the festive occasion was rounded off with approval from Reverend Father O'Leary who was personally gratified by the singing and the exceptional talent provided. He thanked the performers, individually and collectively, for the really excellent results of their efforts. Shortly before the entertainment opened, an army of youths who had congregated outside were admitted by a good-natured nod from the doorkeeper. They returned their thanks later on, by disturbing the music loving public in such a manner as to call forth from the Chairman a very forcible rebuke. Yet the catcalls and disturbance continued. *Miss Dobell, a child of tender years, acquitted herself very creditably and pleased the audience well with the song 'The Cows are in the Clover'. The virtues of the duet 'The Moon has raised her Silvery Lamp' by Messrs Jenvey and Jensen, were lost altogether by the uncouth behaviour of a number of youths who were severely chastised by the Chairman.* Whether the youths who engaged in uncouth behaviour, were ejected from the hall by the organisers of the event or a mob of angry patrons, the newspaper report does not state.

Larrikin behaviour would sometimes lead to serious crime and attempted murder. The memory of Ned Kelly and other notorious bushrangers still had salacious newspaper currency well into the early years of the 20th century. Before then those emulating bushranger behaviour could expect no leniency from the custodians of law and order. A series of letters sent to the Editor of the *Gippsland Times* in July 1885, attest to the still prevalent fear of Kelly style criminals present in rural communities. Only in this particular case from Sale, there was a clemency plea to reduce a harsh sentence of 15 years imprisonment on *a foolish young fellow* (whose larrikin misbehaviour brought) *such disastrous results upon himself. We, in Gippsland, who have watched the entire progress of the case, can surely not unconcernedly allow a young man to be the unfortunate victim, as we can only suppose him to be, the victim of the Kelly Scare. Can nothing be done to secure some considerable mitigation of such a terrible sentence? Common sense and the instincts of humanity revolt from the idea of visiting the hare-brained escapade of this youth with imprisonment for nearly half a lifetime.*

A more serious incident that took place in Warragul in April 1922, appeared in newspapers under the heading 'The Boy Bushrangers'. *An inside story of the bushranging exploits of Henry Maple was told in the Neerim South Police Court today, when William Banks, who was Maple's associate during a portion of the latter's career of crime, was charged with breaking into and stealing from a store. A statement signed by Banks was read in court, in which the accused said after Maple fired at Constable Bartils and sent a bullet through his hat, Bartils fired back and knocked a cigarette from Maple's mouth. Maple said he intended shooting Bartils. And also said to Banks 'if I shoot you, I will bury you in the bush and nobody will be able to find you'.*

oooOOOooo

In March 1931, the Melbourne *Argus* newspaper published a pioneer remembrance of the early days of Korumburra.

When the coalmines were in full blast, Korumburra was a different place. Day and night the streets were filled with miners and their folk, who talked in the dialects of Wales and Northumberland. Farmers drove up the slushy road in mud sleds; the shops were crowded; the hotel bars were always full, and the patrons were often full. There were dogfights and fights between men; Salvation Army bands played on vacant allotments; Coal trains clanked and shunted at the siding; rowdy strikers met in and around the miner's hall. The directors of collieries dined at Radovick's hotel. Once a week the police magistrate arrived on the night train from Melbourne, accompanied by a band of lawyers, to attend busy sittings of the district court and to settle many differences varying from petty debt to deeds of violence. Settlers from the heavy South Gippsland Forest country, their faces eye deep in whiskers, pioneers who could swing an axe and drink a pint, gathered at 'Rads' with the miners and the commercial travellers over pots and poker games. There were lodge meetings and card games; syndicates were formed to exploit new coal outcrops; racing club committees dealt with the running of local thoroughbreds; dances were conducted in the adjacent hall; and the balcony above the entrance to the hotel was reserved for flirtations.

On weekly paydays at the mine, social life in Korumburra reached its climax. In the main street the hotel, the stores, the circus, and the revival meetings were filled to overflowing. So was the lockup. The capacity of the lockup and the small but active police force were inadequate upon these festive occasions. Only 15 prisoners could be crammed into the lockup at one time, so when one batch had sobered a little it was cast out, bellowing and brawling, into the bush to make room for the next batch. It was the blending of coalmining and agriculture, rarely found on coalfields, that gave a special charm to old Korumburra and spiced its social life. Men who delved in rich surface soil formed companionships with men who burrowed beneath it. Both gloried in a common belief in the approaching greatness of Korumburra, the future metropolis of Gippsland. Korumburra coal they agreed was the fiercest burning coal in the world. Korumburra trees were the tallest in the world and the bulls of the district were world champions.

Gippsland families would tell city folk, that cows in the Strzelecki Ranges had one leg shorter than the other to cope with the hilly countryside. They would beguile the unwary with bush tales of three-headed goats and dogs with two tails. When researching family history for the Ned Kelly books I was to write, my wife Joy a city girl born and bred, fell victim to one such bout of tall tale bush storytelling. The north east family we were visiting in the 1970s were renowned for growing oversized pumpkins. A prize pig went missing when about to give birth to a litter of piglets. Old Jack related: *Grandad was passing by the pumpkin patch, when he heard a commotion coming from inside one of the pumpkins. On investigation the missing pig with ten young piglets were found hidden together inside a hollowed out pumpkin shell.* Jack looked over at me with a knowing slyness in his eyes. Joy, still under the spell of Jack's bush blarney yarn, exclaimed *Really?*

Main Street Korumburra 1895 State Library of Victoria

4

Tambo Crossing and Warragul Pioneer Stories

Ten miles from Ryan's Crossing and five below the peak, I built a little homestead on the banks of Rocky Creek. I cleared the land and fenced it and ploughed the rich red loam — and my first crop was golden, when I brought Mary home

A B Paterson

In August 1884, after a short sojourn in Melbourne and the Queensland outback, Hugh Maxwell, a Protestant Irishman from Bangor County Down in Northern Ireland, wrote home to his Irish relatives discussing the prospects of selecting land in Victoria. *There is only one district where there is any good land* (left) *for selection* (and) *that is called Gippsland. I believe it is very heavily timbered, although the land is said to be good when cleared. A selector of government land is not to pay all the money at first but to pay in instalments the paying is not so heavy, as getting the right kind of land and in the right place not too far from the railway or good markets. I have rather better prospects* (here) *than in Belfast and by no means regret the change. The Australian bush impresses newcomers very much on their first run up country. It is so different from the scenery at home. The evergreen forests of Australia are so very different to the home woods, when one does at home come to a wood, which is very seldom. The dead trees which have been rung* to let the grass grow have such a weird appearance. The scenery here does not come up to the home scenery generally, as far as I have seen any rate.

Hugh, joined by his brother John *started for Sale Gippsland by the early train on Thursday; arrived there about 1 o'clock; took the boat which plies on the Gippsland Lakes between Sale and Bairnsdale. We arrived at Bairnsdale about 8.30 pm stopped there all night and started next day at 7.30 pm by coach for a small township called Bruthen; arrived there about 10 o'clock the same evening. On Saturday morning we again started by coach at 5 o'clock and got to Tambo Crossing at 9 o'clock in time for breakfast. We were now at our journey's end. We soon found Mr Wilson a young man that had taken up a block of land there. John and I started off have a look at the lands available for selection. We were rather disappointed, as we found it all extremely hilly indeed mountainous in some places.*

In April 1888, John Maxwell was granted a license for a selection of land in Gippsland. *I am going to turn farmer in the course of six months. The land is not very good not as regards the nature of the soil, but it is very hilly. It isn't much, but it may be a good deal someday. It was the best I could get except* (for) *scrubby country which would take a man with big capital, a stout heart and plenty of muscle. The first and last commodities, I am a bit deficient in. I believe when I get the fences up and timber killed off, it will be good grass country. The block contains 800 acres. One half is very good, but the other is almost valueless. It will be under a government lease for 10 years or 14 years from the passing of the Act, which came into operation at the beginning of 1884. Out of the leasehold, I can select 320 acres which will be excised from the leasehold and subject to a yearly payment of one shilling an acre per year for 20 years when it will be a freehold. The remainder of the land, I will be paid improvements for up to the value of 10 shillings an acre.*

In November 1888, Hugh sent another letter home to his relatives in Ireland. *John has made a start on his selection. He has got a horse and is now making ready to erected his little house. He stays at the hotel at Tambo Crossing where the post office is also, a kind of wayside hotel where the mail coach stops on its route. He has his horse to ride to and from the land.* In February 1889, Hugh and John's brother William takes up the tale. *I went out to Tambo Crossing to see John, found that he was well, only* (with) *a little cold he had got after a wetting he got some time previous. When there, we had a ride over some blocks of land that he wanted me to buy. We settled on one; if John and the present owner can come to terms. There is only one block of 550 acres between him and this one. There is quite a lot of kangaroo and wallaby. Anybody that was good with a gun, could make a pile of money shooting them for their skins. John has got a splendid Martini Henry rifle that can hit a kangaroo at 200 yards away. He seems pretty comfortable, only the cooking does not suit him and he does not care too much for the heat. Bob Wilson and him are often together. He lives on the other side of the river from John. Sometimes, he stops all night with John.*

oooOOOooo

James, another Maxwell brother in partnership with his sibling John, wrote. *John has let a contract for tree ringing of the block. It is nearly completed and the men will soon start a contract for fencing. John has been looking after some cows, as we propose putting on cattle instead of sheep for a few years, as there are wild dogs (or dingoes) in the district and we could not afford to lose any of our little flock. Speaking about John's house, I can give little information on it only to say that the fireplace and chimney is just like a blacksmith's hob, only the hearth is on the floor instead of being raised. The back and sides of the fire is lined with clay instead of mortar and stone, to prevent the wood (with which the walls and chimney on the house is built) from catching fire.*

A short time later James wrote in another letter on the 9 May 1889. *John has now 350 acres rung and also about 1½ miles of fencing done. He had men cutting down some trees and grubbing a bit of ground for an orchard and garden. Mr Thomas was surprised to see the vegetables John had grown, turnips that could not be surpassed, also French beans and vegetable marrows, the latter being the length of his forearm. Now dear mother with reference to John and his hut: I mentioned it before, but I know you would like to hear something fresh. His house, some would call a hut, but I think the proper name for it is a house for it is big enough to accommodate three people to sleep in. Mr Thomas says it is very comfortable. I sent John 20 yards of Hessian to line it with, which will also add to the comfort. I also sent him another pair of blankets to keep him warm during the winter. I forwarded John his socks* (you sent from Ireland).

John described his fledgling Gippsland home as remarkably different from the land tenure arrangements in Ireland. *A young farmer starting on a piece of new land* (here) *has a great many inconveniences to contend with, but there is one grand thing about it. The land is becoming your own and there will be no landlord craving you for the rent. When one compares this land with yours* (in Ireland); *it seems a marvel that there is not an even greater amount of immigration from the old country. I am helping Mr Wilson* (John's neighbour) *with his sheep. They are now lambing and we have great trouble guarding them every night on account of the dingoes, which killed no less than 14 or 15. They are a great pest to sheep owners. I find the soil around my hut very productive, rich black soil with a surface of a gritty clay subsoil. I now have proof of it, in the shape of turnips, cabbages, cauliflowers and vegetable marrows. The cabbages are as big as my head, grown without manure.*

In Gippsland, a land that might be said to be flowing with milk and honey, it is impossible to procure for either love or money, a bit of butter. Meat is an article of food that is on the Australian table at every meal. It seems to me the longer you are in the country, the fonder you get of meat. Most people never think the table properly furnished unless there is meat. However, I restrict myself to eating it twice a day, breakfast and dinner. My third meal being generally bread and treacle. I find the treacle acts as a medicine and prevents any lodgement of bile. The Maxwell brothers were not the healthiest of men. Hugh in particular often wrote of medical treatment and good nutrition.

oooOOOooo

John sent his impression of the natural beauty and harsh rigours of the Gippsland landscape to those among his Irish relatives and friends contemplating immigration. *You have no idea what bush life is* (like) *in Australia. Fancy you are in the midst of a big forest, thousands of square miles in extent with trees growing as thick as they are in Portavoe* (a treed estate in Northern Ireland). *That you are looking down from the top of a very big hill, very steep on the side you are looking down, that you see a creek flowing in towards the big hill and runs right up against it. It bends round at right angles to your left and flows about half a mile, then joins the waters of the Tambo River. In front of you is another nice hill, which slopes gradually back for about half a mile. About 100 yards up the sloping hill from the creek, imagine you see a very little house with walls built of small trees laid parallel with one door, one small window about the size of the window above the slope trough, looking out on your back grounds. This little house has an iron roof. Not far from the little house, imagine you see a shed about 20 feet and 15 feet wide built of bark. When you do this, you will form a better idea of how new selectors are housed in Australia. Although I live in this humble way, I have no reason for complaint. This being the most improved block of land in the district. It can boast of what no other can about here, a garden. But you all have had enough about this place, so we will speak of something else.*

Hugh Maxwell closely followed the Irish political situation. On 17 March 1886, he wrote a letter home discussing the latest Irish political news. *I noticed by the Melbourne papers, that the Protestants of the North of Ireland are arming themselves with all possible haste, in prospect of the Home Rule Bill passing. What is your opinion at the prospect of Home Rule? I don't think the Home Rule Bill can possibly be passed. The North seems to be as much against it, as the rest of Ireland is for it.* Hugh a loyal Orangeman remained true to his Scots Presbyterian roots. He opposed the Home Rule Bill, which subsequently failed to pass into British law.

His brother John, no radical Orangeman and a moderate Protestant in his political thinking, wrote regarding Irish Home Rule. *It is most extraordinary how people differ at home from people out here, or rather how they are situated and how they act. Every man who is over 21 and has his name registered has a right to vote at the time of parliamentary elections. Every man votes for the candidate who he believes will look after his interest, irrespective of religion (save for the Catholics who are as greatly influenced by their ecclesiastical dignitaries, as they are in Ireland).* John, clearly impressed by colonial democracy in Australia, perceived only injustice and oppression in the harsh English laws that governed Ireland.

It is a grievous thing to think that (Protestant) *Irishman should stand between men and their own interests. The majority of those Orangemen who talk of upholding Protestantism and the Protestant ascendancy are men, who may see the inside of a church once in 12 months. And though* (others) *may be strict churchgoers; what Christianity can there be in their hearts, if they persist in upholding unjust laws. If injustice is part of Protestantism, it is high time there was an independent body of Christians* (established). *Injustice was the cause of Protestantism and now to uphold the same said Protestantism, injustice, its origin, is again practised. There are a great many people who think they are fighting for God and Christianity, when in truth they are fighting for their own bigoted opinion. How can it be Christian to oppress?*

oooOOOooo

In response to questions from Ireland in 1890, William wrote *although we have so much land it is all bush; you would understand it better by looking at the inside of Mount Stewart or Lord Dufferin's demesne, only the trees are box and gums from 12 to 36 inches in diameter. Many gentlemen at home would be proud to have such bush* (at their disposal). *Mother would like to know about John's young lady. She is a very nice quiet girl with dark eyes and brown hair, plump cheeks and always a smile playing about her face and seems healthy looking.*

John was 29 years old and planning to get married on 21 April 1891, when on 6 April he died suddenly at his Tambo Crossing selection, preparing his property for his new bride. The cause of his death seems to have been a ruptured blood vessel from hard work splitting logs for fencing. William's letter home on 11 April was heart rending. *Please break the following news to mother and the rest as gently as possible. I received a telegram from Robert Wilson stating that John had died suddenly* (Monday) *morning and to come at once. I shall give you the particulars. Jock Anderson* (who had been working for John) *put the kettle on and made the tea. John took a hearty meal and remarked with a laugh, that he was nearly dead. He thought he had burst a small blood vessel* (and was) *spitting up a little blood. Anderson said to John that he must be making fun. He never saw John look better, for John had just took off his beard that same day before his departure to Melbourne to get married to Miss Wilton on April 21st. The invitations were sent* *on Monday morning before James told her to their friends to attend the ceremony. On Monday morning at 8 or a quarter past 8 o'clock, Anderson heard John vomiting and jumped out of bed. John called him to come as he was dying* (saying) *that his hour had come. Anderson held him in his arms and asked John, if he had any message to leave to any of his brothers. John answered him no, 'all you can do is to pray for me'.*

To make a sad situation even more emotionally unbearable, news came from Ireland that due to the recent immigration to Australia of several younger Maxwell relatives the brother's father had for the first time in 20 years to sow oats on the family farm without help. *We thought we should go home; as it would be only right to do so as father, mother and aunt Grace was getting not so able to look after things as they used to. It was our duty to look after the old people, but financially speaking we were better* (off) *here.* The practical suggestion was made that the older Maxwells should emigrate to Australia. Feeble health, however, prevented such a hoped-for family reunion. It was decided that William would return to Ireland with his family to take over the running of their parent's Ballygannah farm. Meanwhile, the other Maxwell brothers struggled on helping out financially by regularly sending money home. In 1920, Hugh Maxwell, now an old man comfortably settled in his adopted land, wrote to a friend about Ireland's continuing political woes. *A good country spoiled by a lot of fanatics. Here in Australia, we have our share of fools. People that are never content no matter what the conditions may be. Indeed, the whole world seems topsy turvy. I suppose it is the result of the war.*

oooOOOooo

On 2 September 1930, Mr William Gibson, son of a pioneer, gave an address to the Warragul Australian Natives Association titled 'Old Pioneer Days'. The *West Gippsland Gazette* published the lengthy speech in its entirety. This section with some word and sentence changes, consists of selected excerpts from the newspaper. It tells the story of an intrepid pioneer family, as they worked the land to bring the dense Gippsland Forest around Warragul under agricultural production.

Mr Gibson said the family to which he belonged was undoubtedly among the earliest settlers in the district, his father having been granted 320 acres of previously selected and then abandoned land, when the vast bush territory had been thrown open for selection in the 1870s. He asked his audience to go back with him and trace the movements of his family from the 14 March 1876. That was the date on which they had left their old home on the Koroit Creek near Melton and started out for the wilds of Gippsland.

He could remember the starting out one morning 54 years ago. The Clydesdale mare was in the shaft of the dray, and a neighbour's horse in the lead pulling a cart. The neighbour's horse was to be left in a yard in Melbourne. The tyre (rim) *came off the wheel of the dray, while coming down the Keilor Hill and there was some delay in getting it fixed. That night they arrived in Moonee Ponds where they stayed until next morning. There were steep hills to face and the difficulty was overcome by taking the Clydesdale horse out of the shafts of the dray and hitching it to the cart. On reaching the summit of a hill, the Clydesdale was unhitched and brought down again to bring up the lighter vehicle. They were getting into the better class of country. Walsh's Gully the terror to all who passed that way had to be crossed. They got safely over it and another gully had to be ascended. The road was getting worse. They pulled up on a Saturday night, that being as far as the road was cleared for vehicular traffic. The vehicles were left there for some weeks if not months, the horses were sent out to graze indefinitely.*

There was a selector's hut a short distance from where they camped, which belonged to Mr Charles Sargent and it was the only habitation. The next morning after having partaken of breakfast, they started out on foot to walk the remaining 2 miles to their selected block of land, taking with them a few things which they needed. Once there, they discovered a small bark hut. There were three bunks inside, also a table. The legs of the table were four stakes driven into the earthen floor. The top was a sheet of bark, which had been stripped carefully off a gumtree and nailed to the stakes. The overlapping edges, however, rolled up in the process of drying like a roll of paper. The hut could not accommodate the large family, so the men got to work and soon erected a framework of timber obtained from the bush. A large tarpaulin, which his father had bought coming through Melbourne, was thrown over a ridge pole, a large tent was made which was fairly comfortable. That place was where they dwelt pending the building of a house. There was but little clearing done on the selection. At the nearest point the scrub was within two chains of the door. The denizens of the forest comprised wild cattle, native bears, dingoes, tiger cats, flying squirrels, possums, lyrebirds, pigeons and some say a few emus.

The roads were in a very bad state, owing to the sun not being able to penetrate a dense wall of scrub growing close in on both sides. Some of the scrub attained a height of 40 feet. The seasons were very wet and the soil soft, the horses went down in the mud right up to the girth. The road from the selection to the spot where Warragul now stands was not put through at that time and the Warragul/Korumburra Road was not then surveyed. Mr Gibson touched upon the various bush sounds of the early days. Those sounds did not disturb them. What struck terror into the hearts of the younger members of the family, was the bloodcurdling howls of a pack of dingoes, which were forced by hunger to come out of their hiding place in the scrub and wander over the selection's clearing in search of food. Sometimes it was a settler's sheep that had to provide supper for those ravenous animals.

oooOOOooo

The early settler had a liking for exploring the bush. Sometimes he went unarmed, and sometimes he carried a rifle in the hope of meeting some wild cattle. It did not matter about the condition of the beast, or whether it was an ancient male that would not take very kindly to being regarded as beef. Mr Gibson's father said he counted 42 head of wild cattle on a clearing near a spring not far from his selection. One day in the bush, he said he was walking through the scrub, passed around a big tree and found that he stood facing a wild bull which was lying there. The brute jumped up, poised himself as if to make a charge, and then dashed off through the scrub. The speaker mentioned the different varieties of scrub and their peculiar perfumes. A number of stone tomahawks were picked up on the selection and Mr Gibson had one on display. When the family first saw Warragul, there was a small general store on the road at a point near the Railway Hotel. This little business was the nucleus of a successful later business venture. There was another business carried on in conjunction with the Crown Hotel. Mr Gibson said the name of the Crown Hotel, during the occupancy of Daniel Kennedy, was changed to the Oriental Hotel.

Through Daniel Kennedy there is a Warragul connection with Ned Kelly and his infamous story. Charles Hope Nicolson and Francis Augustus Hare visited Warragul in the late 1880s as Police Magistrates. Nicolson and Hare had earlier been Police Superintendents engaged in searching for the Kelly Gang (1878-1880). Nicolson was in charge of the hunt for the Kellys for many months. He ran an elaborate north east spy system from Benalla that included the former Greta schoolteacher Daniel Kennedy. Hare was wounded in the wrist during the first volley of shots fired by the outlaws at Glenrowan. To escape Kelly sympathiser reprisal Kennedy fled the north east district. Both men knew Kennedy well and no doubt the acquaintance was renewed in Warragul. Nicolson and Hare may have stayed at the Oriental Hotel on their visits to the town.

Prior to stores and shops being opened in Warragul, Mr Gibson's father walked all the way to the old Brandy Creek settler's store for his provisions. Some transportation carriers came from Melbourne with bullock and horse teams. People by the name of Miller had a carrying business in Warragul and a notable thing was the unique dress that was sometimes worn, which comprised a hessian bag with three holes cut in it, one for each arm and one for the head. This was put on as an overall to protect them from the flying mud from the horse's feet and to keep off the rain. Some of the settlers had a few cows. A milk dealer from Melbourne came to the district and enquired of Mr Gibson's father, if he could supply him with milk. There was not sufficient milk to be had from one selection, so Mr Gibson and a neighbour between them made up a can of milk and sent it by train as far away as Oakleigh where the dealer had come from. That was the first can of milk that left the Warragul Railway platform.

There was a sawmill where Harry Elliott now has his business. A heap of logs was drawn from the area in which Warragul is now situated. There were some very fine milling trees. Mr Gibson used to see the logs coming into the mill on high wheeled jinkers hauled by bullocks. Howitt Street occasionally flooded. Instead of bitumen which is now used, there was wooden plank roads. The planks in flood time lifted and floated on the water. It was impossible to get a horse across the road with safety. As dairy herds became more common, the settlers met and decided to start a cheese factory. A log building was erected for the purpose. The price of cheese was four pence halfpenny a pound. William Hamilton operated a saleyard in Napier Street. The first stock Mr Gibson bought at the saleyards was a small flock of sheep. The sheep did not turn out a success. The young grass was too rich and caused trouble. Later, a plague of caterpillars took everything before them and this occasioned mortality in livestock.

oooOOOooo

In those days there was no bowling or croquet club. Nor were there motorcars, telephones, picture shows or the wireless. Concerts and dances were popular. Every young man in the town could ride a horse. Everyone who could afford it owned his own hack. Mr Gibson owned an old race horse called 'Micky'. He once lent his horse to a friend named George King. (Coincidently, Ned Kelly's horse and cattle stealing stepfather was named George King. He disappeared, never to be heard from again at the time of the Kellys' trouble with the police. George physically abused Ned's mother Ellen and the suspicion is he was murdered by Ned and buried in an anonymous bush grave.) *When that gentleman returned the horse, he said. 'My word that horse puts you away old man'. 'How's that' he was asked. 'Well' replied Mr King. 'He knows every pub and grog shanty in the district. What's more he won't go, till I get off and go and have a drink'.*

Those were the good old days. A suit of all wool Ballarat tweed could be purchased for 24 shillings. A five roomed house could be rented for seven shillings and sixpence per week. Firewood cost two shillings and nine pence a ton. A three-course meal at the hotels and a glass of beer could be had for one shilling. If you wanted a drink on a hot night, a quart of beer cost 3d. Council rates were set at one shilling in the pound.

I wish to briefly refer to a few of the outstanding personalities of the time. David Connor the 'Father of Warragul' took an active interest in municipal matters. To him the town is indebted for its beautiful avenue of trees at the approach to the town and main street; for the splendid assortment of trees and shrubs around the Shire Hall, Post Office and Courthouse. He saw every brick laid in the Shire Hall. Around his own home, he had the finest collection of roses, flowers and shrubs to be found in Gippsland. He rendered great service as an Honorary Justice of the Peace. In social functions, he was always a familiar figure. He was the best horseman in the district in his youth and he died penniless.

James Copeland was one of the earliest Gippsland pioneers. He chose the wilds of the Gippsland bush for his retirement. A man of high intelligence and refinement, he was one of the first honorary justices to preside over the police court at Brandy Creek. He was known as 'Warragul's Gentleman'. He took a great interest in his church and died at his home at the ripe old age of 93 years. Joe Dale known as 'Gooseberry Joe' was the town's bellringer. He was a graduate of Cambridge University and a brother of the celebrated Dr Dale of Birmingham. One wonders how he came by the nickname 'Gooseberry Joe'? Mr Gibson ended the evening honouring the pioneers. The pioneers have bequeathed a noble example in a glorious heritage. Take example and inspiration from the pioneers, in the great achievements of men and women who claim this great country as their own native land.

5

Cobb and Co:
A Gippsland Coach Journey 1873

A land of sombre silent hills where mountain cattle go. By twisted tracks on sidelings deep where giant gumtrees grow. And the wind replies in the river oaks to the song of the stream below.

A B Paterson

The Cobb and Co coach line was established in Victoria, by Freeman Cobb, a 23-year-old American in 1853 to take passengers and mail between Melbourne and the newly established goldfields of Ballarat, Castlemaine and Bendigo. Cobb's spectacular success over his competitors was due to imported lightweight stagecoaches built to traverse the rigours of the American west. Secondly, by placing changing stations at 10 mile intervals where fresh horses were obtained, Cobb's coach and horses with faster speed could outrun the opposition. When Cobb and his partners sold the business in 1856, they realised £16,000, which is more than 2 million dollars today. In 1861 a consortium of businessmen paid £23,000 — a sum in excess of 3 million dollars. With ups and downs Cobb and Co continued to operate until 1924, when the last Queensland coach run was made. Railways and the advent of automobiles and aircraft sounded the death knell of the coaching industry.

In the *Argus* on 10 June 1922, Harry Peck, the son of John Murray Peck, one of Freeman Cobb's original partners, published an article titled 'Old Coaching Days: The Story of Cobb and Co', which brought to light some interesting background information about those involved in setting up and running the coaching firm. *John Lamber, John Swanton and John Murray Peck (my father) were with Freeman Cobb in New York, in the service of Adams and Co or Wells Fargo and Co. They came out to Australia in 1853, with the idea of entering into the carrying business to the goldfields. However, after a few months of hauling their wagons through the mud, as my father often said 'practically up to their floor' from Liardet's Beach* (the present Port Melbourne) *to the city, they gave up and began coaching on the Bendigo road on January 30 1854.*

After Mr Cobb returned to the United States and the business was sold to Thomas Davies, my father followed him, and purchasing a large cargo of the famed Abbott coaches returned to Victoria, forming a new company which comprised 13 partners, all Yankees and Canadians, which took over the Bendigo road run and branches in 1857 and carried on under the old name Cobb and Co. Mr George Woodworth who died only last year, was the last survivor of Cobb and Co's original drivers. And the first to drive a 'Jack' (a coach carrying 40 passengers pulled by six horses) *into Bendigo. He often related that when he first took the ribbons on a 'Jack', she rolled 'so like a ship at sea' that for the whole of his stage from Castlemaine to Bendigo, the sensation of top heaviness was so strong that he felt all the time he was going to lurch over the wheels. 'But' the old man added with pride, 'never a 'Jack' was known to leave her braces or lose her centre of gravity'.*

James Rutherford (a later partner) *did more to extend and spread the name and fame of Cobb and Co throughout Australia than any other man. Of the original four partners of Cobb and Co, John Murray Peck was the only one to really adopt Victoria as his home. John Lamber died in San Francisco some 25 years ago. Mr Swanton in New Zealand and Mr Cobb in South Africa.*

oooOOOooo

The morning star has vanished the frost and fog are gone. A flask of friendly whisky — each other's hopes we share — and throw our top coats open to drink the mountain air. The roads are rare to travel and life seems all complete. The grind of wheels on gravel the trot of horses' feet. By clear ridge country rivers and gaps where tracks run high, where waits the lonely horseman cut clear against the sky. Past haunted half-way houses where convicts made the bricks, scrub yards and new bark shanties we dash with five and six. Through stringybark and blue gum and box and pine we go. A hundred miles shall see tonight the Lights of Cobb and Co!

The Lights of Cobb and Co (Abridged) by Henry Lawson. The *Sydney Bulletin* 11 December 1897.

Henry Lawson's iconic poem is a romanticised story of a Cobb and Co coach journey. The reality was not nearly so romantic and was often far more tiresome and drearier than Lawson's literary words reveal. When travelling through the rain soaked, dank and boggy Gippsland Forest, there were ordeals to be endured that bush poets tended to shy away from in marked contrast to Lawson's whimsical description of a stirring coach ride through the Aussie bush. We have the revealing diary comments of Thomas Mills, a Cobb and Co traveller in 1873, whose coaching experience was bleak, exhausting and far from idyllic.

Thomas Mills was an immigrant Englishman who was to manage the Heyfield pastoral station owned by James Tyson the millionaire squatting tycoon. He arrived in Victoria as a new chum in 1873, with little understanding of either the Australian bush or the pastoral task he was about to undertake. It is said of him *when he arrived off the ship, he was so green that when the boys put his saddle on back to front, he tried to ride it.* Mills quickly acclimatised to the colonial life and he became a good property manager and an excellent judge of livestock.

On 10 March 1945, the *Argus* newspaper published extracts from Mill's diary narrating his 1873 coach journey from Melbourne to Rosedale in Gippsland, known as the Cobb and Co Gippsland Run. It was a difficult journey of 150 miles that took a day and a half to accomplish. The rough bush tracks of the Gippsland Forest were an obstacle unlike anything Mills had experienced before. The *Argus* journalist described the beginning of Mills Cobb and Co adventure. *At 1 o'clock on a fine September day, he boarded the coach at the old Albion Hotel in Bourke*

Street Melbourne. *The whip cracked and the horses set off at a good pace down the hill. Mills said people on the street 'quizzed' them for the reason; they had done the journey themselves and did not envy the travellers.*

At this point, Mills takes up the narrative. *Going at a good galloping speed through St Kilda soon opened up the country, and after an hour's run brought us to the pretty little village called Oakleigh. Here we delivered mails and exchanged horses. At 5 o'clock we reached the small village of Dandenong. We reached the next stage Berwick, at 8 o'clock. The horses were changed, but no time was allowed for refreshments. Patience is a virtue so I thought, as we pulled up at the longed-for stage called Bunyip Creek.*

I was not long finding my way into the parlour of the comfortable inn, where a blazing log fire was burning to welcome weary travellers. The table was spread with a fine joint of beef and potatoes. We eagerly did justice to it, and followed it with a good cup of tea. I drew up to the fire, prepared to have a warm, when the driver called 'All on board!' So, we had to go or be left behind.

I tried to get a nap to help pass away the dreary time, but with the jerking of the coach and the tumbling about of the luggage inside, and the splashing of dirt from the wheels, sleep was out of the question.

Later on, we passed the homeward bound coach on the road, and were warned by the driver that the roads were very bad indeed. We were not long in finding that out, for the coach came to a sudden halt. The coachman jumped down, and when I heard him exclaim 'Here's a bonnyfix!' I jumped down too. I landed up to my ankles in thick mud, to find that a sapling had become tangled in the wheels of the coach. Axes were brought out, and after an hour's work the wheels were free. Every mile the road got worse, and it was with great exertion on the part of the horses that we arrived at Brandy Creek.

We changed horses, and as a passenger left here, I took his seat on the box, thinking that the time and journey would not be so fatiguing. But in this I was disappointed. It was now 1 o'clock at night and very cold. I was delighted when morning dawned, and felt better able to bear my troubles. The forest seemed full of life. Wild birds sang, cockatoos shrieked. There came the unearthly row of the laughing jackass (kookaburra) *and the scrambling of monkey bears* (koalas).

By 9 o'clock we reached the small village of Shady Creek, where there was just time for a warm. When we started out, I took an inside seat, as I could not keep my eyes open. I thought I might get a nap by sleeping on the mailbags, but that was quite impossible owing to loose boxes and parcels falling about. I became very sick, and was pleased when we pulled up at the village of Moe. It was a source of great gratification to me, when I became aware that the worst perils of our travels had been attained.

My spirits began to revive, knowing that in a few hours my troubles would cease. At Traralgon village we had a few minutes refreshment, then made another start for the last stage for me. An hour's run brought us to Rosedale, where horses were waiting to take me to my destination at Heyfield. The 33 hours in a stagecoach across the Australian Forest, was quite enough to satisfy my ambition in that direction.

There was a further 12 miles to be traversed from Rosedale to the Heyfield squatting run. The *Argus* journalist completed Thomas Mills narrative, stating *food and warmth waited for him behind the sturdy stone walls of the old station on the banks of the Thompson River. The station maintained the reputation for the lavish hospitality of those days.* — Through stringybark and blue gum and box and pine we go. A hundred miles shall see tonight the Lights of Cobb and Co!

Part Two
Irishmen, Pioneer Women and Anzacs

There's a little Irish mother that a lonely vigil keeps in the settler's hut, where seldom strangers come. Where the settlers battle gamely beaten down to rise again, and the brave bush wives the toil and silence share. Where the nation is a building in the hearts of splendid men; there's a little Irish mother always there.

John O'Brien

6
Irish Catholics, Daniel Mannix and Ireland

Tell Ireland! Tell her in her desolation! That hearts within the south for her have bled.

Henry Lawson

A deep sense of my own Irish heritage was something I grew up with in Gippsland. It was all around me at home, in school, church and the playground. Along with the Catholic saints, Archbishop Daniel Mannix and the Irish Fenian heroes fighting for Ireland's freedom dominated my Aussie childhood years. Mum had a strong emotional passion for all things Irish. She would relate colourful stories of her Byrne and Murray ancestors, telling Mary and me of their undying affection for Catholicism, Saint Patrick, the Shamrock and the Old Country. My great aunt Aileen Bridget Byrne, known as Sister Mary Kosta, was a Catholic nun who died at the young age of twenty-seven. Sister Mary was held in high regard almost akin to sainthood by the Byrne family. For many years after her passing, money would be donated and masses said for the repose of her soul.

What was happening in Ireland was a hot topic of conversation, whenever Australia's Irish diaspora met. The Dublin Easter Rising of 1916 was spoken of as if it happened yesterday. The execution sitting in a chair of wounded rebel leader James Connolly by a firing squad of

English soldiers was remembered as a spiteful act of political malice.

> *He went to his death like a true son of Ireland. There was many a sad heart in Dublin that morning, when they murdered James Connolly the Irish rebel.*

Patriotic sympathy for the old country was raw, visceral and emotional. For me and other Catholic Aussie/Irish kids, Ireland was a place of wonder and fantasy tinged with centuries of cruelty and oppression. We knew of Fenian convicts and the suffering they endured when transported to a distant penal colony half a world away. The crimes they committed were often petty and the punishment unduly harsh. For the most part, what we knew was an exaggerated version of the convict past but one that we firmly believed in.

> *By a lonely harbour wall, she watched the last star falling, as the prison ship sailed out against the sky. For she lived in hope and prayer for her love in Botany Bay. It's so lonely round the Fields of Athenry.*

Each Irish family felt the sorrow and the anguish of leaving the old country and loved ones behind. It was a heartbreak and sadness long remembered and passed down the generations. Those who set sail on immigrant ships did so with the unhappy knowledge the farewell was forever.

> *It's not for the parting that my sister pains. It's not for the grief of my mother. Tis all for the loss of my bonny Irish lass that my heart is breaking forever.*

The Emerald Isle, its troubled history and the promise of a new beginning in a faraway land framed the Irish imagination with a sentimental nostalgia every migrant understands. The emotional homeland bond is a deep and enduring legacy, lessened as previous generations pass away but never entirely forgotten. Erin Go Bragh! Ireland Until Eternity!

oooOOOooo

From the pulpit, spurred on by his August 1920 attempt to visit Ireland which was blocked by the British Government, Catholic Archbishop Daniel Mannix fanned the flames of Irish discontent in Australia. The Byrnes and Murrays, along with countless other Irish Australians, supported Mannix and the Irish rebel cause and they would continue to do so in the decades to come. In the Byrne home at Ballarat, an oak framed photograph of Irish Free State President Éamon de Valera proudly hung on the wall next to the Byrne ancestors. De Valera was Commandant in charge of Boland's Mill during the Dublin Easter Rising. Family tradition has it that one or more of the Boland's Mill defenders was an Irish relative of the Australian Byrnes. Fourteen men with the surname Byrne were awarded the Irish Medal by the Irish Free State for their defence of Boland's Mill.

In 1916 the Mount Street Bridge over the Grand Canal and Boland's Mill at Ballsbridge witnessed a significant skirmish during the Easter Rebellion. Two hundred and forty casualties were sustained by British soldiers, which according to one source was approximately two thirds of all British army casualties during Easter week. One author wrote *British casualties lay all over Northumberland Road, on the house steps, in the channels along the canal banks and in Warrington Place. Witnesses recalled the place was literally swimming with blood.* The popular song Raglan Road based on a poem by Irish poet Patrick Kavanagh, is named after Raglan Road in Ballsbridge Dublin.

> *On Raglan Road on an autumn day, I saw her first and knew. That her dark hair would weave a snare that I might one day rue. I saw the danger, and I passed along the enchanted way. And I said, 'Let grief be a falling leaf at the dawning of the day'.*

My great, great grandparents Hugh Byrne and Ellen Byrne nee York (it may have been Elizabeth) were Dubliners residing at Ballsbridge in the parish of Donnybrook. Their son Michael (my great grandfather) was born in 1830. The Griffiths Valuation Book for Irish properties for 1847 has three revealing entries for Hugh Byrne. The most likely Hugh to have a family connection with the Australian Byrnes is the most prosperous and respectable of the trio. Hugh is recorded as being the proprietor of three separate Ballsbridge properties: a house and yard, a house, and an office valued at £5. 5 shillings, £9 and £1. 10 shillings respectively. Rather than hand to mouth labouring for a living, Hugh was a shrewd business man renting property, employing labour and operating an office workshop. There were several other Byrne family property owners residing in Ballsbridge at this time, Patrick, John,

David, Michael and Mrs Byrne to name just a few. My guess is they were respectable, prosperous and related.

Hugh harboured strong Fenian sympathies. The name Hugh Byrne of Dublin appears just once on a clemency petition signed by 80,000 Irishmen to free young Irelander leader William Smith O'Brien. O'Brien led a rising in three Irish counties in July 1848. Captured and convicted of High Treason, he was sentenced to be hanged, drawn and quartered. In June 1849, the sentence was commuted to Transportation for life to Van Diemen's Land. 42,560 Dubliners signed the petition and my great, great grandfather Hugh appears to have been one of them.

The nearby notorious Beggars Bush district was the haunt of gangs of unruly beggars and highwaymen. The residents of Ballsbridge would not venture into Beggars Bush without a pistol to defend themselves. Robbery and murder awaited the unwary and the gullible. Ballsbridge had numerous workshops for printing calico, linen and cotton. By 1837 100,000 printed cloth products were being produced annually. The Hammersmith Ironworks and a gunpowder factory were located close by on the banks of the Dodder River. By the middle of the 19th century these industries employed around six hundred skilled craftsmen and labourers, with a small contingent of workshop entrepreneurs operating independently. The latter is the employment followed by my Byrne ancestors before some of them emigrated to Australia, bringing with them to the new country a passionate love of Ireland and an undying loyalty for the Fenian cause.

> *Oh, see the fleet-foot host of men who march with faces drawn. They come with vengeance in their eyes; Too late! Too late are they! For young Roddy McCorley goes to die on the Bridge of Toome today.*

oooOOOooo

It was still possible in the 1950s to hear the rhythmic lilt of Irish brogue being spoken by Gippsland's older residents, who had emigrated to Australia from Irish farmsteads many decades before. Irish folklore and Irish history were remembered as a living tradition and passed onto the next generation. William Butler Yeats the famous Irish poet wrote in the London magazine *The Leisure Hour* in October 1890. *When I* tell people that the Irish peasantry still believe in fairies, I am often doubted. They do not imagine it possible that our highly thought of philosophies so soon grow silent outside the walls of the lecture room, or that any kind of ghost or goblin can live within the range of our daily papers. They are quite wrong. The ghosts and goblins do still live and rule in the imagination of innumerable Irish men and women, and not merely in remote places, but close even to big cities.

> *Up the airy mountain down the rushy glen. We daren't go a hunting for fear of little men.*

At certain times of the year, offerings of beer and cakes were placed outside Gippsland doors for the 'Little People' as we youngsters were told. The children were amazed when the food and drink was gone the next morning and of course, the fairies and leprechauns were responsible.

> *Pixies in the ferny hollow, Brownies on the hill. Every track we used to follow keeps its fairies still.*

Korumburra children loved to hear fairy stories. Irish fairy stories in particular captured the folkloric fantasy and engaging charm of fairies dancing in the woods. *Once upon a time the fairies of the west rested in Dooros Wood for three days and three nights. They spent the days feasting and the nights dancing in the light of the moon, and they danced so hard that they wore the shoes off their feet, and for a whole week after the leprechauns, the fairies' shoemakers, were working night and day making new ones, and the rip, rap, tap, tap of their little hammers were heard in all the hedgerows.*

I remember my five-year-old sister Mary came running into the house breathlessly one day to tell Mum she had found a fairy dancing circle behind the hayshed.

> *I wandered out into the bush to see the morning sky. All roundabout I heard the sound of fairies dancing by.*

We went outside and sure enough, there behind the hayshed was a circular ring of mushrooms, a fairy dancing circle, covered in moist morning dew. The mornings seemed much brighter, fresher and more vividly alive when you are a child. The crisp country air was damp with the smell of perfumed wattle mixed with the wafting scent of newly mowed hay. It was a magical moment and Mum said nothing to spoil the enchantment. Mary remained convinced that fairies danced not at the bottom of the garden but behind the hayshed wall.

> *The fairies went from the world because men's hearts grew cold; and only the eyes of children see what is hidden from the old.*

Old Mrs Ryan was born in County Tipperary, the illiterate daughter of an Irish tenant farmer who lost his tenancy during a round of landlord evictions. She was nearing 100 years old in 1956. She spoke with an Irish accent so old country and Gaelic, we children found it difficult to understand everything she said. The typical Hollywood movie image of an Irish grandma, she told wonderfully evocative stories of pioneer days and her family's sailing ship journey from Liverpool to Melbourne in the 1860s to begin a new life in colonial Victoria. She revered Ireland all her long life and would frequently reminisce about her childhood among the Irish hedgerows. Tears were visible in her fading blue eyes, as she recounted memorable tales of the Emerald Isle across the Irish Sea. Decades later I would wonder if she encountered Ned Kelly's relatives in Tipperary. Splendid stories such as Mrs Ryan told fuelled my boyhood imagination and love of history.

The stories we enjoyed most were Mrs Ryan's captivating tales of the banshee, fairies and leprechauns, none of whom were all that friendly to humans. W B Yeats relates stories of fairy pillaging and human abduction. *I have quite a number of records picked up from the faithful memories of old peasants. Brides and new born children are especially in danger. Peasant mothers, too, are sometimes carried off to nurse the children of the fairies. At the end of seven years, they have a chance of returning, and if they do not escape then, are always prisoners. A woman, said still to be living, was taken from near a village called Ballisodare, and when she came home after seven years, she had no toes — she had danced them off. The splendour of the fairy kingdom is a magical delusion, woven to deceive the minds of men by poor little withered apparitions who live in caves and barn laces. But this is, I suspect, a theological opinion, invented because all goblins are pagans. Many things about fairies, indeed, are most uncertain.*

oooOOOooo

In our childhood imagination, the Gippsland ferny dells and wooded forest landscape were peopled with strange Irish creatures. The Banshee (Faerie Woman) a ghostly woman figure said to wail a dire warning of death in Irish households held a particular fascination for enthralled children. A nervous shudder and the hairs on the back of your neck would stand on end, as you contemplated where these Irish apparitions might be hiding. *The wailing lament of the banshee sigh; How sad and mournful is the screeching cry.*

In Irish folktales the banshee is variously described as a haggard, old woman wearing a black dress and covering her face with a black veil. An old woman with long white hair and glowing red eyes; a deathly pale woman with long red hair dressed in a shroud; a beautiful woman with white hair, wearing a white dress and carrying a silver comb; and the scariest of all, a headless woman with breasts exposed carrying a bowl of blood. The screeching wail of the banshee was said to send chills up the spine of whoever heard it. These sinister folktales were designed by Irish storytellers to scare the daylights out of their superstitious audience.

The tale of the banshee old Mrs Ryan relates was a family story told by her Tipperary grandmother. *One dark and stormy night as grandma and the children were huddled by the fireside, an unearthly scream was heard coming from the yard outside. The deathly wail was heard again and the face of an old woman with shiny red eyes and a grim look on her face appeared at the window. She slowly raised a crooked finger and pointed in our direction. The finger and her starring gaze fell on Bridget. Three days later she sickened and died. The banshee wail foretold the death of darling Bridget as she will for all of us.*

The Irish brought to Australia many folk superstitions often predating the arrival of Christianity in Ireland. Some were universally recognised; breaking a mirror was the cause of seven years bad luck, a black cat crossing one's path was seen as a harbinger of disaster, spilling salt and not tossing some over your left shoulder would bring bad luck. Shamrocks and a rabbit's foot were considered to be lucky charms. Religious medallions bearing the image of Catholic saints and the holy crucifix of Christ were personal protection from life's misfortunes. Second sight — the ability to discern the future — was particularly valued among Irish pioneer women of a peasant background. The unnerving image of the wild eyed, Irish seeress dispensing prophecy and unsettling the present was a legendary figure in Celtic mythology.

The supernatural and other unworldly things were ever present in the Irish mind. The physical world was seen as a dangerous place where ghosts, menacing sprites and other frightening creatures required to be constantly appeased and pacified through incantations, spells and Druidic magic transformed in later years by the civilising cloak of the Christian religion. Samhain or Halloween celebrated in pagan Ireland in the month of November was an unsettled time, when the souls of the dead walked the earth in ghostly apparition and were mostly feared during the twilight hours.

> *Samhain is here, cold is the earth, as we celebrate the cycle of death and rebirth. Tonight, we speak to those through the veil. The lines between worlds are thin and frail.*

The older Irish pioneers of Gippsland, many of whom could not read or write, had in their hearts and minds a strong oral tradition of the old Celtic ways which came out most often in storytelling. As a child, I heard legendary folktales of heroic warriors, cattle stealing raids and clan warfare. I would later discover the mediaeval source of many of these traditional Irish stories, to be The Ulster Cycle (Rúraíocht in Gaelic) with its mythical hero Cú Chulainn who had seven fingers on each hand, seven toes on each foot and seven pupils in each eye. He was a mighty Irish warrior feared for his ferocious battle lust which cost countless men their lives. Of course, we children loved the blood and gore of it all as our hero vanquished his enemies. Stories of the Kings of Tara would also feature, mistakenly conjuring up in impressible young Aussie minds, a Gaelic fairytale of King Arthur and his Roundtable Knights. For the wrinkled old Irish storyteller, the fictional Celtic past was as real as the pioneer present and for some more so.

Family stories told by Korumburra's settlers, of life in Ireland shaped by these long ago and more recent events, were passed down through the generations. What they related was often tragic, occasionally humourous and always heartfelt. Their love for Ireland and the Catholic religion that sustained them in good times and bad was inspirational. The passing of the last of these remarkable old people in my childhood was keenly felt by the Korumburra community. It was the breaking of the living link with the old country and the new.

oooOOOooo

The colonial Irish retained a deep love for their Irish homeland, a love that over the ensuing years never diminished and was passed onto their children and grandchildren. During their pioneer sojourn in Australia, homesick Irishmen and women wrote sentimental and nostalgic poems and sent them to colonial newspapers. What these amateur poetic offerings lacked in polished skill, was more than compensated for by raw emotion and patriotic fervour.

> Yes, I'm weary 'mid the revel in the stranger's land today. Not one dear voice of those I loved all hushed all passed away. The aching breath of sadness wakes with its deep yearning spell. The hour I breathed to Erin's isle the whisper of farewell.
>
> Thou art distant now but still I cling to thee my place of birth. I've sought but I've never found a second home on earth. The hopes which gave to life it's worth and brought the soul-lit smile; now calmly sleep beneath the turf of Erin's sunny Isle.

Irishmen and women who came to Australia as convicts or emigrated as free settlers in the 18th and 19th centuries brought with them the memory of a long history of crushing poverty, cruel torment and English oppression. They remembered England's harsh penal laws (beginning in 1607) that denied Irish Catholics basic civil, political and religious rights, the last of which were not repealed until 1920; Daniel O'Connell the liberator and the struggle for Catholic emancipation in the 1820s; the young Irelander rebellion of 1848; the Irish republican brotherhood (1858) and its successor Clan na Gael (1867); Charles Stewart Parnell and the home rule for Ireland movement (1870-1918).

From Australia they watched as the 1916 Easter Rebellion unfolded in Dublin. W B Yeats wrote of the struggle *a terrible beauty was born*. They saw Ireland descend into bloody civil war in the 1920s and the winning side celebrate the proclamation of the Irish Free State (1922-1937) without the six counties of the north. Most of all, they remembered the catastrophe of Ireland's Potato Famine (1845-49). The death of over a million Irishmen and women from starvation and the emigration of 2 million more during the harsh famine years.

> They died in their mountain glens, they died along the sea coast, they died on the roads, they died in the fields, they wandered into their towns, and died in the streets; they closed their cabin doors, and lay down upon their beds, and died of starvation in their houses.

The cruel and forcible eviction of tenant farmers and their families by merciless landlords resonates strongly in Ireland's national memory.

> It's well I do remember on a bleak November's day. The landlord and the sheriff came to drive us all away. They set my house on fire with their cursed English spleen. And that's another reason, why I left Old Skibbereen.

> Oh! father dear the day will come when in answer to the call. Each Irishman with feelings stern will answer one and all. I'll be the man to lead the band beneath our flag of green. And loud and high, we'll raise the cry, 'Revenge for Skibbereen!'

Henry Lawson, an Australian born nationalist and republican who was not of Irish ancestry, felt a strong rebellious affinity with Ireland's fight for freedom. He published a politically rousing poem in the *Sydney Bulletin* in 1890 sympathising with the Irish cause titled 'Ireland Shall Rebel' in the expectation of an Irish rebellion that failed to eventuate. A year later in 1891, Lawson penned a tribute to Ireland.

> And though 'twas not in Erin that my forefathers trod. And though my wandering footsteps ne'er pressed the 'dear old sod'. I felt the wrongs the Irish feel beneath the northern sky; and felt the rebel in my heart when the Irish flag went by.

Religious, political and social events in Ireland were extensively reported in the Melbourne Catholic newspaper The *Advocate*. The *Advocate* was founded in 1868 as a forum for Irish Catholic news and opinion. Sir Charles Gavin Duffy, a young Irelander rebel leader and later Premier of Victoria, had a strong personal connection with the publication. The newspaper continued to be published and read by most Catholics as a weekly newspaper by the Melbourne Catholic Archdiocese until 1990. I remember Mum coming home after Sunday mass with her copy of

The *Advocate* tucked away in her black leather bag.

oooOOOooo

The doyen of Australian Catholicism during the last century was Irishman Dr Daniel Mannix, Bishop then Archbishop of Melbourne for 46 years. The son of a prosperous tenant farmer, Mannix was born in County Cork on 4 March 1864 and ordained a priest on 8 June 1890. In 1903 he was appointed President of Saint Patrick's College Maynooth, the Irish national seminary, a position he held until August 1912. On Easter Saturday 1913, Mannix, a newly minted bishop, arrived in Adelaide on his way to Melbourne where he was to administer to the Catholic faithful for the rest of his long life.

Daniel Mannix, a patriotic Irishman and a traditionalist Catholic, saw himself as a crusading defender for both. He took an activist stance advocating state funding for Catholic schools. He became an outspoken opponent against the introduction of conscription by the Hughes Government in the first world war, and successfully campaigned against it. He meddled in state and federal politics for decades, was stridently anti-communist and abrasively critical of the Labor Party's socialist platform. He was a vocal supporter of the Labor breakaway Democratic Labor Party (DLP). It is however, his militant advocacy to set Ireland free from centuries of English tyranny that strongly dominates memory of Mannix today.

The myth that Mannix at the time of the 1916 Dublin Easter Rising was a rabid Irish nationalist advocating violence and bloodshed is false. Before the first world war Mannix believed in a nonviolent Home Rule solution for Ireland. He opposed nationalist violence and was disapproving of the blood sacrifice of the Easter Rebellion. This however did not stop him from shedding tears for the fate of republican leader Padraig Pearse when told of his execution. Pearse prophetically said *If you strike us down now, we shall rise again and renew the fight.* Mannix became Archbishop of Melbourne on 6 May 1917. More than anybody else in Irish/Australian circles, Archbishop Mannix became the lightning rod to renew Pearse's fight. Although Mannix did not agree with the republican rebel's resort to violent revolution, he set up an Irish Relief Fund to raise money for the families of republicans shot or gaoled by the English.

Mannix became ever more sceptical of the British Government's promise to deliver Home Rule to Ireland, as he enthusiastically embraced the republican cause. At a meeting on Richmond racecourse on 5 November 1917, which attracted 100,000 friends and supporters of the Irish cause, Mannix delivered a speech denouncing England's treatment of the Irish. *The time has passed in which we could wait with patience. The tragedy of Easter week has not been all loss to Ireland. She lost some of her bravest, best, most brilliant sons. She wept over their graves, though their bodies are buried in prison yards.* (My) *strong advice to the Irish people is to say 'Now or Never'. They have an opportunity now that they are not likely to have again.* The *Argus* newspaper reported on the closure of proceedings. *The Mayor of Richmond on behalf of the Roman Catholic ladies of Hawthorn, presented Dr Mannix with an Irish flag and an Australian flag. As the flags were unfurled, there was a burst of cheering, which was followed by the singing of 'God save Ireland'.*

On the 25 March 1920, the first contingent of the hated 'Black and Tans', ex British soldiers recruited by Winston Churchill the Secretary for War as an auxiliary force to assist the Royal Irish Constabulary (RIC) arrived in Ireland. They were called Black and Tans because the uniform they wore consisted of a combination of British khaki and RIC black and green. The Black and Tans engaged in a war of terror and revenge against the Irish Republican Army (IRA) randomly attacking civilians and committing war crimes. They carried out targeted assassinations and sacked and burned Irish villages.

> *Come out you Black and Tans! Come out and fight me like a man! Show your wife how you won medals down in Flanders. Tell them how the IRA made you run like hell away from the green and lovely lanes of Killashandra.*

It was into this brutal climate of political and paramilitary terror, that Daniel Mannix set out from Australia in May 1920 to visit his Irish homeland. Mannix's reputation as a troublesome Irish Republican led to him in August 1920 being refused entry to Ireland by the British Government. He was arrested aboard *RMS Baltic* as it approached Cork harbour, transferred to a British destroyer and detained at Penzance in Cornwell before being allowed to return to Australia. As a consequence,

Pope Benedict XV donated 20,000 lire to Irish charitable causes. For the first time in Vatican history, a Pope openly criticised the British Government for their heavy handed treatment of the Irish.

oooOOOooo

The Christian religion, Catholic and Protestant, was more deeply entrenched in Australian society than it is today. People attended religious services on Sunday and special holidays in their tens of thousands. The religious significance of Christ's birth was celebrated with strong church attendance. On 24 December 1954, the Melbourne *Argus* reported 'All City Services will be packed out on Xmas Day'. *There will be standing room only in Melbourne churches for Christmas services. Most clergyman will preach three or four times the usual number of sermons.* A year earlier in December 1953, the Catholic *Advocate* advised. *There will be a midnight mass at Saint Patrick's Cathedral. Immediately preceding the midnight mass, the following Christmas carols will be sung. The First Noel, Angels We have Heard on High, O Come, all Ye Faithful, O Lovely Infant, Silent Night and Adeste Fideles. Before the carols, the Cathedral organ will be played commencing at 11.15 pm. The music of the mass will be sung by Saint Patrick's Cathedral Choir.*

While in Melbourne as a special treat on one of these Christmas eves, my sister Mary and I were taken to midnight mass at Saint Patrick's Cathedral. The bluestone cathedral with its elevated roof and religious statues was awe inspiring and menacing. To children's eyes at night, it was a vast cavernous, dimly lit space with many dark corners, where it was possible to imagine the ghostly figures of Catholic saints lying in wait to deal with misbehaving Catholic children. We were seated on the aisle towards the back of the cathedral, which quickly reached seating and standing capacity. The Stations of the Cross adorned the walls, alcoves contained statutes of Mary and Joseph. Christ on his golden Crucifix dominated the scene. St Patrick's choir sang hymns as the packed congregation waited for Archbishop Mannix and his entourage of priests and altar boys to arrive and in procession proceed down the centre aisle to the flower bedecked, candle lit altar. The atmosphere was expectant and to me watching from an uncomfortable hard-wooden church pew dreamlike, magical and mysterious. It became more so, when priests wearing green robes embellished with shamrocks occasionally passed by.

When the Archbishop's procession arrived outside, we stood as one as the cross bearer approached and the great man in a mitre cap and garland robes made his grand entrance. It was all so different back then, in solemn tone and religious feeling, before the sexual abuse of children by paedophile priests rocked the Catholic Church to its hierarchical core. The organ played and the choir sang as Mannix greeted the faithful with his raised hand dispensing a blessing. As an innocent three or four-year-old I had no idea who this sanctified being might be. It was my first glimpse of Archbishop Mannix and I thought to myself he must be God. Mum would correct me later. She left me with the distinct impression, however, that there was very little difference between the saintly Archbishop and the Christian God we all worshipped. I have no recollection of what Archbishop Mannix said from the pulpit that day but it must have been inspiring as the congregation seemed to hang on his every word. I do remember a thick Irish brogue and an animated tall spindly man who occasionally raised and lowered his fist in emphasis. Mannix was a gifted speaker and a charismatic leader who knew how to sway and motivate his audience. Daniel Mannix was an Irish patriot and Catholic hero combined.

Later when I learned more of the Archbishop's deeds, I succumbed to the Mannix myth and legend. It was the same mythic acceptance that led me in my youth to believe that Ned Kelly was a deserving Irish Australian hero. Catholics admired Mannix for his fortitude and principled stand on the controversial issues of his time. Ned Kelly on the other hand was a hollow man, a career criminal and murderer with attitude, who masqueraded as a hero when the opposite was true.

When as an adult PhD student and lapsed Catholic of more than two decades, I was researching the Irish Catholic side of Ned's north east community, I arranged to visit the Catholic Historical Commission situated in a terrace house in Carlton not far from Saint Patrick's Cathedral. I arrived bright and early one weekday morning to be met by Curator Father Keen's assistant priest. Father Keen has been delayed and he would see me later I was informed. In the meantime, would I like to see the exhibits room? We entered a dark and nostalgia filled room packed full of Catholic and Irish memorabilia. In the middle of the room individually spotlighted stood the builder's model replica of Saint Patrick's Cathedral, surrounded by a variety of chalices and valuable looking pieces of silver and gold plate. I learnt that the spire on top of Saint Patrick's was a people's gift from the Irish Republic, received through the intimate friendship of Archbishop Mannix and Eamon De Valera the President of the Irish Free State. It was known as the republican spire. Adorning the walls were countless crucifixes and photographs of Church dignitaries. Mannix memorabilia was everywhere. It seemed to me the room was a sacred homage to Mannix's memory and the Irish connection.

As the tour ended, I was led into a small room no bigger than a broom closet where the paper records were kept. You can begin your research Father Keen will speak with you when he arrives, I was told. The cramped room had several filing cabinets, an uncomfortable chair and a rickety desk. A single tiny window through which a small beam of light penetrated the gloomy darkness was framed by two large portraits. To the left was Saint Patrick in full priestly regalia with his foot firmly planted on the serpent's head. To the right looking down from upon high was a stern looking Eamon De Valera. I looked through the records for the best part of two hours becoming ever more nostalgic and slightly emotional about my lapsed Catholic past and Ireland's fight for freedom. Just then the door was flung back and there stood a formidable looking Father Keen. I got up from my seat and extended my hand. The good father stared at the proffered gesture of friendship, curtly looked me in the eye and said *of course, you know there will be a charge for this service don't you!* Nostalgia and sentimental feeling evaporated immediately as I thought to myself yes, this is the Catholic Church I know and remember!

oooOOOooo

Archbishop Daniel Mannix died on 6 November 1963 at the advanced age of 99 years, just a few months before his 100th birthday. The cathedral bell tolled 99 times at one-minute intervals. He was buried in the crypt of St Patrick's Cathedral. At his request there was minimal public ceremony acknowledging his death. Among the possessions listed in Mannix's will was a cheap mantel clock inscribed 'God Save Ireland'.

My childhood view of Mannix fostered by those around me, saw him through rose tinted glasses as the champion of Australia's downtrodden Catholics and the saintly leader of the noble struggle for Ireland's freedom. The post Irish civil war republican myth, firmly entrenched in 1950s Irish Australian minds, predisposed me and countless others to accept this assessment without question. The Catholic community went into deep mourning for a revered and beloved leader who never waived in his devotion to the Catholic Church and his Irish homeland. Commiserations were sent from Ireland and the loss of an exceptional Irishman was felt worldwide.

As Mannix lay in an open coffin at St Patrick's Cathedral, my sister Mary along with her convent school classmates, was taken by the Presentation nuns to kiss the episcopal ring on the dead Archbishop's hand. This act of religious devotion greatly traumatised Mary and angered my mother. She remonstrated with the Mother Superior who in her wisdom had not seen fit to consult with parents before subjecting their children to such a morbid ritual. Mannix was an icon to Catholic Australians, thus the insensitivity of the nun's gesture was carried out in remembrance of a great man of Catholic faith and Irish and Australian political conscience. To Mary however it was an unwelcome close contact with the dead and the memory of it still haunts her today.

7
Priests, Nuns and Christian Brothers

As the howling young cub ran away to the scrub where he knew that pursuit would be risky. The priest as he fled flung a flask at his head that was labelled 'Maginnis's Whisky!' And Maginnis Magee has been made a J.P., and the one thing he hates more than sin, is to be asked by the folk who have heard of the joke. How he came to be christened 'Maginnis'!

A B Paterson

When Mary and I left Mr Fielding's small rural state school to attend the much larger Saint Joseph's Catholic primary school in Korumburra, it was something of a school experience shock. There were many more schoolchildren, school uniforms were required and the rules were stricter. The Good Samaritan Sisters were Irish or Australian born of Irish parents. There was sternness and severity in their voice that would brook no opposition. Nevertheless, I loved to hear the rhythmic Irish cadence as lessons were taught and prayers intoned. Religion took pride of place at the beginning of each lesson.

We blessed ourselves and recited a Hail Mary or Our Father watched, by vigilant nuns on the lookout for boys and girls not taking their devotions seriously, and of course that meant corporal punishment. *You would be called up in front of the class, made to face the blackboard and Sister*

Aloysius would set about the back of your legs with the cane handle of a feather duster. Sometimes, she would call up several offenders against the rules and collective punishment would be administered. She would continue whacking at bare legs, until she was satisfied justice had been done. I don't remember the girls being punished in this painful way, but they may have been. They were definitely struck on the hand with the wooden part of a feather duster, the nun's punishment weapon of choice.

It was here at a tender young age that I began to seriously question the compassionate tenets of Christianity and the clip around the ears and feather duster therapy administered by the nuns for the slightest infraction of a multitude of rules. The feather duster, strap and act of corporal punishment were the accepted methods of instilling discipline in those days. It would be misleading to construe such punishment as sadistic bullying, at least for the majority of Catholic nuns and brothers. There were some who took pleasure in wielding the instrument of punishment. Brother McCabe a booming voiced, red-haired Christian Brother carried a leather-bound iron strap inside the sleeve of his religious robe and produced it at the slightest sign of rule breaking. Other nuns and brothers seldom resorted to physical punishment, preferring instead to use words to resolve discipline problems. Catholic children feared the former and appreciated the latter.

As time wore on, it became an ongoing battle between my Irish heritage stubbornness and the born and bred Irish strictness of the Good Samaritan Sisters and later Christian Brothers. Aggrieved, I accepted corporal punishment but could never understand why for Catholics, it was considered a mortal sin to eat meat on a Friday. Would eating a meat pie or a steak sandwich really condemn its consumer to everlasting hellfire? I never felt comfortable during the confession of sin and invariably told the priest what it was I thought he wanted to hear. My thoughts were my own, to share them with a priest, a nun or Christian Brother seemed unnatural and an unwelcome intrusion. Was confession and repentance truly required for entry into the Christian Paradise? Catholic belief said Yes! I would repent, but to me that was a private affair. Some boys would openly brag of the lies they told in confession; but there always remained even in the most jaded of hearts, an innate Catholic sense of guilt and impending damnation.

oooOOOooo

St Patrick's Day was a red-letter day celebrating Catholic religious and Irish cultural identity throughout the district and beyond. In Korumburra and Warragul street marches were organised by the local Hibernian Society with the Irish tricolour flag prominently displayed, pipe bands, Irish dancers, colourful banners behind which clubs and societies decked out with shamrocks, some marchers wearing green sashes and carrying shillelaghs, and contingents of schoolchildren from the Catholic school parading down main street to applause and cheers from a crowd of onlookers. There was always someone dressed as a Leprechaun performing an Irish jig and dispensing sweets. For us schoolchildren dressed in our school uniforms, we marched with civic pride and eager excitement, pleased to be part of such a prominent public event dedicated to Saint Patrick the patron saint of Ireland.

For Catholic children St Patrick's day began solemnly with mass, communion and a votive prayer to St Patrick, followed by gathering together in columns waiting for the parade to begin. The pipe band pumped up their bagpipes sounding for all the world to hear like a banshee in pursuit of a damned sinner. Amidst this cacophony of noise and other distractions, the nuns kept order patrolling the ranks of the schoolchildren enforcing a silence, which stood in marked contrast to the clamour and commotion going on all around. The musical march down main street was sublime and spinetingling for children, whether spectators or participants. Parents lining the street would cheer and clap as their children marched by. Heads would swell and chests puff out as Mum and Dad wearing an item of green clothing were spotted in the crowd. It was a magical Aussie moment of Irish Catholic tradition.

As the day wore on men and women, usually with their children safely home in bed, would gravitate to pub or private functions to drink beer, dance to Irish music and listen to Irish songs, some of them sung in Gaelic. There were jigs and reels that made the wooden floorboards creak and bend with the stamping of dancing feet. As the celebratory atmosphere became evermore boozy, smoky and impassioned. American ballads, particularly those of Bing Crosby from his 1940s Hollywood priest movies and Irish recordings, brought a sentimental nostalgia and flood of tears to people's eyes.

> *When Irish eyes are smiling tis like a morn in spring. With the lilt of Irish laughter, you can hear the angels sing.*

Towards the end of the evening, songs celebrating the Irish Republican Army and rousing ballads depicting Ireland's fight for freedom were sung with gusto and fervour by now inebriated men and women.

> *Armoured cars and tanks and guns came to take away our sons; but every man will stand behind the men behind the wire.*

As Saint Patrick Day festivities came to an end, the same Irish heritage Australians who cheerfully guzzled beer and enthusiastically sang Irish rebel songs proudly sang the Australian national anthem, which at that time was 'God Save The Queen'. There was no racial or political contradiction in this ending to an evening's entertainment. We all stood silently at the end of picture shows as the national anthem was played. Commonwealth British identity was not the same as English identity, and respect and loyalty for the Queen were patriotic givens in people's lives. Nevertheless for patriotic Irishmen and women, there was always a shrouded ambivalence to be navigated.

Convivial public occasions such as Saint Patrick's Day celebration, would sometimes degenerate into alcohol-fuelled, grownup bluster push and shove fights. The police would be called and law and order restored. On one occasion, I witnessed a roughhouse brawl in the street with crude words and fists flying brought about by feuding neighbours and too much grog. Disturbances of this sort usually followed a visit to the pub. Whenever Dad made a pub visit, I would wait outside and he would bring me a glass of lemon squash. I have tasted many pub and lemon squash drinks since those days of waiting patiently on the footpath, but it is those much-anticipated childhood pub treats I still regard as the most enjoyable.

oooOOOooo

There was a holiday tolerance extended by the district's Protestants, which allowed everyone to enjoy St Patrick Day festivities without opposing belief or prejudice intruding. The usual slurs and insults traded by Protestant and Catholic children from different schoolyards were on this special day frowned upon by adults and actively discouraged. *Catholic dogs sitting on logs eating maggots out of frogs* were Protestant taunts. Catholic children would reply *Protestant cats sit on mats eating maggots out of rats*, finishing the confrontational chant with *When Catholics ring the bell all the Proddies go to hell!* Protestants retaliated with insults directed at the Virgin Mary and the Catholic prohibition against eating meat on a Friday. Sometimes stones were thrown and fights would break out, girls and boys from both sides would join the fray in defence of their ancestral religion, but more often the childhood motive was the sheer thrill of the scuffling encounter.

All this childhood religious bigotry stood in marked contrast to earlier pioneer times when country people, Catholic and Protestant, worked cooperatively together to establish schools, churches and community infrastructure. It was a time of rural necessity, of community success or failure. At the Korumburra dedication ceremony of Saint Joseph's Catholic Church in May 1895, Archbishop Thomas Carr in his pastoral address said *there were present a very large and representative gathering from the district, irrespective of the religious denomination to which they belonged. In fact, the congregation was composed of as many non-Catholics as adherents of the Church.* He thanked *on behalf of his people the non-Catholics of the district, who at all times assisted and cooperated in every movement having for its object the erection of the noble building they were engaged in opening.*

In July 1914, Archbishop Carr again visited Korumburra to officiate at the opening ceremony of the Good Samaritan nun's convent and St Joseph's Catholic primary school. *Members of all congregations were included in the gathering.* In his speech the Archbishop said *he blessed the day the Catholic children of the district would commence receiving such a splendid education at the hands of the nuns. To his mind there is nothing better than a good religious and secular education. Catholic schools were really state schools in respect of secular education. The only difference was that Catholic schools did more than state schools in religious instruction.* Forty years later, when I was growing up in the district, such denominational cooperation was a thing of the past.

Although for most of the time community relationships between Catholics and Protestants remained cordial, religious sectarianism was a smouldering issue always there under the surface. Within religious communities of the faithful, 'mixed marriages' between Catholics and Protestants were looked upon with a jaundiced eye, particularly if a change of religion as usually happened was included in the mix. Families on both sides of the religious divide would find themselves torn apart by the contentious issue. Fathers threatened their offspring with disinheritance and some never spoke to the offending relative again. It was a stigma and a shame that Catholic and Protestant orthodoxy actively discouraged.

The Catholic Church encouraged its priests to perform 'not in front of the altar' mixed marriage ceremonies. A side altar, the sacristy or the presbytery was the chosen venue. It was not until 1966 and the sweeping reforms of Vatican 2 that this prohibition was relaxed, and mixed marriages with a special dispensation from the Church were acknowledged. Many years later, Mum would tell me of an early 1960s confrontation with a holier than thou Catholic priest who refused to give her confessional absolution when she was seeking a divorce. The clash of two strong Irish Australian personalities was not conducive to religious or conversational harmony.

Vatican 2 (1959-65) brought about monumental change in the Catholic Church. The mass was delivered in English and not in Latin. The altar and priest now faced the congregation. Women no longer had to wear hats during church services and many pastoral and doctrinal reforms were made. There was an exit and short-term decline in the number of priests entering holy orders. More significantly 90,000 nuns left the church after the liberalising decrees of Vatican 2 came into effect. Traditionalist Catholics felt much of the spiritual awe and pious mystery of Catholicism were undermined and lost, by crusading church reformers intent on bringing the Catholic Church into the modern world. I left the Catholic Church around this time of significant religious upheaval. The memory of my Catholic upbringing related in the book is from before major changes wrought by Vatican 2 came into effect.

oooOOOooo

During the 1950s people went to church on a Sunday as a religious duty and a social outing combined. Living on a distant dairy farm located between two regional towns made attending to one's religious devotions difficult. Every second Sunday, a priest from Korumburra or Warragul would arrive at the Seaview community hall to hear confessions and say mass. Confession was a solemn matter; a makeshift curtain was hung across the kitchen doorway for privacy. Adults and children would wait their turn to confess their sins, putting them in a state of grace to receive Holy Communion. Our Fathers and Hail Marys could be heard coming from all corners of the hall before mass began. Kneeling on hard wooden floorboards with knotholes and occasional beetles moving about, with hands clasped together in prayer while pretending to be holy was the pious game Catholic children played. Some probably believed it, but I was more interested in watching the holier than thou expressions on the faces of penitents emerging from behind the confessional curtain. When the curtain was pulled back, I could see the priest sitting there with his rosary beads in his hand and an icy stare on his face that would scare the dead. It was with a mixture of nervousness and suspense that I took my turn behind the curtain.

In those far off days mass was celebrated in Latin. The priest in his gold braid and heavily embroidered vestments with shamrocks and crosses decorating the collar stood with his back to the congregation assisted by two altar boys less sartorially clothed. The ringing of bells heralded the moment of greatest sanctity: the priest raising the communion wafer above his head and intoning the sacred words 'The Body of Christ'. The congregation lined up in rows to receive communion. The communion wafer was placed on the tongue never touched by other than a priestly hand. Because it was a Catholic service no wine was dispensed. This was Catholic mystery, spiritual awe and priestly ritual, as it existed before Vatican 2 changed and diluted centuries of Latinised Catholic worship.

The priestly sermon, delivered in front of a cloth covered table that served as a makeshift altar with a crucifix, flowers and a variety of gold and silver vessels, was a mixture of teachings from scripture, local diocesan news and the latest on the situation in Ireland. Some priests were better than others in delivering an interesting sermon. If the sermon was fiery and rousing the congregation would be wide awake and listening intently. If on the other hand, the sermon was monotone and boring, fidgeting could be heard and the congregation would tune out. Hymns were sometimes sung but they were the exception at Sunday mass. I spent my time during mass reading the narrative histories of the lives of the saints contained in the Catholic Missal. It was history rather than saintly action and the doctrinal words of the priest that intrigued me most, an interest which would occupy me my entire life and become my profession.

When the Seaview mass and sermon were finished, the children were ushered outside to play as tables heavily laden with cakes, buns and sandwiches were set up. Tea was brewed, as the sound of Cowboys and Indians and skipping ropes permeated the noisy conversation of farmers discussing cows and milk prices and the women other things. The visiting priest would partake of the bounty and join in the conversation, which always started with the weather and later turned to politics and other issues. Like John O'Brien's classic bush poem 'Said Hanrahan' there was always a farmer whinging *We'll all be rooned, before the year is out*! Tea and cakes were served and eventually everyone went their separate ways. As I grew older mass and confession were never quite the same elsewhere. The Seaview community hall service was a bush religious experience, no longer available to the present generation of Catholics.

oooOOOooo

Although not a particularly religious family, we would occasionally make the short trip down the road to a neighbour's house to participate in a Rosary night dedicated to Mary the Blessed Virgin. On our knees, with Rosary beads fingered and sets of Hail Marys uttered in unison, we prayed for all manner of things. It could be an hypnotic experience, with rhythmic chanting of prayers and dimmed lights falling in shadow across a statue of the Virgin Mary, adding a supernatural mood to the focused religious devotion. It was not the prayers that occupied my attention but the soreness of my knees and a disguised attempt not to fidget which brought stern looks from the adults present. We children would sneakily try to distract our peers which inevitably occasioned a sharp rebuke from cross parents. Prayers were said on one memorable occasion for a safe journey to the Holy Land soon to be undertaken by our host. An exciting boat trip as a pilgrim to the other side of the world fired the imagination of children as we realised we had an adult celebrity in our midst.

First Communion was an exciting time of religious initiation for Catholic children. After months of religious instruction children were deemed ready for this solemn ceremony. My First Communion was a morning service: the boys wearing white satin trousers with shiny waistcoats, the girls in pure white dresses, each of us swelled with pride carrying a candle lit lantern as we sidestepped slowly down the church aisle towards the Bishop in his mitre cap grandeur, who anointed us as worthy to partake of the Christian Eucharist.

Eventually the time came for me to make my Confirmation — the next important Catholic initiation ritual. The Confirmation class was a day or so beforehand assembled in the church for doctrinal instruction. A visiting Jesuit priest from the Society of Jesus with a thick Irish brogue stalked the church's aisle teaching the boys and girls a Latin version of the Lord's Prayer. He was a short tempered, bald headed man with the gaunt look of an ascetic, who readily clipped around the ears those who faltered in reciting his barely comprehensible version of the sacred prayer. Needless to say, he frightened the bejesus out of all of us. One boy wet himself and was taken away crying by the good sisters. The girls were too terrified to speak. Parents complained and angry voices were raised. Unabashed, the Jesuit priest left the church without apology or comment and thankfully we did not see him again.

In order to avoid the impression that Catholic priests, nuns and brothers were all Irish ogres and collective abusers of their young charges. Today's sexual abuse claims against priests and some nuns make it seem so, and obvious. We should acknowledge that only a small percentage of the Catholic clergy worldwide have been accused of sexual abuse. An American study reports that between 1950 and 2002 the number of accused US clergy was 4%. In an exhaustive investigation into 75 Australian archdioceses, dioceses and religious institutes *some 7% of priests who had worked in Australia between 1950 and 2009 were found to be alleged perpetrators.*

Catholic Church leaders have done irreparable harm to the church's reputation in covering up decades of clergy abuse. The laity rightly feel betrayed and the religious bond of trust has been greatly shaken. Sexual abusers were a power misusing minority, shamelessly shielded and moved from parish to parish by protectors in the church hierarchy. As a consequence, paedophilia was allowed to flourish unchecked. Such serial sexual predators, however, do not represent the many decent men and women in religious orders with a genuine spiritual calling and a strong belief in Catholic dogma. Cardinal George Pell's miscarriage of justice rape trial resulting in a guilty verdict, a prison sentence and belatedly a unanimous High Court acquittal, is a salutary warning to thoroughly investigate sexual abuse claims made against the clergy and not simply substitute anti-Christian intolerance, judicial prejudice and a trial by media witch hunt.

The conduct of the priests, nuns and brothers I knew was in the main both commendable and caring. Some I really liked and admired for their benevolence and sincere piety. I saw this side most often and along with other Catholics regarded religious people with reverence and respect. I never experienced or heard sordid stories of sexual abuse in my youth or of inappropriate behaviour by the clergy from my childhood friends. Clearly such things happened but they were not part of my growing up years in the Catholic Church. Sexual abuse and strict discipline from the Catholic clergy were not the reasons I decided during the 1960s to leave the church in my teenage years and dispense with religion altogether.

oooOOOooo

I attended the Christian Brothers College in St Kilda during the early 1960s, where I came in contact with two very different kinds of Christian Brothers. Brother Maginnis was a young man in his early twenties with a friendly personality and a gentle kindness towards the boys he taught. He taught me English in a relaxed and easy-going classroom situation. When he heard I was to go to boarding school, he called me up to his desk during the lesson and spoke in hushed whispers. He told me what to expect at boarding school, not to neglect my prayers and to make my parents proud. I later found out; Brother Maginnis left Holy Orders not long after. He married had a family and died in his early thirties. I remember him as a good teacher and a true Christian who practiced his religion with genuine compassion and piety. There were many brothers and nuns in the Catholic school system who were equally likeable as teachers and religious persons.

On the other hand, Brother Guerin, a fearsome 6 foot 6 inches giant of a French/German man, scared the daylights out of the boys he taught mathematics. He had the look of an angry troubled man about to explode. Every time he entered the classroom you could feel the mounting tension. It was as if he sensed our fear and enjoyed bullying his students. Being one of the taller boys and unable to blend into the classroom background I became a special target for Brother Guerin's always bad-tempered remarks. It was obvious he felt superior to and disliked his students. He should never have been let loose in a classroom of young boys. He was scornful in his language, used the leather strap on a whim and would box a boy's ear for no apparent reason other than he felt like it. Today such intimidating classroom behaviour would be labelled as abusive and sadistic.

One day Brother Guerin made the mistake of striking me on the side of the head. When I told my parents my mother, her Irish blood well and truly up, rang the school immediately and demanded an audience that night with the Head Brother and Brother Guerin. I sat anxiously on a chair outside the interview room and heard raised voices inside. After about half an hour Brother Guerin emerged with a chastised look on his face. He eyeballed me with none of his usual arrogance and swagger. Clearly, the fearsome Brother Guerin had met his match in my red-haired mother. He never struck me again and as far as I can recall, he never spoke with me again after that tumultuous night time confrontation. When next day I told my classmates, Mum in particular and I by being present outside the room, became schoolboy heroes for a day or two.

8

Pioneer Women, Casterton and a Bush Lunatic

A land where gaunt and haggard women live alone and work like men till their husbands gone a droving will return to them.

Henry Lawson

Today's feminist historians criticise the notion of the bush heroine calling it romantic and fanciful. They acknowledge that the pioneer woman's life was one of constant drudgery, childbirth and farming chores. However they belittle respectable pioneer women who are described as 'God's Police' and celebrate Ellen Kelly, the sly grog selling mother of bushranger Ned, as a pioneer role model and Irish heroine. Ellen Kelly belonged to the lawless underbelly of her community. A criminal fringe group engaged in horse and cattle stealing from their neighbours rich and poor alike. She was foul-mouthed, unruly, promiscuous and dismissive of women outside her badly behaved circle of friends and relatives. She was not representative of the law-abiding lifestyle and community building behaviour of the majority of pioneer women, nor was she admired by them.

While researching Ned's Greta community, I came across many pioneer women who do not fit the rebellious persona attributed to Ellen Kelly. I wrote of two such praiseworthy Irish pioneer women in an earlier work *Ned Kelly: Selectors, Squatters and Stock Thieves* Connor Court

(2018). Their story is the typical pioneer woman's story of ordinary women rising to the challenge in extraordinary times to live decently and raise a family to be proud of. This traditional womanly task was paramount in their lives. They took their caregiver's role seriously and earnestly devoted their lives to family and community service in equal measure.

Mary Graham née Dinning who emigrated from Ireland to Australia in 1866 at the age of nineteen was to marry and settle at Greta. She came on her own as a cabin passenger on the steamship Great Britain. The passenger manifest records her status as a 'Lady', a genteel term used to refer to a gentlewoman of sensibility and in this case a woman of no great wealth. Mary travelled cabin class, which allowed her to avoid the usual long voyage interactions with the rowdier elements in steerage and to maintain respectable standards mingling with other cabin class passengers. Her future sister-in-law Mary Ann Dinning née Wallace who was to marry and settle at Glenrowan shared a similar decent woman's outlook. She also referred to herself on her marriage certificate as a 'Lady' rather than using the more usual term 'Spinster'.

Neither of these Irish women came from wealthy privileged families, nor were they ladies of leisure with spare time on their hands. They were hardworking wives, mothers, housekeepers, farmhands and much more besides. Mary Ann was to have twelve children. They regarded themselves as respectable women with a conventional sense of Victorian propriety, principled, virtuous and morally attuned to maintaining decent standards and traditional family values. They neither sat on Victorian pedestals nor inhabited a shady underworld of crime and debauchery. They were in equal partnership with their husbands to succeed in farming the land, raising a family and establishing a viable pioneer community.

They brought up young families in a pioneering community where life was raw, demanding and uncompromising. Both women were regular churchgoers and active participants in church and community affairs. Mary Ann helped with the church and school, organised tea meetings, fetes, picnics and a variety of other neighbourhood fund raising activities, which shanty women such as Ellen Kelly shunned as the work of religious 'Mugs' and meddlesome 'Do Gooders'. Along with her sister-in-law Mary, she delivered clothing and food packages to the poor, including needy Kelly Sympathiser families, perhaps even visiting the Kellys themselves on such charitable occasions.

Rural women like their respectable husbands sought to maintain decent standards in the home and in public. They were the moral compasses of family life and far from being under the thumb of domineering Victorian husbands. Law-abiding, pioneer women did what was communally expected of them not as repressed doormats, but with a sense of pride and achievement different in kind and attitude to Ellen Kelly and her badly behaved shanty women friends. Respectable rural women lived a harsh life of drudgery and isolation in the wilderness of the Victorian bush and were determined to maintain and improve their family's social standing in the local community. Despite their isolation, they maintained contact with the community through schools, a myriad of local events, their churches and charitable work. Hard work and demanding times do not have to be associated with a lowering of community standards, particularly during the Victorian period.

oooOOOooo

Clement Semmler in his book *The Banjo of the Bush: The work, life and times of A B Paterson* Lansdowne Press (1966), wrote of the epic struggle and love for the Australian bush of Emily Barton, Banjo Paterson's pioneer Scot's grandmother in the Molong district near Orange in New South Wales in the 1840s. Emily was a relative of Sir Edmund Barton, Australia's first Prime Minister. *Emily's home was a hut* (on the Boree Nyrang pastoral run) *to begin with, her nine children were born and brought up there. Emily's courage and patience must have been monumental. Undaunted by droughts and failing crops and all the discomforts so engendered, Emily, who did not leave the station for twenty-five years, clothed and fed her large family, looked after their every need (there was no doctor within nearly 100 miles) and, above all, educated them. She would have the boys stand around the kitchen table reciting their French and Latin verbs while she made the bread and puddings.*

Prowling Aborigines were always a threat to the homestead. On one occasion the Boree tribe, pursued by a tribe from the Yass country, turned at bay and waged a pitched battle in the homestead itself; many were slaughtered in the garden until jackaroos came to the rescue flourishing guns. The Aborigines had, however, ransacked the house taking all the food and tobacco. Emily with her children found safety in a back room. (Later) her lot was made harder because her husband broke his leg when thrown from a horse and he was lame thereafter.

As remarkable as Emily Barton's experiences in the New South Wales bush seem to us today, they were the common experience of all pioneer women when their menfolk were away working or attending to other business. Pioneer women and their young children experienced loneliness and aloneness in the bush. Neighbours helped one another in times of need, but it was hardworking and determined bush women who kept their heads in a crisis and managed family life on their own.

George Essex Evans in his haunting poem 'The Women of the West' (1906) reveals the careworn toll of pioneer women's lives. *The red sun robs their beauty, and, in weariness and pain, the slow years steal the nameless grace that never comes again; and there are hours men cannot soothe, and words men cannot say. The nearest woman's face may be a hundred miles away. For them no trumpet sounds the call, no poet plies his arts. They only hear the beating of their gallant, loving hearts. But they have sung with silent lives the song all songs above. The holiness of sacrifice, the dignity of love.*

Pioneer women of all ethnic backgrounds coped with all manner of farming emergencies from Aboriginal attack, livestock theft, raging bushfires, snakes in the house, to troublesome swagmen intent on taking advantage of the situation. Bush women had to be tough and resourceful in all circumstances; the challenges they encountered were often of the life and death kind. What they accomplished was indeed heroic and courageous. My grandmother Theresa Murray nee Byrne was such a strong willed and practical bush woman. In her middle of the night dealings with a lunatic madman threatening her life and those of her children, she remained surprisingly calm and took charge of a potentially deadly situation.

oooOOOooo

Theresa Byrne my mother's mother came from a well to do Ballarat farming family. Theresa was born at Haddon, a few miles from Ballarat, on 1 September 1890. She was the daughter of William and Winifred Byrne and was the fifth child of a marriage that would produce thirteen children. Her Irish grandfather Michael Byrne was born in 1830 and lived in Dublin. At the age of twenty-four Michael emigrated from Ireland seeking his fortune during the gold rush. He married in Dublin a month before his departure. Somewhat appropriately, he arrived in Victoria aboard the immigrant ship *Bride of the Sea* on 11 August 1854. Theresa Thompson, his newlywed eighteen-year-old bride, remained in Dublin with her family. Two years later in July 1856 she arrived in Port Phillip aboard the *Mindon*. Michael must have been lucky on the Ballarat goldfield. He and Theresa settled in the Ballarat district farming the land and raising five children, including my great grandfather William who was born in 1859. Michael died at Ballarat aged 70 years on 1 January 1900, living just long enough to see the dawn of the new century.

William and Winifred Byrne married in 1883. Winifred, the daughter of Scarsdale's goldminer James Feeley, was born in 1863, when the Ballarat/Scarsdale diggings were at their most productive. The Byrne children were all born at Haddon (previously the Sago Hill gold diggings) between 1884 and 1906, so it is fairly certain that William and his family remained in the Ballarat area to be near relatives. In 1913, the family was living in the Western District at Blackwood Farm, Bella Vista, Carapook near Casterton.

According to an article in *The Pastoralist Magazine* December 1912, William's family was involved in *a model farm experiment set up by the science trained McDonald brothers of the Bella Vista Estate. As the name implies Bella Vista commands a view of one of the most beautiful valleys in the district. This magnificent estate, the property of Messrs McDonald Bros, is situated seven miles from Casterton. Within the last two years the Messrs McDonald have established four dairy farms on the estate. Each of these farms is fitted up with the most modern appliances, and neither time, trouble, nor expense has been spared in perfecting the general equipment. Water has been laid on to the various buildings, yards and enclosures, and everything has been carefully thought out and planned with the object of economising the time and labour of the dairy farmers. Including employees and the families of the dairy farmers there are now more than forty persons resident upon the estate. The splendid results and the success attending Captain McDonald's efforts are bound to have a beneficial effect on the dairying industry in the Casterton district.*

For William to be selected to participate in the McDonald brothers model farm experiment suggests he had extensive dairy farming experience in either the Ballarat or Casterton districts. In all likelihood, he had farmed land near Casterton for quite some time before signing on with the McDonalds. William died on 24 July 1920, presumably, still tending to his dairy cattle on Blackwood Farm. Winifred outlived her husband by 10 years, dying on 6 April 1930, 9 days before her granddaughter my mother Magdalene (Madge) was born. Theresa's sad loss of her mother may have affected her advanced pregnancy and brought on a hurried birth. Both William and Winifred are buried in the Ballarat cemetery. Some of their children remain in the Casterton district as farmers.

oooоOOOooo

James Murray my grandfather was born in 1881 into a far from prosperous farming family at Eden in New South Wales. His father Thomas and mother Elizabeth were Irish Catholic immigrants, with possibly Scottish ancestors added to the mix, who became pioneer dairy farmers. Where they came from in Ireland was never discussed within the family circle. Presumably some dark secret prevailed that is now lost to the present generation. They may have come from tenant farms or city slums, escaping the Irish famine or lured by goldfield riches. Whatever the reason they came singly or together seeking a new beginning and a better life in Australia. Thomas and Elizabeth instilled in James a hard work ethic and respect for law and order. James was a quiet and gentle man and his skill as a farmer was admired by all who knew him.

In 1912 James, single and 31 years of age, pioneered a Western

District closer settlement block that contained 347 acres of land. He called it Dunrobin after the squatting run on which the property was situated. Dunrobin was the first Victorian pastoral run established on the banks of the Glenelg River. In 1856 the squatter James Murray (as far as I know no relation to my grandfather James) built the Dunrobin Homestead. On the 19 January 1849, the *Argus* newspaper described the Dunrobin Pastoral Run in the following terms. *Established and Leased by Addison and Murray in 1848. Estimated area — 153,600 acres. Estimated grazing capability — 37* (sic) *head of cattle, 14,000 sheep. On the west side of the river Glenelg, commencing 55 chains north of the junction of the rivers Wannon and Glenelg, and bounded on the south by a perpendicular line of 11 miles due west along land occupied by John Macpherson, on the west by a perpendicular line of 24 miles due north, partly along land occupied by John McLellan and unoccupied land, on the north by a perpendicular line of 9 miles due east, thence by a road to Mr Pearson's crossing place on the Glenelg river aforesaid and about 60 chains north of his home station, on the east by the Glenelg river to the point of commencement, distant 24 miles in a straight line with the exception of the border of the river much of the above run consists of extensive heaths and sandy stringybark forests.*

The Closer Settlement Act of 1904 enshrined in law the partition of the remaining squatting runs by the Victorian Government into smaller farming allotments. The blocks were sold under the administration of the Closer Settlement Board. The Dunrobin Estate near Casterton came up for the board's consideration in 1912. The 11,118 acres was subdivided into allotments of different sizes, all of which were to become successful dairy farms. According to a Glenelg Shire centenary publication in 1963 *well over half* (of the farms) *are still owned by the original settlers or their descendants.*

On the 17 January 1912, the *Argus* carried the following notice. *The Closer Settlement Acts Subdivision of the Dunrobin Estate into Allotments ranging from 5 acres to 724 acres. — The Dunrobin Estate* (excised from the Dunrobin Pastoral Run) *comprises an area of 11,118 acres, and adjoins the rising railway town of Casterton, the most distant allotments being within seven miles. The estate consists of land suitable either for dairying, mixed farming, fruit-growing, or* grazing. Good roads intersect the property, leading to various centres in the district. The Butter Factory at Casterton provides an outlet for dairy products. Agricultural produce and meat may be despatched by rail to Melbourne, Geelong, or Portland to the principal markets of the State or to overseas destinations. The rainfall is good, and the climatic conditions suitable for all kinds of farming and stock raising. A special feature of the subdivision is the provision made for Agricultural Labourers Allotments close in to Casterton. Provision has also been made for Sites for Schools, Municipal Sale Yards, and an Agricultural College. The Local Land board to deal with applications will be held at Casterton on Wednesday, the 21 February 1912.

The Border Watch (Mount Gambier SA) wrote on the 28 February 1912. *The Dunrobin Land Board has completed its work of dealing with the applications for this land. The Mechanics Hall was packed to the door with applicants and others. The interest shown recalled the old land boards of the sixties. The homestead block, on which the valuation for the buildings was £150, was recommended to J. Hart, of Ballarat. The estate contains 11,118 acres. About 8,000 acres had previously been sold by auction. There were 160 applicants. Many of these, however, applied for a number of blocks, in order to increase their chances. The estate was cut up into 68 blocks of 5 acres to 724 acres; and the values placed upon them varied from £2 10 shillings per acre to £25. A German, who had been in Canada and Cape Colony, was an applicant for a small block. He remarked to a person who advised him to preserve his railway ticket to enable him to return home. 'I won't return home; I am satisfied with this place'. Another applicant brought with him his whole family and furniture. Others camped on the blocks they had applied for, under the impression that it might strengthen their chances.*

Under the banner headline 'Homes for Life' the *Argus* described the Casterton proceedings. *The eventful day, long awaited at Casterton had arrived at last. The members of the Land Board had arrived, and Dunrobin estate, purchased by the Closer Settlement Board after years of hesitancy was to be allotted among the land seekers, who had flocked into the town to urge, with all the impressiveness of men seeking to establish homes, their claims for the block into which the estate had been subdivided. There was excitement not only among the applicants,* many of whom were from remote districts, but among the business people as well for Dunrobin estate stretches right into the town, and city folk should understand that its settlement means more mouths to feed and more bodies to clothe, more business in every way to the people of Casterton. Even the visitors, the commercial travellers, and the holiday makers, found their interest in the event increase hourly, and soon they were as much wrapped up in the proceedings as if they were among the applicants for the most sought-after block, and believed that their future welfare lay in the decision of the board.

A man's face lit up when his name was called, and hands were thrust out to shake with him. 'Good old ___' was always the refrain as the block and its owner were called, and if the applicant did not happen to be known, if he were a stranger to the town, he was 'a party of the name of Brown or Smith', as the case might be. In half an hour the fortunes of 100 men and their wives and children had been determined for some time to come and the audience dispersed. There was no mistaking the feelings of one fine looking fellow as to his fortune. He drew himself up to his full height on the steps of the hall as if there had not been room enough inside, and said 'I've got a home for life'. On the list of successful applicants was *James Murray: Allotment 1, Parish of Casterton, 347 acres, £5 15 shillings per acre.*

James was determined to succeed as a farmer. Six years after his arrival in the Casterton district, he married 28-year-old Theresa Magdalene Byrne on 8 April 1918. It was considered within the Byrne family that Jim Murray was not a particularly suitable match and this caused tension within the family circle. A community minded man, his greatest joy was his family who admired and respected him as a loving father and devoted husband. Despite an age difference of 9 years, James and Theresa were soulmates. When Theresa died in 1942, James was inconsolable and family life was never the same afterwards.

My Mum would occasionally speak of her 1930s Western District childhood on her father's Dunrobin sheep and dairy farm near Casterton. Mum's life at Casterton was spent in the usual childhood pursuits. She rode a piebald pony to and from school in the early years. She went to Sunday mass in her best clothes holding a Catholic missal in her gloved hand. Along with her brothers and sisters, she helped her mother with kitchen chores and her father around the farmyard. Outside in the fresh air with her father Jim tending to the animals, carting haybales and occasionally going with him in a horse drawn wagon into Hamilton for supplies was what she liked most. Money was tight during the depression years and Mum learned early not to ask for treats on excursions away from the farm. Nevertheless, on the return journey home, Jim always produced a bag of boiled lollies *to be shared with your brothers and sisters* he said. By the time the wagon returned to the Murray homestead the bag of lollies had somehow disappeared.

Jim Murray doted on his red-headed, freckle-faced, feisty youngest daughter and the bond between them was strong. So strong that in later years when Mum would dream of her father or felt his presence, it was always taken as an omen that something bad was about to happen. Invariably something did. More often than not somebody we knew died. As a family we came to trust Mum's intuitions. She believed it was second sight brought about through her Byrne Irish heritage. There were women in the Byrne family down the generations who it was said possessed a similar gift. Not quite believing we nevertheless paid attention to any warnings she passed onto us.

Many years later as we stood halfway down the lengthy driveway of the family's long ago sold Dunrobin property, Mum would relate to us the poignant story of her father's death in 1946. Mum and two of her sisters were sitting in a horse drawn wagon driven by their father James. The day was sweltering hot and sultry; this was to be the foremost memory of a painful tragic event. They were returning from a farm errand in Casterton and were at the point where we were now standing, when James fell from the wagon unconscious. He had suffered a massive stroke. Shocked and upset, the girls all of whom were teenagers, stood by their father as he lingered for less than a minute and died without speaking a word. It was a traumatic and not to be forgotten moment for my fifteen-year-old mother. She had lost her mother Theresa four years earlier in 1942 at the young age of 52 years. Now with the sudden death of her beloved father James at 65, the family farm would soon be sold and life for Mum would begin anew as a student nurse in Melbourne.

In many respects, the life Mum led at Casterton was similar to the Korumburra childhood my sister Mary and I grew up with in the

Strzelecki Ranges during the 1950s. School and farm life went on unrelentingly for adults and children alike, regardless of community progress and scientific innovation. Times had definitely changed, a world war and depression had come and gone, but really not all that much about the fundamentals of 1950s country life was different. Living through those serendipitous times, the separation of past and present seemed rock solid and obvious to all. A decade later only the outward appearance of a provincial country lifestyle remained as the outside world increasingly intruded.

ooooOOOooo

There was one Dunrobin story Mum told that both intrigued and scared my sister Mary and me. The night madman Bushy Daniels made a surprise midnight visit with an axe when Mum, her Mum Theresa and some of her sisters were alone in the house. Jim and the Murray boys were many miles away camped out in the bush on a hunting trip. Bushy Daniels (I never knew his Christian name) was a nomadic swagman travelling the country roads with madness in his eyes, a full beard and an insatiable thirst for alcohol. He suffered mental problems and would today if the authorities could catch him, have been institutionalised and prescribed a regime of drug therapy. They never could as he rarely stayed in one place for more than a day or so.

It was common knowledge amongst Dunrobin children, you never spoke to Bushy Daniels or in any way upset him when he was undergoing one of his many violent episodes. Even grown men and women would cross the street in Casterton to avoid his unpredictable behaviour. With a bellyful of grog, Bushy who more than likely suffered from paranoid schizophrenia, would leave behind him a trail of violent assaults, petty theft and property destruction as he gave into his fantasy world of imagination. He would shout obscenities outside closed doors and on one occasion he punched in the face a priest he said was the devil. On another he allegedly set fire to a farmer's haystack. Bushy would spend a short time in the Casterton lockup for his eccentric behaviour and be on his way the following morning. He was never gone for long. He would return unexpectedly a month or two later, to visit more havoc and mayhem on the community. Jim sternly warned Theresa and the children to *stay well away from that drunken swagman as he only brought trouble.*

One cold and frosty June night in winter, Bushy Daniels was again out of control muttering to himself and wandering in the darkness carrying an axe. Around midnight, several hours after Grandma Theresa and her daughters had retired for the night, a loud crashing sound was heard coming from the farmyard directly outside the backdoor. With no men or a gun in the house, Theresa followed closely by her startled young daughters cautiously went to investigate. Someone or something was moving around on the verandah and incoherent words filled the air. The plodding tread of heavy boots could be heard stomping across creaking wooden boards. Then came a short period of uneasy silence. Suddenly a grotesque and twisted face with wild and staring eyes appeared at the kitchen window, deranged and sinister looking in the dappled moonlight. It was Bushy Daniels, axe in hand, looking for all the world like Jack Torrance, the axe wielding Jack Nicholson character in Stanley Kubrick's horror movie 'The Shining'.

Mum and her sisters screamed and hid under the kitchen table. Grandma Theresa was made of sterner stuff and not wanting to frighten her daughters further, she picked up a large kitchen knife and put it in the pocket of her dressing gown. In true pioneer spirit, she was ready to do whatever was necessary to defend herself and her young daughters from harm. Meanwhile Bushy Daniels was at the backdoor, which in those days few country people kept locked. He turned the doorknob and carrying the axe before him came into the kitchen. Theresa now shielding her daughters behind her said in a quiet calming voice as with a shaking hand she lit a candle to illuminate the scene. *What do you want Bushy? Do you want something to eat?* With a quizzical look on his face, the armed intruder raised the axe in the air and muttered something inaudible. Theresa tightly clutched the handle of the concealed knife determined to defend herself and her daughters against Bushy's midnight madness.

Grandma Theresa, a hospitable country woman even to an unhinged swagman, had in more settled times supplied a more lucid Bushy with bread and vegetables when he called at the backdoor. Country people knew it was a wiser course of action to part with a few groceries, than to refuse such a request and risk a burnt haystack, an injured animal or worse. Bushy in his deranged state of mind remembered Theresa's kindness. The madness in his eyes began to diminish a little, as he abruptly sat down with his hand to his head and the axe gleaming in the candlelight laid menacingly across his knees. Theresa motioned to her daughters to quietly leave the room. To one of the girls she silently mouthed the words to fetch Constable Murray (no relation) from Casterton several miles distant.

Alone in the middle of the night with a mentally disturbed and unpredictable swagman, who was talking to himself in a delusional state of mind while stroking the handle of an axe, Grandma Theresa knew what stood between her family and disaster was to keep Bushy Daniels distracted and calm. She talked to him attentively about everyday things, never mentioning or even looking at the axe he occasionally fondled to his breast. Was Constable Murray on his way and what would happen when he arrived? Were the children safe she wondered as she went about the task of pacifying a madman?

For two uncomfortable hours, Theresa acted as hostess and unwilling confidante to the agitated swagman, serving him cups of tea and whatever she could scrounge from the kitchen larder. On several occasions the hairs on the back of her neck stood on end and a cold shiver went through her body as Bushy paced the room wild eyed and dishevelled, brandishing the axe and uttering frenzied words to an invisible adversary. What he said had something to do with a broken picture frame and a stolen photograph. *Do you know where it is? He is watching! I'll kill you!* was the angry tone of an imagined conversation repeated over and over again.

Things were beginning to spiral out of control, when Constable Murray and another man appeared at the backdoor and silently entered the kitchen. Bushy who was facing away from the entrance did not see or hear them. Without uttering a word, both men tackled the deranged man and his menacing axe to the floor. Bushy let out a wild yell as he tumbled downwards, flailing out and cursing. It took some time for Bushy to accept the situation and calm down. The axe was immediately picked up by Grandma Theresa and safely placed out of reach. Greatly relieved, she returned the knife hidden in her dressing gown to the kitchen drawer. Fortunately, no blood was shed and nobody got hurt. Manacled and in the hands of the police, Bushy still in the grip of his personal fantasy was taken away in a police van and lodged in the Casterton lock-up. With women and children's lives at risk the authorities acted decisively. Bushy was sent to an asylum for the insane. What happened to the disturbed swagman after that remains a mystery.

Having narrowly escaped what could have been a gruesome scene of bloody murder, Theresa and her children were unable to sleep for the rest of the night. They huddled together around the kitchen stove and watched the winter sunrise, as they anxiously waited for Jim and the boys to return home. The reunion was poignant and a relief to all. The Bushy Daniels encounter was a pioneer story of fear and near tragedy passed down to future generations. From that day forward, at Grandpa Jim's insistence, a loaded shotgun was kept above the fireplace in case madman Bushy Daniels returned. He never did.

9

Anzacs Khaki Brave and Aussie True Blue

Did you leave a wife or a sweetheart behind? In some loyal heart is your memory enshrined? And, though you died back in 1916, to that loyal heart are you always 19? Or are you a stranger without even a name, forever enshrined behind some glass pane, in an old photograph, torn and tattered and stained, and fading to yellow in a brown leather frame?

Eric Bogle

At the outbreak of World War 1 in June 1914, the Korumburra Caledonian Society held a Patriotic Concert in the Mechanics Institute Hall. *There was a very large attendance. The programme was a good one and the respective items keenly enjoyed, the audience demonstrating their appreciation by frequent encores. 'The Men of Harlech' opened the concert and Miss Jesse White's pupils sang 'Australia, Grand Australia'. Mr B R Smith immensely pleased the audience with his original recitation 'The Korumburra Boys' in which reference was made to the local lads who had volunteered for the front. The Reverend H Williams said 'When Britain calls, she could always depend on an immediate and loyal response from Australia'. A feeling reference was made to the self-sacrifice of Mr and Mrs McHarg in allowing two of their sons to proceed with the Expeditionary Force.*

Not everyone was happy with Korumburra's patriotic treatment of their young soldiers. Six months later in December 1914, an irate letter signed 'John Bull' was sent to the Editor of the *Great Southern Advocate* newspaper. *It is with deep regret I express my disappointment with the people of Korumburra for allowing our fine young men, who have enlisted to serve the Empire, to leave our town* (for training bootcamp) *without a single word being said in public by way of a social send off. In reading the daily papers one sees that in almost every little country town and hamlet, where even one young fellow has felt the call of his country, the people have risen to the occasion and given him a splendid send off. For the people of our town to say it was an oversight would not be fair, seeing we have not only sent one lot away but two. It is too late now they are gone and the opportunity is lost forever. I would suggest that a card be sent to each mother with these words: 'Your brave son will do his duty to his King, his Country and his Fellows'.*

It was not quite as grim a situation as the John Bull letter writer declares. On one of these occasions, Korumburra's newly minted soldiers were not allowed to return home by the military authorities prior to embarking for overseas battlefields. Confusion over leave dates rather than wilful neglect was the cause. Korumburra soldiers generally received a well-attended and heartfelt community send off before departing on what they saw as a great overseas adventure.

On 11 February 1915, two months before Australian soldiers landed at Gallipoli on 25 April, the *Great Southern Advocate* published a letter from a Korumburra Soldier who was then stationed in Egypt. *It took us about three days to disembark and everything was sent to Cairo by train. We had to wait for our horses, which were on another boat, and she did not arrive until a few days after. We are camped in the sand and as far as we can see on one side of us is nothing but sand, but on the other side is the village of Maadi which is very pretty with nice green shrubs and trees and irrigated from the Nile. I have not been over to the pyramids yet as we expect to be shifting over there shortly, but we can see them quite plainly.*

In August the newspaper published a letter from Private H Pam, *who is about the only one who went from Korumburra with the first contingent still left in the firing line. He writes to his mother as follows: 'My dear mother we have been having warm weather here but the flies are awful. The Turks have been sending us a few 9-inch shells lately. They throw great stones and clods of dirt in the air when they burst. We also get some high explosive shells. You don't get many bullets our way only a few strays. Alex Jones was wounded the other day; he is likely to lose his leg. Cecil Scott also got wounded. C Wilkinson from Jumbunua got killed. All the rest of the boys are keeping well. Things are going as well as can be expected. I reckon the Turks get more than they expect. The place here is a maze of trenches. They will take some filling in.*

In the same issue the *Great Southern Advocate* published a letter from Sam Makeham who was recently wounded. *I was in our front trench within 40 yards of the Turks. At night we could hear a phonograph they were in the habit of playing; you never heard such gruesome noise in all your life! At 12 o'clock on Monday, June 28 at midnight, another chap and I had just finished our watch when we heard a cry of 'Here they come!' The Turks yelling to Allah were coming at us in all directions. The moon was full and you could see their bayonets gleaming. Then commenced continuous firing for four hours. The taller men remained up over the trench shooting like blazes; the shorter men remained down in the trench reloading and changing rifles to keep them cool. The chap firing on my left was hit and toppled back into the trench. I haven't heard of him since. Shortly after he dropped, they got me. The first thing I knew I was sitting in the trench. They took me down to the doctor, where I found out there was nothing seriously wrong with me. I am now at Gizeral Palace Hospital, Cairo.*

Korumburra boy Henry Fowles, a serving Victorian police officer before the war, died at Gallipoli. His grieving parents and police colleagues attended a solemn memorial service held at the Richmond police station. *A memorial framed photograph of the late Constable H Fowles was unveiled by Superintendent Gleeson. The Superintendent said Constable Fowles in a noble spirit of patriotism, offered his services in the defence of King and Empire and was a member of the first contingent that left these shores. The fortunes of war went against him and he fell storming the heights of Gallipoli. Sub Inspector Currucan who was in charge of the Richmond police station, bore testimony to the sterling qualities of the deceased whose death he said was a loss to the police force.*

In his emotionally charged 1976 ballad 'No Man's Land', songwriter Eric Bogle captures the lingering generational sorrow of the 'War that was to end all Wars'. *The sun's shining down on these green fields of France; The warm wind blows gently and the red poppies dance. The trenches have vanished long under the plough; No gas and no barbed wire, no guns firing now. But here in this graveyard that's still No Man's Land. The countless white crosses in mute witness stand. To man's blind indifference to his fellow man. And a whole generation who were butchered and damned.*

oooOOOooo

Anzac Day is a day of solemn ceremony and remembrance throughout Australia. Crowds gather in solemn commemoration of those who served and acknowledge the sacrifice of those who lost their lives. The 'Ode for the Fallen' recited each Anzac Day has a special place in the national memory and hearts of all Australians. *They shall grow not old, as we that are left grow old: age shall not weary them, nor the years condemn. At the going down of the sun and in the morning, we will remember them. We bring our thanks this day for the peace and security we enjoy, which was won for us through the courage and devotion of those who gave their lives in time of war. We pray that their labour and sacrifice may not be in vain, but that their spirit may live on in us and in generations to come.*

By 1950 the younger soldiers who served in the first world war were approaching 50 years of age. I had seen a tattered old photograph of my Anzac grandfather Stanley on leave in Egypt in 1916. He was a cocky-looking young man sporting an Aussie slouch hat and wearing a crumpled AIF khaki uniform. Stanley was soon to be sent to the hell of the western front trenches in France. Nobody spoke of him in later years, I suspect he deserted his family when he returned home from the war. Stanley was dead long before I was born.

Another world war was fought and won. The end of the second world war was a decade ago by the mid-1950s, when World War 2 soldiers had returned home to their families and farms. They brought with them dreadful memories they would not share. Not a few, following in the despairing footsteps of earlier Anzacs, took the 'long walk down the paddock' with their rifles and ended in suicide the trauma they could and would not talk about. Those who got on with life were never the same young men they had been before the war.

My Uncle Albert Pye was a conscript a 'chocolate' soldier. It was said by regular army soldiers the 'chocos' would melt in the sun when they came under fire. Yet they defended Australia with courage and resolve. Albert took part in the New Guinea jungle campaign. He was sent there to defend Australia from the Japanese, when British Prime Minister Winston Churchill stubbornly refused to send home Australian troops serving in the Middle East. Their duty he said was to defend England the mother country, defence for the colonies came a poor second. In Australia this was regarded as Churchill's darkest hour and it resonates still among many older Australians.

Australia's wartime predicament was dire. Japanese planes bombed Darwin and other places in northern Australia on more than 200 occasions. Ships were sunk, massive damage was caused to Darwin's port and town, and hundreds of people were killed and wounded. The Northern Territory bombings which began at Darwin in February 1942 did not cease until June 1944, when the last Japanese aircraft was brought down on Australian territory. The Japanese enemy was in New Guinea and Timor and invasion of the Australian mainland seemed imminent.

Uncle Albert did not participate in the bitter fighting along the Kokoda Trail (also referred to as the Kokoda Track), where outnumbered, poorly trained and inadequately equipped Australian 'chocolate' soldiers valiantly fought alongside regular army soldiers and stemmed the tide of the Japanese march towards Australia. Albert encountered the Japanese invader in other jungle battles across the rugged Owen Stanley Ranges. For the rest of his life, he could not forgive nor could he forget the appalling Japanese brutalities inflicted on Australian troops during the war, particularly the slave labour barbarity of the Burma Railway atrocity. Like Gallipoli in Turkey the Hellfire Pass in Thailand where many Aussie soldiers died from cruelty and malnutrition is a place of pilgrimage for Australians. This was a sentiment and wartime trauma Albert shared with his generation. Forgive and forget was not in the lexicon of men who bravely met the brutal ferocity of the Japanese in battle.

On the battlefields of Papua. On the shores of Milne Bay. On the track to far Kokoda and down Gona Buna way. Through the fever-stricken jungle, where the Nippon lurked unseen. Into slime and slush and slaughter went their faded suits of green.

When the war came to an end Albert's infantry platoon was flown home and landed at Essendon airport. Without being officially demobbed, Albert arrived at the family farm at Bessiebelle near Portland with a stubbly beard, wearing a battered slouch hat, his faded suit of green, carrying an overladen backpack and his 303 rifle. His arrival was unexpected and he walked in the door a conquering hero. The fresh-faced young farm boy was no more; in his place was a battle-hardened stranger.

A new fear born between the doorstep and the door; far from the night patrol, the terror, the long sweat — and far from the dead boy who left so long ago.

Like many ex-soldiers, Albert would never speak of his wartime experiences not even when his sons as grown men asked him. The memories forged under fire were his and his comrades' memories alone, sacred and tormenting in equal measure.

In the 1950s servicewomen were acknowledged but not yet accorded the recognition they deserved for their wartime service. My Aunt Mary, Mum's sister and Albert's wife, served in the Australian Navy as a Wren. She would occasionally speak of her wartime experience but never in any depth. I once overheard a conversation between veterans describing how young boys and grown men as they approached battlefield death would suddenly cry out for their mothers. Later I was to read of Royal Airforce staff during the Battle of Britain, listening in horrified silence on loud speakers in the war room to the final radio transmissions of pilots as their planes spiralled out of control. The last word many of them said was 'Mother!'

For countless Australian families, the heartbreak sorrow of the death knock visit or delivered telegram remains vivid today. Parents would refuse to open the door to a postal worker, a military man or a priest in case he was the bearer of bad news. They would cross to the other side of the street to avoid meeting any one in authority fearing the worst.

Most often it was bad news and the family was inconsolable. Mothers disbelievingly collapsed to the floor; fathers retreated outside to weep alone. Brothers and sisters tried their best to cope as each word they heard came from afar and seemed alien.

> *The old man died at the table when the old wife's back was turned. Face down on his bare arms folded; he sank with his wild grey hair outspread o'er the open Bible, and a (treasured son's) name written there.*

My mother's twin brothers, Dermot and William Murray, were volunteer soldiers who served in the Middle East. I wondered whether they were to be numbered among the celebrated heroes the Rats of Tobruk. I know they fought in Crete and Greece. As a kid, I saw old black and white photographs of them in military uniforms wearing Aussie slouch hats. They appeared young, eager and optimistic. War had not yet reached out to trouble or weary them. Keen expectation and excitement was plainly etched on each face. Later when I asked 'what did you do in the war?' They would slowly turn away and say nothing. I soon learned that like my Uncle Albert, silence was golden with these hard-edged men. There was no breaking through the impenetrable barrier they so tightly placed around themselves.

oooOOOooo

The Korumburra War Memorial inscription reads: *Erected to the glorious memory of the 165 men of the Shire, who nobly fought and sacrificed their lives in the cause of freedom and Empire during the Great War of 1914-1918. And to the men of the Shire who nobly fought and died during the 1939-45 war. Greater love hath no man than this, that a man lay down his life for his friends.*

A dawn service was held each Anzac Day at the Korumburra War Memorial, followed later in the morning by a street parade with a pipe band and veterans wearing medals and marching to applause from an assembled crowd of onlookers. Wreaths were solemnly laid to honour the dead; prayers were said and a lone bugle sounded the Last Post. The Diggers, all still relatively young men, would adjourn to one of two pubs, the Korumburra or the Austral Hotel to drink beer, reminisce and play two up for the rest of the day. Wives and children were never in attendance on these purely male, boozy, old comrade pub sessions.

These were tough, single-minded men who despite everything they had been through remained strong in faith and fiercely loyal to the Australia they had fought for and loved so well. Edward Meagher a captain in the Australian Imperial force (AIF) during the second world war, was a Japanese prisoner of war forced to labour on the notorious Burma Railway (1942–45) known as the 'Death Railway'. Aussie POWs suffered unspeakable horror and torment at the hands of brutal and bushido driven Japanese camp guards. POWs were tortured, beaten, starved and left to die when they could no longer work, or rise from their sickbeds.

On an emotional pilgrimage to the Hellfire Pass railway cutting in 2019, Aussie POW and artilleryman Jim Kerr summed up the feelings of many ex-soldiers. *People say do I hate the Japanese? I look at it in this way: I'll never ever forgive the Japanese for what they did. They didn't give to our people what should have been given — adequate food, medical attention — and I'll never forget as long as I'm alive. You soon learned as a POW that you couldn't survive on your own, that you had to have a mate or mates. If you were sick or in need of some help; anything you managed to steal or scam or whatever, you shared among your mates. The others the British and Dutch troops soon realised this was the way they* (too) *had to function.*

Edward Meagher who was not from Gippsland, later became a prominent Victorian Liberal Party politician and government minister. In heated political debate with his Labor Party opponents, he famously and patriotically said, *I didn't get filled full of bullet holes on the Burma Railway, to see a bunch of socialists take over this country!* I worked as a humble filing clerk for Edward Meagher when he was Minister for Aboriginal Affairs in Victoria (1967-72). He was a genial and straightforward man, who oversaw the granting of land rights to indigenous Victorians in 1970.

oooOOOooo

I have an enduring Gippsland childhood memory of a mid-fifties stormy Korumburra Anzac Day. Of standing in the pouring rain with my parents watching from the sidelines as soldiers from both world wars marched by. A few wore ragged slouch hats and seen better-days khaki uniforms. The world was grey and bitter that day. Thunder rumbled loudly overhead. Lightning flashed in layered sheets across the cloud dark sky. The wind howled around in gusting gales. Flags fluttered perilously; umbrellas were blown inside out and back again. The rain came down in torrents, cascading off shiny medals and turned up collars of overcoats. Standing there in the driving rain, I was utterly transfixed by the column of marching men, rigidly in step with their heads held high, clearly proud of themselves and their fallen comrades. There was no question in my boyish mind; these men were true Australian heroes.

Our heroes from Australia who faced the Turkish shells have left their names forever on the Shores of the Dardanelles. They heard the bugle calling and the National Anthem played. They boldly reached the front amid the shrieking shells; (and) *fought and died for the Empire on the Shores of the Dardanelles.*

I have an earlier childhood memory of an Anzac Day March in Melbourne. I was four years old and we were watching row after row of Anzacs march down Swanston Street. I remember Mum's faux leopard skin coat and the peacock feather she wore in her hat. A lean and ruddy faced man wearing a tilted slouch hat and medals left the parade of marching soldiers and walked over to where we were standing. With his rough hands, he patted my curly blond locks and pressed a ten shilling note into my tiny hand. With a friendly smile, he turned to the crowd and said *This young boy is what we fought for and some of us died for!* Those around us applauded as he re-joined his mates. I remember Mum's glowing pride and of course the chocolate purchased later with the ten bob note.

On one occasion when I was eight years old, I was taken by Mum to visit 'Scotty' who had experienced the wartime terror that was besieged Tobruk. Scotty (I never knew his real name) was a shattered man suffering from a variety of physical ailments and what was then called 'War Nerves' a decade after he returned home. The conversation was tea and biscuits small talk. Scotty was fidgety and paying very little attention. As we left, I heard Scotty's wife say to Mum in a soft tone: *He has dreadful nightmares. He sits all day and can't sleep more than an hour or so at night. That's his life on a good day. As for the rest, you don't want to know about it.*

I have seen men that could laugh no more. I've seen them die quickly. I've seen the face of death, lying by my side in deep holes. I have seen the gauze wrappings of men that have gone, lying in one great heap. I've been too afraid to move for fear.

oooOOOooo

Mum and Dad would occasionally take my sister Mary and me on a visit to a neighbour's rundown dairy farm. Mum would take a freshly baked cake and Dad a couple of bottles of beer. Jimmy was a soldier who had been captured by the Japanese in World War 2 and underwent unspeakable cruelties at their hands. For Aussie soldiers like Jimmy held in the living hell of Japanese prisoner of war camps, mateship was the key to their survival. Aussie POW Duncan Butler, who along with others was tasked by the Japanese to build the infamous Burma Railway, wrote a poem he deferentially called 'Mates'.

Me mind goes back to '43 to slavery and hate; when man's one chance to stay alive depended on his mate. With bamboo for a billycan and bamboo for a plate; a bamboo paradise for bugs was bed for me and mate. You'd slip and slither through the mud and curse your rotten fate. But then you'd hear a quiet word 'don't drop your bundle, mate'. And though it's all so long ago, this truth I have to state; a man don't know what lonely means 'til he has lost his mate.

Jimmy was a middle-aged Irishman, thick in brogue and red headed, who had settled in Australia years before and came home from the war prematurely aged, emotionally traumatised and downright angry at the world. His wife and children had left him before I was born, unable to cope with the savage outbursts of physical violence, verbal abuse and overpowering bouts of tears that would erupt out of nowhere.

We children were cautioned before each visit to be on our best behaviour, make no noise and don't stare. What I remember most about these visits was the torment in Jimmy's eyes and the tomb-like silence of the house. Mum would do the dishes while Dad and Jimmy drank together barely speaking a word. I watched Jimmy's hands shake uncontrollably and felt his embarrassment as the tears welled up in his eyes and rolled down his cheeks. Psychologically balancing on a knife edge of fear and mental turmoil, I heard him say the nightmares were the worse. He would wake soaked in sweat and screaming. Day or night, the horror and a barely held down feeling of dread never left him. Before there was such a word, Jimmy was in the vice like grip of a post-traumatic stress disorder (PTSD) that he was never to get over.

A year or so after our visits ceased Mum told us Jimmy had let loose his farm animals onto the road. He took a length of rope, slung it over a wooden beam in the dairy and hanged himself. His body was not discovered until the next day with his Kelpie dog lying next to the chair from which Jimmy had launched himself into eternity. Even sixty-five years later, I can still see Jimmy's sad face and feel the melancholy of those long-ago visits, to a troubled soldier utterly crushed by his wartime experience and the survivor's guilt he brought home with him.

I attended Jimmy's funeral with the family at Saint Joseph's Catholic Church in Korumburra. A sombre mass was celebrated, kind words were spoken by those who said they knew Jimmy before his life turned to tragedy. The Returned Services League president praised Jimmy's war service and spoke of his painful struggle to readjust to civilian life. I do not remember the exact words that followed the eulogy, but they were in accordance with today's RSL graveside sentiments. A red poppy is placed on the coffin and a pray intoned. *Valiant Hearts, who to your glory came. Through dust of conflict and through battle flame. Tranquil you lie, your knightly virtue proved. Your memory hallowed in the land you loved.* The tragedy of Jimmy's post war life is that he never really came home. He remained forever emotionally crippled and mentally trapped behind Japanese barbed wire.

The congregation at Jimmy's funeral, many of whom barely spoke more than a word or two to him when he was alive, respectfully honoured his troubled life in death. As Jimmy's coffin left the church for its final resting place; those gathered together sang Danny Boy, the traditional Irish song of farewell.

But come ye back when summers in the meadow; or when the

valley's hushed and white with snow. I'll be here in sunshine or in shadow; Oh Danny boy, Oh Danny boy, I love you so. — Rest in Peace, Jimmy.

Part Three
Aborigines and the Colonial Frontier

A simplistic view implying as it does that Aborigines were without volition, mere tools of a white agenda and mere objects at the disposal of Europeans. It is an outdated way of looking at the past — good and simple Aborigines and awful Europeans. We know that situations were more complex than that, and we have learned to look for and respect evidence of Aboriginal volition. We are in the presence here of mature adults, intelligent men, black and white with their own agendas.

Marie Hansen Fels

10

Colonial Frontier Warfare

Mr Thomas informs me that Mr Smith is very kind to the blacks and rewards them liberally for any little service they perform. It is therefore not surprising the blacks should take up their station near to Mr Smith when he affords them such liberal encouragement.

George Augustus Robinson to Charles La Trobe, 16 September 1840

The colonial frontier which officially lasted from 1788-1934 was not a peaceful place or an idyllic paradise for Aborigines or white settlers. Cultural contact brought with it misunderstanding and apprehension on both sides. When communication broke down, violence and aggression ensued. In recent years the demonization of the frontier as white settler colonialism, whose aim was to destroy Indigenous people and their culture, has overshadowed an earlier more benign pioneer narrative of Aussies working hard to tame the land and build modern Australia. European settlement, frontier warfare and the misnamed 'stolen generation' of Aboriginal children are equated with British Empire tyranny and the genocidal horrors of the Nazi holocaust. A more balanced history-based view of land settlement and cross-cultural contact is dismissed as racist and discriminatory.

For white men to survive on the colonial frontier an upheaval in outlook and accommodation to a new and alien lifestyle was required. Senior Lecturer in History at James Cook University Mervyn Bendle writes of the colonial struggle to establish farms and bush communities. *The settlers were faced with unprecedented challenges as they confronted a vast wilderness extending on a continental scale from their initial tiny settlements. As they became aware of the opportunity that lay before them, they quite consciously went about creating a New World, with each advance of the frontier entailing a steady movement away from the influence of Europe. And inevitably, a very specific set of personal characteristics came to dominate amongst these people, as they moved out from their beachheads to create a new nation. Primary among these were individualism, independence, self-sufficiency, resourcefulness, a suspicion of centralized authority, a democratic temper* (and) *values. Outback conditions exercised a kind of natural selection upon the human material. The qualities favouring successful assimilation to frontier society were adaptability, toughness, endurance, activity and loyalty to one's fellows. Frontier conditions fostered and intensified the growth of the distinctively Australian outlook.* Australian pioneers were tough-minded resilient men and women, who like the Blues Brothers, saw themselves on a 'mission from God' to cultivate luxuriant nature and civilise their adopted land.

The study of Indigenous history is currently under the literary spell of Bruce Pascoe, who in his book *Dark Emu Black Seeds: agriculture or accident* Magabala Books (2014), disputes that Aborigines were stone age hunter/gatherers. Pascoe sets out to rewrite history and make the case that Aborigines were sophisticated agricultural farmers, lived in stone villages of 1,000 inhabitants, extensively cultivated the land and erected large storage granaries. *Aboriginal people were farming, there's no other conclusion to draw.* Pascoe misquotes his sources and misrepresents facts. He invents and exaggerates a false narrative that has no historical or archaeological credibility.

oooOOOooo

The Aboriginal presence in Australia is estimated to be between 40,000 and 60,000 years. In that time no significant social or cultural contact occurred with the outside world. Indonesian and Malay fisherman and possibly some others occasionally visited Australian shores, mingled with Aboriginal tribes for a time and were eventually killed or driven away with spears. Conflict between clan and tribal groups resulted in successive waves of Aborigines being pushed south. Some crossed the Bass Strait land bridge which 30,000 years ago was inundated by an ice age rise in sea levels to occupy Tasmania. Different language groups suggest two or more distinct waves of Aboriginal occupation in Tasmania. *Evidence for contest over territory is reflected by the presence of 'Nara'* (a tribal language spoken in Western Tasmania) *in 'Mara'* (a tribal language spoken in Eastern Tasmania) *territory suggesting a pattern of occupation and hostile takeover that mirrors traditional hostilities during colonial times. Colonial settlers found two main language groups in Tasmania upon their arrival, which correlates with broader* (mainland) *clan divisions.*

Unlike primitive societies who evolved technologically and socially over time and experienced successive waves of outsider conquest, Aboriginal society throughout Australia remained relatively static and unchanging. Survival strategies devised over thousands of years left the land undeveloped and Aboriginal society unprepared for the arrival of strangers with a desire to tame and settle the land. In 1969 Professor John Mulvaney, touted as the father of Australian archaeology, argued in his *Prehistory of Australia* Thames and Hudson London (1969) that Aboriginal society made changes and did sometimes engage in innovation. The rate of change over time however was exceedingly slow even by the sluggish standards of medieval Europe.

The myth persists of a peaceful and unified Aboriginal culture, exercising a harmonious tribal sovereignty over the continent. Clan warfare and tribal disputes were rife in Aboriginal Australia for many thousands of years before white settlement took place. There was no tribal clan or community entity in existence representing a unified Aboriginal 'First Nation' (an imported idea from Canada and America) before British settlement. This was a later invention promoted to serve an activist political purpose. *It is dramatically over-simplifying Indigenous culture to suggest that they didn't have their own endless territorial conflicts and tribal wars that had an equal or worse impact than the coming of the Europeans. Fighting for resources and territory is a universal trait.*

In his recent book *Justice and Warfare in Aboriginal Australia* Lexington Books (2020), French Economist Christophe Darmangeat cites the words of a western desert Aborigine on the fear and chaos generated by tribal warfare before European settlers arrived. *Before it was permanent war; you didn't sleep at night because your brother would come and kill you to take your wife and daughters. But when the whites came, everyone calmed down.* The calm was no more than a short-lived pause in a volatile situation of ongoing clan and tribal violence.

Christian missionary George Taplin wrote in his book *The Narrinyeri: An Account of the Tribes of South Australian Aborigines* J T Shawyer (1874). *In 1849 I saw a battle where about 500 of the Narrinyeri met some 800 of the Wakanuwan, and it was very evident that if the conflict had not been stopped by the colonial authorities the Narrinyeri would have been signally defeated by their opponents. They bore a special enmity to* (their opponents) *because these latter had a propensity for stealing fat people and eating them. If a man had a fat wife, he was always particularly careful not to leave her unprotected, lest she might be seized by prowling cannibals.*

Ruthless tribal warfare and territorial conflict continued unabated as European settlement swept across the country. In his 1969 book *Journey to Horseshoe Bend* Anthropologist Ted Strehlow, whose father Carl was a Lutheran Pastor and from 1896 to 1922 Superintendent of the Hermannsburg Mission 80 miles from Alice Springs, wrote of an 1875 massacre of tribal Aborigines by other Aborigines that occurred near the Finke River in Central Australia. *The warriors turned their murderous attention to the women and older children and either clubbed or speared them to death. Finally, according to the grim custom of warriors and avengers they broke the limbs of the infants, leaving them to die 'natural deaths'. The final number of the dead could well have reached the high figure of 80 to 100 men, women and children.*

In 1891 Strehlow's fellow missionary, Louis Gustave Schulze, wrote a monograph for the Royal Society of South Australia. *The natives to the south eat human flesh. It is said that they engage in regular human hunting parties for this purpose. It is even said that they roast and eat their own infants, if they succeed each other too quickly. Only last year a woman not far from here did it, and when reproved for so doing, she was surprised at being found fault with, as she considered the roasting and eating of her own child as something quite natural.* In the following chapters there are many such cruelties and barbarities directed at Aborigines by their own people.

oooOOOooo

Aboriginal Australia was not a tranquil and nonviolent land. The pre-colonial situation was socially and culturally fragmented by incessant clan disputes, tribal warfare and property/women stealing raiding parties. Nowhere was there a collective sense of Aboriginal nationhood or a cohesive monoculture of kinship and dreamtime experience. Diversity of belief, attitude and behaviour proliferated across the country. The iconic pre–European Didgeridoo was a ritual wind instrument developed around 1500 AD and until recently was found only among Aboriginal tribes in northern Australia. Cooperation would sometimes occur between Aborigines, but it was fleeting and subject to the pursuit of individual and tribal self-interest.

The idea of the noble savage living in peace and harmony in a state of pristine nature is an 18th century fiction without historical foundation. Peaceful interludes of Indigenous coexistence always collapsed into aggression and warfare as one side or the other felt themselves strong enough to prevail. Some of these brutal regional conflicts could even be described as genocidal in their destructive rivalry and clan disruption. When the frontier clash began Aboriginal groups friendly to Europeans watched with satisfaction as white settlers drove traditional clan enemies from their tribal lands. They would sometimes join white settlers in bush skirmishes, aggressively pursuing tribal enemies with vengeance and enthusiasm. On other occasions, the tribes formed temporary alliances to attack European settlers. Violence and occupation did not arrive with the English First Fleet. Both were an entrenched and accepted norm in Aboriginal tribal society long before Europeans began to explore the Pacific Ocean region.

Horrendous physical assault, domestic and sexual abuse were practices deeply embedded in Aboriginal culture for ritual, revenge and rape purposes from the very beginning of tribal society. Captain Watkin Tench who arrived in 1788 with the First Fleet, wrote of the wretched plight of Aboriginal women at the hands of violent tribal men. Aboriginal women *are in all respects treated with savage barbarity; condemned not only to carry the children, but all other burthens, they meet in return for submission only with blows, kicks and every other mark of brutality. When an Indian* (Aboriginal) *is provoked by a woman, he either spears her, or knocks her down on the spot; on this occasion he always strikes on the head, using indiscriminately a hatchet, a club, or any other weapon, which may chance to be in his hand.* Marine Lieutenant William Collins confirmed the savage conduct of Aboriginal men towards their womenfolk. *We have seen some of these unfortunate beings with more scars upon their shorn heads, cut in every direction, than could be well distinguished or counted.*

Congregationalist minister George Taplin wrote of the exploitation and mistreatment of Narrinyeri women in his book *The Native Tribes of South Australia* E S Wigg and Sons (1879). *Amongst them the woman is an absolute slave. She is treated with the greatest cruelty and indignity, has to do all laborious work, and to carry all the burthens. For the slightest offence or dereliction of duty, she is beaten with a waddy or yam stick and not infrequently speared. The records of the Supreme Court in Adelaide furnish numberless instances of blacks being tried for murdering lubras. The woman's life is of no account if her husband chooses to destroy it, and no one ever attempts to protect or take her part under any circumstances. In times of scarcity of food, she is the last to be fed, and the last considered in any way. That many die in consequence cannot be a matter of wonder.*

Anthropologist and Anglican clergyman Professor Adolphus Peter Elkin, a meticulous 20th century observer of Indigenous tribal culture, kinship and ritual, recorded many examples of the tribal abuse of Aboriginal women, from the temporary swapping of wives to cement clan warrior solidarity and settling disputes with clan enemies, to engaging in ritual sexual intercourse during religious ceremonies and sending women to have sex with visitors as a mark of hospitality. The role of Aboriginal women was one of tribal and communal subservience to the arbitrary dictates of elder authority and male control.

Author Robert Hughes wrote in his prize-winning book *The Fatal Shore* Random House (1986), *the unalterable fact of tribal life was that women had no rights at all and could choose nothing. She was the absolute property of her kin until marriage, whereupon she became the equally helpless possession of her husband. Before and after* (marriage), *she was merely a root-grubbing, shell-gathering chattel, whose social assets were wiry arms, prehensile toes and a vagina. If a woman showed the least reluctance, if she seemed lazy or gave her lord and master any other cause for dissatisfaction, she would be furiously beaten or even speared.*

Anthropologist Alfred Howitt, wrote of the forced removal and licentiousness of Aboriginal marriage custom in his book *The Native Tribes of South-East Australia* MacMillan *(*1904). *When a betrothed girl is of a marriageable age, the man to whom she is promised, having received her father's consent, or even that of her mother, which would suffice, took her away when she was out from the camp with the other women. He was accompanied by a comrade. Having seized her, they dragged her away, she screaming and biting as much as she was able to. No one interfered, the other women looking on and laughing. The marriage was then consummated by the Abaijas* (relatives)*, who remained with her for one or two days of ceremonial dancing, during which there was between her and the men of the camp unrestrained license, not even excluding her father.*

Explorer Edward John Eyre, the first European to travel the coastline of the Great Australian Bight and Nullarbor Plain in 1840–1841 was sympathetic to Aborigines, but deplored the brutal treatment of tribal women by their menfolk. *Women are often sadly ill-treated by their husbands and friends they are frequently beaten about the head, with waddies, in the most dreadful manner, or speared in the limbs for the most trivial offences. Few women will be found, upon examination, to be free from frightful scars upon the head, or the marks of spear wounds about the body. I have seen a young woman, who, from the number of these marks, appeared to have been almost riddled with spear wounds.*

oooOOOooo

Four years after white settlers arrived in Melbourne in 1835, an Aboriginal camp incident occurred that highlights the use of rape as a weapon and its cultural acceptance by tribal women. Historian Marie Hansen Fels describes a wild night of disorder and turmoil in a mixed tribal clan Aboriginal camp in what would later become Melbourne's central business district. *On the night of 17 December 1839, there were around 400* (Aboriginal) *people encamped near the surveyor's paddock* on the north side of the Yarra, including Barrabools from Geelong and Goulburn blacks. They had congregated in Melbourne since September, hoping for good things from La Trobe, the 'Big one Gubernor'. There had been night after night of drunkenness and violence, followed by corroborees.

This night, Derrimut and Mr King (Aborigines) *arrived at the encampment drunk, and the Westernport chief Budgery Tom, irritated, threw a wonguim* (boomerang) *which happened to hit Derrimut. A fight ensued between the Westernport men. Budgery Tom was so badly wounded that* (William) *Thomas* (Assistant Protector of Port Phillip Aborigines) *thought he would die. The encampment settled down eventually, then about 11 pm two Westernport youths held down a thirteen-year-old Goulburn girl while ten or more ravished her. Thomas and Surveyor Smythe rescued her and Thomas proposed putting her in Mrs Thomas' tent. Her brother and sister refused, and insisted she be placed in their care. Then Thomas discovered that the alleged sister was negotiating with the males for a repeat. The encampment quietened down again, only to be disturbed half an hour later by a fight between the women, naked in front of banked up fires, the cause being the girl. Some of the women were roundly abusing her for not keeping quiet while she was being assaulted. The sister was seriously cut open and a Westernport woman seriously injured as well.*

In October 1845, the *Port Phillip Patriot and Melbourne Advertiser* reported on a not uncommon occurrence of Aboriginal domestic violence in Melbourne that appalled all who witnessed it. *On Saturday last an aboriginal, well known in Melbourne as Bob Cunninghame, was reeling about Little Flinders Street in a state of intoxication and beating his lubra* (wife) *with a waddy, who thereupon took refuge in the home of Mr Peacock, the teacher of the aboriginal school, and the door was closed upon her intoxicated husband. Cunninghame became furious, and forced it open, he rushed into the house, overthrew a child six years of age, knocked down a nurse with an infant in her arms and frightened Mrs Peacock into fits, then* (grabbed) *his lubra by the hair, he dragged the unfortunate female into the streets towards his miam* (hut) *on the Yarra. Passing through Richmond, he was so brutally using the poor woman that a sailor passing interfered and gave Bob Cunninghame a sound thrashing.*

In his 1908 book, *The Miracle at Mapoon or from native camp to Christian village* Christian missionary Arthur Ward, writes *at Mapoon* (Queensland) *the* (Presbyterian) *missionaries could not believe that Aborigines could ill-treat their women so badly. The cruelty displayed towards women was at times almost fiendish. One man in a fit of rage seized his 'gin' by the head and poked a red-hot firebrand in her eye. If a mother tried to punish the children for anything, the men beat the mother and let the children abuse her. Telford speared Toby's dog. Therefore, Toby speared Telford's sister.*

oooOOOooo

Lieutenant William Bradley, a British naval officer who arrived with the First Fleet in January 1788 aboard HMS Sirius, initially formed a positive impression of the Botany Bay Aborigines he came in contact with. After several not so favourable encounters, he changed his mind. He wrote in his journal on 1 October 1788. *What has been experienced lately in several instances of meeting with the natives, has occasioned me to alter those very favourable opinions I had formed of them, and however much I wished to encourage the idea of their being friendly disposed, I must acknowledge, now convinced, that they are only so when they suppose we have them in our power or are well prepared by being armed. Latterly they have attacked almost every person who has met with them that has not had a musket and have sometimes endeavoured to surprise some who had.* Lieutenant Bradley was disappointed by this ugly turn of events, but he was realist enough to accept the fact that such encounter clashes were inevitable.

There is always community circumstance and cultural nuance to be considered when assessing racial relationships. *The Port Phillip Patriot and Melbourne Advertiser* reported *a party of natives to the number of seventeen or eighteen visited Mr Brock's station at Mount Rouse. Much humanity was shown to them by Mr Codd who supplied them with food. Mr Codd was my overseer. He was murdered by the aboriginal natives on the 19th of May 1840. I saw him struck down with a leanguil* (hatchet) *a weapon used by the natives.* There were others who like Mr Codd treated the Aborigines around them with kindness and compassion only to be attacked and killed for their Christian good deeds.

Governor of New South Wales Lachlan Macquarie (1810-21) pursued a humanitarian policy towards Australia's Indigenous inhabitants. A later historian assessing Macquarie impressive legacy wrote *Macquarie's policy concerning the Aboriginals was an expression of the humanitarian conscience. He organized the Native Institution (a school for Aboriginal children), a village at Elizabeth Bay for the Sydney tribe, an Aboriginal farm at George's Head and a sort of annual durbar* (a formal meeting place) *for them at Parramatta. Orders of merit and even an old general's uniform were bestowed on deserving chiefs. No other Governor since Phillip had shown them so much sympathy.* The relationship between white colonists and Aborigines was never perfect; but neither was it founded on a government policy of genocide and unprovoked massacre.

Bloodshed carried out by whites against Aborigines and by hostile Aborigines against whites came about in response to an unpredictable and volatile climate of fear and retaliation present on both sides of the frontier conflict. Crime, whether committed by Aborigines or white settlers seldom went unpunished. White men were arrested, tried, convicted and hanged for murdering Aborigines. So called white privilege did not excuse or protect them from the full rigour of the law. Woke histories conveniently overlook the colour-blindness of colonial legal proceedings and paint a false and misleading portrayal of colonial justice. White settlers were not the sadistic genocidal killers of today's popular myth. A frontier clash of contrasting cultures and lifestyles was as inevitable as it was unfortunate and many lives were lost. There was brutality and callousness on both sides of the conflict sparing neither women, children nor the elderly.

All however was not relentless violence and endless bloodshed. A significant degree of cooperation and racial tolerance was present in colonial society. A compassionate sympathy existed in 19th century white Australia concerning the plight and humane protection of Aborigines. Aborigines obtained jobs, shelter and supplies from white settlers and their knowledge of the land particularly their tracking ability, was greatly admired by the early settlers. This well documented but inconvenient truth of paternal and peaceful coexistence does not fit comfortably with the divisive invasion day/massacre narrative and is mostly left out of the national story.

oooOOOooo

The culture wars have changed the way Australians view their history. As one author succinctly puts it *the consensus has created a new, genocidal version of the Australian past: a history full of massacres and killings.* Professor Geoffrey Blainey and Prime Minister John Howard have criticised this 'black armband' view of history as an over simplification of the colonial past — a revisionist narrative, where pioneer men and women are demonised as brutal murderers and Aborigines hailed as heroic frontier resistance fighters. Professor Blainey has rightly said genocide is not applicable in the Australian context.

In his 1999 Times Booksellers book *In Our Time* Professor Blainey writes *to some extent my generation was reared on the Three Cheers view of history. This patriotic view of our past had a long run. It saw Australian history as largely a success. While the convict era was a source of shame or unease, nearly everything that came after was believed to be pretty good. There is a rival view, which I call the black armband view of history. In recent years it has assailed the optimistic view of history. The black armbands were quietly worn in official circles in 1988* (at the time of the bicentenary of Australia). *The multicultural folk busily preached their message that until they arrived much of Australian history was a disgrace. The past treatment of Aborigines, of Chinese, of Kanakas, of non-British migrants, of women, the very old, the very young, and the poor was singled out, sometimes legitimately, sometimes not. The black armband view of history might well represent the swing of the pendulum from a position that had been too favourable, too self-congratulatory, to an opposite extreme that is even more unreal and decidedly jaundiced.*

In the 1970s Historian Henry Reynolds put forward his claim that the colonial frontier was a place of perpetual conflict, unredemptive violence and xenophobic hatred — cherry-picking violent and bloody examples of the black/white frontier encounter. Reynolds painted a one-sided evil picture of white colonisation, depicting it as no more than a deliberate colonialist plan of cultural destruction and racial genocide. His sympathy lay with Aborigines whom he saw as innocent victims of premeditated massacre and white settler tyranny. He introduced a view of the colonial frontier that no other historian before him saw in such overarching confrontational terms. Reynold's flawed and overstated history has become the woke version of the colonial past, denigrating and belittling every aspect of European settlement in Australia.

There is no denying that violent frontier encounters were brutal and gruesome affairs, nor that Aborigines suffered horrific bloodshed defending their tribal lands. Tens of thousands more died because they lacked immunity to European diseases and all of these Aboriginal deaths are to be regretted and lamented. Aboriginal massacres exaggerated and embellished in many cases have been well documented in books, films and the media and are today the prevailing trope in Australian history studies. To call white resistance to aboriginal violence, terrorism, genocide and oppression is to buy into an identity politics version of colonial frontier warfare. In academic circles with a few notable exceptions, there is a preoccupation with blaming and shaming pioneers and painting an admiring portrait of Aboriginal defiance. Rarely is the reporting done with objectivity and an even-handed search for truth. Morality tales and activist political agendas emphasising Aboriginal deaths, victimhood and white inhumanity predominate. The past has become condensed, one-sided and abridged in interpretation and explanation.

On the Indigenous side of the equation a simplified notion of Aboriginal identity prevails. In his book *On Identity* (Melbourne University Press 2019), celebrity journalist Stan Grant with part Aboriginal ancestry, writes he is sceptical of urban Aborigines like himself trying *to reconfigure, reconstruct, reimagine more romantic visions of some lost mythical past. A construction, not entirely a work of fiction, but selective in its facts* (accepting of a colonial story of) *loss and exile, rape, pillage and massacre*. Grant disavows the search for *the* (Holy) *Grail of an inner 'Aboriginal' self.* He sees himself as a *Wiradjuri man, a Kamilaroi, an Irishman and an Australian.* Stan Grant eschews modern cultural definition and Aboriginal identity as confining myth constructions. Like Australia's premier bush poet Banjo Paterson, he wants only to be an Australian, and rightly so.

oooOOOooo

It is a truism to say that history needs to be balanced, truthful and inclusive of both sides. The history of the pioneers has been usurped and unfairly maligned, a casualty of the modern obsession with identity politics and politicised victimhood. The national school curriculum is currently fixated on including multiple references to Indigenous history, culture and lifestyle in every subject and topic. Not as a means to be inclusive and truthful as is claimed, but rather to malign and revile white society, its history and Christianity. This biased and uncritical inversion of the educational process will be discussed in detail in a later chapter.

Pioneers have been denied natural justice in a politically charged rush to judgement that is flawed and confrontational. The research pendulum needs to be brought back to the factual centre, with pioneer history recounted without denigration, fabrication and mythic overlay. Putting front and centre, a dramatic colonial frontier story only half told and little appreciated in today's national narrative. The frontier experience of white settlers is every bit as authentic and valid as that of the Indigenous population. We need to know both sides of the frontier experience, the good and the bad, if genuine and honest historical truth is to be revealed. In the book, I explore the colonial frontier encounter from the neglected perspective of pioneer settlers presenting their side of the story as they perceived and lived it.

History is most rewarding and at its most complex and revealing when examined from a neighbourhood perspective where people's daily lives are most compellingly impacted. The focus of this and the following two chapters is on the murder and mayhem carried out by hostile Aborigines against white settlers — to give a dark and foreboding sense of the colonial reality of the pioneering lives of white settlers that is overlooked and derided in today's history books — revealing the fear and anxiety generated by the uncertainty and unpredictability of the frontier encounter. The advantage was with the white community but not exclusively so. Revenge attacks occurred on both sides and frontier violence escalated exponentially. It was an unequal contest in which there would be winners and losers and the result was never in doubt.

Patrick Morgan has said *we should tell the truth about the past, but not moralise about it, nor feel personally guilty.* Nor should we generalise and malign white motivation as hypocrisy and genocidal because Aboriginal deaths occurred. Modern cynicism concerning the tenets of 19th century god-centred Christian theology and social darwinism, should not be allowed to obscure the strongly held principles of pioneer men and women, nor be presented as an excuse to belittle their many achievements. Enlightenment thinking and the campaign to abolish slavery dominated the century and was morally persuasive in colonial Australia. Today's community standards were not the community standards of the time. The ethical benchmark of 19th century people's daily lives should be how well they adhered to the values and beliefs they professed. The literal truth of the Bible and a Christian way of life was important to these people. We should allow them the strength of their Christian beliefs and convictions.

On the whole, pioneer men and women lived respectable and principled lives within a cooperative rural community, dedicated to what they truly believed to be the progressive advancement of Christian and British civilisation. They believed in God as a supreme being of universal truth and power and in an orderly and law-abiding society. Without such cherished beliefs and genuine conviction, it would have been impossible for them to establish viable neighbourhood communities. Messy reality and human frailty sometimes fell short of such high-minded goals. That however is no reason to dismiss white culture and white behaviour as inherently pernicious and badly intentioned towards Aborigines.

oooOOOooo

The pioneer settler's overlooked account of bloody frontier warfare reveals a more multi-layered and varied experience than the history books relate. The mistake made by many writers of Aboriginal history today is to unfairly tarnish all pioneer men and women, those in government positions and those farming the land, with murderous intentions towards Aborigines, when clearly there was a plethora of diverse opinion and wide-ranging behaviour present in white colonial conduct. Just as there was in Indigenous tribal clans opposing each other over women, territory and the distribution of warfare booty.

There was a multitude of nonviolent daily encounters between whites and Aborigines that led to accommodation and adjustment, not perfect or equal in outcome, but Christian in focus and generously and kindly meant nevertheless. Such encounters took place more often than encounters of the violent kind and were not always or even primarily about subjugation and dispossession. Professor Geoffrey Blainey writes *in some districts no fighting is known to have occurred; the wide Monaro* district of southern New South Wales seems to have been occupied peacefully. In scores of large squatting stations, the relationship with Aboriginals was uneasily peaceful or even harmonious. The surviving knowledge of the Aboriginal's habits and beliefs and language in many places comes from sympathetic squatters who did everything to befriend and help the Aboriginals, feeding and caring for all who camped near the main homestead.

Dr Bob Reece, Emeritus Professor in History at Murdoch University Western Australia writes, of Aboriginal practicality, and the *coming in or accommodation* of Indigenous people in Western Australia during the 1830s. *Far from retreating from white settlement, Aborigines were attracted to it, although their movements were still very much conditioned by (tribal) territorial boundaries and punishment for 'trespassing'. Those groups closest to the main centre of settlement adjusted their traditional pattern of seasonal movement in response to the relatively easy availability of European food. The Aborigines were ready to make pragmatic arrangements with the whites to compensate for the loss of their land and the livelihood which it represented, and this readiness was acknowledged by the white authorities. Aboriginal 'attacks' on livestock and 'thefts' of flour and other property on the edge of the settlement seem to have been a response to the whites' refusal to share their resources rather than any 'guerrilla' effort to drive the whites away.*

John Allen, a Police Constable at Wallis Plains (NSW) in the 1820s reported that *while the settlers were 'much annoyed' by Aborigines at harvest time, in general the settlers were on good terms with them, Aborigines occasionally labouring for the settlers.* Cleve Hassell, a descendent of Albert Hassell, pastoral tenant of the Jerramungup squatting run near Albany in Western Australia, spoke of his family's relationship during the 19th century with Aborigines who occasionally speared station men and livestock. *The family had a great interest in the natives and got on very well with them. Some were employed as shepherds, some helped with the lambing and shearing and many stayed on the station for all their lives. They were good at stock handling and horse riding and were an important source of labour for the station. They also knew the country but their use was limited by their unpredictable nature.*

Western District pastoralists John Eddington of the Ballangeich squatting run, James Dawson of Kangatong, Joseph Ware of Minjah, Colin Hood of Merrang, John Dixon of Wyselaskie and Charles Burchett of The Gums, exercised a compassionate restraint and understanding towards Aborigines. They distributed blankets, tobacco, flour and shirts in a gesture of friendliness, not as some lurid accounts claim, to poison and destroy the Indigenous population. (More will be said concerning deliberate poisoning in a later chapter.) Squatter John Eddington acknowledged *they* (the Aborigines) *were entitled to a share in some of his stock as he had taken their food away.*

Squatter James Dawson and his daughter, Isabella, took a keen interest in the Aboriginal language and collected tribal stories from the Port Fairy Aborigines. In 1866, Dawson a humane and forward-looking man with strong Christian values, reserved a portion of the Kangatong squatting run as an Aboriginal camping ground. However, Dawson was no dreamy eyed colonial romantic. He saw the unequal division of labour between men and women in Aboriginal society, and wrote about it in his book *Australian Aborigines: The Language and Customs of Several Tribes of Aborigines in the Western District of Victoria* George Robertson (1881). *After marriage, women are compelled to do all the hard work of erecting habitations, collecting fuel and water, carrying burdens, procuring roots and delicacies of various kinds, making baskets for cooking roots and other purposes, preparing food, and attending to the children. The only work men do, in times of peace, is to hunt for opossums and large animals of various kinds, and to make rugs and weapons.*

oooOOOooo

Church of England clergyman the Reverend Joseph Docker settled his family on the Bontharambo squatting run near Wangaratta in 1838. George Faithfull had earlier occupied the run but abandoned it when several of his shepherds were murdered by local Aborigines. Aware of this unsettling news, Docker it was said *by his kindly and judicious treatment avoided any trouble with the blacks*. Joseph had an enlightened Christian view of the Aborigines who for many years held corrobborees on an island in a lagoon on his run. Docker hired Aborigines in the running of his station. In December 1840, *having difficulty obtaining* station hands he began employing blacks as shepherds. He supplied food and clothing to 14 of them, who tended 6,000 to 7,000 sheep and employed 8 others on casual work.

Frederick George Docker, Joseph's third son, *remembers the blacks were allowed to come about the homestead whenever they liked, sometimes chopping wood or rendering other light services, but if they saw any horseman riding up to the station they always hurried away and swam over a creek, fearing the arrivals might be mounted troopers after them. On one occasion a black fellow was at the back of the hut and did not notice the arrival of two troopers in time to make the usual method of escape, so he rushed into the hut and hid under my mother's bed for about two hours until the troopers departed. My father, mother and sister Mary knew he was there but did not betray him.*

Victorian settler James Kirby in his book *Old Times in the Bush of Australia: Trials and Experiences of Early Bush Life in Victoria During the* (Eighteen) *Forties* Robertson and Co (1896) records an encounter near Swan Hill, where Scotsman Andrew Beveridge was murdered by a group of Aborigines. Beveridge had earlier warned them he would in future kill those who speared his sheep. A later author accused Andrew of providing poisoned flour to Aborigines. James Kirby gives a heroic account of 'Black Beveridge', an Aborigine who tried to protect his white boss Andrew from those intent on spearing him.

At dawn on Sunday morning, Aborigines crept through bush and set up a cordon at Andrew Beveridge's tent. Andrew went out to meet with them and was immediately threatened with death. Black Beveridge came to Andrew's assistance. *He clasped Andrew in his arms. The blacks called him to let Andrew go, but he would not, and at last they said they would spear him also if he did not let Andrew go, so he very reluctantly had to let go of his friend, and as soon as he did so a shower of reed spears was sent into Andrew; some struck and entered his body, and two entered his skull. Before he was quite dead Black Beveridge caught up his body and carried it into the tent, where he died in a few seconds. No man could possibly have done more for another than did Black Beveridge for Andrew.*

In his book *Dark Emu,* fanning the flames of culture wars discontent, Bruce Pascoe blames Andrew Beveridge for his death accusing him of sexually molesting Aboriginal women. He tells us James Kirby *revealed Andrew Beveridge 'molested' native women, or, at least that the Aborigines claimed he had.* Pascoe also claims the Aborigines smeared Beveridge's dead body with red ochre as revenge symbolism for his sexual misdeeds. None of this is true and Pascoe is yet again revealed for the revisionist fantasist he is.

Journalist Georgia Moody writes of a failed British settlement at Port Essington (1838—1848) on the Northern Territory's Cobourg Peninsula. *In 1838, the British came to colonise northern Australia. Doomed to fail, they sailed home 11 years later. And as they left, the local Indigenous people didn't celebrate they wept.* Aboriginal women were said to have *shown their grief by cutting their heads and faces with sharp flints. You would have thought,* Aboriginal Historian Don Christopherson declared, *Aboriginal people would have said 'They brought all this sickness, we lost so many people', but they still wanted them to stay. At times, there was great humanity shown between Aboriginal people and the English. And we need to tell those stories of great humanity not just the stories of how we kill each other, but the stories of how we help each other.* There was always another more peaceable side to frontier contact between white men and Aborigines to be considered.

oooOOOooo

In January 1950, the Melbourne *Age* published an article remembering the Reverend Joseph Orton, the first Methodist Missionary to visit Victoria in 1836. In discussing the Aborigines, Orton expressed a Christian evangelist message. *These poor creatures will come to a knowledge of the truth, and they and their successors will participate in the blessings of the Light of the Glorious Gospels.* However condescending these words may sound today, the Christian message was for Orton and his congregation a heartfelt one of duty and genuine compassion. It was a Christian message of salvation and assimilation that resonated throughout rural and outback Australia.

19th century Christian Missionaries were men and women of moral conviction and an impassioned religious faith. It is easy with hindsight to point out the flaws in the Christian mission to the Aborigines — to label them as culture destroyers and worse. With sacrifice, self-denial and an overzealous paternalism, Christian men and women devoted their lives to spreading the Christian gospels. The philanthropic object of their endeavour was charitable, educational and the saving of souls. They did not choose this tough evangelist outback life lightly and many devoted their entire adult lives to the altruistic task.

Catholic Archbishop John Bede Polding wrote of this Indigenous soul-saving task in an 1869 Pastoral Letter. *Some of our fellow colonists believe that these black men are not of our race, are not our fellow creatures. We Catholics know assuredly how false this is. We know that one soul of theirs is, like one of our own, of more worth than the whole material world, that any human soul is of more worth, as it is of greater cost, than the whole mere matter of this earth, its sun and its system or, indeed, of all the glories of the firmament.*

There were those such as the Wesleyan Missionary the Reverend Francis Tuckfield, who were scathing and critical of the effects of colonisation and white settlement on Aborigines. Tuckfield wrote in his journal in 1837: *The Government is fast disposing of the land occupied by the natives from time immemorial. In addition to which settlers under the sanction of government may establish themselves in any part of this extensive territory and since the introduction of the numerous flocks and herds, a serious loss has been sustained by the natives without an equivalent being rendered. Their territory is not only invaded, but their game is driven back, their marnong and other valuable roots are eaten by the white man's sheep and their deprivation, abuse and miseries are daily increasing.*

Nineteen years later in March 1856, philanthropist Edward Wilson expressed a similar anger and sorrow at a colonial situation he saw as spiralling out of control. He wrote a letter to the *Argus* newspaper deploring the worst abuses of colonisation on the Aboriginal population. *In less than twenty years we have nearly swept them off the face of the earth. We have shot them down like dogs. In the guise of friendship, we have issued corrosive sublimate in their damper and consigned whole tribes to the agonies of an excruciating death. We have made them drunkards, and infected them with diseases which have rotted the bones of their adults, and made such few children as are born amongst them a sorrow and a torture from the very instant of their birth. We have made them outcasts on their own land, and are rapidly consigning them to entire annihilation.*

The truth of frontier encounter was far more complex and multifaceted in nature than these two contemporary accounts allow. Strong religious conviction and humanitarian benevolence pervaded Victorian society. Men and women with strong British values and a genuine sense of compassion and empathy, prominently displayed in the anti-slavery and working class trade union movements in England, lamented the inevitable social darwinian disappearance of Australia's primitive stone age Aborigines.

These were law abiding, altruistic 19th century Victorians with a forward-looking view of themselves and evolving humanity. Injustices were committed and diligently called out by morally upright colonists such as Reverend Tuckfield and Edward Wilson. Those who write only of Aboriginal massacre, dispossession and cruelty, ignore the good intentions and the good works of Britain's colonists, who on the whole were sympathetic to the plight of Indigenous people everywhere. To slander Christian missionaries and professional women like Daisy Bates as insensitive racists, reveals more about the woke nature of modern politics and the rewriting of history than the lived reality of the time.

The *Sydney Morning Herald on* 20 April 1951, published an obituary of Daisy Bates (who for a short time was married to Harry 'Breaker' Morant), which attests to her lifelong compassionate commitment to Australia's outback Aborigines. As we will discuss later, she did not however shy away from the more unsavoury side of Aboriginal infanticide, cannibalism and other disagreeable practices. *Mrs Daisy Bates, C.B.E. 'Kabbarli'* (grandmother) *to Aborigines throughout Western Australia, South Australia, Central Australia, and the Northern Territory died in her sleep in an Adelaide nursing home yesterday. She was 92 and had devoted 40 years of her life to helping the Aborigines. She lived amongst them in a tent, went walkabout with them, and wrote books about them. She was their guide, counsellor, friend, and universal provider. She clothed them and fed them at her own expense. Initiated into several tribes, she witnessed ceremonials taboo to Aboriginal women. She spoke 188 Aboriginal dialects. Daisy Bates died a pauper. Everything she owned she sold to care for her* (Aboriginal) *friends.*

Daisy Bates was what the Aborigines called a 'Good Fella Missus'.

There were other pioneer women from a generation earlier, who were respected by and took a charitable and humane interest in Aborigines. A Mrs Dunlop from Port Fairy saw it as her Christian duty to civilise and educate the Aborigines in her employ. She dressed them in European clothes, taught them to read and write, read the Bible and took them to church on Sundays with Christian prayer books in their hand. Mrs Dunlop's Aboriginal employees did not resist her Christian benevolence or as far as we know return to a tribal life in the bush.

Ellen MacPherson a Scots squatter's wife on a remote bush station, wrote in her book *My experience in Australia* J K Hope Publisher (1860) of regularly visiting Aborigines in their camp. *One of the most interesting features of the landscape in the vicinity of our station was an encampment of Aborigines, about a quarter of a mile from our cottage. I was naturally very anxious to learn all I could about this strange race, and their encampment was a source of great interest to me. It used to be a very favourite resort of ours in the evenings, and my husband would get into conversation with some of the more sociable individuals, and try to extract from them all the information likely to interest me, but they were very chary in communicating anything touching on their ways and custom.* Ellen MacPherson was curious about Aboriginal culture. She and her pastoralist husband were welcomed into the Aborigine's camp as friends who occasionally brought gifts and food. The relationship was respectful, harmonious and beneficial to Aboriginal welfare and white safety alike.

oooOOOooo

Alexander Crawford, a 22-year-old well-educated young Irishman from Belfast, arrived in Australia in 1880. He went to work on a relative's farm near Ballarat. In November 1881, seeking to make his own way in the world and earn enough money to get married, Alex entered into a business partnership with others. He took on the role of station manager of the Erridabubba pastoral run in the Murchison River district of Western Australia. The pastoral run was extensive, catering for 9,000 sheep accompanied by shepherds, free ranging over many miles of unfenced wild desert country.

In a series of letters Alex wrote to his sweetheart in New South Wales, he describes his relationship with the local Aborigines, which was humane, practical and from a white man's law and order perspective, just. *The natives up here are very troublesome. They are killing the sheep wholesale. On Friday I had four killed, a black fella came in and told me about it and where he thought they* (the Aborigines) *were camped. I have had some heavy losses, nearly 700 sheep killed by the natives, most of them ewes heavy in lamb, beside several other severe losses of horses.* These were not insignificant livestock losses. They amounted to 8% of the pastoral run's 9,000 sheep population.

I had rather a serious encounter with 13 natives the other night, wrote Alex. *I had my left arm rendered useless for days and my left knee badly hurt. It has swollen up considerably and gives me a great deal of pain, besides receiving sundry knocks on the back and the head. I had to fire six shots at them wounding some and then I had to fight them off with my revolver, which I had by the barrel and knocked 2 down with it when it broke. I would have been finished I think outright, had not my native boy hearing the firing come galloping up shouting as he came. The natives sent in word with one of my shepherds, first spearing him, to say they would come down altogether and kill all the white men on the place.*

At the same time as he was writing these words of violent frontier conflict Alex wrote *you ought to see me morning and evening feeding the blacks. There are about a dozen around the station who do anything that is wanted. I give them damper and meat and boiled over tealeaves and sugar. I gave a couple of the best of them, a shirt and trousers to keep them warm these cold nights; but to my surprise when they were going to sleep, they took all off and lay down in the cold absolutely naked.* This he considered his religious duty, compassionate and at the same time pragmatic in the running of the pastoral property.

Alex was young man with strong Methodist scruples. He had a reputation for imposing Christian morality on those he employed. *I will tell you the principal reason for me being called a tyrant, because I will not allow any of the labouring men* (on my station) *to keep black women, which on nearly all the other stations both masters and men do. I have got rid of all the bad men I had and the ones I have now are all rather decent men.* Aboriginal hospitality and tribal custom enforced by Aboriginal men for personal gain was the primary reason Indigenous women cohabited with white men. White men and Aborigines were expected to show respect for the law and adhere to 19th century Victorian principles of self-discipline, decency and virtue. As the morally principled station manager disapprovingly believed, 'sinful' human nature and the ever-present proximity of Aboriginal women encouraged some white men to keep black women as mistresses.

In discussing Aboriginal religious belief and the use of an evil spirit deterrent known as a 'bullroarer' *a sacred object consisting of a piece of wood attached to a string, whirled around to produce a roaring noise.* Alex Crawford recounts *the women are not allowed to see them. If they do and a man gets to know about it, he will kill her. They have no idea of God; they are afraid of an evil spirit they call 'Gingle'. Sometimes they indulge in cannibalism, but not often, and they only eat black fellows that's one consolation.* Crawford had little understanding of Aboriginal religious beliefs. There are many accounts of white men's bodies being mutilated and eaten in ritualistic cannibal feasting.

Although the wounding and killing of Aboriginals occurred on the Erridabubba pastoral run Alex and his men, wherever possible, would apprehend the offenders and hand them over to the law courts. Sentences of between 3 and 6 years hard labour in gaol were handed out for the spearing of livestock. Alex wrote of a typical encounter not involving killing or serious harm: *I made inquiries and found they* (three or more Aborigines) *had killed some sheep some months before. The first two I let go; the other native I gave half a dozen cracks with a whip and told them all if I ever knew them to kill a sheep again, I would beat them and send them to gaol.* In some cases, this retaliatory biblical punishment was enough of a deterrent to stop the spearing of both white men and livestock.

oooOOOooo

For white settlers, particularly during the early squatting era of the 1830s and 1840s, contact with hostile Aborigines was a visceral and fear-provoking experience. In 1831 the *Launceston Advertiser* published a letter simply signed 'Correspondent'. *We are at war with them: they look upon us as enemies as invaders as their oppressors and persecutors they resist our invasion. They have never been subdued; therefore, they are not rebellious subjects, but an injured nation, defending in their own way, their rightful possessions, which have been torn from them by force.* It was not a statement of racist intention, but a compassionate white man's understanding of Aboriginal motivation and hostile behaviour towards all white people.

On the 3 May 1833, the Sydney newspaper the *Australian* reported on the brutal murder and mutilation of five bushmen by Aborigines. *A dreadful murder has been committed at Mr Renkin's Station at Liverpool Plains* (New South Wales), *called the Barber's Stock Yard, the overseer and four assigned servants were found dead in the hut; and from the horrible manner in which their bodies were mangled, there can be no doubt but that the murder was committed by the natives. A quantity of ammunition and firearms were in the hut which were not touched, every other portable article was carried off.* An Aboriginal desire to possess the white man's property was nearly always a major consideration in these murderous sneak attacks. In this case the white man's weapons were not deemed to be valuable booty.

Charles Franks, said to be the white settler after which the Victorian City of Frankston was named, succumbed to Aboriginal violence and was buried on Melbourne's Flagstaff Hill. *Early in 1835, Mr Franks, one of the first immigrants, and his shepherd were killed by some of the Goulburn tribe of blacks. His station was near Cotterill's Mount, Sugarloaf, near the river Exe, now Werribee. They were both killed at one moment by the blacks, who while pretending friendship, smote them down by driving their tomahawks into the backs of their heads.*

On 18 July 1837, the *Australian* carried a horrific account of a treacherous and premeditated attack on sleeping farm workers. *On the 9 February, four persons, named John Spokes, John Pocock, Charles Somerville, and William Lennox, free persons, in the employ of Magnus McLeod in the neighbourhood of Port Macquarie, were asleep in their hut. About break of day, a native black entered the hut, and asked for a drink of water; he was directed by the man John Spokes who was the only one awake, to help himself out of the bucket; while he was doing so; seven more natives entered the hut, accompanied by a boy about ten years of age, and they all, with the exception of the boy, commenced an attack upon the white people with their waddies and nullas, without uttering a sentence, and continued beating Pocock, Somerville, and Lennox, over the head, until they supposed they were dead, the skulls of each being frightfully fractured; they went outside the hut and joined several others, the boy before mentioned having been employed conveying every portable article out of the hut.*

On the 6 November 1839, the *New South Wales Colonist* reported on 'Black Depredations: Extract of a letter dated New England, October 13, 1839'. *I have met with a severe loss a few days ago, 250 of my best ewes in lamb were driven off and slaughtered by the blacks, and the best shepherd in my employment murdered by those savages. We are really in a miserable condition in this district at present, nothing but terror and dismay on every hand, occasioned by the ravages of those ruthless murderers.*

Pastoralist Samuel Rawson wrote of the trepidation of a December 1840 night time attack on Squatter Robert Jamieson's hut by Gippsland Aborigines that lasted for four hours. Jamieson was *asleep when the raid started, he was woken by a yell and rushed out of his hut, to find himself surrounded by 100 savages and seized: he knocked two down and got safely back to his hut.* From inside the hut, Jamieson fired his gun and used it 'club fashion' to prevent the marauders from entering. Nevertheless, through open windows they were able to steal an 'immense amount of things including blankets, bedding, watch glass, brushes and razors'. Jamieson survived the dreadful night. Rawson wrote to his sister Elizabeth informing her *the cattle are recovering* from the disturbance.

In a 5 May 1928 interview with the Maitland Weekly Mercury, a pioneer of the Maitland district in New South Wales spoke of his family's encounters with hostile Aborigines. *The early pioneers did not complain they just worked and worked and kept on working. It was a case then of working out your own salvation. The Aboriginals were very bad in those days. Some of them were most troublesome. My father had many narrow escapes from being killed by the blacks in the very early days of settlement. The blacks on one occasion killed a man at Long Flat on the Upper Macleay* (River), *cut his head off, and stuck it on a pole. The blacks also killed two shepherds and their wives at Kunderang Station. My father once left Wabra station on the Upper Macleay with a mob of cattle for Port Macquarie. He left an old man in charge during his absence. My mother was also there. A party of blacks evidently knew my father had gone away, and came to the homestead, asking for 'bacca' (tobacco). The old man left in charge cleared out when he saw the blacks. However, just when it looked as though there would be trouble, a whip cracked, and the blacks made off thinking that stockmen were coming. — My mother used to put on men's clothes when the men were away from the station, and she also knew how to use a gun.*

On 10 April 1841, the *Port Phillip Gazette* declared *an account of a murder committed by the natives at the station of Mr Oliphant at the Loddon has reached Town. It is stated that they met the hutkeeper laden with some wood with which he was proceeding to the hut, when he was suddenly felled to the ground by a blow from a waddy, and his assailants forthwith put him to death and cut the body in pieces, giving them to his own dogs to eat.* The desecration of the hutkeeper's body in such a despicable and demeaning fashion, was considered to be a particular barbaric act of deplorable Aboriginal frontier violence.

As if this Aboriginal brutality was not bad enough, worse was yet to come. On 14 June 1841, the same newspaper carried a gruesome letter from Thomas Grant *with feelings of horror, I acquaint you with the murder of* (bark strippers) *Mr Morton and his servant Larry by the blacks it happened on Friday or Saturday last. I went over this morning with Mr Cowan and a man who followed the track of the dray to where they had stripped a little bark about six miles from the station. I found the bodies; I observed what I considered at first a white log with a large Eagle Hawk pecking upon it; upon my approach the bird rose slowly from the mangled remains of Mr Morton. He was stripped quite naked and was lying on his face, the greater part of which was actually cut away. His head was one mass of frightful wounds with many bruises on different parts of his arms and body, which were torn by birds of prey. About fifty yards nearer the dray lay the remains or skeleton of Larry, from whose bones the flesh had been completely cut off. The skin was cut a little above the wrists and ankles with a sharp knife or instrument. From all other parts, the flesh was cut and nothing left but bare bones. God only knows whether they did this before life was extinct, as the struggle with him had been long and dreadful. His arms were extended and speared through the wrists to the ground.*

Aboriginal cruelty and murder of the innocent and defenceless remained so throughout the colonial warfare period. In 1860, the *Armidale Express* (NSW) reported: *a shepherd, his wife and their infant at the breast, were murdered in a most brutal manner by the blacks. Their bodies were then chopped up into small pieces, and left in a heap where they were found. Subsequently, another shepherd was murdered by the blacks.*

oooOOOooo

In July 1842, the *Portland Bay* newspaper comprehensively reported on the constant state of fear and terror Aboriginal murders and robberies were causing Western District settlers. The lengthy article quoted here in full, was a summary of recent Aboriginal attacks and a desperate appeal to Governor Gipps to do something to stop the robbery, violence and human and animal bloodshed. The frustration and growing anger of station owners who were alone in the bush with their large flocks of sheep and only a few shepherds to tend them was fear filled and intense.

On the 4th July, Mr Ricketts' station, on the Glenelg, was visited by a tribe of natives who had for some time been very troublesome to the neighbouring settlers. They were under the direction of one of their number, named Bob, who had formerly been domesticated at the station, and had received at Mr Ricketts' hands innumerable acts of considerate kindness. Under the guidance of this base ingrate, the natives drove away a flock of sheep, and forcibly carried with them the shepherd, a man named Freeman.

As soon as intelligence of the outrage reached Portland, Mr Blair dispatched a party of mounted police to capture the marauders, and liberate Freeman; but unfortunately, success did not await their exertions. A party of men, however, who had started from the station of Mr Ricketts, shortly after the perpetration of the outrage came upon the track of the sheep, and found the boots of Freeman, with the strings broken, as if they had been taken forcibly from his feet. By the side of these laid a faithful dog, owned by the unfortunate shepherd, covered with wounds, it had evidently been received in a spirited defence of his master.

On the following day they came upon the camp of the natives, who saluted them with a shower of spears, and then took to flight, all escaping save one woman, who was not sufficiently swift to elude pursuit. The only trace of Freeman at the camp was his gun, which the party found with the breech taken out, but the woman they had taken prisoner informed them that the tribe had killed Freeman, chopped him into pieces, which they had eaten as they proceeded on their march with the sheep. The sheep were all recovered with the exception of forty, and these had their legs broken, and were otherwise so dreadfully mutilated that the men found it necessary to put an end to their sufferings on the spot.

About a week since Mr Ricketts' station was again attacked, one of the shepherds speared, and a quantity of sheep driven off. A few of those were destroyed, but the greater portion regained. A short time since Mr Winter's station, adjoining that of his cousins, the Messrs Winter Brothers, upon the Wannon, was attacked by the blacks, and two hundred sheep taken away. A party of four persons started on horseback to recover them, but being surrounded by the savages, were glad to escape unharmed. A second party, six in number, afterwards ventured in pursuit, and found the lifeless carcases of the sheep, but the natives had disappeared. A number of the bodies of the stolen animals had been thrown into a swamp, evidently for the purpose of forming a bridge, over which the blacks might pass.

Mr Carey's station, at the head of the Crawford, has recently been attacked, and upwards of one hundred sheep taken away, none of which have been recovered. Mr Cameron's station on the Crawford, which has been subject to repeated depredations, was recently visited by about two hundred and fifty blacks, among whom were identified several of the men concerned in the murder of Mackenzie; they endeavoured to drive off the sheep, but Mr. Cameron taking the alarm, procured assistance from an adjoining station, and kept them at bay.

Foiled in this part of their design, they proceeded to the huts, the whites remaining to guard the sheep. They drove the hut keeper away, robbed the huts, and then burned them down. Elated by their success, the rascals then returned to the men in charge of the sheep and holding up the ammunition they had taken from Mr Cameron's hut, defied them to fire, as, if they did so, they said their ammunition would be soon exhausted. One fellow, named Charley, who had been in the habit of frequenting the station, exhibited from behind a tree a portion of his body, and told the whites to fire at him, saying, if they dared, Mr Sievewright (Charles Wightman Sievewright, Protector of Western District Aborigines 1838-

1842) *would plenty 'wigel'* (prosecute and hang) *them.*

The blacks at last left the run, and the sheep were driven to Mr O'Neil's station. They are at present near the crossing place of the Crawford, almost in a state of starvation; and there we suppose they must remain, until a new run has been discovered; for after the repeated outrages committed by the blacks at the abandoned station, it would be imprudent in the highest degree to return thither. Mr Cameron, we understand, is now endeavouring to affect a sale of his sheep, at about half their value, being fully determined to quit the province forthwith. Mr Thomson's station on the Yohoo Ponds has been attacked, and two hundred old sheep, and three hundred lambs driven off: these have not been regained.

A short time since the blacks visited the station of Messrs Corny, of Wando Vale, at about nine o'clock at night, and drove off one hundred sheep. As soon as the theft was discovered, several persons on the station set out in pursuit, and succeeded in tracing the blacks, by means of their firesticks, to the head of the creek. The natives, on observing their pursuers, immediately fled, and the dead bodies of the sheep were found lying in and about the creek.

The station of Mr Norris, on the Glenelg, was attacked for six consecutive nights. We are not aware of the amount of injury sustained, but we believe it to be considerable. Two flocks of sheep were driven from the station of the Messrs Henty, on the Wannon; the shepherds tending the sheep received spears through their clothes, and were compelled to seek safety in flight. Fortunately, the sheep being accustomed to the run, made off to the home station instead of to the scrub, and were all recovered with the exception of twelve.

Mr French's station on the Grange has also been attacked, and a considerable number destroyed and driven off. Seven hundred sheep have been destroyed in recent and repeated attacks on the station of Messrs Winter Brothers, on the Wannon. A few days ago, a shepherd in the service of Mr Desailly, was entrusted with the care of fifteen hundred wethers. Not returning at the usual hour, an alarm was created, and on a search being instituted, the lifeless body of the unfortunate shepherd was discovered in a state of nudity, every article of clothing having been taken off, with the exception of his shoes. The body was much mutilated, being covered with spear wounds, and the back of the head laid open, apparently by the stroke of an axe.

A party went in search of the sheep, and tracked them a distance of sixty miles, into one of the Grampians, where a body of natives had encamped but who immediately fled on the approach of the whites. A double-barrelled gun, which had belonged to the murdered man, was found at the native camp, and, somewhat to the surprise of the party, was loaded. As the sheep were feeding in an almost treeless plain at the time of the attack, it is supposed that the nipples of the gun had been rendered useless by a shower of rain, and had in consequence misfired. Eleven hundred sheep were recovered, many of these were dreadfully mangled.

The station of Mr Hunter, near Mount Eccles, has been attacked, the shepherd speared, and five hundred sheep utterly lost. Mr J. H. Patterson's sheep station on the Grange has been subject to repeated depredations and a large number of sheep taken away. A tribe of Aborigines have encamped on the same gentleman's cattle station, near Mount Napier. The cattle, with the usual and singular aversion entertained by all of their kind towards the effluvia arising from the sable race, are scattered over the run. The blacks kill and eat them as they want them. This is putting Mr Patterson's lately published scheme for their amelioration into operation with a vengeance.

Two hundred sheep have been driven from Mr Riley's station on the Wannon, and totally lost. A large number of sheep were driven away from Mr Purbrick's station on the Wannon, but were fortunately recovered. The station of Mr T. W. Watson, on the Wando, was recently visited by a tribe of blacks, and a large number of sheep driven away. Mr Watson, accompanied by two of his servants, started on foot, in pursuit, and came upon the blacks at night. They were sitting round their fires, and were supposed to be about one hundred in number. The men, appalled at the sight of so many natives, when they expected to meet comparatively few, refused to approach the encampment. Mr Watson was consequently compelled to return home, and to give up all hope of regaining his property.

Several nightly attacks have been made upon the station of Mr Duncan McCrae, situated on the borders of the Merino Downs, and upwards of two hundred sheep have been destroyed. Since the murder of the ill-fated Mackenzie, the station occupied by him at Emu Creek has been abandoned, and the sheep removed to a station on the Smoky River, under the charge of a Mr O'Neil, the tribe of natives who were concerned in the murder of the deceased, having intimated to Mr O'Neill their intention of driving the sheep away. Messrs Henty, the executors to the estate, have consequently been compelled to send additional men to the station, that efficient resistance may be offered to the blacks in the event of their endeavouring to carry their threat into execution.

The latest accounts from Port Fairy state that the blacks are extremely troublesome, driving away sheep at their leisure. During the past four months, 3,500 sheep have been destroyed, four men have been killed, and two men seriously wounded. To use the graphic language of one gentleman possessing large flocks in the district, 'the country might as well be in a state of civil war, as few but the boldest of the settlers will move from their home stations'. Many of the principal sufferers from the depredations of the blacks, are now running from two to three thousand sheep in a flock, and these are tended by as large a number of shepherds as they can afford to hire. As it is impossible that such large flocks can be properly fed, the consequences will soon evince themselves in the ill condition of the animals, the prevalence amongst them of scab, and the consequent deterioration, both in quality and quantity, of their wools.

We would earnestly implore the attention of His Excellency Sir George Gipps, and the Executive Council, to the fearful list of murders and robberies we have narrated, and which we have purposely worded in as matter of fact a manner as possible, lest it might be said of us that we were dealing in gross perversions of truth. Can it be expected, we would ask, that the settlers of this district, that any man, any body of men, with the feelings universally implanted in our nature, will sullenly fold their arms, and look passively on while their friends, their servants and themselves know not the hour nor the day when their hitherto peaceful homes may not be converted into houses of wailing, dismay and despair. God forbid that we should advocate other than an implicit obedience to the laws. But, if protection is longer withheld, if victim upon victim is to be added to the hecatomb already reared, we much fear that a cry of vengeance will shortly ring throughout the length and breadth of the land, the disastrous sating of which will long be remembered with horror and awe.

A tipping point of white anger, loss of human life and significant property loss had been reached in the Western District. The feeling among white settlers as stated above was *the country might as well be in a state of civil war* — and for many it truly was.

oooOOOooo

The *Portland Guardian* under the heading 'Trials of the Pioneers' wrote in 1933. *The years 1841-43 were the peak years of murders of settlers and shepherds and for sheep and cattle stealing. South from Mount Eccles was one of the chief resorts of the Aborigines. Frequently they speared or stampeded or drove the cattle into swamps. In four months, four shepherds were killed, two seriously wounded, and 3,500 sheep were stolen or destroyed. Settlers were terrorised from Portland Bay to Merino Downs. from Port Fairy to the Grange, from Glenelg to Geelong, and also as far north east as Swampy River near the Ovens River.*

On the 19 April 1930, the *Weekly Times* in a lengthy article titled 'The History of Casterton' gave an account of the early days of land settlement and frontier warfare in the Western District of Victoria. *The Whyte Brothers were annoyed by the blacks as early as 1840.* (The Aborigines) *tracked them on their journey from Melbourne, harassing them in every way, setting fire to the grass around them, throwing spears at their shepherds and stealing their sheep. It was not until 1841, that aggressions became of frequent occurrence. Shepherds were repeatedly murdered, their sheep driven off, sometimes 50 or 60 miles and as they were usually found with their legs broken, they were valueless to their owners.*

Thomas Ricketts, the original proprietor of Clunie (a squatting run), *lost so severely that he became insolvent in 1844 and James Blair purchased the estate from his trustees. Mr Blair described Aborigines as sly and stealthy, holding no intercourse with whites, and seldom seen by the settlers unless when detected in committing an outrage or overtaken when retreating with their plunder; and as they frequently travelled long distances to commit outrages, no one could tell to what part of the district they belonged. The squatters had to band together for protection, there being no adequate police for the purpose. The natives carried off their sheep and burned the grass to cover their tracks. The* early squatter carried his life in his hands; at any moment a sneaking native crouched behind a tree might put an end to his existence.

In 1842 white settlers at Port Fairy sent an anxious letter to Charles La Trobe, Superintendent of the Port Phillip District, asking for police protection. *The settlers and inhabitants of the district of Port Fairy, beg respectfully to represent to your Honour the great and increasing want of security to life and property which exists here at present, in consequence of the absence of any protection against the natives. Their number, their ferocity, and their cunning, render them peculiarly formidable, and the outrages of which they are daily and nightly guilty, and which they accomplish generally with impunity and success, may, we fear, lead to a still more distressing state of things, unless some measures, prompt and effective, be immediately taken to prevent matters coming to that unhappy crisis.*

A native police corps with some Port Fairy Aborigines in the ranks was established in 1837 and reformed in 1842, but the settlers felt in need of greater protection. In just a few months they had sustained the loss of 3,600 sheep, 100 cattle, and 10 horses from Aboriginal raids on their properties. In New South Wales the *Bathurst Advocate* reported that one pastoral run had lost its entire herd of milkers and young stock to Aboriginal depredation. These were serious stock losses and tensions continued to rise in rural communities, as rampaging bands of hostile and aggressive Aborigines roamed the countryside stealing, looting and wilfully committing murder.

Some squatters were more concerned about their personal affairs and maintaining their Aboriginal workforce than in sacrificing for the good of the community. In a September 1838 letter to the Melbourne Police Magistrate; Mornington Peninsular Squatter George Smith complains *of unwarrantable interference by Christiaan Ludolph Johannes de Villers in attempting to recruit* (Aboriginal) *man Boudeor and wife and family from Smith for the native police; Smith has clothed and fed him for upwards of two years and he has lately become very useful.* This short-sighted approach was not looked upon favourably by distraught settlers suffering property loss, the death of loved ones and much needed employees.

As the stock losses continued to grow, the *Sydney Morning Herald* published a report from its Queensland correspondent that settlers had learned from conversations with Aborigines, they were *determined to annihilate if possible, the whole of the* (live)*stock in the district.* Frederick Isaacs wrote a letter to the *Moreton Bay Courier* outlining what he knew of Aboriginal intentions. *I have since heard, that the plan of the blacks was to murder first all the men at my head station, and sack the store; and then, having waylaid the shepherds, to take possession of the whole of the sheep.* This was bloody frontier warfare focussed on murder and pillage. Not by white settlers but by Aboriginal warriors intent on creating fear, havoc and chaos.

oooOOOooo

The white settler community felt exposed and vulnerable. Settlers lived in a menacing climate of fear and apprehension, with the constant threat of Aboriginal attack hanging over their head. Charles Melton and his wife living in Brisbane in the 1840s, said people in the town rarely went out after dark for fear of Aboriginal violence. *Aborigines thought nothing of entering the hut or garden and removing all the food and produce in sight. Residents were often alarmed by half a dozen stalwart blacks coming to their doors and demanding flour, tea, sugar, tobacco, and rum.* (They) *frequently swooped down on the huts of the settlers and carried off all they could lay their hands on, sometimes killing those who offered any resistance.*

Rosa Campbell Praed remembers her nervous Burnett River childhood in Central Queensland, where her family lived in a perpetual state of fear of Aboriginal attack. *The women practiced at targets with firearms, and the men would ride home with a sinking feeling in their hearts, fearing for their wives and children. Often, I heard father describe how each evening coming in from the run, he used in cold fear to mount the hill overlooking the humpy, and draw free breath when he saw it lying quiet and unharmed.*

Settler's huts were fortified with barricaded doors and port holes to fire on Aboriginal attackers who could number 100 or more. The fear of Aboriginal attack was an ever-present reality not to be taken lightly. An Aboriginal tactic that struck terror into the hearts of the entire white settler community was the practice of lighting bushfires and following up with a fusillade of flaming spears to burn down their huts. Dr Raymond Kerkhove writes *flaming spears and firebrands fixed to spears were hurled at white combatants or more usually onto the roofs of their huts to burn them out. Huge fires were also lit to halt progress. For example, when (Squatter) Ross tried to reach the Darling Downs around 1860, Aboriginals set fire to the surrounding fields, forcing him to drive his flocks into the scrub.*

Dr Kerkhove has mapped the violent nature of Aboriginal frontier warfare in Southern Queensland and shown it to be coordinated and designed to terrorise white settlers. *The Southern Queensland black war manifested elements that equate with military strategy, inter-tribal coordination, and military adaptation. It consisted mostly of economic sabotage, the disruption of transport, and a great deal of harassment.* It was in essence, guerrilla and psychological warfare carried out with the intention to drive white settlers from the land and for a time it proved successful.

Sometimes Aboriginal vindictiveness against the innocent and vulnerable was unspeakably cruel. In March 1846, a New South Wales coroner's inquest was held on the body of Baby Devlin, a 9-month-old Clarence River infant, taken by Aborigines from his Irish parent's bark hut and callously abandoned in the bush, only to found alive 3 days later. The family's loyal cat was with the child and had tried to keep the baby warm throughout this period of time. Lengthy exposure, physical exhaustion and cold nights were too much for the infant's tiny body and death occurred a day later. Community sympathy for the distraught parents and anger against Aborigines reached fever pitch.

On 23 August 1845, the New South Wales *Paramatta Chronicle* wrote of continuing frontier violence and growing white settler frustration, at the futile attempt of the authorities to bring to justice hostile Aborigines engaged in rape, robbery and murder. *The blacks are still, as they have always hitherto been in this district, peculiarly distinguished for rapine and murder. A few days since a gentleman residing at the Richmond (River) received a spear wound in his arm, and Commissioner Fry only escaped being dangerously wounded from a similar weapon, through its falling between him and a person riding by his side. In an encounter which subsequently took place, a policeman was most severely wounded, and the marauders signalled to a black boy who was attached to the party of border police, that they would spear cattle whenever they pleased in spite of the settlers or police. Within two years, eight white men have been murdered by these savages and as yet not one of these black scoundrels has had as much as a hair of his head injured. The cattle and sheep speared by them is innumerable.*

Fifteen years later, in June 1860, the *Armidale Express* (NSW) reported on Aborigines carrying firearms in their encounters with white settlers. *In January last, Mr J Perrett of Tyringham, was shot at by blacks when about a mile from his house. It appears that the McLeay blacks, whose predatory incursions are numerous and sudden, have been for some time past a pest and continual source of apprehension to many settlers on the Grafton line. They have frequently been seen with a large number of firearms, and we are informed that some of their guns have a bore of an inch in diameter, carrying an ounce bullet. On leaving the vicinity of Armidale, a short time ago, the blacks were seen to have plenty of firearms. One respectable settler on an adjoining creek states, that he particularly observed one gin who was loaded with no fewer than three guns.*

oooOOOooo

Colonial frontier warfare was brutal, violent and ongoing. People suffered and died horrible deaths on both sides of an escalating bloody conflict. Aborigines were victims and aggressors, who plundered and killed white settlers with a premeditated callousness not recorded in today's history books. Truth and not politicised myth of colonial encounters peaceful and bloody, should be of paramount importance in relating the pioneer settlement story. Victimhood fairytales, genocidal fantasies and race-based fabrications serve no one's interest, least of all Aborigines. We can empathise with the past, and recount it with honesty, candour and integrity. To do otherwise, is to invent a false narrative that romanticises the Aboriginal past ala the Bruce Pascoe delusion. The past then becomes obscured and trivialised, no more than a modern-day polemic of genocide and inhumanity.

11

Aborigines and White Settlers

The Gippsland blacks are very bad men, steal and kill white man's bullocks and they (the Bonurong warriors have) *gone to helpem white man too much frightened to gogo bush.*

'Berberry', Westernport Bay Bonurong Tribe (1846)

Henry Meyrick, a 23-year-old Gippsland pioneer, wrote a letter to his family in England on the 30 April 1846, in which he expressed sympathy for Aborigines. *The blacks are very quiet here now, poor wretches. No wild beast of the forest was ever hunted down with such unsparing perseverance as they are. Men, women and children are shot whenever they can be met with. I have protested against it at every station I have been in Gippsland, in the strongest language, but these things are kept very secret as the penalty would certainly be hanging.* He added *for myself, if I caught a black actually killing my sheep, I would shoot him with as little remorse as I would a wild dog, but no consideration on earth would induce me to ride into a camp and fire on them indiscriminately.*

Henry Meyrick was a devout Christian, a compassionate and highly principled young man with a cultivated sense of law and order. His brother James wrote of him *he never lost sight of his duties as a Christian. Night after night before bedtime, under the pretence of seeing that the sheep were all right, he went out to pray.* Henry's father and grandfather were Wiltshire clergymen and Henry was expected to follow the family tradition. Instead, he followed his adventurous cousins Maurice and Alfred, 20 and 19 years old respectively, to Australia. At the tender age of just 17 years, Henry set sail for Port Phillip arriving there in April 1840. Neither Henry nor his cousins Maurice and Alfred were destined to become prosperous in Australia. They took up squatting runs, ran cattle and sheep and endured many hardships. The Melbourne boom of the early years of settlement was over and although the cousins did not become bankrupt, they lost much of their capital.

In 1847, Henry lost his life in the flooded Thompson River. He was trying to swim his horse across the raging waters to bring a doctor to a woman in childbirth. She too died a few days later. Henry and his cousins Maurice and Alfred were not among the few Gippsland squatters who killed Aborigines and there were many others just like them. They were young men with clear-cut traditional values and a code of honour but if they were wronged or threatened there would be consequences. Maurice eventually returned to England, became a clergyman and settled into the life of a country parson in a village four miles distant from Ramsbury, where Henry's forebears had preached. Alfred became a civil servant in Victoria.

oooOOOooo

Gippsland was named after New South Wales Governor Major Sir George Gipps (1838-1846). Count Paul Strzelecki, a self-promoting Polish explorer/scientist, is often feted as the European discoverer. Angus McMillan was the overlander who opened up Gippsland for pioneer settlement. Strzelecki relied on information supplied and trails blazed by McMillan's expeditions to traverse the Gippsland wilderness. Angus, a Scottish squatter with an intemperate 'eye for an eye' Old Testament attitude, was to become a merciless killer of Aborigines.

Patrick Morgan writes *Gippsland's most unusual feature was its founders they were Gaelic speaking Scots from the Highlands and Islands of remote north west Scotland, coming here after the Highland clearances. These 'children of the mist' came from a culture very different from the mainstream of the British Isles and Europe. The founder of Gippsland, Angus McMillan, called it 'Caledonia Australis' (Scotland in the South), as its contours and inland waters reminded him of home. In an allusion to the Highland clearances, he wrote 'here was a country lying dormant capable of supporting all my starving countrymen'.*

Angus McMillan's ancestral home was in the Cuillin Hills on the Isle of Skye located in the Inner Hebrides. According to the 10 September 1874 issue of the *Gippsland Times*, Angus was born at Glen Brittle on 14 August 1810. *He was one of 14 sons of* (Ewen McMillan) *an extensive sheep farmer, with a 40 year* (croft) *holding under MacLeod of MacLeod. Colonel Roderick McNeill advised him to emigrate to New South Wales. With a very slender purse and an old* (Highland) *lament ringing his ears, he sailed for Sydney in the Minerva on 5 September 1837, landing at Port Jackson on 26 January 1838.*

With a letter of introduction, McMillan went to work for Isle of Skye military émigré Captain Lachlan Macalister, on his Clifton pastoral station in the Monaro district of New South Wales. Macalister was a friend of the MacArthur's of Camden and he was in charge of the mounted police contingent that shot bushranger Jack Donahue dead. Macalister was wounded in the gunfight. Angus soon became a trusted overseer. *His discrete conduct and amiability of character won the confidence of the neighbouring tribes of blacks and in a few months, he mastered a good deal of their language.*

Angus came to know something of the blackfellow's history and traditions. From the old men of the tribe, he heard that when they were boys they had been attacked, with great loss, by the wild Warrigals (a Gippsland Aboriginal tribe) *who inhabited the seacoast. They described how* (in retaliation) *the Yass, Monongola and Omeo tribes joined together and made a raid; how they pursued the coast natives travelling down the Snowy River until they came to Buchan, and following the coastline how they crossed what are now called the Tambo, Nicolson, Mitchell and Avon Rivers until they finally reached the* (Gippsland) *lakes. The Warrigals had, however, fled to the mountains. Years after, the Omeo tribe made another incursion, caught their enemy on the Tambo* (River), *and slaughtered scores of men, women and children; and McMillan saw the battlefield covered with their bones.* Witnessing the aftermath of such a ruthless Indigenous massacre convinced McMillan and others of the constant danger posed by hostile Aborigines, and the vigilance that was required to combat sneak attack.

It was from Clifton that McMillan set out on several expeditions to Gippsland, exploring and seeking good pastureland, creeks and rivers. Describing the Gippsland lakes, he said *on the north side of the lake the country consists of open forest and the grass was up to our stirrup irons as we rode along. The country was absolutely swarming with kangaroos and emus.* Remembering the Highland Clearances on the Isle of Skye, he added *Oh, how I should like to see my starving countrymen at home turning up the* (Gippsland) *sod!*

This was the beginning of the Highland Scots influx into the Gippsland region. McMillan was driven off his first squatting run at Nuntin near Stratford by hostile Aborigines and for a time he retreated to New South Wales. In 1840 when establishing his Bushy Park pastoral run, he on several occasions clashed with the warlike 'wild Warrigals' (the Gania sometimes referred to as the Kurnai) tribe of aggressive Gippsland Aborigines. The Gania attacks were savage, cattle were speared and deaths occurred on both sides of the frontier conflict. At Glencoe, a pastoral property near Sale, a large group of Gania twice attacked the homestead and were driven off by nails and bits of iron fired from a brass cannon.

In July 1843 following the repeated loss of livestock and the spearing death of his friend and former Isle of Skye resident Ranald Macalister (nephew of Lachlan) by Ganai Aborigines at Port Albert. McMillan rode with a party of Scotsmen known as the Highland or Gippsland Brigade to exact revenge. The Gania it was said speared Ranald in reprisal for a previous incident by a Macalister employee who had allowed them inside his shepherd's hut, and when they refused to leave was forced to evict them by pouring hot coals over their feet.

Max Milton Macalister citing Macalister family tradition writes of the death of his pioneer ancestor who was manager of his uncle Lachlan's Boisdale pastoral run. *The Aborigines ambushed Ranald, speared and killed him with waddies. Ranald's bloodstained horse made it back to Boisdale just on sunset minus its rider. Darkness had fallen and it was too late to send out a search party, but first thing next morning at 5 am a party went searching for him. What the party found was a bit of a shock and this infuriated the Scottish Highlanders, as this type of thing brought back memories of the butchery after Culloden back in Scotland.*

The Aborigines had cut out his kidney fat, as evidently this was a prize piece of meat. They also cut off both his hands as these were found worn around the neck of one of the Aboriginals shot (these gruesome hand necklaces were a common Aboriginal trophy. McMillan encountered Gippsland Aborigines wearing sundried hands around their necks) *when the so-called Gippsland Brigade caught up with them at Warrigal Creek. Ranald's bloodstained Macalister's Tartan shirt was also recovered off another Aboriginal who was shot. These items were recovered and sprinkled with pepper and wrapped in brown paper* (to preserve them).

Ranald's remains or what was left of them, as the wild pigs had been having a nore (sic) *at his remains overnight, were hastily buried on the side of the track. They were later dug up and taken by boat up the river to what was to become Alberton cemetery. The ambush and mutilation of Ranald Macalister was the final straw as far as the Scottish pioneers were concerned, as they had been putting up with the spearing of their cattle and several white settlers had also been murdered beforehand.*

The Warrigal Creek massacre was the bloodiest to take place in Gippsland. Accounts differ, but the toll on the Ganai tribe was devastating with around 60 Aborigines (some say more) killed at five different locations. As an old man in 1925, William Hoddinott the son of Warrigal Creek squatter Uriah Hoddinott, wrote a second-hand account of what happened. The account, written 82 years after the event, is used as evidence to accuse McMillan of taking a leadership role in the slaughter. Hoddinott says McMillan discovered Ranald Macalister's body, not that he led the Highland Brigade which comprised *everyman who could find a gun and a horse*. McMillan was a participant and that is all we can say with certainty. Macalister's ugly murder and mutilation was the pivotal event in the Gippsland settlers pioneer struggle. A Gaelic sense of moral panic demanded immediate action and revenge.

Nevertheless, the Warrigal Creek massacre is bloody and shocking in Hoddinott's account of its gruesome details. *The Highland Brigade coming up to the blacks camped around the waterhole at Warrigal Creek surrounded them and fired into them, killing a great number, some escaped into the scrub, others jumped into the waterhole, and, as fast as they put their heads up for breath, they were shot until the water was red with blood.* If an accurate description of the Warrigal Creek encounter, it was an atrocious act of murder and massacre. A disproportionate and brutal slaughter of Aborigines that no amount of white settler anger and revenge can justify. Clearly a breaking point had been reached and a savage vendetta of pent-up violence took over. True or not, Gippsland legend has it that for many years afterwards, Angus McMillan kept a sugarbag containing several Aboriginal skulls in his shearing shed.

Another passage in Hoddinott's account concerning Aboriginal encounter with white settlers outlines a different view. *When Angus McMillan first settled in Gippsland blacks were very numerous, hostile and treacherous, attacking homesteads and spearing livestock. On several occasions, they speared hutkeepers. White settlers retaliated and many of the blacks were killed in subsequent raids.* (As time wore on) *the blacks were noticeably becoming more accustomed to white people and were more friendly. They gradually began to congregate around the homesteads at the stations.* If genocide was the singular purpose we attribute to white settlers, then these friendly Aborigines would have been murdered instead of living peacefully side by side.

On his first expedition to Omeo in Gippsland in May 1839, Angus enlisted Jemmy Gibber, an Aboriginal Elder from the Monaro district, to act as his guide. In a letter to Superintendent La Trobe, McMillan complained that upon reaching the New South Wales/Victoria border, Jemmy refused to go any further for fear of the Ganai tribe who were warlike and hostile to blacks and whites. McMillan insisted they proceed and reported to La Trobe that Gibber tried to kill him with a club. *Jemmy says we are in the neighbourhood of wild natives and is very restless. Tired out I fell asleep. I awoke to see Jemmy standing over me with a club raised. Another moment and my brains would have been dashed out. I had just time to present a pistol at his heart.* Jemmy's explanation was that he had been dreaming that someone was carrying off his favourite 'gin'. A day or so later, Jemmy surreptitiously 'decamped' and the Scotsman went on alone.

oooOOOooo

Jemmy Gibber had reason to be afraid of the Gippsland Ganai Aborigines. During a journey through Gippsland in 1844, George Augustus Robinson, the Chief Protector of Aborigines in the Port Phillip District (1839-1849), wrote in his travel dairy: *the natives of Gippsland* (Ganai) *have killed 70* (77 is the correct number) *of the Boongerong* (Bonurong) *tribe at Brighton*. William Thomas, Assistant Protector of Port Phillip Aborigines (1839-1849) and later Guardian of Aborigines, wrote in an 1840 letter to then Superintendent Charles La Trobe: *the blacks remember the awful affair near where Brighton now stands, where in 1834 nearly a quarter of the Westernport blacks were massacred by the Gippsland blacks who stole up on them before dawn of day*. Nine years later in 1849, Thomas told Governor La Trobe of an earlier 1820 massacre near Arthurs Seat on the Mornington Peninsular, where *nearly half the* (Bonurong) *tribe was killed*

Such bloody Aboriginal encounters occurred all over the colonial frontier and can best be described as genocidal in nature. In an article published in the *Australasian Anthropological Journal* in 1897, Anthropologist Robert Brothers wrote of a New South Wales clash between rival Aboriginal groups. *About eighty years ago (circa 1817), a certain tribe near Monaro, numbering about two thousand people, were exterminated, man, woman, and child, for having killed a Myell-Wallin* (Aborigine) *who was travelling. They called this tribe mountaineers for they lived in the mountains,* (and) *were said to be cannibals. Warriors came from all parts, even from Bathurst side and from the Tweed, and they mustered around the cannibals in five armies, each numbering three or four thousand men, and they slaughtered the whole of them. The white people at the station nearby were uninjured, but the warriors flocked through the house searching for their victims. An old* (Aboriginal) *man who died at Ulladulla a few years ago is said to be the only one who was not killed, and was a child at the time, and escaped notice by being hidden in a tea chest.*

William Thomas, a god-fearing and compassionate man, earned a reputation as an outstanding friend and advocate for his Aboriginal charges who called him 'Marminata' (Good Father). Responsible for the Westernport Bay region, Thomas' primary contact was with the

Bonurong tribe on the Mornington Peninsular. He became proficient in two native dialects, translating the Lord's Prayer and Bible verse into Bonurong. He was horrified when he learned of a massacre carried out at the Tarwin River (South Gippsland) by his Westernport Aborigines.

Historian Marie Hansen Fels writes that Bonurong warriors *had followed tracks and come upon a sleeping encampment of 14* (Ganai Aborigines) *at the Tarwin River. They killed nine with spears and tomahawks, one man, two lubras and six children the rest escaped. The bodies of two of the children were quartered and brought back to Kunnung* (near Kooweerup). *The whole body of a little child was brought back and planted in the bush not 20 yards from where Thomas was camped. They 'showed no remorse', in fact, 'exulted in their triumph' but were 'dreadfully frightened' of what La Trobe would do when Thomas reported* (it).

Journalist and author Tony Thomas provides us with a colonial account of a Ganai/Kurnai retaliatory raid similar in ferocity and cold-bloodedness to that described above. *In the 1870s,* (Anthropologists) *Lorimer Fison and Alfred Howitt studied the Kurnai* (Ganai) *tribe in Gippsland Victoria. They described feuds and whole groups fighting. In one-episode, fresh tracks indicating trespassing into the tribal territories were revealed and a spy was sent to reconnoitre. He found the intruders, with 'lots of women and children'. The Kurnai men 'got their spears ready in the middle of the night they all marched off well armed'. After several marches, 'when near morning they got close to them. The spies whistled like bird, to tell when all was ready. Then all ran in; they speared away, and speared away! They only speared the men, and perhaps some children. Whoever caught a woman kept her* (for) *himself. Then they eat the skin of the Brajeraks* (the trespassing tribe)*'.*

Squatter Samuel Rawson witnessed the return of the Bonurong warriors *bringing immense quantities of human flesh with them. The blacks stayed several days at the station and feasted with the women and children on the flesh they had brought back and seemed to enjoy it amazingly, and were much surprised that I would not join them. It had exactly the appearance of a piece of fat pork with a very thick skin.* William Thomas wrote they *returned with pieces of mutilated bodies of their victims with arms, legs and pieces of flesh principally of female children eaten by them and their friends. The Gippsland blacks, Omeo and others are cannibals, so far as eating their enemies — all my blacks that they have killed they eat and when they capture any of another tribe, they watch over him at night, making him sleep in the middle of them. Their victim was always killed by a tomahawk at the back of the neck.*

The Bonurong raid into Gippsland in February/March 1840, a brutal and blood-thirsty revenge raid, was not an uncommon occurrence among Aboriginal tribes across the country. A land of milk and honey cooperation and civilised tribal harmony in Aboriginal society, both before and after white settlement took place, is no more than a modern-day fantasy. There were tribal quarrels, ruthless conflicts and bloody clashes throughout all periods of Aboriginal history. The Ganai and the Bonurong were aggressive warrior clans, territorial and vengeful to outsiders. They were a force to be reckoned with by white settlers and Aborigines alike.

oooOOOooo

A proud Scot and staunch Presbyterian, Angus McMillan in 1859 was elected to the Victorian Legislative Assembly as the first representative for South Gippsland. In 1948, in recognition of his pioneer exploration of Gippsland, the Federal Electorate of McMillan was named after him. Several decades later with the rise of Aboriginal activism and in deference to identity politics, the Federal Seat of McMillan in July 2018 was renamed Monash. Somewhat perversely, given one-sided modern criticism, later in his life McMillan was appointed to the post of Protector of Aborigines.

McMillan is today portrayed as the archvillain in a frontier clash with a ferocious and warlike Gippsland tribe of Aborigines that was bloody and cost many lives. Caroline Dexter a close female friend defended Angus when she wrote, he *was compelled in his early struggles to destroy numbers of treacherous natives.* The Gunai were the biggest losers but that does not make them simply hapless victims. McMillan was an unforgiving man; he experienced Gunai hostility as a life and death struggle in keeping with his strongly held Scot's heritage. The freedom loving Highland Scots and the dispossessed Ganai Aborigines both claim to inhabit the moral high ground in a brutal frontier war. The truth is there was no high moral ground to inhabit; just a monumental clash of cultures, competing motivations and survival strategies.

Angus McMillan and the Highland Scots were well intentioned, religious minded and god-fearing people, living in a harsh and dangerous pioneer setting believing in the literal truth of the Bible and following the tenets of the Ten Commandments. They were robust men and women of fervent conviction who eschewed sinful behaviour, at the same time as they defended their rights, family and property from those who would do them harm. In his travel journal the Reverend William Bean wrote of the pious devoutness of the Gippsland Scottish settlers. *Sunday December 17; Mr Macalister drove me down in his gig to Flooding Creek for the morning service. Had a respectable congregation of about 40 adults, some of whom, male and female, had waded across the morass* (riverbed) *above their knees for the purpose of attending. Indeed, nothing could be more encouraging than the general conduct of all those present.*

Novelist Leslie Hartley's observation *the past is a foreign country; they do things differently there* has important relevance here. Peter Crowley who grew up in Gippsland writes *the allegations against Angus McMillan are of the utmost seriousness, but there is no evidence that he was a gratuitously cruel man. One of the thorny problems in making moral judgements about the past is that good people say and do things we find appalling.* Cal Flyn, McMillan's great, great, great niece, writes in her book *Thicker than Water: History, Secrets and Guilt* Harper Collins (2016). *I suppose what I really want is to understand how a person can do these things. Evil things. Because Angus McMillan was not evil. I've read his diaries. He seems like a normal guy. A bit like me in many ways.* Flyn too readily accepts the genocide version of her ancestor's guilt while struggling to make sense of it.

Reconciliation and forgiveness are about acknowledging the past honestly and transparently, without scapegoating one side or the other. It is just as easy to see Angus McMillan as a rigidly stern man of strong personal conviction, as to see him as a sadistic monster without a conscience or a moral compass to guide him. History is always a complexity of competing motivations and perplexing behaviours; to see it otherwise is to gravely misread people's lives.

In August 1858, William Dexter an artist friend of Angus McMillan, wrote a poem praising his pioneering endeavours, which was published in the *Gippsland Guardian* as 'The Pioneer' dedicated to Angus McMillan.

> *Let onward, onward, be the cry, of each brave heart today! There is land and room for all does not McMillan say? Then come o'er the mountains; come where the green wattles grow. Come where sweet birds are singing; come where the rivers flow. The beautiful land appears in sight. Cheer up! We'll soon be there. Now old Clifton's step is light; God heard McMillan's prayer. Now toil and dangers they are passed, from want and troubles free. And may your name forever last, a double health to thee. Then hurrah! hurrah! for the pilot that first set foot in Gippsland. And three cheers for the boys that were with him with our glass, our heart, and hand.*

oooOOOooo

In 1840, the Aboriginal slaughter of 26 survivors of the shipwrecked Brigantine *Maria* in South Australian waters was headline news throughout Australia and beyond. This was to be the largest number of white men, women and children to be massacred by Aborigines in a single incident in Australian history. It could not help but shape the colonial perspective of white settlers, and give strong motivation to uncompromising frontiersmen like Angus McMillan and the Gippsland Highland Brigade.

On 26 June 1840, the passenger ship *Maria* left Port Adelaide on a journey to Hobart Town in Tasmania. High winds and rough seas drove the *Maria* off course and she went aground on the Cape Jaffa Reef. Lifeboats were launched and the passengers and crew reached dry land without any casualties. The ship's company faced an arduous overland trek to Encounter Bay south of Adelaide. With the assistance of some friendly Aborigines, Captain William Smith, the crew and the passengers began their long journey. After covering 60 miles, the group split up and later split up again going in different directions. Aborigines from the fierce and aggressive Milmenrura Big Murray Tribe attacked, killed, mutilated and buried in the sand each group in turn. Men, women and children were speared, clubbed and hacked to death in a most brutal fashion. There were no white survivors left alive to tell the tale. Those savagely murdered were Captain William Smith, his wife, Samuel Denham and Mrs Denham, their five children Thomas, Andrew, Walter, Fanny and Anna, Mrs York widowed sister of Mr Denham and her infant baby, Mrs Denham's servant James Strutt, George Green and Mrs Green, Thomas Daniel and Mrs Daniel, a passenger named Murray and the ship's crew John Tegg, John Griffiths, John Deggan, James Biggins, John Cowley, Thomas Rea, George Leigh and James Parsons.

A rescue party was dispatched from Adelaide and upon discovering the massacre site of one party *a sickening spectacle presented itself. There, partially covered with sand, lay legs, arms and portions of several human bodies. On gathering these remains together, they, by the aid of the doctor who was with them, made out that there were the bodies of two men, three women, and a female child of ten. One woman's body was almost denuded of flesh, except for the hands and feet. Two male children one apparently about fifteen years of age and the other about ten* (were found together). *A little distance away lay the body of a female infant. All were dreadfully bruised about the face and head, and they were stripped of every rag of clothing.*

It took upwards of a year for search parties to discover the other massacre sites, which were no less horrifying, with mutilated human remains found sticking out of the sand. *The bones that bleach the sandhills, the spears redden with blood.* As they searched *the expedition saw large numbers of ferocious looking men who hung about the skirts of the scrub. Almost all had some article of European clothing. At last, they came to some native huts, and found male and female clothing which had been drenched with blood.* (They) *obtained a watch from the natives, the dial was stained with blood.* Two Aborigines said to be leading participants in the massacres were hanged from Sheoak trees growing beside the graves of the buried bodies at one of the murder sites.

On 31 May 1843, Squatter Bromfield from the Geelong region visited the camp of Aborigines he knew, where he witnessed the gruesome cannibal ritual aftermath of a tribal battle between two hostile Aboriginal groups. His graphic description supports the cannibalism and mutilation claim of Max Macalister cited above. *Directly after breakfast I started accompanied by the natives to within a short distance of their huts. I* (saw) *such a disgusting scene as can scarcely be imagined. The whole encampment was deluged with blood; first lay the body of a middle-aged man named Codjajah, speared through the breast in many places, his bowels taken out and the fat drawn off them, and a few pieces cut out of his thigh. The next body was that of a woman speared in many places, quite dead. A short distance from her stood a young lubra with two spears through the belly, the whole of her intestines hanging to the ground — she was perfectly sensible, and it would have been a charity to have shot her then, but she departed this life in the evening. Besides these three, within a short distance of the huts lay the bodies of two more men, known by the names of Jim and Big One Tom, they were partly eaten, their fat being taken out by their Christian brethren!* Bromfield was appalled by the savage mutilation of bodies. *These are civilized Aborigines, who have been well instructed by our assistant protectors, and certainly have profited no little by the time and expense that have been lavished upon them.*

Dame Daisy May Bates, Irish born author/Anthropologist and a strong advocate for Aborigines, who lived and travelled with tribal Aborigines for four decades, wrote a letter to the *South Australian Register* in March 1928, which was published under the title 'Mothers Who Eat Their Babies'. *I have written many articles on Aboriginal cannibalism during the years since 1900. I am making this statement from personal knowledge of the* (Aboriginal) *groups* (of Central Australia). *At the Beagle Bay Mission, a woman who had recently killed and eaten her newly born infant was pointed out. When I asked her how she could kill and eat her baby, she replied 'I only ate one'. Pointing to another woman, she said 'that Jandu* (woman) *ate three'. Among the Beagle Bay Mission women were others who also killed and ate their babies.*

In his book, *The Aborigines of Victoria* Volume One Victorian Government Printer (1878) Robert Brough Smith wrote *in parts of New South Wales such as Bathurst, Goulburn, the Lachlan or Macquarie, it was customary long ago for the first-born of every lubra to be eaten by the tribe, as part of a religious ceremony; and I recollect a blackfellow who had, in compliance with the custom, been thrown when an infant* on the fire, but was rescued and brought up by some stock-keepers who happened accidentally to be passing at the time. The marks of the burns were distinctly visible on the man when I saw him, and his story was well known in the locality.

Walter Edmund Roth, eminent physician, internationally renowned ethnographer with a long scholarly interest in Australia's Aborigines, was appointed Northern Protector of Aborigines (Queensland) in 1898. In this position, Roth travelled extensively, recording all he could of Aboriginal culture, as he sought to benevolently protect Queensland Aborigines from exploitation and intolerance. Roth's ethnographic observations of Aboriginal culture, although acknowledged today as scientifically important, are rarely discussed in the politically correct narrative of Aboriginal history. In addition to his acclaimed 1897 monograph 'Ethnological Studies Among North West Central Queensland Aborigines', Roth produced a series of Bulletins and Reports between 1901 and 1910, graphically detailing many distasteful aspects of Aboriginal culture, including cannibalism, infanticide, wife beating, abortion and the ritual pack rape of young girls.

Roth wrote *new born babies may be killed and eaten. The midwife would screw the infant's neck round, breaking it by holding the jaw and back of the head. If the mother died in childbirth, the child was deemed guilty of murder and immediately killed and eaten by the old women. The reason given for eating the dead,* Roth tells us, *was so survivors knew where the dead actually were, and so could not be frightened by their spirits. The liver was eaten but the rest of the innards were buried, and the spot was marked by three sticks about a foot high, each wound round with grass rope and stuck closely opposite each other in the ground.*

Albert Barunga, an Elder of the Kimberley Worora tribe in north west Australia who died in 1977, wrote in his 2015 published memoir of Aboriginal tribal life: *One of the ways the population was kept at a level balance was by killing girl babies, if they were born in a poor season. This was necessary because the women were hunters, just as much as the men, bringing in a large share of the food in yams and small game. A woman with a small baby was restricted, and if the struggle for survival was desperate at that time, the girl baby could not be kept.*

A son was always allowed to live. Cannibalism was practised by my people in a ritual way.

In his book *River of Gold: The Story of the Palmer River Gold Rush* Angus and Robertson (1967), author Hector Holthouse wrote *the Aborigines* (of Queensland) *killed and ate their own women and children and occasionally their men. The older women were often killed for eating purposes like livestock. When a gin was to be killed, she was taken away to a secluded spot. One man seized and crossed her hands in front of her, while another hit her on the back of the head with a nulla nulla or wooden sword. Then she was disembowelled and cut up for roasting. A woman who was unfaithful was killed and eaten. If a man fell from a tree, or was in any other way seriously injured, he was generally killed and eaten.*

Holthouse writes of *a young black girl* (who) *deserted one of the tribes and was brought into Palmerville. After she had picked up enough English to make herself understood, she was asked if she knew anything about two gold prospectors, who had disappeared in the area she came from. The girl giggled happily, but at first would say nothing. After a good deal of persuasion, she at last told them what had happened. The men of her tribe had surrounded the two diggers and tied them up with vines. They were kept tied up until they had been carried to the black's camp, and then, so they would not be able to run away, their shin and arm bones were broken by being pounded between stones. Next day one of the men was knocked on the head and was roasted and eaten, while his mate looked on. The following day the other man was eaten.*

In her 1928 letter, Daisy Bates spoke of her own knowledge of Aboriginal cannibalism. *In steady, quiet, concentrated investigation extending over 27 years among the* (Aboriginal) *groups, I have learned the various methods in respect of cannibalism. They raided and killed and then left their victim to be buried by his or her own group, who leave the camp of the dead immediately after burial. Returning to the spot they dug up and cooked their victim. Every adult and boy and girl now wandering along the east west line has eaten human flesh. In a group of 26* (Aborigines) *who came to my Ooldea camp in 1920, all have eaten human meat. Cannibalism automatically ceases on their entry into civilised areas.*

oooOOOooo

The colonial authorities took a dim view of murder, whether committed by Aborigines or white men. It was a public hanging offence inflicted on both races. James Kirby a white man was hanged on the 18 December 1820 for the stabbing murder of an Aborigine. The Myall Creek massacre of 28 Aborigines which took place in New South Wales on the 10 June 1838, occurred two months after the Faithfull Creek massacre (11 April 1838) of 8 white men by Aborigines in Victoria and was no doubt a factor in the Myall Creek killings. The Myall Creek murders resulted in the hanging of 7 white men. In passing sentence of death, Judge Burton said to the accused men *I sincerely hope that the grace of God may reach and penetrate the hardened hearts that could surround a funeral pile lighted by themselves, and gloat on the tortures and sufferings of so many of their fellow beings.*

The Aborigines learned quickly of the death sentence proclaimed for murder and they used it as a verbal threat in their dealings with white settlers. *Governor Gipps ruled that hanging would be the penalty for any retaliatory shooting of the natives. This information spread like wildfire among the blacks. One of them caught stealing sheep defied an irate squatter 'You touch me, the Gubbha* (white man) *will hang you'.* How the squatter reacted to the sheep thief's words is not recorded. Clearly, this Aborigine understood the fatal consequences of white man's law. He did not as some historian's surmise, take the white settler's sheep because culturally he thought they had been thrown away by white men.

At Whorouly Dr George MacKay, a fiery and bad-tempered man, had trouble with local Aborigines. MacKay reported *the blacks have murdered a number of white men and destroyed many horses and cattle. In May 1840, 21 of them, all armed with guns, beside their native weapons attacked my station in my absence. They murdered one of my servants and burned my huts, stores and all of my wheat. It was their first visit to the station. It was also their last. I followed them for 18 months and apprehended 17 of them. Their capture had such a good effect that depredations* (in the region) *have since been confined to a few cattle for food.*

Cattle were speared to intimidate white men and for food. Three years earlier on October 24 1837, overlander Alexander Mollison wrote in his diary as he brought a mob of cattle across the Murray River into north east Victoria: *Travelled on, still between the swamp and the range, crossed the creek close to the range and camped. Grass good for cattle and abundant. Discovered that a cow had gone out of the herd last night. Sent Coleman (a drover) back to the Ovens River, but he returned without seeing her. There is a cow in the herd with a broken spear sticking fast in the rump. This has been done by the tribe of blacks who were with us at the Ovens. These blacks knew well that four head of cattle escaped and were feeding at the junction of the Ovens and King Rivers. They saw that our cattle were mustered twice a day and that we were prepared to punish them for any aggression.*

Mary Vincent, wife of Jacob Vincent the pastoral tenant of the Glenmore Run in the Upper King Valley 20 years before Ned Kelly's grandfather James Quinn settled his lawless family there in 1864, experienced intimidation by the district's Aborigines. *The Vincent's believed they were in imminent danger at Glenmore, when a large band of Aboriginals came to the house gesticulating wildly and demanding flour and everything else in the house. Finally, the blacks were driven off without doing any real harm, but the memory of that encounter remained with the Vincents. There was constant danger of attacks by the blacks. A group of 300 Aboriginals lived nearby and they were not all harmless characters. One of the Aboriginals was known as Jim Crow, a particularly treacherous fellow, and Mrs Vincent used to tell how frightened she was of him.*

On 11 November 1880, the day Ned Kelly was hanged in the Melbourne Gaol, the *Age* newspaper reported: *News has been received of an outrage by the blacks eighty-five miles south of Barrow Creek* (Northern Territory). *Two men Anderson and Connor were travelling with Bullock drays loaded with rations for Barrow Creek* (Telegraph) *Station. They were attacked at Violet Springs by natives. Anderson received a spear in his left breast, causing a wound which ran along the bone for 3 inches. Connor was wounded twice on the right shoulder. The spearheads were made of mulga, which is believed to be a poisonous wood. Fears are entertained for them both. Anderson's wound became worse but he is now recovering. The blacks are congregating in large numbers near Barrow Creek Station.*

Seven years earlier in 1873, the Barrow Creek Telegraph Station had been attacked by hostile Aborigines and held under siege for 24 hours before help arrived from Tennant Creek and the Aborigines were driven off. Station Master James Stapleton and Linesman John Franks were speared and died from their wounds. Assistant Manager Ernest Flint was speared but survived. This unprovoked, surprise evening attack triggered settler reprisal against Aborigines and further blood was shed. The colonial frontier was typified by bouts of tit for tat retaliation which could be ugly and horrifying. There was also peaceful cooperation where white settlers and Aborigines coexisted without conflict and discord. To exaggerate one over the other is to lose sight of a dynamic situation responsive to change and circumstance.

12
Cullin la Ringo, Hornet Bank and Faithfull Creek Massacres

Settlers on the McIntyre River (in Queensland) *lived anxiously for years. During which time 'not one of them could stir from his hut unarmed; when one milked or went for a bucket of water another fully armed stood over him'.*

Jidah Clark, *Black Nations Rising* (2016)

Confrontation with marauding bands of Aborigines, interfering as the settlers saw it with the progress of land settlement and civilisation, was a challenging and unsettling pioneer reality. The frontier conflict in Queensland was prolonged and merciless. The Reverend John Mathew, who was to become Moderator of the Australian Presbyterian Church, was a sympathetic and compassionate man towards Queensland's Aborigines. He did not approve of massacre, black or white, and preached against it. In his poem 'Corroboree' (1902), Mathew outlined the trials and tribulations suffered by Queensland squatters. Ownership of the land he believed, belonged to those who cleared and settled on it. Queensland Aborigines did not agree, and resisted white settlement with organised violence, rape and ambush murder.

In December 1855, 50 Aborigines attacked William Young's Mount Lacom squatting run in Queensland. Four white men, a white woman, an Aboriginal boy and a station Aborigine were slain, their bodies mutilated *covered with spear and nulla nulla* (a heavy wooden club) *wounds*. The white woman's body was sexually abused after she was murdered. Sheep were driven into the bush; station stores and clothing were stolen. *The People's Advocate* wrote of the brutal ambush massacre 'Another Fearful Massacre by the Blacks'. *Information has been brought to Brisbane by a gentleman from Port Curtis, of another dreadful slaughter of seven persons by the blacks at that locality. The particulars of the murders are as follows. On the 27th December last, a large party of these savages made a rush upon the men at Mr Young's station, killing one poor fellow who was employed slaughtering a sheep, and spearing to death two others who attempted to reach a gunyah* (hut), *wherein was another white man and his wife.*

These poor unfortunates kept the rascals at bay for some time, but the devils at length tore away a sheet of bark at the back of the gunyah, and speedily dispatched them with their tomahawks. It is reported that the person of the unfortunate woman was treated by the black scoundrels with indignity after her death. Two black fellows belonging to the station were also speared, making a total of seven murders in the whole! Lieutenant Murray, with his small party of native police, went in pursuit as soon as intelligence reached him of the outrage; but upon reaching the scene of butchery he found the scoundrels in such force, and so well prepared to receive his attack, that he was compelled to confine his operations to watching them until he could receive reinforcements.

The newspaper went on to voice the state of terror and constant fear felt by Queensland's white settler inhabitants. *Comment upon this outrage would be superfluous; something must be done to protect our frontier, or all the outstations to the northward of Wide Bay must be abandoned, or be each converted into armed garrisons. The aboriginals to the north grow bolder by the successes which have hitherto attended their butcheries, and subsequent escape from detection. The residents at Gladstone are, fearful that the blacks will ultimately assemble in overwhelming numbers and rush the township itself.* White settlers faced a real and present danger. The Queensland frontier crisis was spiralling out of control and there was little anybody could do about it.

In January 1856, the Elliott brothers' run near Grasmere (Qld) was attacked under the cover of darkness by 100 Aborigines. A shearer was killed and William Elliott wounded. Fortunately, the brothers had not yet retired for the night. They managed to marshal a stiff resistance with rifles, otherwise the death toll would have been higher. The *Tweed Daily* newspaper in its centenary year 1923 wrote. *About 1860 there were found in a cavern, about 200 yards from the road near Mount Lindesay (NSW), 14 skeletons of white men and swagmen who had been waylaid, on their way from Queensland to New South Wales or vice versa, and murdered for their personal effects clothing, knives, and tobacco. When the blacks killed a white man, they always chopped off the feet, sometimes the head as well; a precaution they took to 'euchre' the ghost of the murdered foe lest it should be inclined to follow the culprits, as a ghost without feet is obviously severely handicapped in a chase.*

oooOOOooo

The Queensland Cullin la Ringo massacre on 17 October 1861, of 19 white settlers who had travelled overland from Geelong in Victoria with 10,000 sheep, sent shockwaves of anger and retaliation through the white settler community. A tribal band of 50 Gayiri Aborigines attacked without warning, spearing and bashing to death with nulla nullas men, women and children. The settlers fought back with guns and tent poles but were overwhelmed by the bloody violence directed at them. Only 6 out of a party of 25 survived the onslaught. Those killed included Elizabeth Baker 19 years old, her parents David and Catherine Baker, her elder and younger brothers and eight-month-old baby sister. The Mannion family, father, mother, a four-year-old toddler and an infant baby died together under sustained clubbing from their Aboriginal executioners.

The scene of the brutal massacre is described in graphic detail in a letter sent to the *Sydney Morning Herald* on 26 October 1861. *After dinner the blacks scattered themselves among the men, who were working about the place and around the married people's quarters. When upon a given signal, the blow was struck that hurried 15 souls into eternity at the same moment. Mr Wills was killed near his tent; the cook was speared in the act of taking off the camp oven; the bullock driver alongside his team, the whip in his hand; another man while gathering together boughs to make a yard; one mother with an infant in her arms, another sewing, one young female and a child about five years old and an infant lay together. The demons either before enacting this scene or immediately after, must have gone to the outstation and killed Mr Baker* (the overseer) *and his son; also, two men who were out with the sheep swelling the sacrifice to 19.*

'The Cullin la Ringo Massacre Recalled' a paper read before the Rockhampton and District Historical Society in September 1954 spoke of the sudden unexpectedness of the attack. *Of all the acts of base treachery and fiendish slaughter perpetrated by the blacks, there is none so diabolical as that known as the Nogoa* (Cullin la Ringo) *murders. In an unsuspecting moment 19 men, women and children were smitten down. Mr Will's camp was exceptionally well provisioned and equipped, and as the natives were allowed for a period to roam around at will, their curiosity and cupidity were aroused, which generated a thirst for plunder. The absence of any provocation, and, indeed, the fact that the natives were remarkably well treated by the station people, combine to make this tragedy rank as one of the worst episodes of our early colonisation. Colonists throughout the country were horrified, and although retribution was exacted on the blacks, the settlers for many years entertained nothing but feelings of deep hostility and suspicion against the Aborigines.*

Victorian pastoralist, the son of a convict and a former member of the Victorian Parliament (1855-59), Horatio Wills was the leader of the Cullin la Ringo white settlers. He was a devout Christian, a tolerant and compassionate man with a good relationship with the Aborigines of the Port Phillip district before he departed for Queensland. He employed Aborigines as station hands on his 125,000 acre Lexington property in the Grampians and treated them well. Wills, *a few days previous to his death, met a gin in the bush with a baby in her arms. He rode up to her and took a silk handkerchief out of his pocket and put it around the baby; at this she* (the baby's mother) *appeared quite satisfied.* Charles Dutton of Bauhinia Downs Station *a warm protector from anything like cruelty and injustice* (towards the Aborigines on his run) said of the Cullin la Ringo massacre: *The Aborigines have one feeling in common with whites that of deep implacable revenge for unprovoked injury.*

The Cullin la Ringo massacre receives enraged attention from today's political activists, intent on portraying white settlers as cruel, genocidal and obsessed with the total eradication of the Aboriginal race. They disregard white settler anger and retaliation for wrongs committed against them by hostile Aborigines, while simply ignoring Aboriginal atrocities that rank as some of the worst crimes of the colonial period. There were men of blood and violence on both sides and the innocent and the vulnerable paid a heavy price in the ensuing confrontation. Massacres were seldom initiated or carried out by either side, without a provoking sequence of events leading up to violent attack and bloody murder. In the Cullin la Ringo case, it is said Squatter Jesse Gregson of the nearby Rainworth station confronted and killed several Gayiri Aborigines caught in the act of stealing his cattle.

The white men, women and children of the Wills party did nothing to deserve their bloody fate. Their Aboriginal assailants clearly had a premeditated plan to attack, rob and kill them. They wanted revenge, provisions and white lives. The cunning, guile and brutality of the Aboriginal band of murderers was ruthless and indiscriminate. Tom Wills rode with those who set out to track down the killers of his father Horatio. In an 1895 *Chicago Tribune* newspaper article written by an anonymous American correspondent and published 15 years after Tom Wills alcohol induced suicide death; an alleged firsthand account of Tom's participation in the Snake Ridge massacre of 30 Aborigines revealed the sorrow and anger he and others felt at the unprovoked Aboriginal attack.

I turned to the drovers, who were crying like children, and ordered them to gallop to the neighbouring runs to spread the news. Before morning thirty good men and true were at the door, among them two native trackers who were friendly to us, who said there was about forty (sic) in the gang (of Aboriginals). After eight hours' galloping, we caught up with the band about 3 o'clock in the afternoon. I cannot tell all that happened, but know we killed all in sight. Just as we thought they were all settled I happened to see a dirty, shrinking, greasy brute with my Zingari jacket sneaking off. I galloped after him, and when I got alongside, I emptied the whole six barrels of my revolver into him.

The infuriating sight of his stolen Zingari jacket, a prized possession from his sporting days playing cricket in England, led to his intemperate words and the reprisal death of the trophy wearing Aborigine. When the biblical rage had left him, Tom reverted to his sportsman self and Christian principles. Tom Wills was a foundation pioneer in establishing Australian cricket and Aussie rules football as sporting institutions. In 1866 five years after the Cullin la Ringo massacre, he became coach of the first Aboriginal Cricket team that would tour England in May 1868. Today a bronze statue of Tom Wills stands outside the Melbourne Cricket Ground. The Bradman Museum and International Cricket Hall of Fame in Bowral (NSW) describes Tom's mentoring of Aboriginal cricketeers *as an act of compassion and courageous reconciliation; an early act of public reconciliation between Aboriginal people and the English settlers.*

When controversy arose in September 2021 around the *Chicago Tribune* article Terry Wills Cooke, the great grandson of Tom Wills brother Horace, wrote *I have no documentary evidence that Tom took any part in the reprisal but oral history within the family would suggest that he did. There is* (however) *no evidence to point to his participation. I am at the stage now that I do not accept any theories which are not supported by evidence. Show me the evidence and I will accept it, but I won't accept a rewriting of the events to suit today's cancel culture and woke agendas. You need to remember that the days were different* (then) *and there was no feeling that in carrying out this reprisal there was anything other than fully deserved retribution. The family is disappointed that Tom's name and history should be sullied by what is* (only) *half of the story.*

oooOOOooo

At Hornet Bank sheep station (Central Queensland) at 2 o'clock in the morning on the 27 October 1857, widow Martha Fraser, seven of her nine children, Henry Neagle tutor to the family, two shepherds named Munro and Newman and Jimmy an Aboriginal boy were clubbed and speared to death by Aborigines belonging to the Yiman tribe. Martha who was 43 years old and her daughters Eliza 19 years and Mary 11 years were brutally raped and murdered within hearing of their bashed and semiconscious 14-year-old brother Sylvester. The other Fraser children John aged 23, David aged 16, Jane aged 9, James aged 6 and Charlotte aged 3 were murdered in their beds or as they desperately attempted to escape the ferocity of the Aboriginal killing spree. Henry Neagle was bashed and speared to death, his body mutilated and castrated. Munro and Newman were speared as they returned to the homestead a short time later. Jimmy the Aboriginal servant boy knew of the planned attack beforehand and he poisoned the station dogs. His reward was to be speared along with everyone else. In all, 12 people died at the hands of an Aboriginal band that itself suffered no losses during the encounter. The Aborigines stole 100 sheep, clothes, foodstuffs and the white settler's guns. They ransacked the homestead and destroyed whatever they could not carry away. The *Morton Bay Courier* called the night time ambush attack *a fearful outrage committed by blacks under circumstances of peculiar atrocity*.

Twelve months earlier, several Yiman Aborigines had been shot and killed spearing station cattle and there had been other skirmishes. Aborigines would steal entire flocks of sheep and herds of cattle, take them away into the bush, where they would savagely mutilate and slaughter them for food and reprisal. Heavy stock losses and the disruption to farming life angered white settlers, some of whom resorted to morally reprehensible and illegal practices such as poisoning food and water supplies.

A small minority of Queensland pastoralists provided Aborigines with flour and mutton laced with arsenic in order to rid themselves of troublesome Aborigines intent on retaliation, murder and plunder. The Frasers it is said poisoned Aborigines for killing their livestock and stealing station property. In the months before the Hornet Bank massacre occurred, several Aborigines died from eating a Christmas pudding laced with strychnine. In other parts of Australia similar vengeful poisoning occurred. In 1842 near Port Fairy in Victoria, nine Aborigines died after eating poisoned flour supplied to them by squatter James Kilgour. These were deplorable acts of rough justice neither encouraged, condoned nor engaged in by the majority of white setters.

According to white settler neighbours, John Fraser and his younger brother David were *famous for* (sexually abusing) *young gins* (and that) *was the cause of the atrocity*. Castration and rape are a clear indication that Aboriginal retaliation for sexual misconduct was the motive. In South Australia in 1852, a shepherd was killed by Aborigines *his body ritually mutilated, his genitals cut off and stuffed in his mouth suggestive of payback for a sexual crime.* Surprisingly, although Henry Neagle's castration is mentioned, contemporary records reveal nothing about John and David Fraser's bodies suffering the same fate.

It is important to point out that Aboriginal tribal custom provided for the sexual exploitation of Indigenous women. As shall be discussed more fully in a later chapter the experience of Aboriginal women in tribal society was brutal and degrading. While this in no way excuses the predatory sexual behaviour of the Fraser brothers; it adds an element of social complexity to such sexual encounters that is rarely discussed. In any event a white widow woman, her seven children, three men and an Aboriginal boy died horrible deaths, their bodies savagely beaten and mutilated.

When he regained consciousness, Sylvester panic stricken and *without hat or boots and in a terribly bruised state* ran to the nearest station some miles away for help. Greatly incensed by the rape of white women and the murder of young children, a posse was formed and white retaliation was swift and terrible. William Fraser the eldest son and station manager who had been away from home at the time of the massacre, wore out three horses in three days riding 320 miles from Ipswich to hunt down the murderers of his family. Consumed with a burning anger to avenge his family, William rode with the native police (who were responsible for many Aboriginal deaths) and for the next several decades, he shot and killed any Aborigine he suspected of involvement in the rape and killing of his mother and siblings. He became an officer in the Queensland native police to pursue his vendetta against the Yiman Aborigines.

Not all Queensland pastoralists shared William Fraser's zeal to wreak reprisal on the Yiman tribe. In 1867, Fraser who by this time was a Sub Inspector in the native police with a reputation for ruthlessness towards Aborigines, tracked some Yiman women and children to the Mackenzie squatting run on the Fitzroy River. Mrs Mackenzie knowing what would happen if Fraser caught up with the Aboriginal women and children, hid them in her bedroom, positioned herself in front of the door and refused entry to the policeman. Fraser was forced to abandon the pursuit but not before he received an unladylike tongue lashing from Mrs Mackenzie. Sylvester Fraser never got over his ordeal with the Yiman Aborigines. He suffered physical fits and mental problems for the rest of his life.

It has been suggested the Hornet Bank and Cullin la Ringo massacres were linked, with Yiman Aborigines from the Hornet Bank rapes and massacre participating with Gayiri Aborigines in the later Cullin la Ringo murders. The geographical closeness of both locations (approximately 130 miles) on the central Queensland plains, together with the nomadic wandering pattern of the Yiman tribe following the Hornet Bank incident make this a distinct possibility. Aboriginal tribes would join together in coordinated attacks to carry out raids on shepherd huts and pioneer settlers' homesteads. Those who pursued the Aborigines involved in these two brutal massacres believed there was a connection and they could well have been right.

oooOOOooo

In April 1858, six months after the Fraser family's cold-blooded Queensland murder, New South Wales Crown Lands Commissioner William Wiseman, investigating the deaths of two Coolies (Chinese) and two Englishmen by Aborigines, wrote to the NSW Attorney General reporting a further native attack on three shepherds. The attackers refused the shepherds' offer to take *everything they possessed*, saying *they would only have their lives and added they would take the lives of all the bloody white men in the country*. The shepherds survived the attack, killing one Aborigine. Wiseman said some of the Aborigines involved *had long been living with the whites*.

Two stories of white settler encounters with hostile Aborigines near Violet Town in Kelly Country Victoria, reveal the explosive nature of fragile relationships and revenge vendetta which could quickly turn to violence even against their own Aboriginal people. In the Violet Town Centenary Celebrations Programme (1949) Mrs J Weaver wrote *my grandparents lived on the bank of the Honeysuckle Creek. Mr Myers a station holder from New South Wales stayed with them on his way to Melbourne. He had a black boy with him and some members of another tribe had followed him from Albury. When he* (the black boy) *went out to get the horses in the morning, they killed him. The blacks came many* times around the house when grandma was there alone. They often camped near the old homestead.

A published letter to the *Port Phillip Gazette* dated October 1839, 'A Friend to the Independent Press' wrote of a similar murder of an Aboriginal boy:

> Some five or six weeks since a most diabolical murder was committed by three of the native blacks of the Port Phillip tribe, on a boy about twelve years of age, who had been some time with Mr Langhorne, at the mission station. Mr. Langhorne made it a practice to send the boy into the bush in charge of his milking cows. It appears that the blacks followed him and cut his head open with a tomahawk; they then speared him through the side, cut off one of his hands, and stripped him naked, took out his entrails, then dug a hole and buried him with his clothes. The lad was very intelligent, and had been brought down the Country about two hundred miles. He often expressed his fears that the other blacks would kill him, as they had once before made an attempt to do so.

Another Violet Town story tells of an unprovoked murder that took place on Dr Anderson's Honeysuckle Creek squatting run in 1856. *Doctor Anderson's housekeeper was approached by a black one day at the kitchen, who on finding that she was alone at the time, asked for food. Because he did not get all he expected, he drove his spear into her side and killed her.* There are many family tales like these with pioneer women some brandishing guns to guard themselves, their children and farming property against Aborigines camping nearby. As harrowing as these two stories are and despite occasional revenge attacks by both sides, for most of the time Aborigines and white settlers in the Violet Town area peacefully tolerated each other and the relationship between the two races was friendly and cooperative.

A notable exception, which occurred at the very beginning of pioneer settlement in north east Victoria, was the Faithfull Creek massacre of 8 white men, drovers and shepherds by a band of Aborigines near the future township of Benalla on 11 April 1838. News of the brutal massacre heightened community fear and hardened white settler opinion against hostile Aborigines on the colonial frontier. The Port

Phillip Pioneers Group describes the ferocity of what happened that day and its bloody aftermath:

A large mob of sheep and cattle were being overlanded for George and William Pitt Faithfull. It appears that a few days previous, several sheep went missing then an Aboriginal was seen killing a lamb. Thomas Bently, a servant, found a cache of 80 to 100 spears hidden in the reeds. The overlanders ordered the intruders away from camp. They refused to leave and speared John Bass, then began plundering the drays. Several overlanders rushed up and fired their guns. They were hopelessly outnumbered, there being 150 to 200 natives (recent research suggests this figure is too high. As few as 20 Aborigines may have been responsible for the killings) *and were forced to flee, then were speared one by one as they ran. First John Hargrave was overtaken; Edward Laycock; John Freeman and William Macon were heard to say 'Let us die together'. William Smith was overtaken and killed. The remainder of the party split and ran in two different directions. William Walker and John Brown struck off to the right and escaped. Daniel Balmain and Michael Welsh struck off to the left. William Read was speared three times, struck several times with a piece of wood and struck repeatedly on the head with a waddy and left for dead although alive, he died several days later. It would appear that one Aborigine was either killed or wounded. The pursuit of the overlanders was a fierce one, the dead lying over seven miles.*

About 10 days later on the 21 April 1838, Dr William Bowman and A. F Mollison's properties north east of Mount Macedon had their shepherds attacked and their properties pillaged. A month later Thomas Jones, one of Bowman's shepherds was found speared and disembowelled. Shortly after mounted police tracked a party of 50 warlike Aborigines who had stolen sheep from two runs. A pitched battle took place and seven or eight Aborigines were shot dead, the sheep were recovered. All was quiet until 12 November, 1838 when at least 400 natives hacked to death George Mould and drove away his sheep north east of Rutledge and Forster's run on the Goulburn River.

Squatter David Reid wrote of an Aborigine named Merriman said to have been dressed in European clothes at the time of the Faithfull Creek massacre. *This blackfellow had been several years amongst the whites on the Murray River and was to some extent half civilised. From being brought up amongst white people he had the opportunity of judging as to their means of defence and their customs were familiar to him. He had the knowledge as to what would be the best means to attack them with the least danger and the greater certainty of success.*

From the earliest days of settlement Aborigines engaged in deception and 'reconnaissance' against whites. In November 1821, the Port Macquarie Commandant reported to the Colonial Secretary the spearing of two convicts while cutting timber. *The act of treachery on the part of those savages was greatly aggravated by their appearance of friendship having partaken the evening previous to it, of the supper of the poor fellows who became their victims. Taking advantage of the long Grass and thick scrub they were able to come close to the party unobserved, and matching the opportunity offered by the men engaged in falling a cedar tree committed murder.*

In 1826, Captain Foley a military man stationed at Newcastle (NSW), wrote to his superiors *acts of outrage have been committed by natives who are domesticated on the very estates where they have occurred, and not by the incursions of unknown or wild tribes. Every one of these is perfectly and intimately known by names they have received amongst the settlers near whom they have dwelt.* A white settler Robert Scott added *he had known many Aborigines return to tribal life after being with white men, and what is still more lamentable, these very persons have almost invariably been the instigators of and leaders in the aggressions committed on Europeans.*

In a letter to Superintendent Latrobe, George Faithfull in defence of his shepherds and drovers, reveals the fear squatters and their station hands had of being hanged for killing Aborigines, even when an Aboriginal pre-emptive attack was involved. *The Government has threated to hang anyone who dares to shoot a black even in protection of his property, and appointed a Protector to search about the country for information as to the destruction of the natives. These gentlemen resort to the most contemptible means to gain information against individuals, whom the trumpet tongue of falsehood had branded as having destroyed many of these savages.* White men who killed Aborigines in fear of their lives, felt intimidated by a law and investigative process which made no legal distinction between self-defence and intentional crime. In these clearly defined legal circumstances, it is no wonder that secrecy and public denial prevailed among white settlers fearful of Aboriginal attack and seeking revenge.

oooOOOooo

Some historians believe the Australia-wide total for Aboriginal deaths during the colonial frontier war period may have been as high as 30,000. Others regard the Indigenous fatality figure as lower than this. Archaeologist Alan Williams estimates the pre 1788 Aboriginal population of the continent to have been between 770,000 and 1.2 million in the years immediately preceding white settlement. On no less convincing evidence others dismiss this assessment as far too high, opting instead for an overall estimate of 350,000. The 1922 Commonwealth Yearbook, an official government publication, gave 150,000 as the total number of Aborigines present in Australia at the time of European contact.

Even at the highest level of alleged Aboriginal frontier deaths (30,000) and the lowest estimate of the continental Aboriginal population (770,000), roughly 3.89% of Australia's Aboriginal population perished during approximately 146 years of frontier conflict. These figures do not take into account Aboriginal deaths from disease, alcoholism and a myriad of other causes. They do however put into perspective the exaggerated claims and the dismal failure of alleged frontier genocide, which was never an official or unofficial policy of the British or Colonial Governments. Unfortunately, the number of white deaths receive only cursory attention from historians.

The *Australian History Truth Matters* website is in the process of compiling a state-by-state record of frontier attacks and acts of premeditated murder carried out by Aborigines against Europeans. The coordinator writes *I couldn't find any listings anywhere on the internet of non-Aboriginal victims who died at the hands of the natives. Although there is no end of readily available information on the blacks that died. To try to balance the records, I have set about listing the details of everybody I can find who were murdered by the blacks. What I haven't included, is all of those people who were seriously wounded, but didn't die. I have assumed that these victims survived. Many of these people were never the same again, due to head injuries, damaged lungs and spinal injuries, and limbs chopped off. I haven't included the many Australian natives and half castes who were working with the whites and who were also murdered. I should also say here, that there would have been even more white deaths had many of the natives, especially the women, not warned the whites of impending trouble. There are countless examples of that happening, and quite often the women were speared and killed because they spoke out. I found cases where some natives were attacking the whites, while others, from different tribes probably, were trying to rescue the whites.*

The black armband narrative of Australian history is based on questionable assumptions, misrepresented facts and a simplistic oppressor/oppressed model of frontier behaviour. Today's identity politics drives an activist Indigenous movement that values division, hate and recrimination over understanding, reconciliation and unity. The reproachful radical rhetoric does not match the stated peaceable goal. This chapter has dealt with three horrendous incidents of Aboriginal attacks against white settlers. White retaliation followed and colonial frontier warfare escalated into further bloodshed and tit for tat reprisal. White deaths and black deaths should not be exaggerated or denied their place in the nation's history. Neither should Aboriginal deaths be elevated to a higher moral plane simply because they were more numerous and Indigenous people less territorially cohesive.

Bloodshed and murder occurred across the colonial frontier. White men, women and children died agonising and painful deaths defending themselves from fierce Aboriginal tribes. Aborigines for their part suffered a similar wretched fate and a greater mortality, responding to strangers settling on their ancestral land and disrupting the unbroken rhythm of nomadic bush life. This was the ugly and brutal reality of colonial frontier warfare. Prior to white settlement Aborigines engaged in bloody warfare against other Aborigines and no quarter was given. Right or wrong history records the technologically advanced and/or numerically stronger side inevitably triumphs in such contests.

The white settler community and colonial governments do not deserve the harsh judgement of those who see only massacre and inhumanity in colonial race relations. Some white men were killers, as were some Aborigines who revenged themselves on European settlers through robbery, rape, murder and intimidation. Other Aborigines made peace and came to accept the lifestyle and material benefit bestowed by western civilisation. Massacre and retaliation should not be the defining legacy of pioneer land settlement. The majority of European settlers were well intentioned, god-fearing people and should not be remembered as bloodthirsty killers and moral pariahs. They were neither, and their history told truthfully and in accordance with the values and beliefs of their time reflects this.

Part Four
The Changed Face of Australia

The most effective way to destroy people is to deny and obliterate their own understanding of their history. He who controls the past, controls the future: who controls the present controls the past. Every record has been destroyed or falsified, every book rewritten, every picture has been repainted, every statue and street building has been renamed, every date has been altered and the protest is continuing day by day and minute by minute. History has stopped. The past was erased, the erasure was forgotten, the lie became the truth.

George Orwell

13
Universities, Schools and the Demise of Australian History

When little else in the world makes sense, history is the defining discipline. It carries extraordinarily important lessons for us and the future that we seek to shape. It can demolish prejudice. It is a reminder that there are hard decisions that have to be made, and the importance of making them and not shying away from them. We have to be informed by a sense of not only who we are, but from where we have come.

Brendan Nelson

Since I grew up in the 1950s and attended Latrobe University Bundoora as a mature age undergraduate studying history in the 1970s, and later gaining a PhD in the 1980s, Australian history has undergone a dramatic change for the worse. Social history, anthropology, psychology, sociology, politics, economics and postcolonial studies were at the core of the history curriculum I studied. They were taught in an even-handed fashion by openminded scholars canvassing all sides in rigourous scholarly debate. The late Drs John Hirst and Inga Clendinnen, whom I acknowledge in all my books, were gifted Latrobe history department mentors and academic historians without peer. Different interpretations were advanced and through reasoned argument and the presentation of factual evidence, a clarity of historical understanding was achieved. A Marxist view of Australia's past was tempered by a changing and forward-looking liberalism: a liberalism in the true sense of the word that questioned rigid class theory and refined older historical pronouncements. Without sweeping away truth and meaning in a wave of postmodern wokeism, that has for the past two decades muddied and obscured rather than explained past motivation and behaviour.

For a short period of time in the 1970s and early 1980s. I taught Australian history and other history subjects in three Victorian schools (one of which was a progressive school for delinquent teenagers) and briefly tutored in Australian history at Latrobe University. Coming into teaching as a mature aged adult, with a lapsed Irish Catholic, working class, pro-union, Labor Party background and previous adult employment experience allowed me to distinguish left-wing BS from what was genuinely educationally valuable. During the first lesson each year I would tell my university and secondary school students, many of whom came from first generation migrant or refugee families, that what was needed to successfully study history and indeed any subject was to possess a built-in crap detector.

I left teaching before the woke revolution and completion of the left-wing Long March through the Institutions. Before the scholarly teaching of the hard and brutal reality of communism became transformed into the accommodating socialist idealism and heroic Marxism taught to the young today. Vladimir Lenin, Josef Stalin and Mao Zedong were among the greatest murderers in history, responsible for the suffering and death of tens of millions of people. Yet their monstrous crimes are glossed over in the Socialist/Green/Woke narrative. In classrooms across the nation, these ruthless mass murderers are held up as worthy role models and praised as enlightened political leaders. The communist narrative replaces reality while truth and justice languish in the shadows.

Socialists avoid using the word communism because they know the negative connotation it conjures up in the minds of older Australians. Not to teach socialism which is really communism in a factual and unbiased way is flimflam history-teaching at its worst. Left-wing academics and activist teachers make no pretence that they hate Australia and despise Aussie culture, values and history. They use 'group think' education as a means to indoctrinate the young into accepting socialism and a woke view of the world. The infiltration of the education system runs deep and it is changing the community face of Australia. I avoided experiencing the PC trashing of Australian history and the national education system at first hand. If my suggestion of a built-in student crap detector was a prerequisite to classroom study four decades ago then how much more necessary is it in today's woke indoctrinated classrooms?

oooOOOooo

Wokeness insists on 'decolonising' everything. *The decolonisation movement* writes Dr Bella d'Abrera from the Institute of Public Affairs (IPA) *has come out of our universities. It's born from post-modernism. It basically says that all the institutions of western civilisation, the rule of law, equality before the law, individual rights were all created to oppress minorities and that they're racist. The aim of this movement, pulling down statues, burning churches, graffitiing statues, is to eventually destroy these institutions of western civilisations. That's what we're seeing playing out on the streets of Canada* (where in July 2021 churches were burnt down and statues of Queen Victoria, Captain Cook and others were toppled by woke radicals) *and of course in Australia as well. The movement has no logic, it's just pure hatred, pure anarchy. It's a rolling revolution that has no discernible end.*

In a jointly written article published in the *Sydney Morning Herald* in June 2020, Jacinta Price and Tom Switzer wrote *in university history departments across the western world in the last decade or so, there has been a determination to 'decolonise the curriculum'. This is an approach that politicises the subject by imposing a Marxist slant on it. Far from paying attention to the main facts of history, it concentrates on imposing the 'woke' values of a noisy, self-advertising minority on a very different past. Context is irrelevant to these people: historical figures who had attitudes or performed deeds of which today's society rightly disapprove are to be vilified and despised, with no quarter given. The purpose of history is not to seek the truth, but to deploy it as a weapon however crude and distorted to manipulate the present. Much of history was horrible, but it is why western society is as it is. Removing evidence of that history is the construction of an alternative reality. It is not reality itself.*

University history departments, teaching colleges, primary and secondary schools across the nation have become enthusiastic flagbearers for a new version of Australian history: denigrating white pioneers, preaching skin-based victimhood, gender transition, migrant inclusiveness and frightening school kids with end of the world climate change extinction. Group think prevails in every classroom, stifling free speech and policing language and behaviour. Students study the past without proper nuance, layered complexity or appropriate context from the woke perspective of white oppressors and oppressed victims of colour. Factual distortion, misrepresentation and politicised fantasy abound in a brave new world devoted to destroying western civilisation and crushing its time-honoured traditions and values.

Universities are supposed to be a beacon for a free and frank exchange of ideas, unencumbered by restrictions of bullying political correctness. Professor Barry Spurr, who resigned from the University of Sydney in 2014 amidst a politically incorrect email controversy, writes *one of the astonishing ironies of social and intellectual history of the last half century is that the university, once the stalwart and outspoken defender of unfettered freedom of thought and expression, has now become the principal persecutor of those freedoms. Where censorship triumphs, freedom dies and the rest is silence.*

The unfair treatment of Marine Physicist Dr Peter Ridd, Head of the Physics Department at Queensland's James Cook University (2009-2016) and the University's Marine Geophysical Laboratory for 15 years, who was sacked by his university in 2018 for questioning the climate change orthodoxy of his woke colleagues over the ecological health of the Great Barrier Reef is nothing short of disgraceful. Dr Ridd's environmental message was based on real science and on the ground research that the Great Barrier Reef was not only alive but thriving. In response to a 2021 alarmist report warning that coral reefs were in danger of disappearing, Dr Ridd replied *the idea that coral reefs are close to extinction is just completely ridiculous!* The latest reef research by unbiased scientists vindicates Dr Ridd's position. In October 2021, the High Court of Australia agreed with the James Cook University sacking citing *the problem with* (Dr Ridd's) *submission is that it treats intellectual freedom as though it were freedom of speech generally.* If a respected scientist is denied by legal quibble and university gagging constraints the right to call out factual inaccuracy, then where does intellectual freedom and honesty reside?

Following the High Court decision then Federal Minister for Education and Youth, Alan Tudge, declared *if universities are not places for free, robust speech, then their very purpose is jeopardised. You cannot advance knowledge without challenging existing orthodoxies, and risk causing offence in the process. Freedom of expression is the most fundamental foundational principle of a university. Academics who don't believe in free speech, or cannot handle someone challenging their work, should not be at a university. There are few things more important for the advancement of truth and knowledge than having open, robust debate at our universities.*

Dr d'Abrera expressed her concern at the loss of free speech on university campuses. *Last year* (2019) *the IPA ran a survey and we found out that 41% of students fear saying anything in class because of retribution from their teacher. 31% of students are scared to say anything on campus and 59% of students are scared to say anything around their fellow students that might be conveyed as the wrong thing to say. There is clearly a free speech crisis on campus and our universities owe it to taxpayers to actually endorse a free speech code of conduct.*

In June 2020, *Quadrant* Online carried an article written by 'Anonymous' an undergraduate student at Sydney University titled: 'My University's Betrayal of Truth'. For obvious reasons, the young writer was reluctant to attach his or her name to an exposé article, which revealed the state of Australian tertiary education in such a poor academic and scholarly light. What follows is an abridged version of what was said.

> *As an 18-year-old studying both history and education at the University of Sydney, I've quickly come to realise the greatest intellectual challenge my generation faces is the barrage of cultural revisionism, left-wing indoctrination, postmodernism and the fabrication of history. All this and worse at what is supposedly the most prestigious university in the southern hemisphere. What my experience so far has brought to mind is the slow indoctrination, generation by generation, that truth is a matter of relativity. I am now in a position to confirm that there is indeed a crisis in liberal education.*
>
> *Let me illustrate with an examination of my own two areas of*

study. It has only taken a single semester for me to realise just how tertiary education is saturated with the relativist rhetoric of Marxism, Foucault, Freud and others. In my education course, the leftist trifecta of knowledge, truth and sexuality all taught from a decidedly 'progressive' perspective has dominated my readings. An unhealthy obsession with sexuality and identity politics is being thrust upon our future teachers and their students and encouraging children (to become) *sexually aware from the time they enter kindergarten. This is the current cultural zeitgeist of my degree in education. Championing political correctness without the courage to see knowledge as the disciplined act of seeking truth.*

I had consoled myself with the naïve hope that the academic discipline of objective inquiry would be safeguarded in the study of history. Well, I was wrong. The historical revisionism started on day one. The course was called 'Age of Empires'. A simple topic, looking at the themes and aspects of significant civilisations spanning the course of time. But I was unprepared for the bombardment of environmentalism, attacks on the evils of Christendom in the Americas, plus a course entirely devoted to showing the atrocities of western civilization, compared with the civil and equal nature of Islamic empires and their purportedly peaceful 'expansionism'. The cultures of Indigenous tribes discussed in the course suggested that traditional Aboriginals lived in some Edenic environment entirely devoid of the corruption that animated white European 'invaders'.

My very first lecture began with a 15-minute diatribe from a climate change activist, who introduced the harangue with a title on the screen, 'Nature's Dominion'. What followed was, in effect, an attack on our current age. The lecturer began with an attack on the Morrison Government, claiming that they were not doing enough to stop bushfires, reduce coal use and emissions, and fully comprehend the ethical impacts of destroying nature. Quite an odd way, I thought, to begin an introductory course on historical empires. As in education, the search for truth has clearly been replaced by ideology, history as viewed only through the monocular lens of politically progressive thought.

The attack on traditional western values today has seeped into the way historians now view the past. European and western society is often attacked as the oppressor, who disproportionately told a story of brutal Europeans concerning innocent native peoples who were 'living in harmony with nature'. Yet universities consistently and intentionally choose to discredit our cultural debt to Europe in general and to Christianity in particular. It's as if we should be ashamed of the Protestant work ethic, the foundation of capitalism and of science and, ultimately, of our search for reason and truth.

Our postmodern age has rejected reason, and we must return to the discipline of scholarship founded on truth. Cultural relativism has made its mark on the tertiary education scene. Children are being taught in the educational curriculum that Australia was founded on genocides, identity is found in sexualisation, and the world is going to end because of old, white capitalist patriarchy and Christian men. This feeds into tribalism, culture wars and cultural relativism through courses that reject truth as an absolute.

Thankfully there are glimmers of hope, with some professors and teachers who do not inject their personal values into history and avoid political correctness for the sake of knowledge and their pursuit of truth. But conclusively, history has lost its discipline, and it shows. What we need to do is to regain the disciplines of history and proper education, that allow us to breathe life into the morbid scene of learning.

Accompanying the article was a comment from a retired university academic offering advice. *I finished teaching at universities in 2002. It was bad then in the way you outline, and seems to have only become worse. Glimmers of hope arise though through students who refuse to submit to nonsense, who read more widely and think more constructively than those lecturing them. Some lecturers will always stay honest to their subject's history and potential and behave in a rational manner, but they are becoming fewer I suspect. Engage with these better lecturers and tutors as much as you can, and let other students know who provides you with the best value. Complain at faculty level if you are demonstrably marked down for your views. Complain concerning the narrowness of your reading lists and suggest alternatives. Ask awkward questions about matters that the lectures have ignored. Hone your skills at fighting back against the current intellectual vandalism of the academy.*

Not all academics or schoolteachers are political activists, but it is an uphill battle for them to be seen or heard in the current educational climate of militant wokeness. In science and technology faculties woke political correctness has less of an ideological hold than it does in arts faculties. Even in history departments and humanities faculties where wokeness prevails, there are academics who reject PC bias and intolerance. Academics and schoolteachers opposed to the politicising of students keep mostly to themselves seldom publicly expressing any criticism of their woke colleagues. They hold the common sense line as best they can in an unsettled time of educational and intellectual disarray.

We should gratefully acknowledge and support dedicated teachers at all levels who daily fight for genuine educational values. Rather than being safe and fulfilling workplaces to promote educational achievement and excellence schools and universities have in the main, become 'blitzkrieg battlegrounds' and 're-education camps' peddling woke propaganda and teacher conformity.

oooOOOooo

In a National Press Club address in 2006, Prime Minister John Howard said *too often, Australian history is taught without any sense of a structured narrative, replaced by a fragmented stew of 'themes' and 'issues'. Too often, history, along with other subjects in the humanities, has succumbed to a postmodern culture of relativism, where any objective record of achievement is questioned or repudiated. Nor should* (history teaching) *be at the expense of ongoing pride in what are commonly regarded as the values, traditions and accomplishments of the old Australia. Part of preparing young Australians to be informed and active citizens is to teach them the central currents of our nation's development. Young people are at risk of being disinherited from their community, if that community lacks the courage and confidence to teach its history.* It was PM Howard's persuasive words and my own past teaching experience that prompted me to embark on the long journey to research and write this book.

In the decade and a half since Prime Minister Howard spoke about Australia's ongoing history wars the history curriculum across the nation has been taken over by an overabundance of left-wing politicised 'themes' and 'issues' that mislead and divide. The national historical narrative has become disjointed, entirely one-sided and no more than a classroom exercise in critical race theory and leftist propaganda.

Activist teacher indoctrination and woke virtue signalling gestures are prevalent in primary and secondary school systems across the nation. In August 2020, an egregious example of teacher activism occurred at Albion Park High School in Wollongong (NSW). Suzi Clapham, the retiring principal, praised students at a special BLM school assembly for 'taking the knee' in solidarity with the Black Lives Matter movement. *The highlight for me, as the retiring principal of APHS, was the Black Lives Matter assembly which was put on by our wonderful year 12 students, and where all of year 12 students bent the knee in respect of lives lost. In America they are marching against hate. Word must be spread on what is happening to our own Indigenous population.*

Clearly, Albion Park High School students were encouraged by their teachers to turn a blind eye to months of BLM firebombing, shop looting, street violence and murder. Parents complained and notified local Member of Parliament Senator Mark Latham, who commented *the principal only had to spend five minutes going to the Black Lives Matter website to see that this is a self-confessed neo-Marxist outfit, that believes in defunding the police, attacks the nuclear family and believes in gender fluidity.* Not to mention the fact that BLM espouses revolution and the overthrow of capitalism as the preferred method to change society.

An even more deplorable example of woke activism in the nation's schools and its demoralising effect on schoolchildren occurred in April 2021 at Parkdale Secondary College in Melbourne. According to media reports, during a school assembly address titled 'Diversity and Inclusion', *A Kingston Council youth services worker held a talk about privilege, pronouns and 'intersectionality'. She told the boys to stand up if they were 'white', 'male' and 'Christian' before telling them they were responsible for being 'privileged' and 'oppressors'. A female Year*

11 student told the newspaper, pupils were 'shocked' by the presentation and that the male students had felt 'ashamed' and 'targeted'. 'It was so messed up, we thought for a moment it was a joke, but then we realised it wasn't and we were so upset and angry by it all', the 16-year-old said. 'She basically said straight, white, Christian males were oppressors and they held all the power and privilege in society. We were shocked but it was quite difficult to say anything, because she was also talking about LGBTQI+ and if you spoke out against that you feared you'd be called homophobic'.

What makes this so inexcusable, is that this exact situation was national headline news only a few weeks ago at Victoria's Brauer College. I wonder what would happen if a male youth worker ordered Year 11 girls to stand up in class and labelled them 'oppressors' for being 'white', 'female' and 'Christian'? Will the Victorian Equal Opportunity and Human Rights Commission investigate this as a breach of Section 18C of the Racial Discrimination Act? Funny how 'diversity and inclusion' classes are anything but that. Why hasn't this youth worker been named, shamed and cancelled? After all, the woke think it's acceptable for people to lose their job over views they deem unacceptable.

In March 2021, Channel Nine's Current Affair program reported on the Brauer school incident. *Male high school students who were forced to apologise to female classmates for 'behaviours of their gender' say their Victorian school made them feel like predators. Brauer College in Warrnambool in rural Victoria, made international headlines after all male students were told to stand and offer a rape apology at last Wednesday's school assembly. Year Seven student Levi, aged 12, said the incident made him feel uncomfortable. 'They told us to stand up and turn to a girl in our class and say sorry. I felt under pressure to stand up and if I didn't, I would feel I was a bad person'. Vini, another student, said many at the assembly were left upset and confused. 'I had girls behind me crying' he said. 'We had to apologise for stuff we didn't actually do'.*

oooOOOooo

The Victorian Curriculum and Assessment Authority (VCAA) website outlines the structure and objectives of the Victorian school curriculum. *The Victorian Curriculum F–10 sets out what every student should learn during their first eleven years of schooling. The curriculum is the common set of knowledge and skills required by students for life-long learning, social development and active and informed citizenship. The Victorian Curriculum F–10 incorporates the Australian Curriculum and reflects Victorian priorities and standards.*

In assessing the Victorian Curriculum Foundation-10 learning agenda. I conducted a keyword search on the VCAA website to determine the educational balance and fairness of what was being taught across the curriculum. What I discovered was a curriculum riddled with Socialist/Green/Woke bias favouring left-wing radical causes, with no attempt made to canvas both sides of an argument or genuinely encourage critical thinking.

Your search for '**Aborigine**' returned 289 results.

Your search for '**critical race theory**' returned 184 results.

Your search for '**Asian**' returned 40 results.

Your search for '**white**' returned 10 results.

Your search for '**pioneers**' returned 2 results.

Your search for '**Invasion Day**' returned 262 results.

Your search for '**Voice to Parliament**' returned 257 results.

Your search for '**Black Lives Matter**' returned 452 results.

Your search for '**climate change**' returned 902 results.

Your search for '**fossil fuel**' returned 4 results.

Your search for '**western civilisation**' returned 34 results.

Your search for '**ANZAC**' returned 28 results.

Your search for '**Christian**' returned 11 results.

Your search for '**Henry Lawson**' returned 4 results.

Your search for '**Phar Lap**' returned no results.

In July 2021, the VCAA announced a proposal to abandon the Victorian Certificate of Education (VCE) chemistry teaching of 'elements in the periodic table' — to be replaced by *the study of metals, carbon compounds and polymers and how they can be recycled and repurposed in a circular economy. Specific 'green' chemistry principles* (will be taught) *in relation to energy production and the design of primary cells and fuel cells. Sustainability of ethanol and bioethanol and the production of 'green hydrogen'* (are a curriculum component). Melissa MacEoin, president of the classroom teachers' group at the University of Melbourne's Chemistry Education Association, sensibly pointed out the periodic table was fundamental to the study of chemistry. Not studying the periodic table, she said would be *like learning a language, without first of all learning its alphabet so you can put it together.*

On 29 April 2021, the *Sydney Morning Herald* announced there was to be a major revision of the national curriculum. In years 7 to 10, history topics will be reduced from 12 to 8 *to allow for depth of study. School students across the country will be taught under proposed changes to the national curriculum that First Nations Australians experienced European colonisation as an invasion. The changes, released for discussion by the Australian Curriculum, Assessment and Reporting Authority* (ACARA) *said the terms 'Aboriginal' and 'Indigenous' will be replaced with 'First Nations Australians' or 'Australian First Nations Peoples'*. The changes were to be made at the expense of genuine historical understanding. They were clearly politicised in content, emotion and classroom presentation.

The national curriculum revision included the following:

- How the ancestors of the early First Peoples of Australia are recognised as the first seafarers on record and how this is considered as one of the greatest achievements of early humans.
- The impact of invasion, colonisation and dispossession of lands by Europeans on the First Nations People of Australia such as frontier warfare, genocide, removal from land, relocation to protectorates, reserves and missions.
- The forcible removal of children from First Nations Australia families in the late nineteenth century/early twentieth century (leading to the stolen generations), such as the motivations for the removal of children, the practices and laws that were in place, and experiences of separation.
- The significant events in the movement for the civil rights of First Nations Peoples of Australia and the extent they contributed to change, including 1962 right to vote federally, freedom rides, 1967 referendum, tent embassy, reconciliation, Mabo decision, bringing them home report (the stolen generations), the apology.
- The change in debate about climate change over time from the 1960s

to the present.
- The debate over multiculturalism that arose in the 1980s.
- The debate over the government policy of mandatory detention of asylum seekers.

An overseas booklet *Building Better Schools with Evidence Based Policy: Adaptable Policy for Teachers and School Leaders* Routledge 2021, was endorsed and its free distribution in Aussie schools and universities facilitated by Monash University Faculty of Education academics. Among other things, the booklet advocates teachers should be 'ordered' to teach students about 'super diversity', declare a climate emergency, banish the words 'boys' and 'girls' from the classroom and replace 'English as a Second Language' with 'Emergent Bilingual'. In response Minister Alan Tudge declared the educational idea woke insanity. *I want people to disregard this woke rubbish. Normal parents call their kids boys and girls and I hope they do so for evermore. They shouldn't be paying attention to this sort of garbage!*

Minister Tudge saw too much identity politics in the proposed national curriculum changes. He sent the proposal back to ACARA to be rewritten. *I'm particularly concerned about the history curriculum because it presents a negative view of our history. I think we should honour our Indigenous history and teach that well; but equally that should not come at the expense of dishonouring our western heritage. I think students should come out of school having learnt our history in an accurate manner. You'd almost have the opposite view by reading the draft history curriculum. In the 84 pages there's barely a positive thing said about our country. Moreover, it doesn't provide the rich underpinnings to teach students about how we became a successful liberal democracy. I want to see love of country embedded in the national history curriculum.*

ACARA was forced to revise its national curriculum proposal. On 4 February 2022, the *Daily Mail* Australia wrote the *history curriculum is set to undergo a massive overhaul with more focus on Western and Christian heritage, while reference to debates over the Anzac legend being 'contested' has been removed. References to Christianity have been restored to the Civics and Citizenship curriculum following widespread backlash over the term 'multi-faith'.* This was clearly a step in the right direction; however, it is state education department bureaucrats and individual teachers who decide what is taught in the classroom. James Ridley, who teaches history to students between years 9 and 12 at Hoppers Crossing Secondary College, said the *curriculum serves as a guide for teachers to use, but that individual teachers and school environments have greater influence on how history is taught. In Victoria we have got our own curriculum which is somewhat guided by the national curriculum, but really it doesn't have that much influence over our day-to-day teaching.*

oooOOOooo

Sometimes the absurdity of educational wokeness is laughable. The Ainslie Primary School (ACT) newsletter message to parents was one of a grovelling political correctness centred on the school canteen. *We acknowledge that our beloved canteen is operated on land traditionally nurtured by the Ngunnawal people. We bow to their superior knowledge of sustaining the land that sustains our life and recognise that sovereignty of this land was never ceded.* Should all school canteens and the 'traditionally nurtured' land upon which they are built be similarly cleansed of racist occupation and European defilement? An inner-city kindergarten located within sight of the Sydney Harbour Bridge became national news, when a group of 4-year-olds apparently penned a letter to then New South Wales Premier Gladys Berejiklian, demanding that the Aboriginal flag be flown from the bridge next to the Australian flag. The premier bowed to the 4-year-olds woke demand and both flags fly opposite one another.

Nobody believes 4-year-olds write sophisticated letters or that schoolkids go on strike and march in the street on schooldays for climate change and anti-racism, without the express approval and organisational assistance of activist schoolteachers. For educational authorities to insist that students come up with these politicised ideas on their own is insulting and untrue. Student attendance is high at these rallies because it is a day off school and exciting. Not surprisingly, when student strikes were called on weekends or holidays, they were poorly attended and dismal publicity failures. Why wouldn't savvy schoolkids take advantage of a teacher-sanctioned 'get out of the classroom' invitation?

So pervasive has the postmodern curriculum become that every subject including English, science and mathematics, has a sustainability, Aboriginal and victimhood component. Aboriginal leader and former National President of the Labor Party (2006-7) now a member of the Liberal Party, Warren Mundine, protested the condescending virtue signalling and disruption of traditional subjects. *What is Indigenous physics? Physics is physics. I agree that we need to reassess the curriculum because we need real units that teach the subjects without this ridiculous insertion of culture, the idea that you have to have an Indigenous or Asian perspective, to be frank, is silly. The sciences and maths should be taught properly. I want to see Australian kids learning about Indigenous kinship systems, not paying lip service to Indigenous culture while learning addition and subtraction. We've got Aboriginal doctors, Aboriginal lawyers and Aboriginal engineers, we've got all these incredible people and yet academia in the schooling system is telling* (Aboriginal kids) *that they are victims and no matter what they do in life they'll continue to be victims. It's craziness!*

Even more preposterous from an Aussie curriculum point of view, was a ludicrous statement from a group calling itself 'The Australian Indigenous Astronomy Website'. *Indigenous Astronomy is the first astronomy* — *the astronomy that existed before the Babylonians, Greeks, the Renaissance and the Enlightenment. We are happy to announce that the new national curriculum incorporating Indigenous astronomical knowledge, is now available for teachers and educators via the University of Melbourne Indigenous Education web portal. The 14 Units are aimed at Years 5 and 8, and show how Indigenous astronomy can be incorporated into the seven learning areas of science, mathematics, the arts, English, technologies, humanities and health.* This is imaginative Indigenous folklore of the absurd Bruce Pascoe kind and not fact-based astronomy. How does so called Indigenous astronomy rate a place in the Aussie curriculum as a genuine science? Let alone as a valid curriculum topic spread across multiple subject areas?

In a series of teacher resource books aimed at propagandising young children, the Primary English Teaching Association of Australia (PETAA) in 2021 published and promoted a book titled *Teaching the language of climate change science* by Julie Hayes and Bronwyn Parkin. Through their teachers, students are encouraged to engage with the school principal in letter writing and make Greta Thunberg a role model to be emulated. The authors suggest that *an earth-focused school or class 'anthem'* (be sung) *at assemblies.* (This) *is a great way to build emotional attachment to the planet.* They even supply clichéd lyrics for occasion.

> *Earth is getting warmer, oceans rising higher. Storms are growing stronger, floods and fire. We know about the dangers, know there must be changes. The future is in our hands.*

Author Tony Thomas slams the teaching resource book as climate change nonsense *oriented towards children becoming activists. The book urges teachers to coax kids to give money to the Polar Bear Institute in North America which is actually just an activist group and elsewhere they encourage kids to give money to international green groups. Since when are teachers allowed to tell kids to empty their pockets for the teachers' pet causes?*

In 2021 the Bill Gates Foundation funded a learning toolkit called 'A Pathway to Equitable Maths Instruction for Grades 6-8' distributed to schools, declaring that problem solving in mathematics is a 'white supremist' undertaking. Finding a logical solution using maths formulae and *focusing on the 'right answer' to math equations is an example of white supremacy.* Classroom teachers were directed to *review all the ways that word problems and context show up in the curriculum.* A core belief of the toolkit is that students of colour interpret and use math differently than white students. If you teach students of colour the 'right' way to do math you are reinforcing white supremacy culture.

oooOOOooo

The Aussie school curriculum is overcrowded with an embarrassment of frivolous subjects that have no academic relevance whatsoever. Two of the most preposterous focus on the teaching of puppetry and circus skills. In Victoria the Little Devil's Circus advertises: *We've spent the last decade adding a pinch of magic to curriculums across Melbourne. Our programs not only bring a huge dose of fun to your school, they improve physical health, increase feelings of resilience and coping. With a focus on teaching perseverance, building confidence and self-esteem, they are an excellent component of your school's wellbeing program.*

The Melbourne Arts Centre offers schools Puppetmaster Workshops at

$500 a session. Learning areas are stated to be: *critical and creative thinking, learning about sustainability, mathematics and geometry.* Puppetry might be an entertaining and enjoyable experience for young school kids. But what has critical and creative thinking, sustainability, mathematics and geometry got to do with puppets?

During the Coronavirus lockdown a regime of computer-based home learning allowed parents to see for themselves how their children were being indoctrinated and brainwashed by race and gender obsessed teachers. For many it was a unique eye-opening look behind the curriculum curtain. A troubled parent complained to the New South Wales Education Department regarding his 13-year-old son's computer-transmitted English lesson. *The first question might have come from a course on identity politics. It asks students to define and give examples of social inequality, racism, segregation, ghettos, discrimination, civil rights, slavery. The second question involved researching the victimhood of African Americans in the United States. Students are asked to research slavery, the civil rights movement, the Ku Klux Klan, Rosa Parks, the freedom rides, and the Black Lives Matter movement. Not one question was directed at literature, texts, poetry, or songs. I don't see how researching Rosa Parks or the racism of the Ku Klux Klan helps children understand poetic techniques or rhetorical devices. The questions do not seek to elicit such information. Neither do they engage with Australian culture.*

Moira Deeming, a high school English teacher with 10 years classroom teaching experience, wrote an online article for the Institute of Public Affairs in December 2019 titled 'Principles over Principals'. *In my fifth year of teaching, I had had enough of teaching the likes of Shrek and Percy Jackson and The Lightning Thief in English. I was sick of my students putting themselves down and wanted them to be able to say they had read a 'classic', understood it and perhaps even liked it! So, I decided to try and get John Steinbeck's The Pearl onto the year 8 curriculum. I badgered my principal relentlessly for an entire semester until, finally, he capitulated. My students and I read every word of The Pearl together. They argued and eventually became silent. They had begun to grasp what makes a 'classic', classic. At the end of that year, my colleagues complained about the lexical density of our curriculum and successfully replaced The Pearl with a graphic novel, and replaced the major writing assignment with a 'drawing' one.*

Melbourne tutor Dr Mark Lopez in his book *School Sucks: A Report on the State of Education in the Politically Correct Era* Connor Court (2020) points out that English text selection is no longer made on great literature criteria, but on what furthers the leftist political agenda. *It seems it was not enough for the Victorian Curriculum and Assessment Authority (VCAA), and its text selection advisory panel, for almost all of the texts on the prescribed list for Year 12 English to be by left-wing authors, or to reflect left-wing perspectives, or to promote left-wing values, or to make left-wing arguments in favour of left-wing positions on issues drawn from left-wing agendas. They decided it was time for text selection to be by politically correct quotas.*

Politically correct text selection, Dr Lopez argues, *is not about choosing historically significant, quality literature regardless of race or ethnicity; it's about choosing texts on the basis of race and ethnicity. Texts should be chosen for educational reasons, because of their literary merit, historical significance, and their cultural and aesthetic value. Choosing texts by politically correct quotas is wrong. It is representative of an education establishment that has forgotten its proper role.*

More broadly, Dr Lopez condemned the revised Aussie curriculum as *an updated version of what was already securely in place. The Australian curriculum severely limits the study of what would broadly constitute western civilisation. Instead, it deliberately favours the study of Aborigines, Asia and environmentalism wherever this is conceivably possible. The Australian curriculum reflects these ideological priorities, which are tactfully and deceitfully presented as educational priorities. Not only does the Australian curriculum represent a scandalous waste of public resources, it is a cruel injustice inflicted on the young. An education system should be widening the scope of inquiry, debate and discussion. Instead, the politically correct agenda is prioritised, promoted, celebrated and legitimised, while other beliefs are ignored, marginalised, disparaged or denigrated.*

In September 2021 Raymond Burns, a senior high schoolteacher, wrote in *Quadrant* Magazine *with the recent release of the draft revisions to the Australian curriculum, there was an opportunity for governments to address the decline in standards. In truth, the changes are not an attempt to address past failures but a doubling down on the quixotic aims of 'progressive' educators achieving ecological sustainability, indigenising the curriculum and dismantling systems of 'social domination'. At one school where I worked, the set* (English) *text for Year 7 was The Lorax by Doctor Seuss, a picture book recommended for children between five and eight years of age. To say that this book would not develop the reading skills of a twelve-year-old is, of course, an understatement, but it was selected for its focus on 'environmental issues', one of the ideological commitments of 'critical' educators.*

oooOOOooo

Like the communists and nazis before them, the intention of woke globalists is to indoctrinate and control the young. When speaking of the coming communist utopia, Vladimir Lenin stressed the importance of brainwashing children. *Give me just one generation of youth, and I'll transform the whole world.* When a group of troubled German parents approached Adolf Hitler voicing concern about many of his fascist policies. Hitler replied, *'Do you think I care what you think? We have your children; that's all that matters!'* Karl Marx spoke more broadly concerning totalitarian control. *Keep people from their history and they are easily controlled.* The strategy of today's woke tyranny is to indoctrinate kids, rewrite history, instil self-loathing in wavering adults and everything else will follow. *We have your children; that's all that matters!*

We are losing our freedoms and young people are being fed an educational pigswill of woke inventions, political distortions and fake history. Schools today are no more than left-wing programming centres churning out juvenile social justice warriors. Parents need to pay close attention to what is being taught in the classroom. They need to become informed, hands on and vocal at school meetings and other school functions; to take the initiative against woke politicians, teachers and education department bureaucrats promoting a Socialist/Green/ Woke agenda designed to usurp traditional values and sow discontent. Radicals label those who respect tradition and fact-based education right-wing extremists. In America heated parental debate occurs at the school board meeting level. Parental involvement in Australia is more nebulous in nature but needs to happen if education is to be delivered from wokeness and mediocrity.

Writing in the *Western Australian* in 2021, Senator Matt O'Sullivan condemned wokeness in the classroom. *What is the core purpose of our education system? We should be able to sum it up in one line — to prepare kids to lead a good and productive life as contributors to our great Australian community. How is teaching our kids radical identity politics, critical race theory, climate politics, and all the usual attacks on western civilisation going to achieve that? How is cancelling from our classrooms any references to Christianity or freedom of speech, association, and religion going to prepare Australian children to think for themselves or to contribute to our society? It's time to get back to basics and arrest our national education decline, not confine our kids to a lifetime of grievance and social activism.*

Greek philosopher Aristotle championed wisdom, virtue and reason not emotion as the measure of all things. Senator Amanda Stoker writes *when politicians offer to solve problems that are properly the domain of individuals and families, they slowly erode freedom of choice and deprive individuals of the satisfaction that comes from personal accomplishment.* The Roman philosopher Epictetus said choice is the only genuine freedom we have because it cannot be taken away. *What really frightens and dismays us is not external events themselves, but the way in which we think about them. It is not things that disturb us, but our interpretation of their significance.* Virtue signalling and wokeness is false interpretation and a denial of choice when reason and choice are our greatest freedoms.

Those of us who write and teach Australian history outside the politically correct bubble of Socialist/Green/Woke revisionism, want nothing more outrageous than a return to reasoned and dispassionate debate. A return to the primacy of documents, factual evidence and critical thinking. Critical thinking outside the box of woke ideology and indoctrinating PC analysis. To be allowed a valid voice in narrating the nation's history, honestly from all points of view, without being subject to academic bullying and social media campaigns orchestrated against legitimate and contrary points of view. We cannot allow the radical left to rewrite Australian history and control the national narrative. We cannot allow our young people to be boondoggled by woke deceit and make believe. If we do, then truth and history will disappear, replaced with nonsense and brainwashed children.

14

Safe Schools, Gender Issues, Woke and Cancel Culture

TV shows are all woke! There is nowhere you can go in the culture anymore movies, television, music where you're not being lectured to or being accused of something. It's completely out of control. People are sick of it! We just want to watch a television show without being preached to.

Scott Baio

Only a small minority (3% or 750,000) of Australia's population of 24.99 million in 2018 claim they are homosexual. The majority of the population (97% or 24,250,000) considers themselves to be heterosexual. Birth records clearly show that 99.9% of Australian births are biologically male and female. Yet a major component of the Australian school curriculum concentrates young minds on age-inappropriate sexuality and gender issues. Many parents worry about a school curriculum that demeans traditional values and presents gender as a social construct rather than a biological certainty. Children are no longer allowed to discover their place in the world, without a politically correct school syllabus stressing inclusiveness, gender and diversity, with woke teachers in every subject guiding their every exploratory step through a scandalous process of classroom indoctrination and psychological confusion.

The federal government-funded Safe Schools Program, under the cover of an anti-bullying agenda devised in university faculties, promotes gender diversity and places undue emphasis on the brainwashing of kindergarten, primary and secondary schoolchildren with gay, lesbian and transgender ideas. Latrobe University academic Roz Ward, the Safe Schools Coalition co-founder, a veteran gay activist and revolutionary Marxist, was suspended in June 2016 from the university's Australian Research Centre in Sex, Health and Society, for advocating getting rid of the 'racist' Australian flag and replacing it with the communist red flag. In July 2020, she proudly tweeted: *Cultural Marxists* (are) *infiltrating the education system and generally causing all the right kinds of trouble.* Ward was forthright in proclaiming *the program is about promoting sexual and gender diversity not about stamping out bullying.*

The Safe Schools Program is the Trojan Horse of identity and sexual politics transposed to an education setting. Cross-dressing, transgender propaganda, biological boys participating in girls' sports and gender free toilets which worry many parents with young children are endorsed and encouraged in every classroom by Safe Schools programming. On the education.vic.gov.au website under the title 'LGBTIQ+ Student Support' it is stated *the use of toilets, showers and change rooms that meet the needs of the student should be based on the student's gender identity and whichever facilities they will feel most comfortable using.*

In June 2021, a 14-year-old American eighth-grade student Jolene Grover protested before the Loudoun County School Board in the US state of Virginia against the board's proposal to allow transgender males to use girls' toilets and changerooms. *Calling girls bigots because they don't want to use the toilet in a stall next to a boy or get undressed next to a boy is cruel and wrong. It is embarrassing enough for a girl to change a* (sanitary) *pad knowing all the other girls can hear the crinkle of the packaging. Telling her that she must be okay doing it in the presence of boys because their preferred pronouns are she/her. How evil can you be?* One could ask why not retain male and female toilets for the majority of students so they can feel comfortable, and make other toilet arrangements for the minority who claim a gender difference? Where is the fairness and equity in making everybody feel uncomfortable?

Clearly that would not be PC inclusive in a woke school system, where boys are told 'it's OK to wear a dress' and to display female characteristics. Where heterosexuality is downplayed as masculine, toxic and not an expression of normality. Where sexual orientation is taught and celebrated as a changeable social construct to kindergarten kids. Where transitioned men identifying as women, such as New Zealand transgender weightlifter Laurel Hubbard formerly competing in the men's competition, are allowed to unfairly participate in women's sports. In America in December 2021, the unfair physical advantage transgender college men possess in women's swimming was clearly demonstrated. When *University of Pennsylvania trans swimmer Lia Thomas* (aka William Thomas previously competing as a male swimmer) *eviscerated her competition in Akron, Ohio, after finishing 38 seconds ahead of her teammate in the 1,650 yard freestyle event. She also left rivals in the dust in the 500 yard freestyle race by touching the wall 14 seconds ahead of her closest competitor.* Women competitors were frustrated and left in tears by the woke pretence of a biologically born male smashing women's college records and blitzing the field.

Ordinary people around the world regard the transgender takeover of women's sport as scandalously wrong. A national poll conducted by Binary Australia in December 2021, revealed that 67% of Australians supported banning transgender athletes from participating in women's sports. Binary Australia Director Kirralie Smith said *almost three quarters (75%) of all people surveyed want legal protections for their mothers, daughters, sisters and female friends in sport. We have separate sporting categories for males and females because there are scientific, evidenced-based differences between men and women. Males are faster, or stronger, than the top females. Whether it is athletics, swimming, rowing or weightlifting, males outperform females every time.*

Men identifying as women are housed in Australian women's prisons. According to the Women's Forum Australia, *experts estimate there are up to 400 trans and gender-diverse people in prison cells around Australia right now* (2020). *This unacceptably exposes women in those prisons to increased risk of harm from inmates who are biologically male.* Women prisoners have been sexually abused and some raped by predatory men who say they are women. In light of all this controversy, students are expected to accept homosexuality as normal and biologically natural. *The Left insists* wrote an offended parent *that we respect 'the Science' — except when it comes to the Science of Biology!*

The previously science based medical profession has given into the wokeness of social construct gender classification. On the 16 June 2021, Dr Sandra Adamson Fryhofer of the American Medical Association (AMA) wrote *designating sex on birth certificates as male or female, perpetuates a view that sex designation is permanent and fails to recognize the medical spectrum of gender identity. This type of categorization system risks stifling an individual's self-expression and self-identification and contributes to marginalization and minoritization.* In May 2020, the Victorian Government made it possible for Victorians to *change the gender on their birth certificate to female, male or another description* without producing a gender affirmation document or transition surgery. In other words, gender classification was flexible based entirely on feeling and emotion.

Safe Schools programming does a grave disservice to children and the genuine purpose of education. Schools are teaching fear and discontent to the happiest people, Kids. We need to establish schools based on teaching students how to think, not what to think. When schools become places of indoctrination, it's doubly harmful. The student not only gets brainwashed, but they also fail to learn real skills on how to think for themselves, how to engage in civil discourse. Children are sexualised in the media to an obscene extent these days. They are frightened by climate change and impending extinction. They should be allowed to be carefree children, without pressure exerted to conform to gender or any other woke expectation from their classroom teacher.

oooOOOooo

The Victorian Department of Education and Early Childhood Development's Handbook 'Supporting Sexual Diversity in Schools' (2008) states *an inclusive approach to school policy is standard across all Victorian Government schools. A commitment to support same-sex attracted young people is integral to this inclusiveness and should be reflected in a school's policies and practices. This includes codes of conduct, curriculum, anti-bullying and sexual harassment policies, student wellbeing procedures, teaching and learning practices, organisation and ethos.* Inclusiveness and diversity in every aspect of the schooling experience goes way beyond the Safe Schools agenda and purview of traditional education.

In the September 2020 Victorian Public Service language guide for gender diversity, the Victorian Government expressed its virtue signalling predilection for inclusive language usage nullifying established language conventions. Teachers are public servants and are required to follow the diversity rules handed down by the Education Department. Why should sexual diversity, gender identity and the tyranny of woke language be an issue for schools at all?

The LGBTIQ+ inclusive language guide is for Victorian Public Sector (VPS) employees. It explains how to use language respectfully and inclusively when working with and referring to LGBTIQ+ people. Don't assume that everyone is heterosexual (straight), or that this is the norm. Avoid using language such as 'wife' or 'husband' that assumes all relationships are heterosexual. Words and phrases such as 'partner', 'parents', 'relationship', 'in a relationship' are examples of LGBTIQ+ inclusive language. Pronouns are one way people refer to each other and themselves. If you're unsure what someone's pronoun is, you can ask them respectfully, and preferably privately. Use a question like 'Can I ask what pronoun you use?' Do not ask 'What pronoun do you prefer?' You can support inclusive policies and practices by getting LGBTIQ+ awareness or inclusion training for your workplace.

An alphabet soup of gender categories numbering in excess of 50+ is truly astonishing to many Australians. Even within the homosexual community, there is confusion around many of these gender classifications. Transgender identity is particularly obfuscating and bewildering. Aussie author and poet Eugene Alexander Donnini writes *transgenderism is defined by a 'spectrum' of feelings-based gender identities between the two binary sexes, under the LGBTQIAPP+ label, short for lesbian, gay, bisexual, transgender, queer, intersex, asexual, aromantic, pansexual, polysexual. Transgender identities can then be represented by an array of corresponding pronouns such as ze, hir, hirs, hirself.*

The enforcement of plural gender pronouns such as 'They' and 'Them'

'It' and 'Its' as personal identity markers simply makes no sense and degrades language to meaningless gibberish. Self-identification should be a private not a public matter that impacts the accepted meaning of words. I might personally self-identify as a 'Penguin' or a 'Table'. Absurdly, to dispute or deny my self-identify marker can be construed as offensive and labelled a hate crime which brings legal penalty. Thankfully, there are those in positions of power unwilling to condone such gender pronoun bullying.

In September 2020, NSW public servant Joann Wilkie sent a memo to Treasury Department staff focussed on explaining the wokeness of personal language. *Things like adding a pronoun preference to your signature block. And not assuming when you're talking to a colleague that they are heterosexual/cisgendered/endosex, so use 'partner' rather than 'wife' or 'husband' and use an introduction like 'welcome folks' rather than 'hi guys'.* Wilkie's boss, then Treasurer Dominic Perrottet, told the media *I'll be making sure people in Treasury are free to call their spouse whatever they like. 'Wife', 'husband', 'boyfriend', 'girlfriend', 'honey', 'babe', whatever. We can't have people get rid of their own identities for other people's inclusion. We won't have Father's Day, if we keep going down this path! We've got to get real here!* Most Aussies have zero understanding of what the terms 'cisgendered 'or 'endosex' actually mean. Why should they face legal penalty for refusing to publicly buy into a jumbled transgender word game?

Australia's Defence Minister Peter Dutton was highly critical of identity politics and wokeness being foisted on the Australian military. *Quasi-political agendas are completely irrelevant in the Australian Defence Force. When you're telling people that you can't use language like 'husband' or 'wife' or you're asking people for pronouns, I'm sorry, it doesn't have a place in the modern defence force. We don't discriminate against people, I don't care about people's sexual orientation, their skin colour, their race, their religion, it's completely irrelevant. We treat everybody the same. We have a professional defence force and that's the focus.*

oooOOOooo

Gender Dysphoria is taught in schools and kindergartens as an explorable natural condition. A transgender view of the world is imposed on young school kids from an early age, who are told they can choose to be either a boy or a girl. The examining of sexual identity arises as a social and psychological issue sustained and promoted by ideas of sexual diversity. The number of those said to be 'uncomfortable in their body' or who identify as a member of the opposite sex is statistically small and, in many cases, no more than a temporary condition. *According to Black's Medical Dictionary, gender dysphoria occurs in one in 30,000 male births and one in 100,000 female births.* In overseas studies that is 0.005% of males and 0.002% of females. Unfortunately, there are no similar reliable statistics for Australia.

The Mayo Clinic in Rochester, New York, describes *gender dysphoria as the feeling of discomfort or distress that might occur in people whose gender identity differs from their sex assigned at birth.* In 2018, Assistant Professor Lisa Littman at the Brown University School of Public Health, in Providence, Rhode Island, published an article titled 'Rapid-Onset of Gender Dysphoria in Adolescents and Young Adults'. It was an influential article that pointed out how gender dysphoria follows a clear path of peer group pressure and social contagion. *It's hard not to notice when a condition* (gender dysphoria) *that was thought to be incredibly rare starts to happen in clusters of people who know each other. Parents were describing a very unusual pattern of transgender-identification, where multiple friends and even entire friend*(ship) *groups became transgender-identified at the same time. I would have been remiss had I not considered social contagion and peer influences as potential factors. Social contagion simply means that behaviours and attitudes can spread through* (populations and) *social networks.*

Social contagion as a fashionable notion among schoolgirls is estimated to be as high as 15% in some Aussie classrooms. Save Women's Sport Australasia co-founder Katherine Deves sees the transgender social contagion problem in schools and women's sports as escalating. *We know that teenage girls are particularly susceptible to social contagion. We are getting reports that up to 15% of girls' classes are identifying as trans at particular schools. It really is the trendy movement to hop upon. Everyone wants to be seen as equally developing and inclusive, but know nobody is stopping to think what that actually means. When we include men and boys in women's sports, women and girls get excluded.*

The gender dysphoria mindset brings on emotional anxiety, restlessness, depression and is a source of personality disorder. Severe gender confusion results for some children, with one set of parents *suddenly receiving a note from their 14-year-old daughter claiming she is trans and wanting to be called a new name.* The girl was transferred by her concerned parents to a school not participating in the Safe Schools Program, and they reported within weeks that *she is largely over the confusion now.* A UK private school principal dealing with several girls claiming to be boys, saw their disruptive behaviour as no more than teenage mucking up and refused to be drawn into their adolescent game. The problem brought on by social and peer group contagion soon disappeared and to the principal's relief was heard from no more.

The height of gender fluidity absurdity was reached in 2017, when the New South Wales Education Department reported on a four-year-old kindergarten child who had identified as transgender. Clearly, it was the kindergarten teacher and not the child who came up with this idea. Classroom teachers are urged by the Safe Schools Program to propagandise their students. They are instructed in teacher training sessions to stress sexual diversity and minority inclusion. *Whatever the subject, try to work out ways to integrate gender diversity and sexual diversity into the curriculum.*

New South Wales primary school students are told by activist classroom teachers' *gender is the way you feel on the inside* not physical biology. One Nation politician Mark Latham deplores the fact that *some teachers think the classroom is a place for political indoctrination instead of education. There's a sickness in our education system where adult teachers think the name of the game is to push their politics, their world view, their ideology upon little kids. I say to those teachers, stick to the basics of education.*

High schoolteacher Moira Deeming rejects Victoria's Safe Schools Program, which she says teaches *incredibly inappropriate erotic sex education* and gender confusion to children. *They're destroying the safe boundaries between teachers and students. There's a survey that can be given to children so that they can tick which ones* (sexual preferences) *they would be comfortable with. Ordinary sex education respects the privacy of students, it does not call upon them to divulge their personal sexual preferences in front of the class. As a teacher I feel that's illegal, that's sexual harassment. You wouldn't be allowed to ask those questions in a staff room. Why are children being disrespected like this?*

In addition to encouraging the sexualising of young children to accommodate transgender politics. The State Government of Victoria enacted legislation to usurp the rights of parents and those concerned with gender transition issues. Parents were effectively denied a voice in a life changing decision involving their children. On 4 February 2021, the Victorian Government passed into law the controversial 'Change or Suppression (Conversion) Practices Prohibition Bill'. Under its stringent legal provisions, a parent, priest, doctor or psychiatrist can be fined and gaoled for giving counselling advice to a gender confused person. In other words, offering sensible therapeutic, parental concern and religious alternatives to hormones and transition surgery was deemed to be suppression.

Premier Dan Andrews wrote on his official website. *The laws empower the Victorian Equal Opportunity and Human Rights Commission (VEOHRC) to consider and respond to reports of change or suppression practices from any person, as well as launch investigations where there is evidence of serious or systemic change or suppression practices.* This of course was a gross overstatement and misrepresentation of the 'conversion' situation today. The sting in the law's rhetoric was that it allowed for no discussion whatsoever by parents or professionals with a gender confused person and criminalised any attempt to do so.

In furtherance of the transgender cause which ultimately leads to hormone blockers and life changing gender transition surgery, Sydney University and the Sydney University of Technology came up with an online study module for secondary and tertiary students designed to help them *understand sexual consent*. Anything that did not fit the gender narrative of homosexual relationships was censured. *Through interactive activities and scenarios, you will be stepped through* (a carefully scripted program). *You will only be able to view your results, if you have completed the four sections and received 100% in the quiz at the end. If you fail to do this, you will receive a consent matters sanction and will not be able to view your results.*

Ten bedrooms are visited and a mouse click is required to hear and read explicit details of sexual activity taking place in each. A troubled parent wrote *seven of the ten examples involve same sex couples. A concerned academic, a Christian, showed* (the study module to) *their 18-year-old daughter who after watching a part of the presentation commented. 'This is misrepresenting young people as if we are all gay, take drugs, get drunk and go around having sex'.*

oooOOOooo

During the 1920s Italian Marxist Antonio Gramsci put forward the abstract concept of *Cultural Hegemony* to explain the social control structures of society. Gramsci's revolutionary focused idea was to claim *whoever controls society's institutions controls society*. In 1967 influenced by Gramsci's insurrectionist notion of undermining the social and cultural edifice of capitalist society from within. Rudi Dutschke, leader of the German student movement, coined the activist slogan *Long March through the Institutions to describe his strategy for establishing the conditions for revolution: subverting society by infiltrating institutions such as the professions*. Today we call this infiltration and the sinister Marxist assault on western society the Socialist/Green/Woke revolution. The Long March was a political reference to the Chinese Communist army's year long march across China (16 October 1934–22 October 1935), which resulted in Mao Zedong becoming the undisputed leader of the Chinese Communist Party.

On 26 December 2021, former ABC Chairman Maurice Newman wrote in the *Daily Mail the extent of Marxist infiltration in western institutions over the last 60 years has left virtually none of them immune. The family is the one institution to hold out against the Marxist infiltration of the west but even that is under threat. The family is under threat, marriage of course is under threat. What we're seeing with the promotion of promiscuity and essentially the destruction of the values which* (have) *served us so well for so many generations —* (that they are) *now cast aside. Replaced by nothing other than the notion that what we have is evil. There is not one example of a* (Marxist) *utopia* (anywhere in the world) *where* (people) *are all better off. We don't value things until we lose them.*

The doomsday climate cult, divisive identity politics, toxic critical race theory, Black Lives Matter and Extinction Rebellion combine together with politically correct wokeness under the activist trope of 'Intersectionality' to forge the globalist agenda. Intersectionality is defined as *the interconnected nature of social categorizations such as race, class, and gender as they apply to a given individual or group, and is regarded as creating overlapping and interdependent systems of discrimination or disadvantage.* While the Marxist attack on faith, family and culture continue to drive the global socialist worldview. The older Marxist concepts of economics and class have been replaced by an all-encompassing identity politics definition of race and Intersectionality.

Intersectionality is the preferred woke path to power and control through political and cultural manipulation of a contrived sense of victimhood. Under its Marxist banner capitalism is to be overturned, society transformed and everything acknowledged as racist, the fault of white colonialists and white supremacists, and must therefore be constantly apologised for by white people. The separation of church and state, the glory of western civilisation, is slated to disappear. The nation state is to be abolished, replaced by open borders and a globalist world government. Whiteness, western civilisation and Christianity are to be usurped, undermined and destroyed as a new socialist world order takes shape.

Since the end of the second world war an existential crisis facing western civilisation and Christianity has accelerated to the point of impending breakdown. Moral decay within the centuries old fabric of western society is everywhere evident in thought, word and deed. The taken for granted social and religious certainties of the past no longer hold sway. Author Rod Dreher writes of global nihilism and widespread spiritual malaise. *We in the west are in the worst spiritual and social crisis since the collapse of the Roman empire. We don't see this collapse clearly, because it is hidden by our wealth. But make no mistake: the fundamental pillars of western civilisation are crumbling, none more consequentially than the Church. It is a crisis of meaning. In the postmodern west, we have arrived at a place where many people no longer believe that meaning exists at all, and that we can know it. It is a crisis of truth. We have lost the ability to determine what is true or false. We can no longer agree on a narrative that allows us to reason together. It is a crisis of fragmentation. In our time, people have lost* a sense of unity and purpose. We no longer feel that we are part of a wider community.

In a review of Douglas Murray's insightful book, *The Madness of Crowds: Gender, Race and Identity* Bloomsbury Publishing (2019), Dr Paul Morrissey, President of the Liberal Arts Institute at Campion Catholic College (NSW), applauds the British author's astute analysis of militant wokeness on the march. *Anyone who has read Douglas Murray's brilliant book would not be surprised by the irrationality of our age. Murray lays out plainly and with numerous examples, the toxicity of identity politics and its deleterious effects on rational discourse. He emphasises how human rights campaigns of equality have given birth to a movement that does not want to limit itself to equality: minorities are not just equal, they are better. This identity movement places limited value on objective truth, preferring to see everything through a lens of power. The only truth is the hierarchical pyramid that needs inversing. Everything else is oppression.*

Douglas Murray describes woke culture as the new religion. *This basically is a new metaphysics, a new religion. At the point when things have never been* (materially) *better, people behave as if they are at the barricades. They want to demonstrate their virtue and by doing so they need to find enemies. In societies like Australia where* (human) *rights issues have never been better, they are regularly portrayed as if they have never been worse. The younger generation are growing up in an incredibly perilous environment, where if they 'wrong think' or 'wrong speak' once, they can have their career and life destroyed forever. We are living through a postmodern era in which the grand narratives of religion and political ideology have collapsed. In their place has emerged a crusading desire to right perceived wrongs and a weaponization of identity, both accelerated by the new forms of social and news media. Narrow sets of interests now dominate the agenda as society becomes more and more tribal.* Murray calls for a return to *free speech, shared common values and sanity in an age of mass hysteria.*

oooOOOooo

The woke madness currently sweeping the western world has the same intensity of emotion and self-righteousness, as medieval religious fanaticism exhibited during the bubonic plague pandemic (1346-53) known as the 'Black Death'. The only difference is that wokeness operates on a much broader political, social and cultural platform than medieval Christianity. The virtue signalling, the mob solidarity and passionate extremism of the cause remains the same, with Extinction Rebellion activists gluing themselves to road surfaces rather than flagellating their bodies.

US mathematician and cultural critic, James Lindsay, describes *wokeness as a fusion of the critical school of Marxism, which is a form of identity politics, and radical activism that has a very particular worldview that separates the world into liberationists verses oppressors and oppressed verses oppressors. It has all of the conflict theory with no ability to agree or understand one another and then it takes on the postmodern understanding of truth just being politics by other means, which removes all of the brakes standing up against it.*

Wokeness proclaims God is dead, traditional religion is irrelevant and socialism compounded by contradiction and deceit, is the way forward for virtue signalling government and mob intolerance to control people's lives. Gender, race and identity in all their repressive victimhood expressions form the doctrinal canon of religious wokeness. In the new order, admission of white guilt is paramount for public contrition. There is however no redemption only guilt-ridden confession. Acts of atonement include white people 'taking the knee', confessing 'racist sin' and performing 'penance for being white'. White privilege is the woke religion's equivalent of original sin. The virtuous feel vindicated in their righteous cultist behaviour, while non-believers are damned and cancelled for their scandalous disbelief. The radical political fervour and cultural extremism of woke believers are the new fascism: convinced, uncompromising and dangerous.

Woke means to constantly obsess about race, gender, push the fear of climate catastrophe and censor and cancel those who don't measure up to woke orthodoxy. Emotive language such as 'Climate Denier', 'Homophobe' or 'Islamophobe' is used to smear a speaker before the facts are even discussed. When woke cultists and sadly government bureaucrats and politicians are asked to define a woman, the request is met with silence and the argument becomes hostile and incoherent. To be called a 'Racist' for each and every woke offence is so common these days that it no longer signifies anything other than a hateful term of cancel culture abuse. Everything traditional and culturally mainstream is by twisted woke definition considered racist and evil.

The woke cancel those who disagree with them in the name of diversity and inclusion, which of course is an act of standardisation and exclusion. Woke people don't discuss or consider issues factually or objectively. They shout down and ridicule everybody with hatred and vengeance. Everything is about 'micro-aggressions', 'trigger-warnings' 'white privilege' and 'the cult of virtue'. They bend and control the narrative, appeal to bogus science and when called out never admit to being wrong. The woke exhibit a fanaticism and intolerance that is astonishing in its ignorance and personal sense of moral superiority. Words and concepts change meaning in their hands and become weapons to be used in a vitriolic way to defeat the 'enemy'. To be woke is to be arrogantly self-assured and perpetually offended by just about everything.

Beverley McArthur, Liberal Member of Parliament for Western Victoria wrote in the *Spectator* on 6 May 2021. *There is a sense that everyday life has become a visit to the cinema. We suspend our disbelief as the daily offering of 'crazy' emerges from the left in the form of new ways or words. New rights and wrongs. Our instinct is to consider them a farce. The absurdities are firing in like spears from multiple angles. Educators are critically aware of their ability to influence young minds. In a New South Wales classroom, students professed their knowledge of social issues on posters emblazoned with slogans such as 'White lives matter too much'. To the woke, there is one way of thinking. One idea. One perspective. One right. One-way streets. One history. One future. Our bubbles of suspended disbelief are bursting to the crude reality that this is no longer a fiction. It is, indeed, a war of words in a world where western civilisation is the battleground frontier.*

The crude reality of wokeness is obvious to everybody. We have got to start using the PC words 'tolerance' and 'diversity' against the woke bullies. Tolerance means to permit another person's opinions without cancelling them. Diversity is more than woke prescriptions of identity politics, gender and skin colour. Fundamentally diversity of opinion and the tolerance to listen to contrary views is the bedrock of democracy. When tolerance and diversity are weaponised for cultural and political purposes, then free speech is curtailed and democracy disappears. Woke radicals seek absolute power and control over our lives and our children's lives. George Washington a founding father of American independence tells us *if freedom of speech is taken away, then dumb and silent we may be led, like sheep to the slaughter.* We need to stand up to woke oppression and say no more!

Bill Leak The Australian 25 April, 2014

A perennial problem for the blinkered socialist left is what it terms the culpable denial of white people. British writer and satirist Andrew Doyle dismisses Robin DiAngelo's 2018 book *White Fragility: Why It's So Hard for White People to Talk About Racism* as promoting critical race theory (dubbed 'crazy racist thinking' by its detractors) and inverse racism. *The basic thesis of the book is that all white people are racist, and if a white person denies that they are a racist, then they're suffering from what you call 'white fragility'. The book is absolutely terrible. It's a fraudulent form of academia full of speculation dressed up as fact.* (It) *talks about acknowledging your own complicity in white supremacy and activating something against it. It divides people up and enforces a kind of segregation.* In a regressive step, some American universities have introduced segregated black and white student accommodation.

On 4 December 2018, the University of Sydney hosted a public lecture by Robin DiAngelo, publicising the event as *Why does race seem to be the hardest word for white people?* The lecture was no more than a factually inaccurate, critical race theory assault on white people as evil oppressors and racist bullies. British journalist and political commentator, Brendan O'Neill, said of the critical race theory DiAngelo espouses: *Critical race theory is the notion that all white people are racist, that society is governed by white privilege and even white supremacy. This is an aggressive ideology which racializes everything. Racializes every person, encourages us to see everything in racial terms, encourages us to judge people by the colour of their skin rather than by their character. This is an incredibly backward, aggressive, destructive and divisive outlook. Everyone should be standing up and challenging the idea that all white people are racists.*

Critical race theory is a sinister doctrine teaching kids to hate each other and the country they live in. White kids are taught to hate their skin colour, flag and heritage. Coloured kids that they are better than whites, yet oppressed victims. There is nothing critical about critical race theory, it is an insidious and underhanded formula for brainwashing. Kids are the innocent classroom pawns of woke teachers, who do nothing to encourage critical thinking or to educationally enrich their students' lives. Some students become depressed and suicidal, robbed of all hope and a bright future.

The woke use the term 'equity' rather than the democratic idea of 'equality' as a means to holler down and silence those they disagree with. Equality means everybody is on the same footing regardless of wealth, skin colour or political affiliation. Equity is discriminatory and divides people into those deemed deserving of consideration and those who should be singled out for punishment. It is racist against white people described as unworthy privileged bigots, while it lumps together all other races as worthy and praiseworthy, victims of white supremacy. Equality of opportunity is considered to be of lesser importance than the equity of division. It should not be in schools — the damage being done to children is incalculable.

American journalist Christopher Rufo denounces critical race theory and its accompanying unconscious bias training as sinister and malignant. *Critical race theory is a neo-Marxist formulation, where white employees are denounced for their whiteness and are forced to write letters of apology. The Sandia National Laboratory, which designs America's nuclear arsenal, sent its employees on a three-day white male re-education camp* (that) *was restricted and segregated on the basis of race and sex. They were told that white male culture is analogous to the KKK, to MAGA hats, to mass killings and white supremacy. They were forced to deconstruct their own identity, their white male culture, denounce themselves publicly, and then at the end of the session to write letters of apology to women and people of colour for no greater reason than their inborn characteristics. Critical race theorists, the so called woke social justice warriors, are reducing people to a racial essence, either whiteness or blackness. They are creating a new racial hierarchy saying that people can be judged based on their group identity characteristic. In critical race theory training sessions and on the streets of American cities, they engage in targeted racial harassment.*

Aussie journalist Rowan Dean condemns critical race theory and unconscious bias training in Australian workplaces as totally unacceptable. *The idea that you're not in control of your own thoughts, that you have no actual rational judgement, that you are a creature of the colour of your skin, and that skin colour has predetermined prejudices and bigotry is sick, it's repulsive, and it's certainly dehumanising. It's insidious; it's verging on evil the way this unconscious bias nonsense has basically run through bureaucracies, the public service and corporations.* White fragility, critical race theory and unconscious bias training are insulting, offensive and complete fallacies.

oooOOOooo

The French philosopher Voltaire famously wrote *to find out who is ruling over you, find out who you are not allowed to criticize.* Politicised minorities behave like the fanatical inquisitors of old condemning everyone who does not share their rigidly held beliefs. It is not about engaging in open debate the presentation of indisputable facts or even logical argument. Nor is it about repentance or revealing truth. Public shaming and the crushing of one's opponent is the exacting goal — cancelling an opponent by denying them a speaking or writing platform. The other personified as inherently evil deserving of neither compassion nor consideration. A simplistic Marxist formula of oppressed and oppressor dominates activist thinking and behaviour. The prejudice and bigotry come from the woke fraternity — from those who preach tolerance, inclusion and diversity while engaged in slander, harassment and the suppression of free speech.

Peter Kurti from the Centre for Independent Studies describes *cancel culture as the idea that you sanction anything, any person, any institution, any product or image that is thought to cause harm to vulnerable people. The idea is to remove it completely. Once we impose a totalitarian clampdown on freedom of speech and freedom of discussion and debate, we're going to end up with a society where there is only one prevailing orthodoxy, and if you dissent from that orthodoxy, woe betide you!*

Senator James McGrath said of cancel culture ideology: *It takes away the essence of the individual, it dehumanises through subscribing to a person 'bad characteristics'. What the left do is they create gulags for words and gulags for thoughts. We are dehumanized and anything we believe in, or say or think, is locked away and you're not allowed to go there.*

Dr Kevin Donnelly of the Australian Catholic University (NSW) writes *the way language is being manipulated is cause for concern. Underpinning the cultural left's incessant drive to change the words and expressions we use, is its intention to radically reshape western societies like Australia according to its utopian image. Political correctness and its offspring cancel culture seek to enforce mindless group think and dominance by taking control of language and radically altering what words mean. The most effective way to enforce totalitarian control and to subjugate citizens is via language. As George Orwell argues 'if thought corrupts language, language can also corrupt thought'.* George Orwell also said *'if liberty means anything at all, it means the right to tell people what they do not want to hear'.* Suppress contrary views, compel the redefinition of words and concepts and the social, cultural and political world changes.

Common sense appears to have gone out of the window. Cancel culture operates in waves of hysteria and name calling, seeking new ways to instil mass obedience and spread fear throughout the community. There is always something else to be cancelled, reinvented and ostracised from woke society. Nothing is sacred or beyond the witch hunt reach of Twitter and Facebook social warrior trolls. There is no common ground where opinions matter and are respected. No even handed debate where impartial facts triumph over ideological fanaticism. We are all the poorer because of woke intolerance and self-indulgent feigned feelings of coercive offence.

oooOOOooo

Everything is deemed to be about racism, oppression and victimhood. When HBO Max removed the 1939 film classic Gone with the Wind from its service catalogue for 'romanticising slavery', Senator Mark Latham, angered by the censorship remarked. *The real bigotry comes from sneering inner-city cultural elites, who basically say we can't trust people in the suburbs. They are so stupid out there; we can't trust them to watch Gone with the Wind without falling in love with slavery!* Within a month due to public pressure, HBO Max reinstated the classic movie accompanied by a woke disclaimer falsely claiming the much-loved picture *denies the horrors of slavery.*

The British Broadcasting Commission (BBC) cravenly caved into cancel culture activism, by removing the much-loved performance of Rule, Britannia! and Land of Hope and Glory from the Last Night of the Proms concert program, *because they might offend some activists by their associations with colonialism and slavery.* The BBC was forced to reverse its hasty decision, when the British public voiced anger at the loss of the iconic songs depicting British national identity. The activist narrative of British colonialism and slavery concentrates only on the dark side of the story and neglects to reveal the whole picture.

Slavery was present in many past white and non-white societies and remains today a multiracial problem still in existence. The British were world leaders in the 19th century battle to combat human trafficking and the horrors of slavery. Jeremy Black, former Professor of History at the University of Exeter (UK) writes *the idea that slavery is simply a construction by westerners as a way in which people who are black are oppressed by people who are white is complete rubbish! The Royal Navy was to lose 17,000 seamen to disease, battle or accident in a lengthy commitment* (fighting against the slave trade) *off West Africa.*

Amazing Grace how sweet the sound that saved a wretch like me. I once was lost but now am found. Was blind but now I see.

The BBC song fiasco occurred in the same week as the British Library's Chief Librarian, Liz Jolley, told her staff racism is the creation of white people. *A racial 'state of emergency'* (has been declared) *so that changes to the library's displays could take place to 'decolonise' the British Library's collection.* Public opinion was again aroused and social media platforms carried denunciations condemning the library's foolishness.

Comedian Ricky Gervais, the master of cringe comedy, called out cancel culture for the cultural bullying and anti-democratic absurdity it is. *There's this new sort of fascism called wokeness, where people think they know what you can say and what you can't. Just because you're offended, it doesn't mean you're right. Everyone's allowed to call you an arsehole. Everyone's allowed to stop watching your stuff. Everyone's allowed to burn your DVDs. You shouldn't have to go to court for telling a joke that someone didn't like, and that's what we are getting dangerously close to today.*

John Cleese has said of the bossy agenda of woke activists to muzzle free speech: *If people can't control their own emotions, then they start trying to control other people's behaviour.* Rowan Atkinson in a passionate public address in 2012 defended the right of free speech. *The strongest weapon against hateful speech is not repression, it is more speech.* Sir Salman Rushdie refers to the *'outrage industry', self-appointed arbiters of the public good, encouraging media-stoked outrage. The problem with outlawing insult is that too many things can be interpreted as such. Criticism is easily construed as insult. Ridicule* (is) *easily construed as insult. Sarcasm, unfavourable comparison, merely stating an alternate point of view can be interpreted as insult. If we want a robust society, we need more robust dialogue, and that must include the right to insult or to offend. To be inoffensive is no freedom at all.*

In March 2017 the late Bill Leak, political satirist and cartoonist at the *Australian* newspaper, gave his view of political correctness, cancel culture and the derangement of the perpetually offended. *Political correctness is a poison that attacks the sense of humour. As the senses of humour of people suffering from PC atrophy their sensitivity to criticism becomes more and more acute until they get to the stage where everything offends them and they lose the ability to laugh, entirely. For people with chronic PC, feeling offended is about as good as it gets. A good cartoon gives them an excuse to parade their feelings of moral superiority in 140 characters or less, scrawled on the toilet door of social media where every other humourless halfwit who's seen the cartoon and felt offended too can join in the fun. And they do!*

Bill Leak The Australian 8 February, 2016

oooOOOooo

J K Rowling, renowned English author of the wildly popular Harry Potter books, became the Twitter target of cancel culture abuse for stating that people who menstruate referred to women not transgender men. The Twitter campaign against Rowling was ugly, aggressive and prolonged. In July 2020 a paid-for poster on Edinburgh's Waverley railway station, stating *I Love J K Rowling* was removed by station officials *after transphobic compliant.* In December 2021, J K Rowling received death threats and further woke abuse for tweeting: *War is Peace. Freedom is Slavery. Ignorance is Strength. The Penised Individual Who Raped You Is a Woman.* It was a tweet pointing out the absurdity plaguing common-sense language brought on by the PC words of Detective Superintendent Fil Capaldi of the Scottish police. *Police Scotland requires no evidence or certification as proof of biological sex or gender identity other than a person's self-declaration. The sex/gender identification of individuals who come into contact with the police will be based on how they present or how they self-declare.* Rapists need only declare themselves to be women to be treated as such.

Cancel culture demands conformity and the rebranding of contrived offensive words and ideas. The Coon Cheese brand name came under fire for being racist despite the fact that Edward William Coon was the name of its original American maker. Some months later, the Saputo Dairy Company Australia, announced it was to retire the brand name Coon. Coon Cheese was relabelled as 'Cheers' Cheese. One wonders why the company's Cracker Barrell Vintage Cheddar brand was not similarly renamed, given the American term of white abuse 'Cracker' is prominent in the title? Activists were not interested in calling out racial slurs against white people so the brand name remained intact.

Gubbah is a racially derogatory Aboriginal word for white people. Wikipedia states *Gubbah is a term used by some Aboriginal people to refer to white people. The Macquarie Dictionary has it as an Aboriginal term for a white man. It has been suggested the word is the 'diminutive of garbage'*. I worked for the then Ministry of Aboriginal Affairs in Victoria during the early 1970s and heard the word Gubbah used often and never in a complimentary way. Woke purists in their language crusade against white society denounce the N***** word as white racism, never mentioning Gubbah as an offensive word on the other side of the race-baiting equation.

The Lake Macquarie Council joined in the woke frenzy against the offensive word Coon, taking up the political cudgel to rename the *genuinely racist and genuinely hurtful* Coon Island and Coon Point Island north of Sydney — despite the fact that a majority of Lake Macquarie residents (56%) opposed the name changes. Councillor Kevin Baker twitted to the woke faithful: *We had a name that was genuinely racist and genuinely hurtful to a lot of people in our community. Healing can only begin after a process of truth telling and I look forward to the process of healing within our community.* There was no truth telling, hurt feelings or community healing involved in the council's woke decision, just virtue signalling local politics.

oooOOOooo

The cancel culture madness became even more pronounced, when chocolate manufacturer Nestlé Australia bowed to Twitter mob pressure and changed the name of its confectionary products Red Skins and Chicos. Nestlé's virtue signalling may have appeased the bullying woke Twitterati but it upset many of its loyal customers. In May 2021 breakfast cereal giant, the Kellogg Company in alliance with advocacy group GLAAD (Gay and Lesbian Alliance Against Defamation), came out with *a 'Together with Pride' product that promotes acceptance of the homosexual lifestyle and encourages children to pick their pronouns. The cereal 'features berry-flavoured, rainbow hearts dusted with edible glitter'.* (Sexual stereotyping which in any other context would be condemned as homophobic is obvious in the marketing language used.) On the side and back of the cereal box were panels listing the pronouns 'He/Him', 'She/Her', 'They/Them' and inviting children to 'Create your own Pronoun'. Parents comments railed against the wokeness of Kellogg and the indoctrination of young children at the breakfast table.

In lecturing its employees in an online program of diversity training based on Robin DiAngelo's theory of white fragility to *try and be less white. To be less white is to be less oppressive, less arrogant and less ignorant.* Coca Cola or Woke A Cola, as the virtue signalling soft drink company is labelled by many of its customers who now boycott the brand, calls its compulsory staff training *a learning plan to help build an inclusive workplace.* A workplace where intimidation, harassment and dissatisfaction prevail and woke bullying is rife. *My father a Coca Cola delivery driver for more than ten years was threatened with being fired if he did not do the required training.* Coca Cola sales fell and public indignation became ever more vocal. 'Go Woke Go Broke' was the commercial message delivered to the Woke A Cola board of directors.

Why do companies react to and do the bidding of a few Twitter narcissists and keyboard warriors who relish arguing with others? Their numbers are small and they seek celebrity for themselves through creating controversy. They hide behind social media devices seeking mob approval for the silliest comments. Companies that stand-up to these computer bullies are rewarded by customer loyalty. So why give into the woke idiocy of the craven few?

The ABC whose coverage of the BLM protests in Australia and overseas was biased and supportive of protesters, violence and anarchy on the streets, felt a pressing need to bring political correctness to the game of chess. John Adams a celebrated Aussie chess player tweeted: *I just received a phone call from an ABC Sydney based producer seeking a comment about the game of chess. The ABC have taken the view that chess is racist given that white always go first! They are seeking comment from a chess official as to whether the rules of chess need to be altered! Trust the taxpayer-funded national broadcaster to apply ideological Marxist frameworks to anything and everything in Australia!*

The woke ABC has lost the trust and respect of everyday Australians. On 13 June 2020, ABC journalist, TV presenter and left-wing historian Julia Baird wrote in the *Sydney Morning Herald: the toppling of statues is enriching not erasing history and it has thrilled my heart. We could remove statues from plinths and place them at our height, or lower. Or we could grind them to dust and mix them with concrete, placing them on paths we walk on to a place, a country, where we not only accept the truth, but welcome it.* Accept the truth by erasing it! The ABC's cultural barbarians are inside the gate and we would do well to remember the collapse of Rome and its centuries old empire.

At the same time as activists were gleefully pulling down statues of the past. Winchester University in the UK was proposing to spend £24,000 on erecting a life-sized bronze statue of Greta Thunberg celebrating the teenager's school climate crusade. Public opinion was scathing of the suggestion. Even the student union opposed the idea and complained that students were not consulted. The world isn't being destroyed by the climate. The world is being destroyed by the climate religion.

The inner-city Melbourne Yarra Council joined in the cultural vandalism, declaring it would carry out an audit of 'problematic' historical monuments in its jurisdiction. *Yarra council declared its support for the global Black Lives Matter movement at a council meeting last night. We are committing to taking a look at all the historical people and events represented in statues, plaques, monuments and other signage, and examining anything that may be associated with oppression of Aboriginal and Torres Strait Islander people.* Under consideration for removal were memorials to Captain Cook, Dame Nellie Melba and others outside the Collingwood Town Hall. Dean Hurlston President of the Victorian Ratepayers Association opposed the council's virtue signalling announcement. *Councils need to focus on roads, rates and rubbish and stay out of this space.*

On 30 June 2020, *The Daily Telegraph* carried the banner headline: 'Woke Dopes Call for Removal of Statue of Bush Legend'. *An online petition was started by Blue Mountains resident Ailie Banks calling for the Blue Mountains City Council to tear down statues of William Wentworth, Gregory Blaxland and Henry Lawson* (erected) *to honour the first successful European crossing of the Blue Mountains. However, instead of William Lawson, the third statue is wrongly identified as famous bush poet Henry Lawson.* Blue Mountains City Council Mayor Mark Greenhill said *the statues won't be coming down, they'll stay where they are. To me it's about respecting the culture of Aboriginal people in the Blue Mountains, understanding the truth of history, the European truth and Aboriginal truth, and telling the true story.*

Johannes Leak The Australian 15 June, 2020

Indigenous spokesman Warren Mundine called out the virtue signalling of white activists on councils and elsewhere. *I laugh at these white people making apologies, bowing and carrying on. People say they are pulling down statues because they are racist, but these people need to learn the facts and the history before running around. Do not pretend you speak for the Aboriginal people. We don't need you to speak for us.* In the frenzy to erase white history 'woke dope' ignorance of history was again found to be wanting.

oooOOOooo

Former Deputy Prime Minister John Anderson contemplated re-entering politics in 2021, because in the age of cancel culture and identity politics, he saw a distressing future for Australia's institutions. *I think we all share a deep concern that those elites who hold the bulk of the microphones seem determined to divide not unite us. We have lost faith in ourselves, at the very time in which those who wish us ill are full of all conviction. Our biggest problem today is that cultural division, tribalism, the poison of identity politics, is constipating our capacity to have a reasoned evidence-based, respectful debate that can lead to good policy.*

The ancient Greek storyteller Aesop offers a timely warning to those caught up in the demoralising thrall of wokeness. *The shaft of the arrow has been feathered with one of the eagles own plumes. We often give our enemies the means of our own destruction.* Aesop's short fable 'The Wolf and the Lamb' tersely sums up the PC browbeating intolerance of today's social justice warriors: *One day a wolf saw a lamb drinking water from the same source. So, he shouted down at the lamb. 'How dare you make the water dirty I am drinking?' 'You must be mistaken, sir', said the poor lamb gently. 'The water flows from you to me and not from me to you. So, I am not making the water dirty for you'. 'Do you remember calling me all sorts of abusive words just a year ago?' said the wolf to the lamb. The lamb replied 'but, sir, I was not born a year ago'. The wolf said in a loud voice 'then your father must have abused me long ago'. The lamb said 'I apologise on behalf of my father'. 'You are arguing with me! Let me teach you and your family a lesson! Saying this the wolf jumped upon the poor lamb, killed him and ate him.* Those who set the rules will always find a way to be offended and destroy their enemies.

For the woke to differ in word, thought or deed is a crime not to be tolerated. In their role as the anti-fun and anti-happiness police everybody must be perpetually angry and offended. The Aussie larrikin sense of poking fun at authority and mocking smug opinion, is under threat from a woke zealotry of intolerance. The humourless and bullying devotees of political correctness and cancel culture seek to impose a regime of permanent censure and constant gloominess on society. Like Henry Lewis Mencken's description of Puritanism, the woke subscribe to the *haunting fear that someone, somewhere might be happy.* They criticise and condemn everything of time-honoured value and respect in order to make us fearful, miserable and intimidated always standing on the crumbling cliff edge of impending destruction. Offence and harassment comprise the new woke normal strictly enforced by doctrinaire faultfinders and nit-pickers.

> *Without freedom of thought, there can be no such thing as wisdom — and no such thing as public liberty without freedom of speech.*
>
> Benjamin Franklin

15

Aborigines, Black Lives Matter: An Era of Smoke and Mirrors

If we want to diminish in the long term the number of Aboriginal people in prison, we have got to have low tolerance of anti-social behaviour and criminal behaviour. We have got to have low tolerance to interference sexually with children. We have to have low tolerance with adults who are behaving badly and affecting sober members of the community.

Noel Pearson

Australia's pioneer past is falsely labelled as genocidal and massacre driven. The savagery and violence of frontier warfare between whites and Aborigines is portrayed as the fault of xenophobic European settlers. Aborigines who committed similar atrocities are exonerated as frontier resistance heroes. The complexity and cultural nuance of pioneer and Aboriginal behaviour is not addressed, resulting in an imaginary Aboriginal past and the defacing of public monuments. Politically correct stereotypes prevail and the Aboriginal activist side claim the moral high ground because of a greater Aboriginal mortality rate.

Today there is little left of pre-colonial tribal society and its Indigenous ways even in remote Aboriginal communities. In 1904 world renowned Anthropologist Alfred William Howitt, who spent several decades during the 19th century studying New South Wales Aborigines on mission and welfare stations, commented on the rapid disappearance of tribal ways. *The tribal remnants have now almost lost the knowledge of the beliefs and customs of their fathers.* By 1904, tribal knowledge was at best passed on in a piecemeal and culturally adulterated fashion. Across Australia the transmission of tribal knowledge deteriorated further in the early and middle decades of the 20th century. Anthropologist William Stanner wrote of the Northern Territory's Daly River Aborigines. *Many of the preconditions of the traditional culture were gone a sufficient population, a self-sustaining economy, a discipline by elders, a confident dependency on nature and, with the preconditions went much of the culture, including the secret male rites.* Young people were no longer taught or valued traditional tribal ways. They sought to adopt the white fellas' lifestyle and went to work for pastoralists or shifted to the towns.

Only in recent years, driven by post war political activism and academic/media romanticism concerning the Aboriginal past, has a fabricated version of tribal knowledge emerged as a central feature of modern Aboriginal identity. This is especially true of radical groups of urban Aborigines, such as the 'Warriors of the Aboriginal Resistance' (WAR) who use a contrived vision of Aboriginal culture as a political bludgeon to advance a militant activist agenda. *We are Warriors of the Aboriginal Resistance. We want to revive the warrior spirit in our people by facilitating a culture of resistance. We draw inspiration from Pearl Gibbs and Malcolm X. Our publication Black Nations Rising is modelled on the Black Panther Party's Intercommunal News Service.*

oooOOOooo

The wrongly named 'stolen generations' debate is infused with dark and sinister overtones of racism and genocide that are more political opinion than factually based. Aboriginal activists present emotionally charged stories of family suffering and childhood trauma. They deliberately ignore the testimony of Aboriginal children who fail to fit the racist narrative of insensitive government cruelty and abuse.

They dismiss such stories as atypical and irrelevant. The fact these stories exist at all, suggests a complexity of childhood experience and favourable circumstance, never acknowledged or discussed in today's black armband version of Aboriginal history.

One such story concerns Alec Ross, an infant removed from his Aboriginal mother at birth, who lived a happy and fulfilling life at the Alice Springs Telegraph Station. Alec wrote in a 2002 pamphlet titled: 'A Living History of the Alice Springs Telegraph Station'. *I came from the hospital. I was very sick. That's why I was taken from my mother. They brought me here because they thought I'd have a better chance of getting better meals to get me back into health again. I can understand why they took us away, because my mother lived like (her people) did centuries earlier her parents and their parents before them. The thing is, I didn't mind that. I think they did the right thing at the time. I never had it bad, I can tell you that. I always loved where I lived and what I did. If I hadn't been taken away, I'd never have enjoyed the life I live today. It was the best thing that ever happened to me.*

Historian Keith Windschuttle writes *Aboriginal children were never removed from their families in order to put an end to Aboriginality or, indeed, to serve any improper government policy or program. Most children affected had been orphaned, abandoned, destitute, neglected or subject to various forms of domestic violence, sexual exploitation and sexual abuse. They were removed for the same reason as white children in similar circumstances. Rather than acting for racist reasons, government officers and religious missionaries wanted to rescue children from welfare camps and shanty settlements riddled with alcoholism, domestic violence and sexual abuse.*

Windschuttle went on to describe the total lack of interest by Indigenous activists in an Aboriginal stolen generation before woke radicalism emerged from the shadows. *At the high point of Aboriginal radicalism in the late 1960s and early 1970s, the attempt to put an end to Aboriginality by removing children never received a mention in any major agenda of aboriginal political grievances. During the lead-up to the successful 1967 constitutional referendum to give the Commonwealth powers in Aboriginal affairs, not one of the political activists campaigning for reform mentioned stolen children as an issue to be rectified. In 1970, neither the ten-point Policy Manifesto of the*

National Tribal Council, nor the Platform and Program of the Black Panthers of Australia, nor the 1972 Five-Point Policy of the Aboriginal Tent Embassy at Parliament House, Canberra, or any other political manifesto of the time, mentioned stolen children, let alone the genocide that Aborigines had purportedly been suffering for the previous sixty years.

Assimilation and the safety of 'stolen' Aboriginal children, not a malicious government policy of exclusion or genocide, was the aspiration. The intention was principled, benevolent and based on Christian compassion. Acclaimed historian and writer on the Jewish holocaust the late Dr Inga Clendinnen makes the salient point: *Intention is all in defining genocidal behaviour.* The philanthropic intention was clearly welfare protection and removal from childhood abuse. Systemic racism, the false notion of official genocide and the removal of Aboriginal children to expedite cultural elimination, are postmodern tropes indulged in by militant activists whose purpose is to rewrite history to suit a modern political purpose.

oooOOOooo

A myth that still prevails today is that Australia's Aborigines were denied voting rights until 1967. Aborigines in South Australia were granted the vote in 1856, in Victoria in 1857 and New South Wales in 1858 by enlightened colonial administrators. Under Federation, the Commonwealth Franchise Act of 1902 restricted voting in federal elections for Aborigines but did not take away the right to vote at state elections. In 1949 the federal parliament legislated that Aborigines who had served in the armed forces regardless of earlier voting rights status be given full voting rights. In 1962 the Commonwealth Electoral Act removed all voting restrictions for Aborigines and Torres Strait Islanders who could now vote in federal elections. In 1965 Queensland was the last state to enfranchise its Aborigines.

A referendum in 1967 was passed to allow the federal government to make laws to assist Aboriginal people and for them to be counted in the Commonwealth Census. Previously it was state governments which exercised sole power in Aboriginal affairs. Professor Geoffrey Blainey informs us *Aboriginals were counted in the federal census right from the start, even though it was impossible to locate and count most of those who lived in the far outback. What the federal constitution specified was that Aboriginals were not included in the national tally when federal seats and federal financial allocations to states were allocated.* The referendum changed the constitutional dynamic. The notion that Aborigines did not receive the right to vote before 1967 is simply wrong.

Following the 1967 referendum Sir Paul Hasluck Governor General of Australia (1969-74) wrote of how things changed. *One immediate change was the sudden transference of a number of fully assimilated persons of part Aboriginal descent into professional 'Aborigines' who, with the entitlement of having one Aboriginal among four of their grandparents, became the confident authorities on 'the way of their people'.* To the detriment of remote community Aborigines, urban Aborigines living assimilated city lives with only partial Aboriginal descent (sometimes as little as 4% or 5%) usurped the process. Then there are those who fraudulently claim indigenous descent with zero credibility. Aboriginality became a politicised vehicle complete with a newly designed land rights flag (1971) for city-based activism and cultural propaganda.

Dr Victoria Grieve-Williams, an Indigenous historian at RMIT University in Melbourne, said of race-shifting: *In Australia the race-shifting phenomenon is pervasive and well recognised by Aboriginal people. The race-shifters hold the power, they stifle debate and resist scrutiny in various ways, including attacking Aboriginal people who ask who they are in our cultural terms. They tend to be urban-based, clustered in southeast Australia, and raised with all the privilege of being white.* Suzanne Ingram, an indigenous health professional, writes *the Wiradjuri people* (from central New South Wales) *have been dealing with this for a couple of decades. What interests me is not simply that race-shifting is happening and on such a vast scale, it is the ways in which it is happening. My analysis in health communication shows how it affects policy, it seems to have started in housing policy but it has soared in the education sector, and the stats show that the east coast of Australia is the epicentre.*

In subsequent years, misrepresentation and falsehood became rife, with remote Aboriginal communities pushed to the periphery. Aboriginality morphed into a popular culture and public event spectacle. Contrary to what many Australians believe the 'Welcome to Country' ceremony is not a traditional Aboriginal tribal ceremony. The Middar Aboriginal Theatre invented the cultural performance in 1976. The 'Smoke and Gum Leaves' ritual, also a modern marketable creation, is portrayed as a traditional Aboriginal observance, and seen on many public occasions, including the opening of the Australian Parliament. Aboriginal cultural groups charge a hefty fee from between $5,000 and $8,000 to perform these rituals. The Aboriginal flag designed in 1971 by Harold Thomas, a Luritja man from Central Australia, was created as a symbol for the political land rights movement. Today it flies as a modern representation of a unified Aboriginal nation that never existed.

Next to Black Lives Matter, the endlessly repeated slogan *Always was, always will be Aboriginal land* is a political rallying cry, based on the misrepresentation that Aboriginal society was a sovereign tribal society with a collective national identity. The archaeological, historical, cultural and ethnographic evidence clearly shows that such was not the case. To pretend otherwise is to indulge in woke identity politics and the falsification of the Aboriginal past.

The 30 December 2021 arson vandalism of the front doors of the Old Parliament House in Canberra, a revered historic symbol of Australian democracy, by a handful of Aboriginal and white activists did nothing to win the hearts and minds of law-abiding Aussies. *Emergency services have extinguished a fierce blaze at Old Parliament House which ACT Police said was started by a group of protesters on Thursday who were heard yelling 'let it burn'. The protesters started a fire at the front doors of the building. It marks the second fire at Old Parliament House after protesters started a blaze outside the building last week. Protesters were reportedly yelling the site of Old Parliament House was on Aboriginal sovereign land. A man who attended the protest explained. 'We come here for no other reason than to get through those doors* (to) *take back that building'.* Prime Minister Scott Morrison voicing the opinion of most Australians commented, *their cause doesn't justify that sort of violence, that's not how Australia works, we have a rule of law in this country, people should obey it.*

oooOOOooo

There is today an activist driven push to enshrine in law and the constitution separate treaties and an Aboriginal Voice to Parliament. Aboriginal academic Dr Anthony Dillon sees no value in forging symbolic treaties, preferring instead to focus on practical outcomes for Indigenous Australians. *The problems plaguing too many Aboriginal communities and people are ones that, I believe, can be addressed without a treaty. In fact, I believe pursuit of a treaty will be a major distraction from addressing the real problems, as a treaty will be seen as a magic bullet. Let's not be distracted by symbolism and 'quick fixes' such as treaties, however alluring they might seem to be. Let's focus on providing Aboriginal people with real hope and help, even if this means tackling the tough issues such as child abuse and violence, or making unpopular decisions like relocating people from dysfunctional and economically unsustainable communities to centres with facilities where they can thrive.*

New South Wales Indigenous lawyer Josephine Cashman, speaking for One Voice Australia and the Big River Foundation, seeks to unite rather than divide Australians. *Australia does not need a Voice to Parliament or constitutional change. It needs to abolish the current Aboriginal funding model and implement measures capable of improving the economic outcomes of my people. Aboriginal families should be allowed to transfer land held by land councils to individual ownership and some freehold title can be returned to local traditional owners to establish local businesses, innovations and enterprises. Traditional owners should become shareholders and be able to use their land in whichever way they see fit. The time is ripe to focus on generating economic independence and overdue lifestyle improvements. We don't want the Uluru statement; elders are voiceless and treated with contempt.*

The Uluru statement from the Heart (2017) advocating a First Nation Aboriginal realignment, the drafting of a treaty as well as wanting privileged parliamentary leverage, uses impassioned and misleading language in the political manifesto of a new round of Aboriginal activism. *Proportionally, we are the most incarcerated people on the planet. Our children are alienated from their families at unprecedented rates. And our youth languish in detention in obscene numbers.* The first statement portraying Australia as an incarcerating race segregating country is preposterous. The other two are just as much an Aboriginal cultural, family and community problem as they are a white political problem. The Uluru statement is communally divisive, politically power seeking and racially confrontational in a way it claims to deplore. It is about enshrining Aboriginal advantage and Indigenous separation in law and not seeking reconciliation the political catchcry of the Indigenous cause.

Recognition of Aborigines as the pre-European inhabitants of Australia is acknowledged by every Australian. The Voice to Parliament proposal puts racism at the very heart of the Australian democratic process. An Institute of Public Affairs poll conducted in July 2021, confirmed that 60% of Australians did not want race of any kind included in the constitution. In 2019 the percentage was 45%. The constitution is not the place to acknowledge the privileged status of one racial group over another. Aboriginal lawyer Dr Hannah McGlade rightly observed *would Indigenous women and children feel safer if constitutional recognition, or even a treaty, eventuated in Australia? The answer must be a resounding 'No'.*

Dr Augusto Zimmermann, Professor of Law at the University of Notre Dame Australia, writes *the Australian Constitution is simply a federal document which is colour-blind and does not mention the history of any ethnic group at all. The constitution is basically the product of a compact between the former colonies to form a federation. Its primary function is not to describe history, but to distribute various powers between the two tiers of government: the commonwealth and the states. It is a practical document designed to establish a federal system of government, not a synopsis of Australian history. Australians should not be bullied into supporting 'group rights' that flow to selected people on the basis of culture, origin or ethnicity. 'We got here first' is a much poorer concept than the great principle of western constitutionalism: 'We are all created equal and endowed by the creator with certain inalienable rights'.*

oooOOOooo

Dallas Scott, a Victorian Aboriginal writer, gives a truthful analysis of the current state of Aboriginal affairs. *Australians have happily swallowed the lie that Aborigines are one big, multi-coloured family who stick together. Those without a voice trust the rest who have one to speak up for them. They are not the ones lecturing on recognition from a function centre, but the people who are often functionally illiterate and unemployed, thousands of kilometres away from where people are listening and deciding what is important for them. I believe that these people, overwhelmingly, call for better housing, protection from violence and corruption, healthcare, jobs, education and the dignity that cannot be legislated into being.*

Dr Anthony Dillon says *when discussing Aboriginal matters there seems to be no end to where offence can be taken and accusations of racism made. Some children have suffered, all in the name of 'culture'. A colour-blind culture or way of life, characterised by love, is a far more important consideration than a culture that is assumed to be Aboriginal simply because the adult potential carers themselves have some Aboriginal ancestry.*

Political activists speak of systemic racism. It is trendy and financially rewarding for those with little or no Aboriginal blood or heritage to declare themselves Indigenous. Bruce Pascoe is an example of race-shifting black privilege that readily springs to mind. Would they do so if they faced systemic racism and community discrimination? Would they do so if there was no personal or financial advantage to identifying as an Indigenous Australian?

Indigenous Australians have the same civil and political rights as everybody else. They are on all occasions accorded equal treatment before the law and receive the same fair play as every other Australian. Cultural circumstances, alcohol, criminal offence and strained domestic relationships and not racism, the police or white privilege are the causes of disruption and turmoil within Aboriginal communities. Aborigines annually receive and poorly administer billions of dollars of taxpayer money for a variety of Indigenous purposes. They have occupied a unique place of black privilege and safeguarding in the nation's eyes for the past 50 years. This inconvenient truth does not fit a racist narrative and therefore is never front and centre of activist media statements or street protest placards. Systemic racism is not real and exists in Australia only for left-wing political purposes.

Essayist and author Peter O'Brien, who has written a critique of Bruce Pascoe's book on Aboriginal history, makes a strong point about the lack of systemic racism in Australia. *Racism is not prevalent or even expanding in Australia, but I suspect antipathy towards Aborigines as a group is increasing, thanks almost exclusively to those entitled* (urban Aboriginal) *demagogues who harangue us at every opportunity. It is hardly an endearing act to proclaim on Australia Day that the country needs to be 'burnt to the ground', a comment made by Melbourne blacktivist Tarneen Onus Williams, who was at the time serving on a consultative committee established by the Victorian Labor Government to craft a treaty with the state's Indigenous.*

Whenever I ask those, I speak to, to point out a concrete example of systemic racism, homophobia, or any of the other fashionable phobias the left so glibly allude to, they are never able to pin down anything beyond mere buzz words and clichés. They try to win an argument by redefining words that are not applicable. The facts are against them and their argument invariably has no merit. Those who protest 'Invasion Day' and blindly follow Black Lives Matter directives, vent a systemic racism in their attention-grabbing beliefs that most Australians find disagreeable and frankly unacceptable.

oooOOOooo

It is politically correct to identify the violent, alcoholic and sexual abuse dysfunction of today's rural Aboriginal communities (80% of those identifying themselves as Aborigines live in cities and towns and are completely assimilated, with only 20% living in remote areas) as an historic white problem to be resolved by spending truckloads of money. The 2014 Australian Government Productivity Commission Report on Indigenous Expenditure, reveals the exorbitant extent of annual government spending on Aboriginal affairs.

Total direct expenditure on services for Aboriginal and Torres Strait Islander Australians in 2012-13 was estimated to be $30.3 billion, accounting for 6.1% of total direct general government expenditure. Estimated expenditure per person in 2012-13 was $43,449 for Aboriginal and Torres Strait Islander Australians, compared with $20,900 for other Australians (a ratio of 2.08 to 1; an increase from a ratio of 1.93 to 1 in 2008-09). Government expenditure on non-Indigenous services was estimated to be $16.1 billion dollars. The annual expenditure figure for Aboriginal and Torres Strait Islanders continued to rise in following years.

Clearly very little of this annual swag of taxpayer's money reaches those most in need. So, what happens to it? Aboriginal councils, and other public entities run by Aborigines, are central to the process of dispensing government money and services to urban and remote Aboriginal communities. In the past however many of these Aboriginal organisations have contributed little towards the betterment of fringe dwelling Aboriginal people. The discredited Aboriginal and Torres Strait Islander Commission (ATSIC) was abolished by the Howard Government in 2004 due to financial corruption, embezzlement of funds and rape charges.

The National Congress of Australia's First Peoples established in 2010 framed itself as the premier Indigenous body until July 2019 when it was disbanded. Chairperson Rod Little wrote of its demise. *We regret that no funding was forthcoming from any source. This meant that congress was unable to continue its business of representing the rights and interests of its members at the national level now or into the future.* Without funding from urban Aboriginal activists not prepared to support their self-proclaimed national congress with their own money the umbrella organisation collapsed.

Meanwhile chronic dysfunction and community turmoil continue to prevail. Aborigines living in rural communities with a generational government handout mentality and a lifestyle centred around alcohol, crime and domestic violence need to take responsibility for their behaviour and not keep blaming the colonial past and racist Australia for their present-day choices and failure. The media-reported alcoholism, domestic abuse and crime ridden lifestyle of badly behaved Aborigines unfairly blackens the copy book of law-abiding and decent living Aborigines in these communities. The breakdown in community behaviour is widespread and in need of urgent attention. Stories of infant rape and sexual abuse of children by their parents or family friends abound in Aboriginal communities.

A Howard Government report in 2007 that led to federal intervention in the Northern Territory found that child abuse was present in every one of forty-five remote Aboriginal communities. In 2006, at Napranum, an aboriginal community 40 kilometres south of Aurukun in Queensland, a 10-year-old Aboriginal girl with an intellectual disability, the daughter of an alcoholic mother, was gang raped by 9 Aboriginal men aged between 13 and 25. The accused men pleaded guilty to the horrendous sex crime. Judge Sarah Bradley *spared them gaol time and said the victim 'probably agreed' to have sex with them. She ruled the men were also victims themselves after growing up deprived and subjected to physical and sexual abuse at the hands of others in their community.* The judicial message to Aboriginal sexual abusers was that victimhood is a 'get out of goal free card' no matter how heinous the crime.

In March 2020, at Tennant Creek in the Northern Territory, a 27-year-old Aboriginal man was convicted of the 2018 rape of a two-year-old girl while her mother was sleeping. The child suffered severe internal injuries. She was airlifted to Adelaide for urgent medical attention and was given a blood transfusion. The toddler's rapist was sentenced to 13 years in prison. In response to this unspeakable child abuse case, community anger across Australia ran red hot and an appropriate sentence was handed down without the usual victimhood messaging.

As if these appalling remote Aboriginal community sexual abuse cases weren't bad enough, in July 2020 again from Napranum on the Cape York Peninsular came a report of the brutal gang rape of a five-year-old Aboriginal boy by four Aboriginal children. The *Daily Mail* newspaper commented: *The community is now reeling from the attack on a five-year-old boy, who was allegedly sexually assaulted by four boys, aged between 10 and 13, on a remote beach on July 1. The alleged attack was so violent the victim required emergency medical treatment and was airlifted to Cairns Hospital, some 800 km away. The group have been taken into police custody, while the 900-strong Napranum community has banned them from returning to the town.*

oooOOOooo

In January 2020, veteran journalist Piers Akerman wrote *a recent report in the Australian* (newspaper) *on a proposal to reintroduce alcohol sales in the historically violent township of Aurukun on the Cape York Peninsula, noted a 2013 Queensland study which found sex crimes against children in the community were reported at a rate 6.6 times the Queensland norm. The incidence of sexually transmitted diseases among children and under-age teens was fifty-six times the state average and included the infection of twenty-nine children younger than ten.*

According to the Australian Bureau of Statistics, in 2016-17 the ratio of age standardised rates for Indigenous offenders was five times the non-Indigenous offender rate in New South Wales and Queensland and almost nine times for the Northern Territory.

On New Year's Day 2020, Aurukun erupted in alcohol-fuelled violence following the stabbing death of an older Aboriginal man by two Aboriginal youths. Police Superintendent Geoff Sheldon said *There were 250 people wandering the streets of Aurukun all armed, all aggressive and it became a dangerous situation, not only for our staff, but members of the public and other government staff. They were seeking vengeance for the stabbing that occurred and they were going house to house looking for what they believed were two offenders responsible for the death of the man. It became a violent confrontation at each and every residence. There's hundreds of men, women and children cowering in their houses.*

Inspector Mark Henderson *said the community was in severe unrest. A number of houses have been totally incinerated after being firebombed by offenders. Extra police are being flown in from right across the north to secure the Aurukun region and return some sort of law and order to the community. Alcohol has played a huge factor in both the Kowanyama* (another Cape York stabbing incident) *and Aurukun matters.* The media reported that the *riots in Aurukun have led to 130 people fleeing six hours west to Coen, with others moving south to Kowanyama and Pormpuraaw. Another 110 people travelled through the night to a makeshift bush camp 80km outside of Aurukun, now being run by former soldiers. There are serious concerns about access to health services, food and personal safety following what police labelled a 'vengeance-seeking exercise'.*

Aurukun is symptomatic of an endemic culture of lawlessness and community disrespect that plagues many remote Aboriginal communities. To protect their family and property from out-of-control violence, worried Aurukun residents have erected 4-metre-high fences topped with rolls of barbed wire. The hackneyed complaint from political activists that systemic racism is to blame for Aurukun's community dislocation and worsening violence lacks credibility. The police and the Queensland Government seem powerless to effectively tackle the escalating violence and ongoing abuse.

Prominent Aboriginal leader and lawyer Noel Pearson points out that low expectation of the Indigenous population, not systemic racism, is worsening the situation in regional and remote Aboriginal communities. *It's a (community) crisis but it's not a crisis that we are on top of. Progressive policies prevail in relation to welfare, education, criminal justice, etc. We are reaping the bitter harvest of progressive policy preferences that oppose the reforms needed in our communities. We have got to shed any hesitation whatsoever about the notion that we should take children away from abusive situations and place them into foster care. In the past 30 years there's been a tendency for the judicial system to take into account the cultural and historical background of Aboriginal offenders and therefore resulting in leniency, when in fact the imperative has all along been to make sure that social norms are observed and maintained in communities.*

Those who suffer most in Aboriginal communities are abused women and neglected children. Aboriginal children some as young as six and seven join teenage gangs to vandalise and destroy. Rarely do they attend school; they terrorise residents, rob shopkeepers, binge drink, sniff petrol and glue, taunt the police and cause trouble in juvenile detention when apprehended. Before the courts and the media, Aboriginal teenagers show little remorse for their out-of-control behaviour. They blame everybody including schools, police and the Aboriginal welfare system and are on their way to an adult life of crime. In crime ridden Townsville Aboriginal youth offenders are subject to a lenient revolving door policy of bail and prosecution. This further diminishes respect for law and order and sets Aboriginal delinquents on a trajectory of greater criminal behaviour.

The 2019 Northern Territory Don Dale Youth Detention Centre disturbances began with unruly Aboriginal youths acting up and quickly escalated into full scale rioting when tensions boiled over. Skin colour and youth were not the issues involved. Bad attitude and violent behaviour with makeshift weapons were the catalyst that led to confrontation and facility lockdown. Media images of young Aborigines wrestled to the ground by warders, detained in isolation and wearing hoods, do not reveal the serious nature of what brought about such a dramatic response from prison authorities. In youth detention centres across the country a culture of violence and defiant disobedience regardless of skin colour has grown up among young offenders that requires a firm hand and suitable response.

The Aboriginal community situation is disorderly, chaotic and self-perpetuating. A social media comment revealed the intimidating extent of community violence and disruption in central Australia. *We have friends living in Alice Springs who claim it is particularly lawless. A close friend lives in a gated community and even though she lives three minutes from work must take a car for safety.* Then Alice Springs Deputy Mayor Jacinta Price spoke of a tense atmosphere of bullying intimidation and anxious fear. *In Alice Springs a member of the public is far more likely to be randomly assaulted, physically or verbally, if they are perceived as 'white' rather than 'black'. Grossly offensive racist insults are used liberally in the streets of Alice Springs against white people. I have walked the streets of this town with my white friends to protect them from this sort of thing.*

oooOOOooo

Jacinta Nampijinpa Price belongs to the central desert Warlpiri Mob. She is an educated and articulate Indigenous woman opposed to identity politics, the misleading deceit of the Uluru statement and the political correctness of urban Aborigines. Jacinta is a moderate voice of reconciliation in an inflamed and politicised cauldron of Aboriginality. She advocates for Aboriginal women experiencing domestic and sexual abuse at the hands of violent husbands, for the alleviation of poverty and crime in rural communities and for Aborigines to be justly proud of modern Australia.

Jacinta has done much to publicly lift the lid on the wretched plight of Aboriginal women and girls living in remote traditional rural communities, exposing the abhorrent nature of outmoded cultural practices that still today allow the sexual exploitation and subjugation of Indigenous females. The 2016 Census recorded that Aborigines represented just 3.3% of the Australian population and the proportion of domestic violence was higher than in the white community. Aboriginal women are 35 times more likely to suffer domestic violence at the hands of an Aboriginal partner than non-Indigenous women. Jacinta writes *ignoring cultural drivers does not allow for robust examination and debate to take place that may carve out better ways of addressing such a debilitating issue.*

At the heart of the problem is Aboriginal customary law written by Aboriginal elders, which discriminates against women and girls and allows all kinds of violence to be used at the discretion of Aboriginal men. Women found guilty of breaking traditional law can be beaten or raped. Young girls from 13 years of age are routinely forced into marriages with older men. If women or girls transgress the marriage law; tradition decrees they be speared through the leg. Other no less barbaric cruelties are inflicted, to keep Indigenous women tightly under the thumb of the Aboriginal tribal patriarchy. To their shame, government and private agencies charged with protecting Indigenous women and children do nothing, claiming colonisation and racism are responsible for the high levels of violence and crime in Aboriginal communities. Jacinta says growing up in the Northern Territory, she saw young girls married off to much older men while still too young to be married under Australian law. She saw Aboriginal women beaten by their husbands and male relatives, young children sexually and violently abused.

Jacinta's mother, Bess Nungarrayi Price, speaks of her remote Aboriginal community upbringing. *My own body is scarred by domestic violence. We Aboriginal people have to acknowledge the truth. We can't blame all of our problems on the white man. This is our problem that we can fix ourselves. The Racial Discrimination Act was there to protect us from white racism and we needed that protection. But it has not protected our people from ourselves. We need an act; we need laws that recognize that the problem now is blackfellas killing blackfellas and killing themselves.*

Aboriginal tribal law was never the romanticised fiction and peacefully benign cultural practice espoused by Black Lives Matter supporters and Aboriginal activists. Jacinta's white teacher-father David Price describes the barbarity of Aboriginal customary law in the following terms. *Women in remote Aboriginal communities are threatened with execution, torture and rape for committing offences against traditional law. A woman who enters a men's punishment camp at night may be punished by being required to participate in sexual acts. This punishment may continue for some time, perhaps months. This is a coy way of describing gang rape, a punishment for the commission of cultural crimes.* Add to this the forced marriage of sometimes pre-teen girls to much older men, and I can't really see how the uncritical acknowledgement of such a law and contemporary adherence to it, would aid in the reduction of domestic and sexual violence and the sexual abuse of children, especially when chronic and wide spread substance abuse is added to the mix. All of the horrific crimes perpetrated against these children were committed by their own people. They were the victims of severe neglect, if not outright abuse, by members of their own families. There is no evidence that any of the Aboriginal organisations offering services to their communities and families, did the jobs that they were funded by taxpayers to do and no evidence that Aboriginal leaders did much to prevent it all from happening.

oooOOOooo

In America, following the death of George Floyd on the 25 May 2020, Black Lives Matter — a hard-left dominated political movement dedicated to anarchy and chaos — quickly descended into looting, arson, murder and street lawlessness. Journalist Alexandra Phillips commenting on BLM's radical agenda wrote *BLM happily self-identifies as a neo-Marxist movement with various far left objectives, including defunding the police (an evolution of the Black Panther position to control the police), to dismantling capitalism and the patriarchal system, disrupting the western-prescribed nuclear family structure, seeking reparations from slavery to redistribute wealth and via various offshoot appeals, to raise money to bail black prisoners awaiting trial.*

British commentor Brendan O'Neill wrote *this no longer has anything to do with Floyd. Rather, we are witnessing nothing less than a power grab by the politically correct machine; an attempt by the new intolerant elites to export their eccentric ideologies into every street and square and corner of the public sphere. The arrogance of the woke elite is now through the roof to such an extent that they think everyone must conform to their way of thinking. They want to force everyone to take the knee, to bow down, to be cognisant of identity. People are tired of the constant woke witch hunts against those who don't share the woke establishment's view.*

At the time of George Floyd's death, a serving Queensland police officer writing in *Quadrant* Online (June 2020) under the nom de plume of Martin Lynch, received unexpected woke abuse from his teenage daughter. *My 13-year-old daughter became particularly rude and disrespectful, telling me that being white, male and a policeman defined me as a hateful racist. It was odd because she spent part of her childhood in Coen* (Cape York Peninsular) *surrounded by indigenous people and has met hundreds of coppers. Indigenous people come to our house to break bread and she played with indigenous kids in our house and their yards. She is a cape copper's kid whose younger daily life disproved the lie that police and indigenous people see each other as mortal enemies. I dismissed this, putting it down to normal adolescent insolence, rebellion and the endless feed of simplistic rubbish she gets from social media.*

The rank-and-file Queensland policeman was offended by the blatant lies being told. *Every interaction between coppers, Aboriginals and Torres Strait Islanders is measured not against the law or even standards of acceptable human behaviour, but as indicators of so-called 'systemic racism'. The idea that cops need to 'just stop killing people' is not just a lie, it is a monstrous, vile, contemptible lie. It's a lie so big even Goebbels and Molotov might have hesitated to tell it, yet the sort of 'black leaders' promoted by the media, especially the ABC, SBS and NITV do not. Can there be any clearer demonstration that white men in blue shirts are not the threat to black lives?* At the time the Aussie policemen made his comments, the American media was reporting that white students were being told by BLM promoting woke teachers a *future killer cop* was sitting in the classroom.

The Black Lives Matter cause was zealously taken up by left-wing circles in Australia. Here it was ostensibly about systemic racism and Aboriginal deaths in custody. Black Lives Matter protestors roamed the nation's streets shouting *F**k the Police! Defund the Pigs!* and carrying placards brazenly and deceitfully denouncing the police as *Murderers and Racists — 432 Black Lives Lost: Murdered by the Police!* Nobody publicly defended the police or called out the fraudulent figure of Aboriginal lives lost. Despite the Aussie activist claim that racism was responsible for 432 Aboriginal deaths in police and prison custody since 1991. The facts presented by the Royal Commission into Aboriginal

Deaths in Custody (1987–1991) and what has occurred since then clearly suggest otherwise.

The final report of the Royal Commission was made public in April 1991, *the Commission concluded that the 99 deaths investigated were not due to police violence. The immediate causes of the deaths do not include foul play, in the sense of unlawful, deliberate killing of Aboriginal prisoners by police and prison officers. More than one third of the deaths (37) were from disease; 30 were self-inflicted hangings; 23 were caused by other forms of external trauma, especially head injuries; and 9 were immediately associated with dangerous alcohol and other drug use. Indeed, heavy alcohol use was involved in some way in deaths in each of these categories.*

In February 2019 the Australian Institute of Criminology published a federal government study paper titled 'Indigenous Deaths in Custody: 25 years since the Royal Commission into Aboriginal Deaths in Custody'. The abstract read *twenty-five years has passed since the Royal Commission into Aboriginal Deaths in Custody. This paper examines the trends and characteristics of Indigenous deaths in custody since 1991–92, using data obtained through the National Deaths in Custody Program (NDICP). NDICP data show Indigenous people are now less likely than non-Indigenous people to die in prison custody. Coinciding with this decrease in the death rate of Indigenous prisoners is a decrease in the* (suicide) *hanging death rate of Indigenous prisoners.*

There was no clear trend in the statistics that police were directly responsible for more than a small number of Indigenous deaths. *The largest number of deaths occurred in 2002–03 and 2004–05 and the lowest in 2013–14. As to the manner of death* (during this period), *47% (68) of Indigenous deaths in police custody were classified as accidental. With 57% (39) of these during motor vehicle pursuits and 19% (13) during another type of pursuit. Natural causes accounted for 21% (31), self-inflicted deaths 19% (28), 'justifiable homicide' 7% (10) and 'unlawful homicide' 5% (8).* Unlawful homicide was caused by miscalculation and only rarely by deliberate intention.

An earlier 2015 Australian Institute of Criminology Monitoring Report, titled 'Deaths in Custody in Australia: National Deaths in Custody Program 2011–12 and 2012–13' reported: *Since 1979, a total of 2,463 deaths in custody have occurred, with 1,487 deaths in prison (60%), 953 deaths in police custody (39%). Of the deaths in custody, 470 were Indigenous people and 1,993 were of non-Indigenous background. (Of) the 1,487 deaths in prison custody, 253 were Indigenous prisoners (17%). There have been 750 deaths in police custody and custody related operations since 1989. Indigenous persons have comprised 20% of the recorded deaths. Overall, the Royal Commission found that Indigenous people were not more likely to die in custody than non-Indigenous people, but were significantly overrepresented in custody compared with their proportion of the total Australian population. This remains true today with the rate of overrepresentation continuing to increase* due to the high crime rate in remote Indigenous communities.

Criminologist David Biles, who for three years was Head of the Criminology Research Group of the Royal Commission, wrote in the *Canberra Times* in May 2016: *The Royal Commission was required to consider the underlying social factors leading to deaths in custody, but the Letters Patent (or terms of reference) made no mention of over-representation or even imprisonment rates. Nor was it required to compare Aboriginal and non-Aboriginal deaths in custody. In fact, in the early days of the Royal Commission, when I and a small team of researchers were able to prove unequivocally that Aboriginal people were slightly less likely to die in prison or police custody than non-Aboriginal people, we were met with derision and disbelief. We were even accused of disloyalty to the Royal Commission.*

On the 30th anniversary of the handing down of the Royal Commission Report in 1991, Aboriginal postdoctoral fellow at The Australian Catholic University, Dr Anthony Dillon, supported the criminologist's claim when he wrote in the *Sydney Morning Herald* in April 2021: *It has been known since the early days of the Royal Commission, that Aboriginal people in custody do not die at a higher rate than non-Aboriginal Australians. We are sick to the eyeballs of each Aboriginal death in custody being cited as evidence of racism against Aboriginal people. Let's work together. Honest reporting on Aboriginal deaths in custody would be a good start.*

oooOOOooo

Jacinta Price tells us Aboriginal incarceration rates *are not the result of systemic racism. The Royal Commission into Black Deaths in Custody did not find that Aboriginal people were being targeted and that it was a racial issue. The Royal Commission (found) there was a tendency for courts to be more lenient towards Indigenous offenders. The majority of Aboriginal deaths occur at the hands of other Aboriginal people. For 85% of Aboriginal victims of crime their offender was known to them; so, they were either family or a partner and 50% of those were a partner. 70% of Aboriginal men and women incarcerated are incarcerated for acts of violence against their loved ones. A large portion of the* (Northern Territory) *police force is Indigenous. There has been growing resentment against police officers for years, but no growing resentment toward the perpetrators within our own communities, who are causing far more destruction toward our people than what our police officers are doing. If we want to see a reduction in incarceration rates, then we have to stop the murderers and the rapists in our own communities and in our own families. It is not racism that is sexually abusing our kids. It's not racism that is killing our people. It is the actions of our own people.*

Jacinta reveals the true plight of Indigenous Australians. *Our people are suffering and their problems are daunting and complex. We will not find the answers, if we are denied the right to take part in an open and honest debate. We can't do that without offending those who are ideologically committed to the party line that has been laid down by the activists of the eastern cities and their white allies. They are educated, speak English and know how to use the system against anybody they disagree with. The most marginalized and least powerful of the Aboriginal population are denied a voice by self-appointed spokespeople who know nothing of the circumstances in which they live. The agenda is dominated by those least affected by these issues. An English speaking, Aboriginal middle class ignorant of the values and issues of remote speakers of traditional languages.*

We've got Indigenous parliamentarians in our federal parliament who ignore (domestic and sexual abuse) *issues, who don't campaign on behalf of young girls like Layla Leering* (a rape and murder victim), *who don't seek justice for them. Instead, they seek justice for black deaths in custody for perpetrators who pass away in gaol, and we know that when it comes to black deaths in custody the majority of those deaths are because of natural causes. These issues are not confronted properly, we're not honest about them, we blame colonisation and racism for our issues instead of getting to the crux of the problem. Indigenous women and children need protection in these communities. Perpetrators need to face consequences for their actions and not be let off lightly, or use customary law as an excuse to get away with crimes.*

Aboriginal people are being told by those removed from traditional culture that assimilation is a dirty word and that being part of the mainstream is bad, while these same people take advantage of the modern world. We have an absolute right to find our own solutions, to find our own way forward out of this misery without being vilified by those who claim to be on our side and claim to speak for us. We live in an era of Smoke and Mirrors, where an industry has arisen that purports to be helping Indigenous Australia, and yet while increasing sums are spent the promised outcomes are nowhere in sight. Why has this happened? Because somewhere within our country's consciousness, a shift has taken place, which has triggered an obsession with our country's historical injustices toward Indigenous Australians and a blindness about the real problems that abound today. As long as we continue to be sidelined by arguments for the need for more symbolism changing the date, replacing the national anthem, finding racism where it does not exist the real issues will not be solved.

16

Migrants: Everyone was an Immigrant at Some Point

When the place and you are strangers and you struggle all alone, and you have a mighty longing for the town where you are known. When your clothes are very shabby and the future's very black. There is nothing that can hurt you like the shame of going back.

Henry Lawson

For most of its white settlement history until the middle of the 20th century Australia felt itself geographically and culturally isolated in the Asia Pacific region. It feared teeming Asian nations, especially as they began to emerge from the long shadow of European colonialism, and that gave rise to the White Australia Policy. The fear was real and imaginary in equal measure. The country was under-populated, sparsely settled away from the fertile east coast and bereft of proper defence. Britannia may have ruled the waves, but Britain was 13,500 nautical miles distant from Australian shores. Australians felt they were on their own and needed to exercise strong immigration vigilance, which meant excluding Asians and coloured people from entering the country. Those needed for essential labour were granted a temporary immigration exemption.

An Australian Government Parliamentary Library online monograph has this to say about the introduction of the White Australia Policy. *The*

Immigration Restriction Bill, which enacted the White Australia Policy, was initiated in the House of Representatives by Prime Minister Edmund Barton on 5 June 1901. The Bill was one of the first substantive pieces of legislation to be introduced to the new Commonwealth Parliament. As there was almost universal support for the immigration restriction of non-Europeans to Australia, much of the parliamentary debate focused on the character of the bill not whether or not it should be enacted. The debate explored the best method of exclusion and whether exclusion was best achieved through the introduction of an education or dictation test. The majority of parliamentarians advocated absolute exclusion; others supported the admission of small numbers of coloured labourers to work in the tropical regions of the north, while a minority argued for admitting a limited number of educated 'coloured aliens'. The Protectionist Government was unified in its support for the Bill. Labor politicians, who were vociferous in their opposition to coloured labour, offered strong support to the Government.

The White Australia Policy restricting European and non-British migrant entry to Australia was the law of the land until 1973, when the last remnants of the policy were abolished by the Whitlam Government. Reforms had commenced in the 1950s and were accelerated by Prime Minister Harold Holt in 1966. The Immigration Restriction Act (1901) was replaced by the Immigration Act in 1958, which dispensed with the language dictation test and introduced a system of visas. The White Australia Policy was already an anachronism and ignored as European migrants and refugees flocked to Australia in the post war years.

oooOOOooo

Immigration and refugees occupy a central place in the modern Australian mindset. In her speech to parliament in 2016 after being re-elected, Senator Pauline Hanson said *in my first parliamentary speech in 1996, I said we were in danger of being swamped by Asians. This was not said out of disrespect for Asians but was meant as a slap in the face to both the Liberal and Labor governments who opened the floodgates to immigration, targeting cultures purely for the vote, to such an extent that society changed too rapidly due to migrants coming in the front door but also the back door.* Hanson faced widespread criticism for expressing a view unpopular with those on the political left. The One

Nation Senator was voicing a fear that was clearly on the mind of many worried Australians.

A 2020 Letter to the Editor expressed Aussie concern at high levels of immigration. *Australia's political class have flung open our borders and embarked on a radical demographic and cultural experiment. With the highest per capita immigration rate and the highest proportion of foreign-born residents in the developed world, Australia is fast being reduced to an international boarding house for an assortment of people with no attachments to each other. An unprecedented colossal immigration wave largely from culturally-distant countries, is rapidly sweeping away the Australia that had evolved by the end of the twentieth century.*

According to the Australian Bureau of Statistics, population growth within a single lifetime (my own) has been astonishing. In 1955 the population of Australia was 9,199,729, in 2019 it is 25,088,636. With the birth rate continuing to grow at around 120,000 and legal and refugee immigration adding a quarter of a million migrants each year, an estimate of an Australian population of 40 million by 2050 and a bewildering 100 million by 2100 is considered conservative. The Coronavirus pandemic brought about a static situation with a policy of quarantine and closed borders instituted. During 2020-21 immigration was reduced by 85% with only 15% arriving before international border closure. An October 2021 poll conducted by the Australian Population Research Institute, as the covid vaccinated nation contemplated reopening its international border to the world, revealed that 70% of Australians were opposed to a return to pre-pandemic immigration levels and wanted to see immigration substantially reduced to a more sustainable level.

In 2016 ABS statistics noted that 83% of those born overseas lived in a capital city. Sydney has the largest overseas born migrant population (1,773,496), followed closely by Melbourne (1,520,253) and Perth (702,545). The 2016 Census recounted that 820,000 migrants *self-reported they spoke English 'not well' or 'not at all*, up from 655,000 in 2011 and 560,000 in 2006. A Tower of Babel language confusion is in the process of undermining English as the dominant Aussie language. Without access to a common language, national identity and cultural unity are considerably more difficult to forge.

In March 2018, the then Federal Citizenship Minister Alan Tudge *warned that many migrants were becoming isolated, living in their own 'cultural bubbles' limiting their interactions with the broader society.* Ethnic enclaves or the *'geographical concentration' of migrants is linked with poor English language standards. If we are to guarantee the social cohesion of this country, if we are to guarantee a successful multicultural country into the future, then the broad Australian population needs to have reasonable English.* This was highlighted in Victoria during the Coronavirus pandemic, when despite repeated health warnings publicised in multiple languages, there was a systemic failure to get the health message across to non-English speaking migrants. The minister went on to say *it is incumbent on new migrants when they come here that they* (should) *want to learn English.*

Political scientist and journalist Dr Jennifer Oriel offers a sombre picture of migrant life inside today's urban ethnic enclaves. *Concerns have been raised about the emergence of ethnic ghettos in Australia, where cultural insularity is the norm. The crime rate of some ethnic groups is disproportionately high. The cultivation of anti-western sentiment among first and second generation* (Moslem) *immigrants devoted to jihad remains a serious national security issue. The problems have broadened the scope of inquiry about immigration reform. At the centre of inquiry is the question of how to balance rights with responsibilities and teach citizens that western freedom is a form of order not an excuse for violent disorder.*

oooOOOooo

In 1988 at the time of the bicentenary of white settlement in Australia, the Australian population was 75% Anglo/Celtic and most of the rest European. By 2025 the Anglo/Celtic population is predicted to be around 60%. The nuclear and extended family, Christianity and western civilisation were admired as the heritage foundation of the nation. There was a strong national bond that had none of the divisive social and cultural hurdles so obvious today from three decades of relentless mass immigration, championed by politicians for economic growth and voting reasons without consultation or approval from the trusting Aussie public.

In 2016 the Australian Bureau of Statistics Census *found that China was one of the top countries of birth for Australian residents. Over the past 20 years, Chinese born residents have overtaken other countries of birth, such as Italy, Vietnam and Greece, highlighting changes in Australia's migration intake.* In 1901 when the *Immigration Restriction Act* (White Australia Policy) was introduced, there 32,700 Chinese residents living in Australia. By 1947 the number had fallen to just 12,100. Australia today is home to more than 1.2 million people of Chinese ancestry and the figure is growing exponentially each year. Australia's annual immigration rate between 2013 and 2019 was 260,000. During that same five year period, Chinese immigration increased by five times and migrants coming from India by a staggering nine times. White immigration from the United Kingdom, Europe, America and Canada dropped significantly.

Since 2016 India has ranked first in immigration to Australia. In the two years between 2017 and 2019, the Indian population in Australia increased by a whopping 30%. Between the Census years 2011 and 2016, Moslem residency and immigration to Australia increased by 15%. In June 2018 the overall migrant population stood at 7.3 million; with around 29.7% of Australian citizens born overseas. If these high rates of Asian and to a lesser degree African immigration continue, then the white Australian population will be overtaken by the pressing tide of immigrants and refugees, resulting for the first time in a loss of majority social and cultural position. The consequences of this will radically change the face of Australia forever.

oooOOOooo

Australia is among one of the most urbanised countries in the world. In 2019 the majority of Australians (85%) live in towns and cities. Around 70% are resident in capital cities, leaving only 15% of Australians with a rural background. Sydney, Melbourne and other capital cities are literally bursting at the seams, as they engage in a futile attempt to accommodate the migrant influx, which predominantly congregates in these cities. Melbourne is Australia's fastest growing city with a migrant population from 200 countries, speaking 233 languages and following 116 different religious faiths. In one Sydney suburb alone, there are more than 100 different migrant nationalities, many without citizenship.

Some deride Australian citizenship as inferior to their own cultural identity. They demand access to our freedoms, but seek language and cultural separation. Others are more than happy to assimilate and they gratefully accept the Australian way of life, become good citizens and contribute to the national prosperity.

The regional city of Shepparton in Victoria with a population of more than 60,000, 10% of whom have refugee status and others drawn from the 1.5 million temporary visa holders currently living in Australia, is hailed as a multicultural success story. *With up to 60 languages other than English spoken in the home, Greater Shepparton City Councillor Chris Hazelman, said Shepparton's demographic profile was 'unique' for a provincial Australian town. 'We have four operating mosques, a Sikh temple and an Albanian mosque, which is actually the longest continuously operating mosque in regional Australia'.*

Behind the multicultural veil of political correctness, a feeling exists among many regional Australians that they are losing control of their towns. No racism is involved; simply a pressing need to understand why regional towns are increasingly becoming bastions of multicultural exclusiveness with all of its associated social and cultural problems. In March 2021, the media reported the newly amalgamated Greater Shepparton Secondary College which caters for more than 2,000 students, 600 of whom come from Aboriginal and other ethnic backgrounds, was in the grip of adolescent racial tensions spilling over into a violent student encounter where the police had to be called to quell the violence. *One boy was taken to hospital with head injuries after a fight and a 15-year-old and an 18-year-old were later arrested by police. Students involved in the affray were also suspended.* Parent Colleen Jones, representing a community group opposed to the new school merger because it denied families a safe schooling choice, said *the violence is unbelievable; it's a dangerous place for our children to be. This education plan should never have been introduced to Shepparton.*

The response of the Victorian Education Department was to accuse its teachers of 'systemic racism'. *The multicultural school is reckoning with a leaked report, commissioned by Victoria's Department of Education and Training, that identified a culture of 'systemic racism' among its exclusively white teaching staff.* The apparent solution was to employ *private security guards, additional teachers and extra multicultural education aides to create a culturally safe and inclusive environment.*

Predicably with the leaked report in its hands, the ABC wrote of a *staff reluctant to confront unconscious biases. The report identifies an unwillingness by existing staff to undertake cultural awareness training.* Shepparton's teachers rightly felt aggrieved by their employer's accusation of racism. Only 3 out of more than 100 school staff agreed to undergo the Education Department's diversity and unconscious bias training course. It was a further insult and teacher morale reached rock bottom. The independent Member of Parliament for Shepparton Suzanna Sheed said *teachers at the schools lacked the resources to deal with the violence and festering ill will within the city's secondary schools* — an ill will that extended beyond school boundaries into the larger community. It is clear where multicultural racism and violence in Shepparton were coming from and it was not from systemic racism of the city's white teachers.

oooOOOooo

During the second world war, Italian POWS taken prisoner during the North Africa campaign were shipped to Australia and some were sent to the Bete Bolong Prisoner of War Camp near Buchan in East Gippsland. There they were assigned work as labourers on Gippsland farms. Repatriated at war's end and sent home, some returned to Australia in the post war years seeking a better life. In April 1950, the Melbourne *Age* carried a story concerning the fate of *Emelio Colangelo, 35, killed by a tractor. The former Italian POW died in the Korumburra Bush Nursing Hospital on Wednesday from injuries he received, when a tractor he was driving capsized and fell on him. He had worked for Mr D Olsen on his property at Poowong North as a prisoner of war and had been back in Australia for nine months.* Emelio returned to Australia because he believed there was opportunity here for a better life.

The 1950s was a time of strong post war immigration from Europe. European migrants and refugees came in ever increasing numbers and the British pre-war face of Australia was set for dramatic change. Many adjustments would have to be made by the new arrivals, many of whom came here with nothing but a suitcase and a dream for a better life. Like British pioneer immigrants of an earlier period, the majority of these uprooted European people through hard work and sacrifice made a new life for themselves and their children now reaching into the third generation.

In June 1950, the staunchly Irish Catholic *Advocate* newspaper compassionately spoke of migrants *pouring in upon us in their thousands and hundreds of thousands. These Catholic 'new Australians' come from many different people with traditions and histories lying far apart; but they are bound to us by two things their common humanity and the heritage of Faith. We, who have ourselves received that Faith from the Irish pioneers the Faith of Saint Patrick, fought for and preserved through ages of oppression have now to make our love of Christ the vital force in a great creative work, the moulding of a new Australian Catholic life to which these exiled people can contribute their richness and colour.*

At an Australasian Women's Association meeting on Australia Day 1950; Mrs D Blackburn in proposing a toast to *Australia and the day we celebrate*, said *many who are members of pioneer families have their roots deep in this country. Today standing beside them, are newer Australians who in the future, would make their contribution to the country's progress. We must be big enough to accept these people from other lands, and to join hands with them in friendship and good fellowship to work together for the future of Australia.*

In the same year an *Argus* journalist wrote *we are friendly to new Australians. Each one I spoke to — English, Ukrainian and Hungarian had the nicest things to say about Australia and Australians. A Hungarian lass Claire Fuchs (once a concert pianist now a domestic servant) said 'everybody is so terribly nice, it is not difficult to get acclimatised to this country. I get along with everybody over here. I did at first find it hard to do the cooking and peel the potatoes, when I had only played the piano for 16 years but I am only sorry I didn't come sooner'.*

oooOOOooo

The refugee immigration target for Australia in 1950 was set at 200,000;

100,000 migrants from Britain and the same amount from war-torn Europe. The nationwide assumption was that integration and unity would govern the immigration process. Once in Australia wrote the *Age* assimilation was the goal. *People coming here must be accepted on terms of equality and opportunity and given full citizen rights as soon as possible. Insular attitudes of mind and prejudices against people of particular races or beliefs must give way to tolerance and a helpful interest in promoting assimilation.* There was a patriotic and national purpose at work, taking in more migrants *is the compelling answer to the incalculable dangers facing an underpopulated country and therefore decreed by the needs of national self-preservation.*

In January 1950, the *Age* succinctly summed up Australia's attitude towards post war immigration in the following glowing terms. *New Australians have come, not to take anybody's job, or to make it more difficult to find houses; on the contrary, they are here to create new jobs, build new houses, stimulate production and assist in the task of developing Australia as a land of vigorous, self-reliant, self-respecting people. New Australians should be welcomed, not only as economic assets contributing to the manpower of the nation, but on a warm basis of common humanity. Once assimilated, they and their children will add to the wealth, culture and mobility of the nation.*

On Australia Day 1950, the Melbourne *Herald* published a letter from E. Leembruggan, Glenhuntly Road, Elsternwick, which praised the principled stand of a migrant unionist at odds with his union. *Australians might learn something from some new Australians as regards divesting themselves of misdirected loyalty and allegiance to causes not wholly aligned with the dictates of Australian conscience. If the action of the new Australian who is defying his union is a stand against communist control, his attitude is an object lesson and highly commendable. It is easy to follow the herd, but often takes character to make an astute stand against what one knows to be wrong. Dictatorships have sprung from too much of the herd mentality.*

Upon arrival migrants faced some discrimination, but mostly their experience of Australia and Australians was welcoming and positive. In January 1950, the *Age* published an article titled 'Union Policy on Migration'. *At first the trade union movement objected to uncontrolled migration, but as there was no unemployment, and the fact that migrants were being selected in a sensible manner, it has no objection to controlled migration. Most unions were very happy to do what they could to assist migrants and help them to become accustomed to Australian standards.*

oooOOOooo

There were of course social and cultural tensions between the newcomers and resident Aussies. The slang terms 'dago' and 'wog' (Italians tasked to work from sunup to sundown were called dagos) became a belittling part of Australian culture, resented and demeaning to those they were directed against. On building sites and in factories across the nation clashes between 'aussies' and 'wogs' occurred, with epithets such as 'go back to your own country' being hurled at newcomers, sometimes good-naturedly sometimes not. The 1966 comedy film 'They're a Weird Mob' features Nino Culotta as an Italian immigrant who *tries to get a job and finishes up laying bricks. Nino works hard and makes friends with lots of locals. Nino and Kay fall in love. Kay takes Nino home to meet 'Daddy' but Daddy hates immigrants and bricklayers (he's now boss of a construction firm). Nino starts to win him over with his charm and determination to marry Kay.* Of course, all ends well with Kay's Irish Catholic Daddy finally accepting Nino when he points to a framed picture of the Pope on the wall saying *If I am a dago, then so is he!*

Still for those who had to endure insulting words there was trauma and hurt. A Greek girl, Maria Georgiadis, growing up in New South Wales during this turbulent time remembers, *sometimes I would go home crying. You became thick skinned, you had to. It offends me still the words dago and wog.* The legal strictures of the Racial Discrimination Act (1975) took the offensive sting out of the term wog. The woke mob define the term wog as hate speech and see it as offensive, when today the slang term is used in a self-empowering way by the ethnic minority it refers to for example the Greek comedies 'Wogs Out of Work' (1987) and 'Star Wogs: The Ethnics Strike Back' (2018).

Everything was not always as rosy and harmonious as politicians and significant others would have liked. Resentment festered on both sides at perceived racial insults, cultural differences and minor injustices. Spontaneous night time brawls would occasionally erupt outside migrant hostels at Heidelberg, Maribyrnong and Fisherman's Bend. The culprits were usually Aussie teenagers locking horns with refugee teenagers colloquially nicknamed 'refos'. Younger children and even adults would sometimes be involved in these scuffles. The police would be called and peace would be restored, only to reignite again in schoolyards, dances, cafés and movie theatres.

British child migrant William Hankins tells us *I remember the kid gang fights. There were kids from the UK, the Netherlands, Germany, the Baltic countries, Spain and Poland and later Hungary. At St Joseph's Primary School* (Fisherman's Bend) *there were lots of kids from Italy and Malta.* Another British child migrant, resident at the Royal Park Migrant Hostel in Melbourne, recounts *I lived at Camp Pell as a child and we used to sing a song. I can't remember it all, but it started like this. 'Camp Pell Kids. Camp Pell Kids. Camp Pell Kids are we. We're always up to mischief, wherever we may be'.* An Aussie resident of Heidelberg remembers *refugees from the migrant hostel as being polite people in the main, with only a few troublemakers on both sides causing problems and disruption.*

Delinquent Aussie and migrant teenagers were frequently front and centre of these wild public brawls. Gang fights would be arranged in advance, where both sides would appear at an agreed upon location armed with knives and clubs. Local dances would occasionally descend into chaos when ethnic tensions arose. Rock n' roll dances at Preston and St Kilda in Victoria were notorious for so called Aussie/Dago clashes. The fighting usually revolved around alcohol, girls and young men posturing. The fights were not always gang related and not all of the patrons would be involved. Migrants as well as Aussies started ethnic brawls. Something offensive was said, a push was involved and punches would follow. On a broader front despite occasional racial and cultural tensions arising, assimilation and accommodation to the Aussie way of life was the national goal of everyone.

oooOOOooo

A new tribalism based on race and woke politics has taken hold of the national psyche which is divisive in the present and derogatory of the past. The partitioning of Australian society into separate warring tribes battling for political and cultural dominance is encouraged by the woke media and daily enacted on the national stage. *Financial Review* journalist Craig Emerson thinks differently. *Tribalism is killing civil discourse in our country and around the world. It is killing progress. When a society reverts to tribes, doctrine supplants logic and reason with such force that rational thinkers deploying scientific tools to inform their views are treated as tribal enemies. Two tribes opposed to rational thought in favour of dogma. It looks and sounds eerily like the pre-Enlightenment period, where tribes were formed around monarchs and religions, predominantly Christianity and Islam.*

In March 2019, Prime Minister Scott Morrison rejected the notion of tribal separation. *I see every Australian as an individual, not part of some tribal group to be traded off against another. If we allow a culture of 'us and them', of tribalism, to take hold; if we surrender an individual to be defined not by their own unique worth and contribution but by the tribe they are assigned to; if we yield to the compulsion to pick sides rather than happy coexistence, we will lose what makes diversity work in Australia. Hate, blame and contempt are the staples of tribalism. It is consuming modern debate, egged on by an appetite for conflict as entertainment, not so different from the primitive appetites of the Colosseum days, with a similar corrosive impact on the fabric of our society. Contempt is defined by the philosophers as 'the unsullied conviction of the worthlessness of another'. The worthlessness of another! That is where mindless tribalism takes us.*

European and British post war migrants were a new generation of Australian pioneers leaving everything behind them to begin a new life half a world away. On a popular culture level, they brought with them food delicacies such as spaghetti, salami, pasta, pizzas, espresso coffee, olive oil and cooking with a variety of vegetables, herbs and spices foreign to Australians that are now an integral part of Australian cuisine. They introduced the Mediterranean café culture, distinctive styles of European clothing and footwear and from the rebellious teenage point of view, hairstylists and barbers not wedded to the Aussie short back and sides. Pre-war British influences were on the back foot in Australia and the post-war European migrant influx was the defining catalyst that brought about rapid social and cultural change.

In Australia over the past several decades, migrant numbers from countries all over the world including Asia, Africa and South America have soared to an unprecedented level. Closing the borders during the Coronavirus pandemic temporarily stemmed the flow. In the wake of the crisis a more measured and cautious approach is required if we are to avoid infrastructure overload and the social and cultural stress of accelerating tribal turmoil. The migrant base is now much broader in ethnic, cultural and religious faith than in the past. Unity and not woke division driven by skin colour and identity politics is the way forward. Migrants have played and will continue to play a significant role in a prosperous country built on immigration and respect for all enshrined in the Australian way of life. Working together rather than against one another is the egalitarian Aussie way and always has been.

17
Climate Change, CO2 and Renewables

Some ideas are so ridiculous that only an intellectual could believe them.

William Francis Buckley

John O'Brien's famous bush poem 'Said Hanrahan' was published in *Around the Boree Log and Other Verses* in 1921. It captured the essence of the unpredictable weather vagaries of bush farming life, the fragile optimism 'of just one good crop away' and in Hanrahan's case the 'We'll all be rooned pessimism' of the pioneer enterprise. Hanrahan's dire warnings of impending doom and gloom are reminiscent of today's climate change alarmists and their despairing prediction of global warming apocalypse.

> *'We'll all be rooned', said Hanrahan in accent most forlorn, outside the church, ere mass began, one frosty Sunday morn. The congregation stood about, coat collars to the ears, and talked of stock, and crops, and drought, as it had done for years.*
>
> *'It's lookin' crook', said Daniel Croke; 'bedad, it's cruke, me lad, for never since the banks went broke has seasons been so bad'. 'It's dry, all right', said young O'Neil, with which astute remark, he squatted down upon his heel and chewed a piece of bark. And so around the chorus ran 'It's keepin' dry, no doubt'. 'We'll all be*

rooned', said Hanrahan, 'before the year is out'.

'The crops are done; ye'll have your work to save one bag of grain; from here way out to back o' bourke they're singin' out for rain. They're singin' out for rain', he said, 'and all the tanks are dry'. The congregation scratched its head and gazed around the sky.

'There won't be grass, in any case, enough to feed an ass; there's not a blade on Casey's place as I came down to mass'. 'If rain don't come this month', said Dan and cleared his throat to speak. 'We'll all be rooned', said Hanrahan, 'If rain don't come this week'.

A heavy silence seemed to steal on all at this remark; And each man squatted on his heel and chewed a piece of bark. 'We want an inch of rain, we do', O'Neil observed at last; But Croke maintained we wanted two to put the danger past. 'If we don't get three inches, man, or four to break this drought, 'We'll all be rooned', said Hanrahan, 'before the year is out'.

In God's good time down came the rain; and all the afternoon on iron roof and window pane it drummed a homely tune. And through the night it pattered still, and lightsome, gladsome elves on dripping spout and window sill kept talking to themselves. It pelted, pelted all day long, a singing at its work, till every heart took up the song way out to back o' bourke. And every creek a banker ran, and dams filled overtop; 'We'll all be rooned', said Hanrahan, 'If this rain doesn't stop'.

And stop it did, in God's good time; and spring came in to fold a mantle o'er the hills sublime of green and pink and gold. And days went by on dancing feet, with harvest hopes immense, and laughing eyes beheld the wheat nid-nodding o'er the fence. And, oh, the smiles on every face, as happy lad and lass through grass knee deep on Casey's place went riding down to mass.

While round the church in clothes genteel discoursed the men of mark, and each man squatted on his heel and chewed his piece of bark. 'There'll be bushfires for sure, me man, there will, without a doubt; We'll all be rooned', said Hanrahan, 'before the year is out'.

oooOOOooo

Australia is a vast dry country of periodic droughts, floods and bushfires. Climate change, variable and fickle as every farmer knows, has always been with us. Nobody questions this undeniable fact. However natural disasters such as storms, cyclones, hurricanes, blizzards, tornadoes and the like vary in seasonal intensity. They are by definition unpredictable and not a reliable measure of cyclic shifts in the earth's ever-changing weather patterns. Weather trends from the distant and not so distant past denote recurring periods of heat and cold, droughts and floods and rising and falling sea levels. Clearly, there is climate change complexity that belies the 'sky is falling' predictions of impending worldwide calamity.

Occurring around 252 million years ago, the Permian/Triassic extinction event was the earth's most catastrophic circumstance with 96% of marine species, 70% of land species and 83% of all genera becoming extinct over a geological period of some 2 million years. There were three distinct phases of the 'Great Dying' as it is called by scientists. A complexity of causes, the most serious of which were massive volcanic eruptions such as those that took place within the 'Siberian Traps', fissure-like basaltic lava and ash-spewing volcanoes, spreading devastation across the land and seascape of the Supercontinent of Pangaea which comprised all the land of the earth existing together in one place. Immense lava flows and swift flowing water erosion over exposed coal beds released a massive amount of Carbon Dioxide, Hydrogen Sulphide and Methane gas, making the earth's atmosphere and oceans toxic.

An alternate and possibly contiguous theory suggests a dimming of the Sun around 250 million years ago, due to the spiral arm of the Milky Way Galaxy passing through thickly obscuring gas clouds triggering a devastating planetary ice age. Whichever theory is the right one, the few plant and animal species that survived are said to have taken between 2 and 10 million years to repopulate the planet. The optimistic message to be drawn from the earth's long-ago calamity is that life on earth is irrepressible and resilient, able to reset itself and thrive again even in the most horrendous environmental circumstances.

There have been six major glacial ice ages (periods with large land ice sheets) in the earth's ecological history. We are living in an interglacial ice age — a period with lesser land ice sheets known as the Holocene. It is an interglacial interlude within the Pleistocene epoch that began around 11,700 years ago; an epoch that in all probability, despite global warmest predictions of pending unprecedented catastrophe, will continue for many thousands of years to come into the next glacial ice age. Ian Plimer, geologist and Emeritus Professor of Earth Sciences at the University of Melbourne, comments *we are getting towards the end of a warm period; the peak of the warmth was about 5,000 years ago and we are heading for the next inevitable ice age. To use the word 'unprecedented'* (in reference to global warming prediction) *shows you have expunged history and geology from your knowledge.*

In the current interglacial period, temperature variations fluctuate between the freezing cold, the blistering hot to milder conditions. Civilisation and agriculture arose in this eco-friendly age of favourable conditions. The earth is presently undergoing one of its periodic warmer phases. Ice sheets in the Arctic and Antarctic grow and retreat on a monthly and yearly basis according to the climatic intensity of the season. In Spring 2020, Antarctic Sea ice was increasing at a rate that confounded scientists. According to the National Aeronautical Space Administration (NASA); *Paul Holland, a climate modeler with the British Antarctic Survey, has spent the last ten years studying Antarctica's sea ice and the Southern Ocean. Lately, he has been scrutinizing the seasons of Antarctica and how fast the ice comes and goes. Holland thinks these seasons may be a key to a conundrum: If earth's temperatures are getting warmer and sea ice in the Arctic has been shrinking fast, why then is sea ice in the Antarctic slowly increasing?* Alarmist predictions of a permanent and irreversible ice depletion at both poles rather than reoccurring natural cycles simply do not accord with the environmental facts.

In November/December 2013, Professor Chris Turney from the University of New South Wales led a summer expedition aboard the Russian ship Akademik Shokalskiy to the Antarctic. The expedition was to study the effects of climate change on Antarctic ice sheets and Australia's weather patterns. The assumption was the Antarctic ice sheet cover was under abnormal global warming stress. 'The Ship of Fools' as the expedition was subsequently labelled became trapped in Antarctic ice three metres thick for several days. At the height of the drama a crew member tweeted *Our rescue boat, the Xue Long* (a Chinese icebreaker) *has had to turn back because the ice was too thick for it to get through. We're are now awaiting Aurora Australis*. The Aurora Australis (an Australian icebreaker) was forced to abandon its rescue attempt and turn back with snow flurries and freezing cold winds posing even greater danger.

In Roman times, climate sensitive crops were being successfully grown in Britain due to a year-round warmer temperate than at present. During the Middle Ages a warming period known as the 'Medieval Climate Optimum' which lasted from circa 950 AD to circa 1250 AD prevailed. In 1965 British paleoclimatologist Hubert Lamb wrote *evidence has been accumulating in many fields of investigation pointing to a notably warm climate in many parts of the world, that lasted a few centuries around c 1000 AD — c 1200 AD, and was followed by a decline of temperature levels till between c 1500 AD and c 1700 AD the coldest phase since the last ice age occurred.* Back then the 20th century climate prediction was that the world was rapidly heading towards another severe ice age.

As the Industrial Revolution got underway around 1760, global temperatures were higher than they are today, despite the period which followed the medieval warming being called the 'Little Ice Age'. The current trend is towards a greening and slight warming of the planet. In February 2019, NASA reported *the world is literally a greener place than it was 20 years ago. This new insight was made possible by a nearly 20-year-long data record from a NASA instrument orbiting the earth on two satellites. It's called the Moderate Resolution Imaging Spectroradiometer, or MODIS, and its high-resolution data provides very accurate information, helping researchers work out details of what's happening with earth's vegetation, down to the level of 500 metres, or about 1,600 feet, on the ground.* The satellite imagery was dramatic *taken all together, the greening of the planet over the last two decades represents an increase in leaf area on plants and trees equivalent to the area covered by all the Amazon rainforests. There are now more than two million square miles of extra green leaf area per year, compared to the early 2000s a 5% increase.*

The Global Warming Policy Forum in July 2019 stated numerous satellite observations have shown that the increase in the atmospheric CO2 (Carbon Dioxide) content has contributed significantly to the greening of our planet over the last decades because the rising CO2 content of the air acts like a fertiliser on the vegetation. Satellite images show that plant cover has become lush all over the world. This increase in green biomass worldwide is equivalent to a new green continent twice the size of the US.

oooOOOooo

As the greening of the planet demonstrates rather than accelerating towards hunger and famine worldwide crop production has never been higher. We are living in a climatic period of marginally warmer global temperatures. For Australia this means the possibility of more intense droughts and hotter summers with greater bushfire risk. It does not mean global cataclysm and the beginning of the end for human and animal life, as Swedish schoolgirl activist Greta Thunberg and others endlessly preach. Thunberg's scaremongering hyperbole: *The World is on Fire! People are dying! Ecosystems are collapsing!* is biblical in its end of days fervour. Sadly, even the Pope and the Dalai Lama now espouse a fake climate change message. Thunberg's climate extremist panic lacks scientific credibility and plain common sense. Nor does it mean that there will not be an eventual return to a colder ice age period, as the global doomsayers of the late 20th century were obsessively predicting and now conveniently neglect to mention.

In 2008, Al Gore, Vice President in the Clinton administration and a prominent climate change alarmist, warned the world that the Arctic would be entirely ice free by 2013. The prediction spectacularly failed to eventuate. Gore's 2006 Oscar winning documentary 'An Inconvenient Truth' which is still being shown in classrooms today as scientific fact, despite a 2007 UK High Court ruling that its false information breached the Education Act, is a sleight of hand drama of questionable statements cobbled together to scare and intimidate. It is an egregious example of fact distortion and appeal to spurious scientific authority. Gore's climate catastrophe documentary is on a fraudulent par with Erich von Däniken's discredited 1970s alien visitation 'Chariot of the Gods' film and book swindle. Both are superficially convincing until subjected to thorough scrutiny and objective analysis when the central argument and 'facts' fall apart.

The hypocrisy of those who claim environmental cataclysm is truly astonishing. Al Gore has made a personal fortune from his failed predictions and he continues to spread a fake message of impending global catastrophe. President Barrack Obama and Al Gore, both strident eco warriors and global alarmists, have predicted a rise in sea levels which will bring about worldwide environmental catastrophe. Genuine science tells us sea levels are stable and there is no need for panic. Both men and their families live in multimillion-dollar mansions overlooking the seashore — so how real do you think the danger is?

In a career spanning several decades Australian palaeontologist and climate alarmist, Tim Flannery, has made many failed predictions. In 2004 Flannery prophesied: *I think there is a fair chance Perth* (WA) *will be the 21st century's first ghost metropolis* due to climate change. Famously in 2007, Flannery proclaimed *even the rain that falls isn't actually going to fill our dams and river systems.* In 2012, he predicted that *Victoria's changing climate is likely to lead to less snowfall.* In subsequent years, Flannery's alarmist predictions became even more strident and ludicrous. The Great Barrier Reef would collapse entirely by 2020. The world was nearing imminent and catastrophic disaster. None of these dire predictions came true and Flannery is revealed for the climate change flim-flam man he is. One critic commented *Tim suffers from what most alarmist suffer from: a complete lack of balance in science, data and facts. He shamelessly predicts things that never come true and never apologises when he is caught out.*

A disgruntled Aussie saw through the sham science and alarmist rhetoric peddling approaching global catastrophe. *It started off with 'global warming' and then morphed into 'climate change' when the 'warming' aspect was not really happening. To think humans can change the climate either for better or worse is a very egotistical sentiment. We can't even predict the weather for the next week correctly, but yet we think we can predict climate? According to alarmists like Flannery and Gore we should have all been dead years ago!*

Environmentalist Michael Schellenberger, described as an eco-pragmatist and *Time* magazine's 'Hero of the Environment' in 2008, wrote in *Forbes* magazine in December 2019 *I started out pretty anti-nuclear. I changed my mind as I realised you can't power a modern economy on solar and wind. All they do is make the electricity system chaotic and provide greenwash* (green marketing spin) *for* (abolishing) *fossil fuels.* In February 2020, Schellenberger again wrote in *Forbes* magazine. *Bernie Sanders called climate change 'an existential threat'. Extinction Rebellion said 'billions will die' and Greta Thunberg said 'I don't want you to be hopeful' about climate change, 'I want you to panic'.*

German teenager Naomi Seibt, mockingly labelled by the world's media as a climate denier and anti-Greta sensation for speaking out against the Thunberg alarmist message, was threatened by the German Government with prison for her video climate posts. *I am not anti-Greta, and we are not climate deniers. We are currently being force-fed a very dystopian agenda of climate alarmism, that tells us that we as humans are destroying the planet and that young people especially have no future: that the animals are dying, that we are ruining nature. Many people are now developing mental disorders, and referring to them as eco-anxiety and eco-depression. I believe it is important, that we act now and change this entire mainstream narrative of fear-mongering and climate alarmism. What is so dangerous about all of this is that we are now doing real politics with fictional science. I don't want you to panic. I want you to think.*

oooOOOooo

Green activists and the current crowd of Extinction Rebellion climate alarmists begun by a small group of Socialist/Green/Woke militants in the UK in 2018, frighten impressible schoolchildren and worried adults into believing they have no future and the planet is doomed. Extinction Rebellion has its followers in Australia whose main preoccupation is vandalising public property, defacing the federal parliament, dressing in weird costumes, barricading city streets, disrupting traffic and gluing themselves to road surfaces.

Dr Patrick Moore, world-renowned scientist and cofounder of Greenpeace says of the environmental movement, it has become a *fraudulent moneymaking scam turned into a racket. The truth is*

Greenpeace and I underwent divergent evolutions. I became a sensible environmentalist; Greenpeace became increasingly senseless as it adopted an agenda that is anti-science, anti-business, and downright anti-human. Greenpeace is so far on the extreme left politically that it isn't an environmental movement anymore. The Greens have got control over management of resources in the hinterland where mining, forestry, fisheries and agriculture are going on and they are living in a completely artificial urban environment. People in the country are being depicted as the enemies of the earth. When in fact what they are doing is supplying people in the city with everything they need. They (the Greens) *are living in a fairytale world.*

In his bestselling book *Fake Invisible Catastrophes and Threats of Doom* Independently published (2021) Dr Moore writes. *The scare stories in the media today are based on things that are invisible, like CO2 and radiation, or very remote, like polar bears and coral reefs. Thus, the average person cannot observe and verify the truth of these claims for themselves. They must rely on activists, the media, politicians, and scientists — all of whom have a huge financial and/ or political interest in the subject — to tell them the truth. We are told that nuclear energy is very dangerous when the numbers prove it is one of the safest technologies. We are told polar bears will go extinct soon when their population has been growing steadily for nearly 50 years. We are told severe forest fires are caused by climate change when they are actually caused by poor management of fuel load (dead wood) in the forest. We are told that all the coral reefs will die by 2100 when in fact the most diverse coral reefs are found in the warmest oceans in the world. And of course, we are told that invisible CO2 from using fossil fuels, accounting for more than 80% of our energy supply, will make the Earth too hot for life. All of these scare stories, and many more, are simply not true. There is no substitute for the truth.*

Climate alarmists use computer modelling to make their dire predictions of global warming catastrophe. Dr Mototaka Nakamura a world-renowned climatologist, who for the past 25 years has specialized in studying abnormal weather and climate disaster events, questions computer modelling predictions and the untrustworthiness of the data upon which climate predictions are made. *The climate system is far more complex than an absurdly simple system simulated by the* (computer) *toys that have been used for climate predictions to date. The take home message is that all climate simulation models, even those with the best parametric representation schemes, suffer from a very large degree of arbitrariness. Since climate models are tuned arbitrarily, there is no reason to trust their predictions/forecasts.*

In much the same way as Australia's Coronavirus computer modelling turned out to be wildly erroneous. Dr Gavin Schmidt head of NASA's Goddard Institute of Space Studies (GISS) regards computer modelling as wholly unreliable in making precise global warming predictions. The models are alarmist and scientifically untrustworthy. *It's has become clear over the last year or so (2021) that we can't avoid this. Many of the world's leading models are now projecting global warming rates that most scientists, including the model makers themselves, believe are implausibly fast* (that is too hot). Journalist and climate change sceptic Rowan Dean agrees with Dr Schmidt's analysis. *Every climate model going back to the 70s and 80s they've all been way, way exaggerated. Someone averaged out all the climate models over the past 40 years and matched them against reality and guess what, reality was lower than even the lowest of all the climate models! So, reality refuses to do what the climate models predict. When empirical evidence doesn't match the theory then the theory must be wrong.*

Climate modelling is only as good as the quality of data input and the parameters used. Extreme weather conditions are not as climate change cultist proclaim convincing proof of accelerated global warming. Environmental disasters have occurred and will continue to occur as part of the natural cycle of evolutionary change. There have been severe weather events in the past such as prolonged droughts, calamitous floods, monster cyclones, mammoth snow storms and rapid onset glacial incursions and they will seasonally come again. The planet and its ecosystems are neither static nor catastrophically failing. They are changing and adapting as they have always done. Nature thrives on change, climatic and otherwise without it there would be no geological transformation, no species variation and no biological future for either humans or animals. Ecological change which can be devastating and life destroying is not the end of the world. It is the natural order of things.

oooOOOooo

There is no doubt that human activity since the Industrial Revolution has added a further dimension to the climate change dynamic. To what destructive degree is the crucial question nobody seems able to answer. Common sense observation and the opinion of many scientists, indicate that C02 emissions caused by human activity is not nearly as disastrous as hysterics of the climate alarmist cult would have us believe. The contested evidence for global warming and catastrophic climate change depends entirely on which group of scientists you choose to talk to: those on Thunberg's alarmist side of the equation espousing faux science or those with genuine fact-based scientific knowledge opposed to obsessed prediction.

Dr Jennifer Marohasy editor of *Climate Change: The Facts 2020* (2020) writes. *The contributors* (to the book) *all share the perspective that* (global) *warming is subject to cycles, and is not unusual in its rate or magnitude, and is not catastrophic. If anything about the climate is unprecedented, it is the notion that something as complex as climate science can be 'settled'. It is better to have questions that cannot be answered than answers that cannot be questioned.*

Professor Ian Plimer addressed the climate hysterics claim that 97% of the world's scientists believe in approaching climate catastrophe. *Trust in the Science!* they say. *You can't argue with the Science!* Yet the science of climate change is not clearly understood and is far from settled. Plimer writes *in my 50-year scientific career, I have never seen a hypothesis where 97% of scientists agree* (on anything). *The 97% figure derives from a survey sent to 10,257 people with a self-interest in human induced global warming who publish 'science' supported by taxpayer funded research grants. Replies from 3,146 respondents were whittled down to 77 self-appointed climate 'scientists' of whom 75 were judged to agree that human induced warming was taking place. The 97% figure derives from a tribe with only 75 members.* Climate cultists endlessly repeat this discredited figure as a green parable not to be questioned.

In November 2019, media headlines across the country reported: *11,000 scientists have signed a scientific paper declaring a climate emergency.* The scientific paper was no more than an online petition. One critic wrote: *I pulled down the list of the supposed 11,258 'scientists' who signed this declaration. There are only 4 who specifically state they are professors or lecturers in 'climate science'. There are 30 doctors, 23 vets. Nearly 1,000 PhD and master's students and 1,300 ecologists. Many are retired. Some work for the World Wildlife Fund. There's even over 100 economists on the list and many other occupations unrelated to science.* However, the most ridiculous entry recorded there has to be *Mickey Mouse, Professor of the Mickey Mouse Institute for the Blind!* We need to carefully scrutinise all such climate alarmist pronouncements, as invariably they turn out to be grossly exaggerated and patently untrue.

oooOOOooo

In August 2021, the United Nations Intergovernmental Panel on Climate Change (IPCC) released yet another of its 'special reports' beating the pessimist drum of impending climate catastrophe, which of course was *unequivocally caused by human activities.* The propaganda message was dire in its shrill urgency and anti-fossil fuel alarmist rhetoric. The earth was warming precipitously, sea levels were rising, glaciers melting and extreme weather events increasing. As a result of rapid global warming, the earth could be boiling and irreversibly damaged by the end of the century the consequence of major environmental crimes committed by planet destroying humans.

Global Socialist and UN Secretary-General António Guterres described the IPCC report as a 'Code Red for Humanity'. *The alarm bells are deafening, and the evidence is irrefutable: greenhouse gas emissions from fossil fuel burning and deforestation are choking our planet and putting billions of people at immediate risk. Global heating is affecting every region on Earth, with many of the changes becoming irreversible. This report must sound a death knell for coal and fossil fuels, before they destroy our planet.* Greta Thunberg called *for massive action to put pressure on governments to act now.*

Critics slammed the report as old news rehashed for the upcoming 2021 Glasgow COP26 climate summit. *The IPCC report was downgraded from their original computer projection, because the original was too high, as is this. But the projection is just that: a projection. There is nothing new in this report that has not been said many times before. The so-called science is just scaremongering computer modelling: weather is just the same as it has always been, unpredictable.*

Around the world 1,900 local councils have taken the knee in declaring a climate emergency. As of June 2021, 32 Victorian councils out of a total of 79 have joined the woke virtue signalling of environmental alarmists declaring a climate emergency and ecological disaster. The City of Melbourne Council came on board with the climate rhetoric in 2019. Interestingly for the purposes of this book, the South Gippsland Shire Council has not bowed to woke intimidation or vowed to spend ratepayer's money on a non-existent climate emergency. Politics and not science clearly govern the ramped-up oratory of climate pessimists shouting doom and gloom from the roof tops. *Only 12 years left to climate Armageddon unless we act now!*

A less than 1% rise in global warming is not the calamitous climate change bogeyman driving drought and bushfires it is claimed to be. Global warming is a contributory factor in a complex and widely fluctuating pattern of dynamic weather conditions. Many cumulative and coalescing factors are involved, fuel load being the most significant in the case of bushfire. The media and politically driven hysteria surrounding Australia's CO_2 emissions and the panic of impending climate catastrophe is overwrought and emotional.

CO_2 or Carbon Dioxide emissions comprise three quarters of the world's greenhouse gas discharge. Of these emissions (97%) are primarily natural in origin. Only 3% of current emissions come from man-made sources. CO_2 computer modelling and climate change prediction are fraught with error and sham parameters. The studies produce a false positive from grossly inadequate scientific data. They fail to take into account the more than 40,000 kilometres of un-monitored mid-ocean ridges, with thousands of submarine volcanoes, which through periodic eruption, leak primeval Carbon Dioxide previously trapped in rocks and mud. The gases are spewed into the earth's atmosphere — a natural geological process that has been going on for hundreds of millions of years. By comparison the man-made CO_2 contribution is minor.

Statistician Bjorn Lomborg, author of *False Alarm: How Climate Change Panic Costs Us Trillions, Hurts the Poor, and Fails to Fix the Planet.* Basic (2020), states *the first great myth of climate activism is that individuals can make a significant difference. The problem is that the changes we can make to our personal lifestyle and habits at best make only a tiny difference* (and this is true) *even if all of us do them.* Lomborg estimates that if every country in the world who signed up to the 2016 Paris Climate Agreement achieved their emission reduction target by 2030 and continued to reduce emissions for the rest of the century, the cost would be between 60-100 trillion dollars for an insignificant temperature reduction of just 0.2 degrees centigrade. The World Health Organisation (WHO) *Special Report on Climate Change and Health* issued 2 months before the 2021 Glasgow climate conference put the global cost of transition to renewables at a staggering 150 trillion dollars.

oooOOOooo

Australia has 0.03% of the world's population and produces just 1.3% of the 3% of manmade global CO_2 emissions. By way of comparison according to the International Energy Agency quoting 2018 metric gigaton (GT) statistics of the world's largest annual Carbon Dioxide emitters. China's CO_2 emissions were 28% (10.0GT), America 15% (5.41GT) and India 7% (2.65GT). Australia's CO_2 emissions figure of 1.3% was rated as sixteenth with 0.42GT. In December 2018 Dr Alan Finkel Australia's Chief Scientist from 2016 to 2020, a believer in climate change and an advocate for reducing CO_2 emissions worldwide, wrote: *on 1 June 2017, I attended a Senate Estimates hearing where Senator Ian Macdonald asked if the world was to reduce its carbon emissions by 1.3%, which is approximately Australia's rate of emissions, what impact would that make on the changing climate of the world. My response was that the impact would be virtually nothing.* In 2017 the CSIRO estimated that the economic cost of transition to renewables in Australia would be one trillion dollars. Destroying Australia's prosperous economy and degrading its functioning power grid for a virtue signalling zero emissions goal is woke lunacy of the first order.

No matter what we do economically or how wisely we use energy it is simply not in our power to save the planet from global warming, even if we were to stop mining coal immediately and achieve zero emissions. The pipedream of a 100% stand-alone renewables power generation system is just that: a green pipedream. The reality is that 80% of the world's power generation comes from fossil fuel production, particularly from natural gas and coalfired power plants. Where practicable we should of course use wind and solar power generation as well as hydropower, a clean and water renewable energy source, in support of the national power grid. Even with these renewable addons available, baseline grid stability will be reliant on fossil fuel and if the debate takes place 'demonised' nuclear power well into the foreseeable future.

Those who demand zero emissions stubbornly refuse to even consider zero emissions nuclear power as a viable alternative to fossil fuelled power stations and prohibitively expensive renewables. Thermonuclear fusion reactors currently in the research development stage are a zero carbon emissions source with a promising future that will add a further dimension to the nuclear resource. Fusion compresses nuclear material together, whereas fission drives nuclear material apart. Australia should develop a fission and fusion nuclear power capacity. Nuclear power generation is now much safer and technologically far superior to the older fission nuclear plants and radiation problems that Australians feared in 1999 when a nuclear ban was imposed. The new kid on the block, a small modular fission nuclear reactor (SMR) that takes up only 1% of the space of a conventional nuclear reactor, operates in linked banks and produces less waste, which makes it a power generation game changer.

UK environmental journalist Lois Parshley writes that small modular gas cooled, pebble-bed nuclear reactors *overcome many of the drawbacks of traditional larger reactors. Their small cores produce far less heat than the cores in large reactors. They are much less likely to overheat because of innovative designs in SMR technology that reduce coolant pumps failing.* Numerous safety protections are included to avoid a Fukushima style calamity. During the 2011 Fukushima tsunami and nuclear reactor meltdown disaster, the tsunami killed 15,893 people; 573 people died from evacuation and stress induced difficulties. As of 2018 only one Japanese powerplant worker has died due to radiation exposure. There have been no noticeable effects on perinatal mortality (stillbirths and infant deaths) and a predicted wave of cancer deaths from the twin disaster has so far not occurred. Australia is a geologically stable country, so the danger of precarious storage and natural disaster is minimal. The small-scale Lucas Heights nuclear reactor situated 40 kms from Sydney was in operation from 1958-2007 without serious mishap. In 2007 it was replaced by a more modern type of reactor again without safety problems.

Overlooked in the discussion concerning the reliability and safety of SMRs, is that the US and navies around the world have used small-scale nuclear fission propulsion for their nuclear submarines for more than 60 years. In September 2021, the Morrison Government announced it would be investing in nuclear power submarines. Australian Workers Union National Secretary Daniel Walton went further calling for a civilian nuclear power capability. *Every nation in the world that has the capacity to build or operate nuclear submarines also has nuclear energy capabilities. Why would we make ourselves the exception?*

Former UK Extinction Rebellion activist Zion Lights, who subsequently saw the light (pun intended), stated *a key part of protecting the natural environment for my children is nuclear energy that is just a fact. it's the only solution. If you're building huge solar farms with huge wind turbines* (in Australia). *I don't see why that's okay, and that's seen as green but nuclear energy isn't. You could have abundant energy and energy independence and not rely on anybody. You could be a world leader in showing how things are done. You can create a decarbonized future that still gives everybody abundant energy, high quality of life, but just isn't causing climate change. You've got loads of space as well, you've got more space than we have* (in the UK).

A 2008 federal parliamentary research paper states: *Australia has the world's largest resources of low-cost uranium. It exports 10,000 tonnes of uranium oxide per year. Uranium is an important export earner for Australia. In 2007–08 Australia exported $887 million dollars' worth of uranium. World demand for uranium exceeds current world production and will ultimately lead to more uranium exports from Australia and greater world prices.* Yet we handicap ourselves by not using for industry and domestic power production uranium resources we profitably export to the rest of world. A clean energy resource for emissions-free nuclear power generation in foreign countries, which we continue to refuse to use ourselves. It is time to rescind the outdated ban on nuclear power and take advantage of our natural uranium resource for zero emissions power generation.

The Australian Government's Geoscience website gives a percentage breakdown of the nation's natural resources and energy production. *Australia produces about 2.4% of total world energy and is a major supplier of energy to world markets, exporting more than three-quarters of its energy output, worth nearly A$80 billion. Australia has an estimated 46% of uranium resources, 6% of coal resources, and 2% of natural gas resources in the world. In contrast, Australia has only about 0.3% of world oil reserves. Australia is the world's largest exporter of coal. Coal accounts for more than half of Australia's energy exports. Australia is one of the world's largest exporters of uranium, and is ranked sixth in terms of liquefied natural gas (LNG) exports. Australia's primary energy consumption is dominated by coal (around 40%), oil (34%) and gas (22%). Coal accounts for about 75% of Australia's electricity generation, followed by gas (16%), hydro (5%) and wind around (2%).* (Solar energy accounts for 5.2% of Australia's total electricity production.)

oooOOOooo

Aussie systems engineer Michael Green, quoting the World Energy Outlook 2020 Report from the International Energy Agency, *reveals demand for* (Australian) *coal in the Asia Pacific* (region) *will grow in coming years and that a global target of net zero emissions by 2050 is unachievable in practice. Demand for coal in the power and industry sectors continues to grow in India, Indonesia and Southeast Asia and China.* In Southeast Asia the report tells us, the demand for Aussie coal is projected to increase by a significant 30% by 2030. There is a bright long-term economic future for the mining, sale and export of Australian coal. Coal's predicted imminent demise as an essential fossil fuel world power source has been grossly overstated by zero emissions green propagandists. In June 2021, Deputy Prime Minister Barnaby Joyce said *we've had record sales of coal. Record sales, at record prices for thermal coal. Guess where they use that? Coal-fired power stations!*

The rest of the world continues to buy Australian coal and to build coalfired power stations, as we run down and decommission the remaining few in grid operation throughout the country. China invests heavily in coalfired power stations. In 2020, China built three times more coalfired power stations than the rest of the world combined. It did so with privileged WTO developing country status, despite being the world's second largest economy and in 2021 landing a satellite rover on the planet Mars. China operates in excess of 3,000 coalfired power stations, a figure that continues to grow exponentially. In 2019, before China placed trade sanctions on Australia for daring to call for an enquiry into the origin of the Coronavirus, Australia exported coal to China worth $13.7 billion dollars. Despite its aggrieved blustering, China's growing economy needs coal and Australia has the best thermal and coking coal reserves in the world. How long China will punish Australia and buy inferior coal from other countries is a question worth asking.

China discharges more CO_2 emissions into the atmosphere in 16 days than Australia does in an entire year and will continue to do so without accountability until 2030. Australian journalist Greg Sheridan takes with a grain of salt that *the Chinese have committed to zero emissions by 2060. Meanwhile simultaneously, they have the biggest coalfired power station construction program of any nation in the world. They are responsible for nearly 30% of* (manmade) *global emissions and responsible virtually for all the increase in global emissions over the last 10 years.* As of 30 June 2020 in addition to its coalfired power stations, China has 50 operational nuclear power plants with 11 more currently under construction.

China pays lip service to climate change and zero omission targets, but clearly has no intention of abiding by any agreement. The Chinese Communist Party strategy is to make use of climate change and CO_2 emissions reduction, in the same unconscionable way the CCP knowingly facilitated the spread of the Wuhan Coronavirus to the rest of the world at a time when climate change and zero emissions obsessed western countries are rushing to deindustrialise and further weaken their economies. China with a global monopoly on manufacturing solar panels and wind turbines, is rapidly growing its economy and strengthening its military in a quest for world domination.

oooOOOooo

Solar and wind renewables are heavily subsidised and backed up by fossil fuels. Between 2005 and 2015, the federal government spent $51.2 billion dollars of taxpayer money on renewable energy subsidies, granting tax incentives for 90% of those taken up. By comparison the government subsidy for the oil and gas industry was $1.8 billion dollars in 2014. Coal mining in 2017-18 received approximately 1 billion dollars in government subsidy. The bottom line is that renewables annually received five times as much public money as reliable oil and gas. On these figures, the annual subsidy for coal is ten times lower than that for renewables.

A trillion dollars will need to be spent on renewable energy transmission infrastructure and the development of lithium battery storage capacity. Household lithium-ion battery arrays costing anywhere from $3,420 to $20,700 (May 2020 Australian prices) have a finite life measured in a couple of decades, as do wind turbines and solar panels. Over time, wind turbines and solar panels become functionally impaired and need scrupulous maintenance in order to continue to operate. The disposal of used turbine blades, solar panels and spent batteries containing lead, cadmium and other toxic chemicals is fast becoming a major worldwide problem. Wind turbines an ugly scar on the landscape, generate a pulsating sound that annoys humans and are annually responsible for killing thousands of birds and other flying wildlife. It is estimated that 1,500 Wedgetail Eagles are killed in Australia each year. In America approximately 330,000 bids die each year from wind turbine strikes.

oooOOOooo

Renewable energy advocates point to the Elon Musk-built Tesla battery facility in South Australia, as the green litmus test for renewable power storage. Renewable energy critic Rafe Champion writes of the shortcomings of battery storage and wind turbine generated power. He tells us there is a not insignificant problem with *wind droughts; frequent periods up to 30 hours in duration with next to no wind across the whole of South East Australia. The big battery has been hailed as a great contribution to the green transition, but it is important to realise how small it is compared with the demand of the power grid. The first Musk battery attached to South Australia's Hornsdale No 3 Wind Farm occupies a hectare, with a capacity of 129MWhrs and a $90 million price tag. It has been upgraded to 190MWhrs at a cost of $70* million, but compare those numbers with the demand of the SA power grid, ranging from 8,000MW to 25,000MW per hour depending on the season and the time of day. The amount of power that the battery can deliver is clearly negligible by comparison.

Renewable manufacture requires high temperatures which are currently generated by fossil fuels. Subject to when the sun shines and the wind blows, renewables are not sustainable even with battery storage backup in the short or the longer term. Grid instability has proven to be a troublesome problem with solar panels in South Australia, which proudly boasts that for one hour on Sunday 11 October 2020, all of the state's power generation came entirely from solar panels. Even with SA's large battery storage facility, a spike in electricity production within the grid when the interconnector link transporting electricity to Victoria was temporarily out of action, as it was for two weeks in February 2020, produced major grid disruption. Energy regulators had earlier warned *without careful management, grid stability could be at risk if there is more electricity going in than coming out.* The inevitable result was interruption to South Australia's power supply.

On Australia Day 2021 with searing heatwave conditions reaching 47.3C in Sydney's western suburbs, brownouts occurred across the suburbs due to heavy power demand. With three quarters of the New South Wales electricity grid operating on coal and a mixture of renewables, the power grid was simply overwhelmed by peak demand. In March 2021 with battery storage, solar power and wind turbine power generation online, South Australia was forced to shut down 1,200 homes with solar panels because of baseline grid instability. At present and for the foreseeable future, renewable energy is neither cheap, stable or dependable. It will always require massive battery, substantial fossil fuel and/or nuclear power backup. To pretend otherwise is to invite power shortages, through the roof electricity prices and ultimately economic ruin for industry and the country.

oooOOOooo

A Victorian Government advisory panel 'Infrastructure Victoria' report in April 2021 recommended banning the sale of new petrol and diesel cars by 2030, to reduce the state's vehicle emissions in line with net zero CO_2 emissions by 2050. Infrastructure Victoria Chief Executive

Michel Masson said *Victoria will not reach its emissions reduction targets unless more people shift away from petrol and diesel vehicles. Reducing Victoria's transport emissions is vital, especially when car use in inner Melbourne is now at risk of surpassing pre-covid levels by 100,000 extra trips a day.* A panel member said *electric vehicles represent an exciting and vital frontier that Victorians need to explore for the sake of our environment.* A big brother prohibition on the sale of new petrol and diesel vehicles and the consumer's right to choose, is more woke bullying from those who demand conformity to the climate change religion.

Electric cars are touted in glossy advertising campaigns as a vital component of the green panacea to avoid climate change catastrophe. Nissan advertises its flagship electric car the Nissan LEAF in glowing green terms while ignoring the prohibitive price, limited highway range, lengthy battery charging times and battery life deterioration at a rate of 2.3% annually and possibly higher. The 2021 price of battery replacement after ten years is $5,500. The manufacture and disposal costs of an electric car which can only be built using base load power primarily generated by fossil fuels or nuclear energy reveal the substantial drawbacks of purchasing and owning an electric vehicle.

The Nissan LEAF can be plugged into any standard 240 volt electrical socket. With a Type 2 charging unit installed, the LEAF 40 kw can reach full charge in 7.5 hours, so you can charge overnight and start the day with a full 270 km of range. From regional highways to major shopping centres and office buildings, there are more than 800 public charging stations across Australia. Many public charging stations offer CHAdeMO charging, a fast-charging system that charges the LEAF 40 kw's battery from 20% to 80% in just 60 minutes. Sixty wasted minutes at a recharging station after just 270 kms is simply ludicrous! While Inner-city green virtue signallers may feel virtuous driving their electric cars around the paved streets of capital cities, regional Aussies, long haul truckdrivers and the vital transport infrastructure of the nation will be disastrously compromised for an impossible dream of achieving a fossil free driving and haulage future.

The proposed battery takeover of fossil fuel driven machinery and equipment has operational consequences for those who run earthmoving and small agribusinesses. With commercial lawn mowers, chainsaws, bulldozers and a host of other petrol and diesel driven appliances targeted for battery transition, everyday work tasks will become more cumbersome and costly to perform. A gardening business owner with a small but sizeable workforce estimates that if divested of his current fossil fuel inventory, his business will require upwards of sixty battery changes a day just to keep his gardening equipment operating.

oooOOOooo

In the wake of the Coronavirus pandemic and China's hegemonic push for global power there is an urgent need to re-establish Australia's manufacturing industry. Thanks to our bountiful natural resources we have the means to do so. Cheap reliable power becomes the key variable to consider. Senator Matt Canavan has said *if we are not going to pursue and fight for the cheapest energy costs, then we are not serious about rebuilding an Australian manufacturing industry. The political battle we should engage in is the one to return manufacturing jobs to Australia. To pursue naive policies that reduce our carbon emissions, regardless of what other countries are doing, hurts our ability to win that battle.*

Greg Sheridan wrote in the *Australian* newspaper: *the abandonment of coal has serious strategic implications for Australia. We will never recover a robust manufacturing industry without cheap energy and we won't have cheap energy without coal. The new lowest common denominator on coal is we continue to export it, but there are no circumstances in which we* (would) *build a coalfired power station. Ultra-supercritical coalfired plants the so called high-efficiency, low-emissions plants create about 30% fewer emissions than old coal and a similar amount more than gas. Such plants are being built in many parts of the world. It is a crazy woke fantasy to think coal is being phased out. We make ourselves poorer economically and weaker strategically, while our competitors, economic and strategic, become richer and stronger.*

The federal government favours gas over coal and has based its economic recovery plan around *new technologies that will cut emissions in agriculture, manufacturing, industry and transport.* On its official website, the Australian Government promotes subsidized green hydrogen energy as the new renewables' panacea. *Hydrogen energy can be stored as a gas and even delivered through existing natural gas pipelines. When converted to a liquid or another suitable material, hydrogen can also be transported on trucks and in ships.*

The famous Hindenburg Zeppelin disaster that took place in New Jersey in America on 3 May 1937 was caused by a spark that ignited leaking hydrogen, which is indicative of the highly volatile nature of hydrogen. Professor Ian Plimer tells us hydrogen energy cannot be safely contained in steel pipes or transported by metal ships and trucks. The reason is because hydrogen leaks into the atmosphere and when enclosed is equivalent to a bomb waiting to explode. *If you were to make hydrogen, you lose a massive amount of energy doing it and then you've got to compress it to only 700 times atmospheric pressure, and that requires a huge amount of energy. Then you've got to liquefy it to 200 degrees Celsius and that requires a huge amount of energy. We have extremely good technology now, where we can convert fossilised sunlight into energy and that fossilised sunlight is called Coal!*

oooOOOooo

Federal Labor politician Joel Fitzgibbon makes the point *ignorance is bliss; most of the people who jump on the climate change bandwagon only talk about the electricity generation system. They don't understand that about 90%* (80% in fact) *of our energy globally comes from fossil fuels. It's not just the generation of electricity, it's all those products just mentioned. Planes in the air, trucks and cars on the roads, the energy used in heating and in our manufacturing sector, it just goes on and on and on. Our global economy and our national economy could not operate without fossil fuels. There may be a day when we can operate without them, but it won't be in our lifetime. It's a long way away. We have to exercise some common sense.*

Jennie George former President of the ACTU (1996-2000) and Labor Member of Parliament for Throsby (2001-2010) called out the myth of renewables, particularly in relation to workers jobs and 'green' steel production. *It is a pity advocates of such technologies don't tell the community the whole truth: that there are no proven and commercially viable technologies to replace coal/coke in the blast furnace steelmaking process at BlueScope in the Illawarra. Renewables are not commercially* viable, nor can they guarantee the required reliability for the smelter's continued operation. The largest South Australian battery today would power that smelter for less than 15 minutes.

In October 2020 the ANZ Bank in a virtue signalling gesture put out a press release titled 'Our Renewed Commitment to take action on Climate Change'. It was a greenwash statement full of anti-coal/carbon emissions reduction rhetoric aimed at denying loan funding to customers who failed to toe the Socialist/Green/Woke transition to renewables line. *To facilitate a gradual and orderly transition (to renewables), ANZ will encourage customers that have coal-fired generation assets to work towards setting medium and long-term emission reduction targets up to 2050. The bank will lend to new customers where their thermal coal operations are less than half their revenue. We will not finance any new build of conventional coal-fired power plants.* Denying customers business loans for climate alarmist reasons has become a new low in the Australian banking sector.

oooOOOooo

In pursuing his woke socialist dream, self-declared Marxist and federal Green leader Adam Bandt, has outlined a green new deal vision for Australia's post Coronavirus future. *A green new deal is a government led plan of massive investment and action to build a clean economy and a caring society. Under a green new deal, the government takes the lead in creating new jobs and industries, getting to zero-emissions as soon as possible and delivering universal services to ensure nobody is left behind. But it's not just a plan for a clean energy transformation it's a plan to right the injustices of the past and rewrite the rules between local communities and Canberra. Under a green new deal, people are in charge of their future and no one will be left behind.* Promising a green/socialist future and taking Australia back to a pre-industrial stone age to control CO_2 emissions, benefits no one and will cause untold misery and a greatly diminished country similar to that experienced during the worldwide Coronavirus lockdown. In Adam Bandt's brave new world we will all be left behind.

The green new deal first advocated in America, *the preferred environmental blueprint of leading Democratic Party politicians, would create a permanent state of near emergency. Environmentalists want to convince Americans that climate change presents an emergency that is the moral equivalent of war, requiring the same worldwide mobilization as the Coronavirus outbreak. It should serve as an alarm for Americans to realize what a policy like the green new deal would do to the U.S. economy, American jobs and our way of life. It would not be pretty.*

Even more ludicrous is the World Economic Forum's pan globalist ideas of 'build back better' and the 'the great reset'. Build back better simply means undermine the nation state, change the face of capitalism and destroy the democratic western way of life. *The great reset,* says Aussie journalist Rowan Dean, *is a program designed to strip us all of our fundamental democratic rights in favour of a new form of society as dictated by the elites. The great reset is a quasi-fascist version of the green new deal. With 80% of the world's energy still reliant upon fossil fuels, these zealots wish to plunge us into some post-covid dystopian nightmare of climate subservience.*

In a short promotional video, the World Economic Forum (WEF) tells us that by 2030: *You'll own nothing and you'll be happy.* Author Colin Todhunter writes *the jobless (and there will be many) could be placed on some kind of universal basic income and have their debts (indebtedness and bankruptcy on a massive scale is the deliberate result of lockdowns and restrictions) written off in return for handing their assets to the state or more precisely the financial institutions helping to drive this great reset. The WEF says the public will 'rent' everything they require: stripping the right of ownership under the guise of 'sustainable consumption' and 'saving the planet'. Of course, the tiny elite who rolled out this great reset will own everything.* In the cautionary words of American historian Daniel Boorstin, *the greatest enemy of knowledge is not ignorance; it is the illusion of knowledge.* Build back better and the great reset are globalist illusions parading as woke knowledge. *You will own nothing; you will be controlled by others and you will not be happy.*

Build back better, the green new deal and the great reset are political boondoggles endlessly repeated by the radical Socialist/Green/Woke alliance. Eighteen months into the demoralising Biden Administration in America, a deteriorating national economy, rising commodity prices, rampart inflation, a surging crime rate and out of control illegal immigration across the southern border attest to the ongoing disaster of all 3 far-reaching platforms. In Australia we clearly see what is taking place in Democrat controlled America. We should avoid the woke trinity of failure at all cost. American journalist Bernard Goldberg writes *sooner or later, the American people — the rational ones, anyway — will say, 'We've had enough of this woke nonsense'*. For many Americans, that day can't come soon enough!

oooOOOooo

Despite the politicised rhetoric and mass hysteria of some, we are doing more than many developed countries to reduce CO_2 emissions. An October 2019 report by the Australian National University (ANU) said that *Australia is leading the world in the installation of renewable electricity. Australian rooftop solar penetration now exceeds 24%, the highest in the world.* In December 2020, Prime Minister Scott Morrison politically obsessed with the inequitable Paris Climate Agreement (2016) and net emissions control said *we have got a great track record. That record is one that has seen our CO_2 emissions fall by 16.6% since 2005.* Elsewhere it was reported, *we are on track to beat our 2030 climate change goals by 145 million tonnes of carbon emissions and achieve cuts to greenhouse gas emissions by 29% below 2005 levels.* Australia is doing its bit, many other are not. In February 2021, Morrison angered many Quiet Australians, when he announced it was his government's policy to adopt a CO_2 net zero emissions target by 2050.

Net zero is an oxymoron, a combination of incompatible words. The dictionary meaning of oxymoron is *a combination of contradictory or incongruous words. Something (such as a concept) that is made up of contradictory or incongruous elements.* English language linguist Kel Richards equates the expression net zero with the fantasy word Unicorn. *We can define it, we can say what it means, but we also know it can never actually exist as such. The net part of net zero means: what is left when you subtract the outgoings and the incomings. The zero half means that when you do that sum, you will get a zero, you will get the two sides balancing exactly. You can never achieve a balance. The zero part of net zero is unachievable.*

Time and again, a majority of Australians have rejected climate change predictions and extremist fears at federal and state elections. Politicians never reveal the true cost of taking the nation down the renewables path of net zero emissions and the lunacy of the green new deal. Senator Matt Canavan said of the lack of cost transparency. *If you don't know what something is going to cost, don't buy it. You don't buy a house unless you know the price. You wouldn't buy groceries unless you knew the price. If you don't know the cost of it don't buy it and if you did know the cost of net zero emissions, you definitely wouldn't buy it because it's astronomical.* Polls consistently show that Aussies are not prepared to sign on to an open-ended renewables future. They care about the environment and understand the economic and social consequences of the imposition of a carbon tax and other green restrictions on their lives. They see through the self-interest of politicians and those who promote net zero emissions and green new deal recklessness at the expense of job security and living standards they want nothing to do with it.

The Morrison Government's feel-good 2050 net zero emissions target has real world consequences and none of them are beneficial to Australia or its power-driven economy.

In December 2021, Labor leader Anthony Albanese, kicked off his party's 2022 election campaign by announcing a 43% net zero emissions target by 2030. The Morrison Government's 2030 target was a more modest 28%. Albanese's 'voodoo economics' 2030 climate plan, which he claimed was based on *the most comprehensive modelling undertaken by an opposition in Australian History,* promised to create more than *600,000 new jobs, cut power prices by $275 a year per household by 2025, boost private investment and cost the government $683 million.* Hidden amongst Labor's pie in the sky promises to the electorate was the lurking spectre of a carbon tax. Worse than Albanese's political hyperbole and rubbery figures was the impending pall of an economy destroying renewables future.

In October 2021, PM Morrison said he wanted to set in motion a 35% net zero emissions 2050 wrecking ball target, that would shatter the economy and disastrously impact people's lives. He offered a hastily compiled and grossly inadequate cost analysis for the undertaking and placed his faith in technology some of it yet to be invented. Morrison's net zero plan lacked substance prompting journalist Jenna Clarke to voice majority Aussie concern. *Just give us something really simple.*

Just give us how much it's going to cost us in our hip pocket. Without nuclear power in the mix, Morrison's proposed 2050 zero emissions strategy lacked credibility. The global appeasement plan the PM took to the COP26 meeting satisfied no one least of all many of his Coalition colleagues, the Liberal Party base and the majority of Quiet Australians.

A Quiet Australian expressed his disappointment at PM Morrison's 2050 net zero emissions policy. *The climate has been changing since the earth formed, and will continue to do so, and mankind (can I still say that?) has next to no influence. But net zero 2050 here we come, at huge cost to achieve nothing. We are doing a great job of destroying what was a reliable supply of energy generation.*

Liberal Senator Alex Antic voiced his opposition to the 2050 net emissions target. *I'm absolutely against net zero, I think it's nothing more than a slogan created by global bureaucrats and crony capitalists. We got China on the other side of the world spewing* (out) *more emissions than all of the developed nations together, and they're not even showing up to Glasgow. A lot of the reductions that we see in net zero targets themselves rely on potential technology that doesn't exist yet. I think Australia does more than its fair share of heavy lifting and should stay the way it is.*

The Glasgow climate talk fest added another back slapping layer of zero emissions deceit from a global elite drunk on power whose aim is renewables profiteering and worldwide control. Follow the money trail of renewables subsidies and investment and all will be revealed. The greenwash virtue signalling of crony capitalist corporations and the promise of tens of thousands of green jobs following transition to renewables are globalist pipedreams. Among others Russia and China the world's largest emitter of CO_2 were not in attendance at Glasgow. COP26 was another round of partying by the world's self-indulgent woke elite, the majority of whom arrived on fossil fuelled private jets to be present for the fun. The false perception of world unity exposed the naked greed of woke billionaires and climate scammers itching to get their hands on truckloads of taxpayer money.

oooOOOooo

At the close of 2021, the climate change emperor was revealed to be wearing no clothes. In Australia with the grass still green, and despite some hot summer days and significant rain falling throughout December into January 2022. The global warming alarmist model again faltered in its doomsday prediction of unrelenting, earth destroying, excessive heat and extreme dryness. No amount of data distortion, media misrepresentation and computer modelling can hide the obvious fact that weather is complex, variable and beyond human control.

An everyday Aussie speaks common sense in a climate debate increasingly devoid of reason and logic. *The climate alarmists have an answer for every variation of how the current temperatures differ from the CO2 driven high temperatures that we should be seeing, year on year from the hyper sensitive CO2 controlled climate models. They simply don't want to admit they are wrong about the predictions of 2C-4C by the end of the century. Record low temperature in Antarctica, a new record for California snowfall last week, Texas freezing and many other places in the world seeing colder than average temperatures. The Earth's climate is simply not driven by an atmosphere CO2 concentration increasing 0.01% over the last century.*

While the rest of the world pays lip service to net zero emissions, we willingly set out on an ecological fool's errand to cripple our economy and undermine the stability of our democracy. We should not delude ourselves that what we do in the field of energy production or CO2 emissions reduction will have more than an infinitesimal effect on the level of global emissions. Green trolls and climate zealots belittle Australia's emissions control measures. It is never enough in their woke eyes more is always demanded regardless of the consequences. What is at stake is not the climate health of the planet, but who governs the country and the increased power they wield over the lives of ordinary Aussies.

American journalist and political satirist, Henry Lewis Mencken, could have been writing about climate emergency, the green new deal and the great reset, when he wisely wrote *the aim of practical politics is to keep the populace alarmed and hence clamorous to be led to safety by an endless series of hobgoblins, most of them imaginary. For every complex problem there is an answer that is clear, simple, and wrong.*

The urge to save humanity is almost always only a false face for the urge to rule it. To which could be added a woke compulsion to save the planet. Perpetually alarmed, continuously misinformed and poorly governed. What could go wrong?

Professor Ian Plimer has said of Australia's future. *Let's not pollute our minds with carbon fears. Carbon Dioxide is plant food. It is neither a pollutant nor a toxin. Without Carbon Dioxide, all life on earth would die. Plants convert Carbon Dioxide, water and sunlight during photosynthesis into sugars, cellulose, fruit, vegetables and grains, which animal life uses as food.* Plimer goes on to say *the grasslands, forests, farms and continental shelves of Australia absorb far more Carbon Dioxide than we emit. The attack on emissions of the gas of life is an irrational attack on industry, our modern way of life, freedoms and prosperity. It has nothing to do with the environment.*

Harvard atmospheric physicist and former Professor of Meteorology at the Massachusetts Institute of Technology (1983-2013) Dr Richard Linzen writes: *What historians will wonder about in future centuries is how deeply flawed logic, obscured by shrewd and unrelenting propaganda, actually enabled a coalition of powerful special interests to convince nearly everyone in the world that Carbon Dioxide from human industry was a dangerous planet destroying toxin. It will be remembered as the greatest mass delusion in the history of the world; that Carbon Dioxide, the life of plants, was considered for a time to be a deadly poison.*

18

A Sunburnt Country of Fire, Drought and Flooding Rain

May the showers in torrents fall and all the tanks run over; and may the grass grow green and tall in the pathways of the drover.

Henry Lawson

Climate alarmists point to the 2000 Millennium Drought and the ravages of the 2019-2020 Drought, as proof positive that Australia is in an unprecedented period of heatwave, drought and bushfire emergency. This is not true. In the past droughts, heatwaves and bushfires have been just as devastating and prolonged. Unprecedented is a much-overused word by those pushing a global catastrophist political agenda and we should not heed such dire pronouncements. Before climate change dominated the nation's attention, drought, bushfire, heatwave conditions and ruinous flood prevailed in seasonal reoccurrence.

The Federation Heatwave and Drought (1895-1902) was the deadliest and hottest drought in Australian history, claiming 435 lives, with summer temperatures soaring into the high forties and outback New South Wales reporting 48.9 degrees centigrade three times in 1896. This drought brought about massive crop failure, animal starvation, widespread bushfires, furnace like wind and dust storms, a critical lack of water and untold settler suicides. South Australian pastoralist Thomas Pearse wrote a desperate letter to the *Burra Record* newspaper in May 1898. *While I am writing this the dust is blowing in clouds; no* lambing for the last three years, and a bad prospect for one this year; high rents, and wild dogs galore; three parts of this country blown further east. It will take three good seasons for the country in question to be of (the) same value as it was before the drought set in. When the drought finally broke in 1902, more than 50 million sheep and around 40% of the nation's cattle had perished from starvation and thirst. The property loss was not calculated.

Reacting to the severity of the Federation Drought, Henry Lawson in his 1899 bush poem 'Song of the Darling River' saw the damming of rivers as a practical solution to drought proofing the country. His vision was of a network of water storage dams and irrigation channels spreading in abundance across a burgeoning land of plenty.

> *We've been drought ruined in the west and ever in my dreaming, I see wide miles of waving crops and sheets of water gleaming. On plains where fortune died of thirst when my brave father sought her; I see painted barges pass along the winding water.*

Lawson's belief in establishing a continent-wide network of drought-busting dams and irrigation channels has yet to be realised. In other poems, Henry Lawson writes of the endless cycle of drought, bushfires and floods.

> *In stifling noon when his back was wrung by its load, and the air seemed dead, and the water warmed in the bag that hung to his aching arm like lead. Or in times of flood, when plains were seas, and the scrubs were cold and black. He ploughed in mud to his trembling knees and paid for his sins outback.*

In the outback township of Bourke during the Federation Drought, the temperature reached above 38C every day for more than three weeks. Horses and people collapsed in the street and the local hospital was unable to cope with the heat-exhausted. In January 1896, the *Bourke Western Herald* wrote *living in Bourke under present conditions is suicide. Since last Friday no less than 14 additional deaths have taken place in and around Bourke, all of which were at least accelerated by the continuous excessive heat. In view of the rapidly increasing rate of mortality, it can scarcely be a matter of surprise that the town is panic stricken. Every morning a large number of our townspeople, especially* women and children, are actually fleeing for their lives from Bourke to some cool retreat.

Australian writer Joanne Nova has said of the 1896 Heatwave: *Newspaper reports of the day showed temperatures that month, before all our CO_2 emissions, ranged from 44C to 51C all across the country. Hundreds of people died from heat apoplexy. Emergency trains were put on in Outback NSW to evacuate people from the unbearable heat, in a time when no one had an air conditioner or a fridge and freezer.* Melbourne University Associate Professor Don Garden writes *during the first two months of 1898, there seems seldom to have been a day when there was not a fire in the eastern colonies, especially Victoria. Much of Gippsland was devastated, with the smoke so thick that daylight turned to dark, and offshore coastal shipping was forced to slow. Smoke from the Victorian fires even created a haze over Sydney.*

The historical record shows other occasions when bushfire smoke in Sydney was so thick that sailing ships were totally obscured and unable to navigate Sydney Harbour. In more recent times, passenger planes at Sydney Airport have been grounded till the bushfire smoke haze cleared. The 2019-2020 New South Wales and Victoria bushfire smoke haze was widespread and severe in its intensity; however, it was not an unprecedented event.

Every year scare mongering predictions are made that the coming summer fire season is shaping up to be the worst on record. We are told time and time again that we are experiencing the hottest day on record when summer temperatures reach 49 degrees centigrade. On the 7th of January 1906, Mildura in Victoria registered a scorching temperature of 50.7 degrees. Officially the meteorological record for the hottest day goes to the New South Wales town of Bourke, where on Sunday 3rd of January 1909 the recorded temperature was 51.6 degrees. The outback Queensland town of Cloncurry claims an even higher temperature, erecting a sign on the outskirts of the township which states: *Cloncurry Australia's Highest Temperature 53.1C (127.5F) 16th January 1889.* In the second week of January, on the eve of the 1939 Black Friday bushfires in Victoria, the temperature recorded at Windsor (NSW) reached 122F or 50C. These documented temperatures occurred in summer periods before global warming and climate change could be assigned the blame.

oooOOOooo

From the beginning of white settlement in Australia there has been a strong focus on drought, extreme heat and bushfires. On his Pacific voyage of discovery, Captain James Cook reported seeing the Australian mainland covered with a thick smoke from bushfires. On 13 May 1770, while sailing past Smoky Cape (NSW), Cook recorded in the Endeavour's logbook the sighting of *a point or headland on which were fires that caused a great quantity of smoke; which occasioned my giving it the name of Smoky Cape.* He does not say whether the fires were lit by Aborigines or caused by lightening or other natural events.

Captain Watkin Tench of the Royal Marines arrived at Port Jackson with the First Fleet in January 1788. In December 1790 he wrote of oppressive summer heat, temperatures above 43 degrees Celsius and searingly hot north winds *like the blast of a heated oven.* In February 1791, *the north-west wind again set in and blew with a great violence for three days. At Rose Hill, it was allowed, by every person, to surpass all that they had before felt, either there, or in any other part of the world. An immense flight of bats, driven before the wind, covered all the trees around the settlement, whence they every moment dropped dead, or in a dying state, unable longer to endure the burning state of the atmosphere. Nor did the perroquets, though tropical birds, bear it better; the ground was strewed with them in the same condition as the bats.* For cool climate Europeans, Australia's hot summer weather, droughts and bushfires were a burden and a tribulation. They also faced freezing cold winter weather in their precarious struggle to survive and prosper.

Arriving with the First Fleet on HMS Sirius, Lieutenant William Dawes, a soldier and scientist, kept meticulous weather records during the formative years of the New South Wales colony. Dawes' 182 pages of hand-written weather observations covered the period 14 September 1788 to 6 December 1791. Six times a day, Dawes would dutifully record temperature, barometric pressure, wind direction and comment on relevant weather events. Dawes' weather journal is a scientific guide to climatic conditions in Sydney Cove at the beginning of European settlement. The journal was found in the archives of the Royal Society in London in 1977. The first journal entry reads: *1788, 14 Sept. noon,*

SSW (wind direction), *4* (wind speed), *heavy cloud,* 29 (barometer reading), *70 degrees* (temperature in Fahrenheit). Dawes was an early advocate for Aborigines. He left the colony following a heated dispute with Governor Arthur Phillip over what he believed was the poor treatment of Aborigines.

In her book *Sunburnt Country: The History and Future of Climate Change (*2018). Melbourne University academic Joelle Gergis writes of William Dawes and the earliest colonial weather observations. She compares them with today's meteorological records. *The First Fleet weather records reproduce the observed modern patterns of seasonal extremes incredibly well. The observations have provided us with a valuable opportunity to cross-check our results against earlier settler accounts. They show us that climate extremes have long been a quintessential part of Australian life.*

In discussing extreme winter temperature fluctuations, Gergis confirms the overall reliability of Dawes' 18th century colonial weather observations, although she does so with a global warming bias. *Looking at the maximum temperatures recorded by Dawes, there was one winter day 12 June 1789 when the temperature only reached a teeth-chattering 6.9 Centigrade. According to long term climatology recorded at Observatory Hill* (where Dawes gathered his weather information) *the lowest maximum June temperature on record was 9.7 Centigrade on 13 June 1899. Even factoring in a cool bias of up to 2 Centigrade as seen in Dawes' record, it is still 0.8 Centigrade cooler than the lowest maximum observed at Observatory Hill since 1876.*

The inference is global warming has been occurring since the early years of colonial weather reporting. The problem that arises is a 70 year gap in reporting from 1792 when Dawes left the colony until the recommencement of record keeping in July 1858. The best that can be said is that Dawes has provided us with valuable scientific observations that are a boon to early colonial climate research. Temperatures fluctuate up and down, but essentially the same temperature patterns repeat themselves in more or less predictable cycles, sometimes in an extreme form and at other times more moderately.

oooOOOooo

Bushfire has always been regarded as the greatest Australian misfortune. In February 1854 in *Cassell's Illustrated Family Paper*, William Howitt wrote of 'Black Thursday the Great Bushfire of Victoria'. *This famous fire took place on Thursday, February 6th, 1851. In one day, a whole country of 300 miles in extent, and at least 150 in breadth, was reduced to a desert. It was one blackened and burning waste. In Melbourne, I have heard those who experienced it say, that the suffocating heat was something inconceivable. The very atmosphere seemed aflame. The country was this year visited with an extraordinary and intense and long continued drought. The grass was dried up to a state of tinder. Waterholes and creeks, which had never been known before, since the white man came into the colony, to fail, were now hollows parched and cracked with heat. We hear of whole flocks of sheep and vast numbers of cattle dying of thirst and starvation.*

It was after the long, severe drought and the tinder condition of the grass and foliage in the summer of 1850-1, that one of the hot winds came (and fanned the flames of bushfire). *Cattle in vast herds were seen careering madly before the fires. Troops of horses, wild from the bush, galloped across the ground with the fury of despair. Flocks of kangaroos, and of smaller animals, leaped desperately along, to escape the horrible conflagration, and hosts of birds swept blindly on, many falling suffocated headlong into the flames, and the rest raising the most lamentable cries.*

Horsemen galloped madly and for scores of miles, till their horses fell under them. The destruction, not only of farms, crops, shepherds' huts, cattle, horses, and sheep, was immense, but the destruction of the wild creatures of the woods, which were roasted alive in their holes and haunts, was something fearful to contemplate, People rushed into waterholes and creeks and sunk themselves to the very mouths, yet in some instances (were) *so scorched and broiled as to perish from the effects. How many perished in this now truly 'howling wilderness' God only knows. Far out at sea, there were driven clouds of dust and ashes, which covered the decks of ships like snow and obscured the midday sun.*

Amazingly only twelve lives were lost, as one million sheep and thousands of cattle were burned to death. On the eve of the goldrush in 1851 the population of Victoria was estimated to be around 77,000, compared to today's 6.7 million inhabitants. With the Victorian population 87 times larger than what it was in 1851, the devastation of this 19th century mega bushfire today would be horrific to behold.

Two days after the Black Thursday bushfire on 8 February, the *Argus* newspaper wrote: *Thursday was one of the most oppressively hot days we have experienced for some years. In the morning the atmosphere was perfectly scorching, and at eleven o'clock the thermometer stood as high as 117F (47.22C) in the shade; at one o'clock it had fallen to 109F (42.77C) and at four in the afternoon it was up to 113F (45C). The blasts of air were so impregnated with smoke and heat that the lungs seemed absolutely to collapse under their withering influence; the murkiness of the atmosphere was so great, that the roads were absolutely bright by contrast. The bushfire flame careering with lightning speed along the tops of the trees, fanned and lashed on by violent hot winds, is said to have been attended by the most appalling roar, more awfully overpowering than that of the ocean in storm.*

oooOOOooo

The same combination of prolonged drought, extreme heat, high fuel load together with catastrophic bushfire weather occurred in Victoria on 13 January 1939, when the Black Friday bushfire burned 7,722 square miles (4,942,000 acres) impacting a large portion of the state. Five townships were completely destroyed, 1,300 homes and 69 sawmills were burned. It was estimated that 3,700 buildings were lost as the main megafire merged with other smaller blazes. The human death toll was 71 with more than a hundred injured. Forty-one years earlier on 1 February 1898, the South Gippsland Red Tuesday bushfire burnt 1,004 square miles of bush and farmland, destroyed 2,000 buildings, killed 12 and left 2,500 people homeless.

In Queensland in 1944, 1 million hectares burned and more than 500 houses were destroyed. In Victoria in 1951, 4 million hectares burned and 11 lives were lost. In 1962, 450 houses were consumed and 32 people died. The Black Tuesday bushfire in Tasmania in February 1967 killed 62 people with 1,293 homes lost. The Lara/Little River bushfires in Victoria in January 1969 burnt 617,763 acres and claimed 23 lives, many of whom died in their cars attempting to flee the bushfire inferno. The 1983 Ash Wednesday bushfires in Victoria and South Australia, destroyed around 2,500 homes and 75 people died. During the 1984-85 bushfire season in New South Wales 3.5 million hectares went up in flames. In Victoria in 2003, 1.3 million hectares were burnt, 41 homes destroyed and three lives were lost. In 2009, the deadly Black Saturday bushfire in Victoria destroyed 4,500 buildings and killed 173 people. The number of farm livestock and wild bush animals killed during these destructive bushfires was inestimable.

The worst destructive bushfire season on record occurred in the summer of 1974-75. Fires burnt across 15% of Australia's land mass, engulfing 117 million hectares (290 million acres) throughout New South Wales, Northern Territory, South Australia, Western Australia and Queensland. The Northern Territory and Western Australia suffered the most damage with 64 million hectares incinerated. The area burnt was mainly lush desert grassland brought about by heavy winter rains which the fire devoured causing significant loss of livestock. According to Bureau of Meteorology records, the 1974-75 bushfire season occurred in a year of above average rainfall and below average temperature. This stands in marked contrast to the climate change narrative that claims bushfire intensity occurs in excessively hot and dry years. The 1970s disastrous bushfire season occurred before the era of climate change alarmism and global warming hysteria arrived on the scene peaching impending doom and disaster.

As horrific as the August to January Black Summer (2019/2020) bushfires were for those who experienced them, they were neither unprecedented nor the worst in the country's bushfire history. Bushfires in Queensland, New South Wales, Tasmania, Victoria, South and Western Australia together burnt 18 million hectares (46 million acres), destroyed 2,779 houses and claimed 34 lives. In addition to lightning strikes and accidents, many of these bushfires were deliberately lit and fuelled by a major build-up of more than a decade of uncleared forest undergrowth and ground litter. True devastation occurred among the nation's helpless animals as the fires were catastrophic for wildlife and farm animals.

In typical Australian climatic fashion, the national emergency abruptly went from bushfire disaster to torrential rain and flooding. In mid-January drenching rain fell across all fire grounds and the situation was brought under control. In the space of 24 hours the Bureau of Meteorology reported *intense rainfall through the early hours of this morning between midnight and about six or seven over the Sunshine Coast, Brisbane and the Gold Coast. We're looking at rainfall totals across that wide area in the of range of 100 to 200 millimetres for a number of locations but coming up to just over 300 millimetres at a couple of locations as well. The highest total that we have recorded is 330 millimetres at Loder Creek on the Gold Coast.* 95 millimetres fell in one hour on the Gold Coast suburb of Carrara and 145 millimetres within two hours at Monterey Keys. The Bureau went on to say life-threatening flash flooding was likely. Drought-affected areas of New South Wales received more than 250 millimetres in a 24-hour period. Victoria and the other bushfire-affected states received a heavy saturating rainfall and within days new grass and plant growth began to appear.

Far from being unprecedented climatic conditions and the product of catastrophic global warming, January rains and a cool summer in 2020/2021 without a major bushfire incident proved once again that Australian weather patterns are cyclical and variable. There is not a cataclysmic trajectory towards a global warming Armageddon. The lesson to be learnt is that drought, summer heat and bushfires have been mild and severe in the past, when the false narrative of global warming and climate emergency could not have been responsible, and they will remain so in the future. The same can be said of national disaster torrential rain and flooding events. The climate fantasy disappears when confronted with climate reality.

oooOOOooo

Bushfires depend on harsh weather conditions mainly in summer and on the amount of dry fuel on the ground. Fuel reduction burns are not being carried out today as they should be around the country, because of green environmental intransigency at the state and local level. For more than a decade prior to 2020, green legislation locked up the nation's forest parklands and prevented farmers from establishing firebreaks and carrying out bushfire hazard reduction burns. In Queensland invasive lantana plants several metres high in many forests, made access and firefighting in emergency bushfire situations wellnigh impossible.

Monash University and CSIRO bushfire expert David Packham has repeatedly warned that not to carry out bushfire fuel reduction burns is the principal reason behind the severity and ferocity of the bushfires we face today. *You need fuel to have a fire and due to gross mismanagement of our forests, we have way too much of it.* He warns of the potential for thousands of deaths and tens of thousands of fire related injuries in high bushfire prone inhabited areas. Sensible policy of autumn and winter fire reduction burns, as has been recommended by more than one Royal Commission Inquiry in the past, should be made a national priority in the cooler months. *The one thing, the only thing people can control, is the amount of fuel* (on the ground) *and that is what we are not doing. I can't understand why we are so silly to allow the amount of fuel to build up like it does. The Indigenous people, the custodians of the land for 30,000 years, never had fuel like we have now. We have fuel that is about 10 times greater than what the Aborigines had at the beginning of colonisation. If you increase the fuel 10 times more than it should be which is the case now, fire intensity is 100 times greater. The maximum you can extinguish and it doesn't matter what you've got aircraft, bulldozers anything; the maximum you can extinguish is 3, so it's fantasyland to imagine we can ever control these fires, when the* (fuel load) *is 10 times greater than what the Indigenous people handed over to us.*

Associate Professor Michael Shawn Fletcher, an Indigenous paleo-ecologist from the University of Melbourne, told the Bushfire Royal Commission in June 2020 that from colonial times, there was *a universal shift from an open to a woody or forested landscape and the removal of cultural burning* (by Aborigines) *from the landscape.* To which he added, *there is demonstrably more fuel in the modern forested regions today than when they were under Indigenous cultural burning.*

Victor Jurskis, veteran Silviculturist (whose task is the care and cultivation of forest trees) worked for the New South Wales Forestry Commission's Native Forest Division. A man with vast experience in both forestry and fire management, Jurskis agrees with David Packham. *The worst drought in 500 years occurred in 1833, but there were no megafires. The 1851 megafires occurred during a period of average rainfall. This was less than two decades after Aboriginal burning was disrupted across Victoria by John Batman's arrival in Port Phillip Bay, the Hentys in the west and Angus McMillan coming south from the Monaro.* The Millennium Drought was not unusual, but the academics have used it to explain the Black Saturday holocaust of 2009 with the tragic and preventable death of 173 people. It is not climate change that is buggering the bush. It is those being lavishly funded to protect it who are doing the real damage.

A Newspoll published in the *Australian* newspaper in February 2020 revealed that 56% of Australians blamed excessive fuel loads and inadequate fire reduction burns for the intensity of Australian bushfires. Only 35% claimed that climate change was the driver of bushfire ferocity. The major recommendation of the New South Wales Black Summer Bushfire Inquiry report handed down in August 2020, was that hazard reduction burns were crucial to reducing fuel load and bushfire intensity. Allowing people to prepare their property for the coming bushfire season each year, unhindered by green environmental regulation is of course the sensible way to go.

oooOOOooo

The other great natural misfortune in Australia is devastating flood. In addition to heatwaves, drought and bushfires, destructive floods periodically wreak havoc on lives and property. The deadliest flood in Australian history occurred at Gundagai (NSW) on the night of 25 June 1852. The *Gundagai Independent* newspaper described a watery scene of death and destruction that claimed 72, possibly 84 lives in a single night. *Gundagai was built on the flat* (and an island), *between Morley's Creek and the Murrumbidgee River.* (Murrumbidgee is an Aboriginal word meaning 'big flood'.) *As the flood waters swirled through the streets, women, clasping their children, rushed screaming to the housetops; only to be swept away as the houses toppled over in the torrent. Appalling darkness hindered attempts at rescue. The flood waters remained high for several days, and bodies of some of the victims were not found until weeks afterwards. Almost the entire population left to sleep in the old town on that memorable night perished.*

Of the 78 houses then constituting the town, most were on the island, a few on the north hill and the south bank. What a sitting shot for water and the rampage. *For several days the river had been so high that the punt could not run and travellers heading for the golden Mecca of Bendigo banked up in Gundagai. With the residents they watched with anxious eyes, but many stayed in the houses and hotels with a blind faith in man's puny structures withstanding the hurtling charge of Nature in its full fury. By evening the water swirled through all the houses, creeping ever higher; with darkness it quickened for a sharp rise of three feet in an hour. Gundagai's night of terror commenced. Cattle and horses swept along helplessly, frenzied with terror, thudded into the walls, with the water at eaves level, tried to scramble to the beckoning safety of the roof. The men on the housetops fought them off, thrusting the demented animals back into the flood.*

The flood waters rose in a great volume in the dead of night. The town was left in ruins. After the waters receded at South Gundagai, the dead bodies of fewer than 19 persons of all ages and sizes were collected in one house. The bodies had been washed up by the ebb water into one spot, but the others, big and little, were carried away downstream. In the 1852 flood, which was the most destructive of life, the river rose to 37 feet. On the 27th of June the river fell but six feet of water still covered the highest point of the island. On the 28th of June most of the day was clear of water and the task of searching for bodies commenced. Twenty-six of the victims were found in the first three days. Eight members of the Thatcher family lost their lives. Mr Thatcher and his family had taken to their loft, which they thought would be beyond the reach of the flood. But from where they had to be removed in a boat as the water was still rising. The boat, however, was swamped before they had gone far and lives were lost.

Mr Kenna, the Nangus schoolteacher, with his family and others totalling nine persons, relied on the staunchness of the Government building for safety. The flood crashed in one end of the school and blasted its way through the other end sweeping the refugees to death; yet it left the other walls and the attic rooms intact. One boy, the son of a sawyer who perished in the flood, was carried downstream during the night and had to cling to the head of a tree near Johnson's corner. No one could reach him in his perilous position and after three days immersion and exposure, he fell off the tree from exhaustion and was lost.

Many more tragic stories of a similar horrific nature were recounted.

In the midst of so much death and carnage there was heroism. At the risk of his own life, Yarri, a local Aborigine rescued 49 Gundagai residents by bark canoe. His fellow Wiradjuri tribesman Jacky Jacky is credited with saving 20 white settler lives. Others were rescued from certain death by Long Jimmy and Tommy Davis. This is yet another example of an Aboriginal and white settler relationship that transcends colonial conflict and hatred. Yarri and Jacky Jacky were presented with ceremonial bronze breastplates in recognition of their bravery. In addition, Jacky Jacky received a medallion which read: *Presented to Jacky by the subscribers to a relief fund as a reward for his assisting the sufferers during the floods at Gundagai on the 25th of June 1852.* In June 2017, the 165th anniversary of the 1852 Gundagai flood, a life size bronze statue of Yarri and Jacky Jacky was unveiled in the centre of the town honouring their courageous act.

oooOOOooo

In the middle of summer, three years before the bushfire devastation of Black Friday ravaged Victoria, Gippsland suffered a major flood. No one died but property and livestock losses were significant. On 30 June 1936, the *Western Argus* newspaper reported 'Floods in Gippsland: Worst Damage in History up to Six Inches of Rain'. *The Gippsland areas, east of Stratford, are being devastated by one of the worst floods in the history of Victoria, the violent storm that passed over New South Wales on Wednesday night bringing heavy rain and snow. Rainfall up to five and a half inches* (approximately 150 millimetres) *has been reported from Eastern Gippsland, which has suffered very severely from floods in the last three years. Large areas have already been inundated by the still rising waters, and worse is expected. The police at Bairnsdale fear there has been loss of life. They say many settlers in the outlying areas were trapped, and that when efforts were made to reach them the rescuers were driven back by the flood waters.*

The damage is already heavy. Many homes are underwater; highways are blocked; telephone and telegraph lines are down, and hundreds of head of stock are reported to have been washed away. The Avon, Mitchell, Snowy, Tambo and McAlister Rivers have each been converted into swirling torrents, and have overflowed, flooding a huge area. Lindenow is the scene of widespread flood desolation. The river has inundated rich and extensive flats, and has almost entirely covered farms and homes occupied by about 30 families. At Bairnsdale the water quickly rose until it almost reached the housetops, forcing the occupants to leave. Some of them, however, were trapped in their beds when the water rose during the night at an unprecedented rate. Several families awoke to find the water already in the houses, and they were forced to climb to the roofs for safety. Here they spent an uncomfortable and anxious time until they were rescued by Constable Reeves.

One man, Mr Harry Barton, an old age pensioner, had to flee from his home and then, finding himself trapped and cut off by the flood waters, had to climb to a tree top for safety. There he clung for more than half the night, almost frozen. When he was rescued, he was in a state of collapse. Constable Reeves rowed to every house which it was possible to reach. He rescued five different families. After he had saved Barton, he returned and rescued Mrs Stewart and her two sisters, the Misses Keating, and took them to safety. Returning again, despite great difficulty, he succeeded in rescuing Miss Kerton, whose home had been almost swept away.

All communications with Orbost, rail, road, telephone, and telegraph, have failed, and conditions in the town are unknown. It is feared, however, that the position may be serious. The flood at Stratford is the largest ever known. The river has broken its banks, and the water has inundated a wide area. A large retaining wall recently built as a protection against the floods has been ruined. The approach to the main Avon bridge on the Princes Highway has been washed away. The river rose with great rapidity giving little warning to farmers. The Avon has washed out crops at Maffra, and two bridges on the road to Rosedale are closed to traffic. Along the course of the Avon farmers on low lying land have been warned to move their stock.

The massively destructive Townsville flood that occurred in February 2019 was responsible for 5 deaths, the hospitalisation of 10 people, damage to some 3,300 and for making many others uninhabitable. As the flood crisis progressed Michael Guerin, Chief Executive Officer of AgForce and spokesman for the Queensland cattle industry, said *the speed and intensity of the unfolding tragedy makes it hard to believe that it's just a week since farmers' elation at receiving the first decent rains in five years turned to horror at the devastating and unprecedented* flood that quickly followed. The latest reports confirm our earliest fears (that) *this is a massive humanitarian crisis and is steadily expanding southwards. The loss of hundreds of thousands of cattle after five, six, seven years of drought is a debilitating blow not just to individual farmers, many of whom have lost literally everything, but to rural communities.*

On the Federal Government Bureau of Meteorology website in March 2019, it was stated *in late January and early February, an intense and slow-moving monsoonal low over northern Queensland caused record-breaking rainfall and disastrous flooding. Areas affected included the Townsville region and westwards right across the state. A phenomenal amount of rain fell. In the seven days to 4 February 2019 our rainfall gauge at Townsville Aero recorded 1,052.8 mm, and 1,257 mm in the ten days to 6 February. There were several sites in elevated areas including Paluma, Woolshed, and Upper Bluewater that reported 12-day accumulations of more than 2,000 mm.*

In February and March 2022, Queensland and New South Wales experienced a La Niña weather event that caused major flooding and devastation on a massive scale. A national emergency was declared by the Prime Minister. Over 20 people lost their lives and property damage was estimated to run into the billions. According to climate activists the flooding was an unprecedented catastrophe for which global warming was to blame. Politicians and journalist spoke of a 'rain bomb'. The West Australian newspaper reported there's no such thing. Meteorologists say it's actually an atmospheric river that's less like a bomb and more like a conveyor belt, delivering a relentless stream of moisture-laden air. The west coasts of the United States and Canada are frequently walloped by one dubbed the Pineapple Express, which transports moisture over 4,000 km from around Hawaii. 'We don't have any names for them here in Australia' says Ben Domensino, a Meteorologist from commercial weather company Weatherzone. 'But it's common for these atmospheric rivers to affect eastern Australia. All an atmospheric river is, is a very long area of winds, blowing in the same direction over the ocean. It drags moisture thousands of kilometres. When those winds meet a landmass, the air rises and the moisture is converted into rainfall. So (when) you've got a low-pressure system strengthening. It's just sitting at the edge of that atmospheric river. As that low pressure system moves in towards the coast it will cause an area of even heavier rain where there's already been lots of rain. We have experienced such destructive La Niña weather systems in the past and will again in the future.

oooOOOooo

Bushfires, droughts and floods are in the DNA of our country. Sometimes they emerge as relatively benign; at other times they are terrifyingly devastating and horrendous. The Aborigines over many thousands of years developed successful strategies to deal with each of them. Our pioneers learned from hard experience and tragic loss the lessons that had to be learned. Ignore predictable warning signs in the leadup to impending natural disaster and a terrible price will be paid. Prepare as much as possible beforehand, and the worst effects of a natural disaster can be diminished. To blame global warming and climate change on what has always been cyclical and seasonally inevitable, is to lose sight of the country's changeable and erratic ecological history. Climate change is not the cause of droughts, floods, bushfires and extreme weather events. Those who claim it is are engaged in playing political games, not espousing fact-based science. They are as one media commentator characterised them common sense deniers.

Torrential rain brings floods. Droughts dry the land. Bushfires burn the flammable landscape. Extreme weather fluctuates between the sizzling hot to the freezing cold. High temperature, strong dry winds excessive fuel load, are all typical of the worst bushfires. Variable wind speeds propel the fire forward. Radiant heat is generated that feeds the fire turning it into a firestorm. More important than reducing our miniscule 1.3% of CO_2 world emissions is the urgent need to better manage the land. Build more dams for water storage for drought and flood mitigation. Carry out annual fire reduction burns to control disproportionate fuel loads. These are essential to a safer and more productive Australia. Ignore the past, prevaricate in the present and the future will become unsustainable: a dry tinder box bereft of manageable forests, stored water, prosperity and hope.

19

It's as Simple as ABC — Australia Before China!

When we liberate Taiwan, if Japan dares to intervene by force even if it only deploys one soldier, one plane or one ship we will not only return fire but also wage full-scale war against Japan itself. We will use nuclear bombs first. We will use nuclear bombs continuously. We will do this until Japan declares unconditional surrender. There will be no peace talks.

Chinese Communist Party (CCP)

The Chinese Government's Belt and Road scheme is an economic investment vehicle set up as a debt-trap to infiltrate every country in the world. Chinese President Xi Jinping calls it China's Magic Weapon. *China's overseas lending has risen from almost nothing in 2000 to more than $700 billion dollars today. It is the world's largest official creditor, more than twice as big as the World Bank and IMF combined. Those who default on China's loans are compelled to hand over vital infrastructure, strategic ports and land for Chinese military purposes.*

In October 2019 Victorian Premier Dan Andrews agreed to a deal with China under the Belt and Road initiative. The premier's media release touted *the shared objective of increasing the participation of Chinese infrastructure companies in Victoria.* In other words, Chinese companies were free to tender for commercial contracts and gain a toehold in the state's business dealings. The premier had earlier introduced laws that Australian procurement for all state government projects was to be strictly adhered to. Despite this Chinese companies tendered for Melbourne's $16 billion dollar north/east road transport link project and to provide raw materials sourced from China for the Melbourne Metro and West Gate Tunnels. The frontrunner to build the north/east road link was the CCP's principal Belt and Road company China Construction Oceania. In October 2020 then Senator Kimberley Kitching, Chair of the Senate Foreign Affairs Defence and Trade References Committee, condemned the Andrews Government trade policy. *The Victorian Government should not have entered into an agreement with the Chinese Government on the Belt and Road Initiative it is bad policy and bad optics.*

Federal Minister Peter Dutton criticised the menacing deal. *Victoria needs to explain why it is the only state in the country that has entered into this agreement.* Melbourne radio talk show host Neil Mitchell was more scathing in his remarks. *Daniel Andrews seems to have a bendable sense of morality. China is brutalising protestors in Hong Kong. China is suspected of hacking into our parliamentary computer system. China is keeping Uighur Muslims in concentration camps. China runs a social credit system. But for money we turn our backs on all the horror! Do we have no ethics? No morality? Where's the decency and fairness in supporting and working in partnership with a brutal, undemocratic, devious regime?*

In 2015 the Northern Territory Government leased Darwin's port facilities for 99 years in a $506 million-dollar deal with the Shandong Landbridge company — a company with close ties to the Chinese Government, the People's Liberation Army and China's sinister geopolitical Belt and Road strategy. China negotiated a bargain basement price and obtained a foothold in a strategic location becoming a threat to national security. It was *a seriously dumb idea by a state government that really hadn't thought through the consequences.*

The Port of Newcastle, the world's largest coal exporting port, was privatised by the New South Wales Baird Government in 2014. A deal worth $1.75 billion dollars gave a 50% shareholding and controlling interest to Chinese company China Merchants Port Holdings, a company with close ties to the CCP that describes itself as a dedicated follower of Xi Jinping. Exorbitant fee increases have added an additional economic burden for the port's coal exporters. In 2016, the Victorian Government leased the Port of Melbourne for 50 years to the Lonsdale Consortium, a domestic and foreign syndicate which included the Chinese Sovereign Wealth Fund. The Chinese fund stake was 20% of the $9.7 billion dollar deal. Premier Dan Andrews enthusiastically hailed the deal and said it was *a $9.7 billion dollar vote of confidence in the Victorian economy.* The federal government decision in November 2019 to allow a Chinese state-owned company the Sinosteel Corporation to invest $10 billion dollars in West Australia's Oakajee iron ore port and rail project now looks quite sinister.

In August 2019 amidst growing controversy over China's influence in Australia, the media reported 'Foreign Investors plan to create rural Chinatown in WA's Midwest'. *Foreign investors have purchased hundreds of hectares of land in WA's Midwest with a view to establishing a rural Chinatown, including an English language school. City of Greater Geraldton Mayor Shane Van Styn revealed the bold plan by developer PIP Holdings to create the suburb on the city's eastern fringe. It includes building homes specifically for Chinese migrants and associated service industries to cater to their needs.* He said *'they're proposing* (building) *anywhere up to 1,500 houses, a commercial centre and a school'*. Cr Van Styn said the school would be separate from the Australian school curriculum and service middle to upper middle-class Chinese residents. The Port of Geraldton is a major west coast seaport with 70% of shipping travelling to and from China. A strong Chinese presence in the region with undisclosed ties to the Chinese Communist Party is a long-term threat to Australia's sovereignty and national security.

Chinese investment in Australian farmland increased by 1.46 million hectares to 14.4 million hectares in 2017, a significant increase from the previous year. In 2019, investment in Australian commercial real estate was $1.5 billion dollars. The iconic Sydney Kidman and Co outback cattle empire, the largest pastoral leaseholder in Australia with 11 cattle stations covering 100,000 square kilometres, pasturing 155,000 cattle was sold in 2015 and now has 33% Chinese ownership. Foreign investment flowing into Australia in 2014 was $5.7 billion dollars, in

2015 $10.9 billion dollars rising to $14.9 billion dollars in 2016.

In August 2020, the *Daily Mail* newspaper reported *China becomes the biggest foreign owner of Australian water as 10.5% now belongs to other countries and drought-stricken farmers struggle to compete with overseas investors.* 1.9% of Australian water rights, an amount equivalent to one and a half Sydney Harbours, are currently in the hands of Chinese investors. Unibale, an Australian subsidiary company owned by the Chinese Communist Party, controls several thousand megalitres of water entitlements including many along the Murray Darling Basin. Senator Pauline Hanson has called this a national disgrace. *We are absolutely stupid to allow any foreign ownership of our water in this country. We should go back to the old way it was. If you don't own land, you should not have water rights to buy and sell on the market. Water belongs to the people of this nation, not foreign interests to make a lot of money out of it.*

In 2019 the federal government approved the purchase of Tasmania's Bellamy Baby Formula Company to Mengniu, China's largest dairy manufacturer which is part owned by the Chinese government, for $1.5 billion dollars. Voicing dissatisfaction at the Chinese dairy company's takeover, Tasmanian Independent Senator Jacqui Lambie said *I don't feel this is good for future Australians. My biggest fear, like the rest of Australia, is that we are being bought by the Communist Chinese and we are being bought up as soon as they open their cheque books. That is absolutely concerning to the future of the country, when it comes to our food security and our national security.*

In 2016, before signing up to China's Belt and Road initiative, the Andrews Government accepted a tender by the Changchun Railway Vehicles Company (CRRC) to build 65 high-capacity Melbourne trains. The multi-billion-dollar CRRC set up in 2015, employs 180,000 workers and is one of 82 Chinese companies profiting from the slave labour of China's persecuted Uighur minority. The United States citing national security fears banned CRRC as a cyber security threat. I remember travelling on Victoria's country rail network when new V/Line carriages were proudly labelled *Made in Victoria*.

oooOOOooo

Dan Andrews's woke/socialist government upsets many Victorians. Dissatisfaction runs deep with a premier who bases policy decisions on polls and spin. He declares health emergencies on a political whim. He has locked down Melbourne longer than anywhere else in the world. He empowers a heavy-handed police force to administer his draconian Coronavirus rules. Nonsensical rules such as imposing a night time curfew, closing down children's playgrounds and banning the playing of golf. When problems arise, Andrews blames everybody but himself censuring and lecturing long suffering Victorians for his own failures and poor leadership. He is the 'Premier from Hell' a narcissist, autocratic and incompetent.

He is the worst premier in the history of Victoria. His cosying up to China, his overbearing control of parliament and the bureaucracy is oppressive. He has mishandled the economy, burdened the state with massive debt and bungled the Coronavirus pandemic. On Andrews watch hotel quarantine has been an unmitigated disaster. He established a drug injecting room next to a primary school. He turned the state's once reliable power generation into a renewables mess. His promotion of identity politics, climate change and wokeness has led to decline in a state that was once a shining beckon of decency and economic success.

In August 2020 the New South Wales Government awarded a $10 million dollar renewables development grant of taxpayer money to Goldwind Australia, a subsidiary of a Chinese company and the largest wind turbine producer in the world. This happened at a time when China was politically and economically bullying Australia and boycotting selected Aussie exports. The grant was for the research and development of a hybrid gas battery storage facility. Senator Mark Latham said of the generous grant. *It's the worst possible timing, because the relationship with China has deteriorated quickly. For Minister Matt Kean to be handing over $10 million of New South Wales taxpayer funds to a Chinese-owned and operated company shows that we are taking a big risk. We shouldn't be encouraging Chinese expansion into essential infrastructure like the power grid.* Some Aussies were critical of cosying up to Chinese companies. *The Chinese company Huawei was banned from entering the Australian 5G communications network. Why then should any government in Australia give taxpayer money to a Chinese owned company for any reason whatsoever?*

Unfortunately, the enticement of Chinese investment money continues to dominate the national investment agenda. In March 2021, Michael Shoebridge from the Australian Strategic Policy Institute was critical of the federal government's decision to approve a 12 year iron ore mining lease near a military training base and strategic gas reserves at Cockatoo Island in Western Australia to a foreign company with ties to China and Hong Kong. *Now seems almost perfectly the wrong time to be awarding a lease to a company with any connections into Hong Kong let alone mainland China around iron ore. Why are we giving them any market power in iron ore; when we want to wield market power against them as they coerce us?* In 2019 before the Coronavirus pandemic struck and China's global intentions became apparent for all the world to see, China accounted for 62.2% of Australia's iron ore exports.

Australian Strategic Policy Institute Executive Director Peter Jennings warns of the national security danger of uncontrolled foreign investment. *There's a whole lot of foreign investment decisions that were taken in the 2010s that I think this government and future governments will have to unpick because the bet they made on China becoming more like Singapore, more open, easier to deal with has turned out to be wrong. China has become more authoritarian, more aggressive, more difficult to deal with. I think it is going to become untenable for us to say that a significant part of our infrastructure can now be in the hands of companies that see their ultimate loyalty as having to rest towards the Chinese Communist Party*

In September 2020 the Foreign Relations Bill was brought before the federal parliament. The bill was designed to tear up foreign power agreements deemed not to be in Australia's national interest. Of 42 agreements scrutinised 27 related to China, chief among them was Dan Andrew's egregious Belt and Road deal. The new laws prohibited federal, state, local governments and universities from engaging in foreign partnerships detrimental to Australia's economic and political goals. The 2015 Port of Darwin lease to a Chinese company was not among the agreements examined. In December 2021, it was reported in the media *the 99 year lease of the Darwin Port is set to stand after a review from the Defence Department. Defence has found there are insufficient grounds to undo the lease.*

Within weeks of the Foreign Relations Bill being passed into law, the

Morrison Government acted to nullify the Andrews Government's 2015 agreement with China's Jiangsu province to provide government grants *valued at up to $200,000 for universities and companies to share their intellectual property with their counterparts in China.* In April 2021, the Morrison Government rescinded Victoria's scandalous Belt and Road deal with China *because it was inconsistent with Australia's foreign policy. The Commonwealth used its new veto laws to cancel four agreements all negotiated by Victorian authorities including a 2004 deal between the state's Education and Training Department with Iran and a 1999 scientific co-operation agreement with Syria.* Dan Andrews courtship of the Chinese Communist Party at the expense of Aussie jobs was called out as a national security threat.

oooOOOooo

On Australian university campuses there are 13 Confucius institutes funded by and promoting the views of the Chinese Communist Party. These propaganda vehicles exert undue influence on campus politics, curricula decisions and orchestrate 'cultural associations' interference in the wider community. Emeritus Professor John Fitzgerald at Victoria's Swinburne University of Technology decries Chinese Government meddling in Australia's tertiary education sector. *Australian universities enjoy freedom and autonomy because they are generally believed to be self-governing institutions not subject to foreign government interference. Anything that undermines that belief risks harming the sector as a whole.*

In August 2019, the New South Wales Department of Education banned Confucius institute programs from its classrooms, citing growing concern the Institutes could be facilitating inappropriate foreign influence. There are 54 Confucius institute 'culture and language' programs operating in secondary classrooms in schools across Australia. South Australian Greens politician Tammy Franks condemns the Confucius institute for its blatant assault on academic integrity. *Confucius institute contracts across the world have shown disturbing levels of control over content, curriculum and hiring practices. The expansion of these needs to be halted and they need an urgent review. We need to make sure the Chinese Communist Party doesn't have control.*

Ross Babbage, former head of Strategic Analysis at the Australian

Office of National Assessments, comments on the growing militancy of Chinese influence worldwide. *While the cover of the Confucius institutes is primarily language and cultural training, they fit into a large framework of scores of other things they are doing in foreign countries, including in Australia things like spying, which is massive and we know most of it is coming from China. They complain vociferously when anyone on campus says anything they don't like about Taiwan or Tibet, or for that matter, the latest estimates that suggest a million plus Uighurs are being held in essentially concentration camps. The shouting down of anyone who wants to talk comes from people associated with these Confucius institutes.*

At the University of Queensland, Drew Pavlou an undergraduate philosophy student, while exercising his right to free speech on campus protesting against China's human rights record was assaulted. *On 24 June last year* (2019), *a Hong Kong democracy protest at the university was crashed by a pro-Beijing group, many of whom could not be identified as enrolled students. Video of the incident shows Pavlou involved in an altercation, after first being set upon by the counter protesters. He is knocked to the ground. The police are called. Emails released by the university this week* (May 2020) *show on the evening of the brawl, a deputy Vice Chancellor sent a message to the Chinese Consulate in Brisbane to explain how it had handled the situation. Two days later the Chinese Consul General in Brisbane, Xu Jie* (appointed in July 2013), *released his own statement praising the 'spontaneous patriotic behaviour' of the pro-China members of the crowd.*

Prior to the Coronavirus pandemic the University of Queensland catered for 7,000 Chinese students, which was 40% of its foreign student contingent. In 2019 Xu Jie was appointed as an Adjunct Professor in the University's School of Languages and Cultures. Pavlou tweeted *where was UQ* (University of Queensland) *eleven months ago, when I was receiving dozens of death threats at Xu Jie's direction? UQ cracked down on me, a peaceful protester, instead of the Consul General. Now, under relentless public pressure, UQ condemns Xu Jie. Nothing but a face-saving PR move, a year late.*

On 29 May 2020, the *Brisbane Times* wrote *Drew Pavlou* a *student activist highly critical of the University of Queensland's ties to Beijing* has been handed a two-year suspension from the institution. Pavlou faced a disciplinary hearing on May 20 at the university over 11 allegations of misconduct, detailed in a confidential 186-page document, reportedly linked to his on-campus activism supporting Hong Kong and criticising the Chinese Communist Party. *'I was six months away from graduation'*, he said, appearing upset in a video shared on Twitter and Facebook. *'Now that's been pulled away from me because I criticised my university's ties to the Chinese government'. 'This is an indication of how deep Chinese government influence goes. I never thought it would get to this point'*. In 2021 with his suspension reduced, Drew Pavlou returned to the University of Queensland to resume his studies.

When in December 2021, Pavlou decided to stand as a Democratic Alliance Party Senate candidate in the 2022 federal election, he became involved in another round of Chinese influence controversy and wrote on his Facebook page. *This week all billboard companies in Australia blacklisted my Senate campaign, today Facebook bans my account for 29 days due to supposed 'hate speech' but won't even tell me what post breached their rules.* In consideration for their financial bottom line, Aussie billboard companies were afraid of offending China. Pavlou's 'crime' was in two benignly designed posters, to call for a worldwide boycott of the 2022 Beijing Winter Olympic Games. Gideon Rozner from the Institute of Public Affairs remarked *if the Chinese Communist Party controls what we can put on billboards, how far and deep will this go? Every Australian should be afraid of such political interference.*

oooOOOooo

Australian universities have for several decades taken advantage of the 'river of gold' flowing out of China due to its strong economic growth. According to Robert Bolton writing in the *Financial Review* in August 2019: *Melbourne University makes 16% of its operating income from Chinese students, that's $410 million. There are 153,000 Chinese higher education students in Australia, 38% of all overseas enrolments.* Many Chinese students cannot speak or write English. Special study arrangements have been made involving written group assignments put together by an English-speaking team leader. This has led to a drop in educational standards and to an assembly line mentality churning out degrees for profit. Surely, a prerequisite to speak and write English should be the minimum requirement for higher education in Australian universities. This is not racism but plain common sense. Academic salaries are the highest they have ever been due to the Chinese financial windfall. All of this clearly handicaps poorer Australian students and denies them access to a university education, in favour of prioritising foreign students and the cash they contribute to university coffers.

Responding to China's growing influence in Australian universities, Federal Minister Peter Dutton said in October 2019. *My issue is with the Communist Party of China and their policies to the extent that they're inconsistent with our own values. In a democracy like ours, we encourage freedom of speech, freedom of expression, thought, etc. If that is being impinged, if people are operating outside of the law, then whether they are from China or from any other country, we have a right to call that out. We want university campuses to be free, we want them to be liberal in their thoughts, we want young minds to be able to compete against each other but we don't want interference in that space, we don't want theft of intellectual property in our country.*

American universities such as Massachusetts, Michigan, Texas and North Carolina and universities in France and Sweden to name just a few, have closed down Confucius institutes on their campuses labelling them China's soft peddling of its worldwide takeover agenda. In August 2019, a U.S. Senate Sub Committee investigation found that *far from being independent centres of learning promoting language classes and Chinese history, the centres are tightly controlled arms of the Chinese Government.* The investigation report went on to ask *whether Confucius institute employees should be registered as foreign agents.*

In August 2020, it was revealed that China's 'Thousand Talents Plan' an espionage and influence based research program recruiting worldwide, was deeply embedded in Australian universities. Dozens of Aussie academics and scientists signed up and agreed to abide by Chinese Communist Party rules. *The program obliges its recruits to abide by Chinese law and requires their inventions be patented in China, but offered recruits profitable salaries and additional perks.* China uses generous financial incentives to penetrate sensitive Aussie research programs and harvest intellectual property. Some of these are defence programs with cutting edge military application. Those who sign the lucrative financial contracts are forbidden to publicly criticise China or disclose the contractual arrangement without prior permission of the CCP. Australians are alarmed that when China is criticized, influential and wealthy Australians pop up to defend them. One mining and business magnate accompanied by a Chinese consular official ambushed a press conference held by Federal Health Minister Greg Hunt to spread CCP disinformation.

oooOOOooo

In May 2020, a Lowry Institute poll revealed that 68% of Australians voiced dissatisfaction with China and its bullying tactics, exerted worldwide to avoid an open and transparent enquiry into the China origin of the Coronavirus. Australia spoke up and called for an enquiry. China unleashed its wrath. Threats were made against iron ore and coal shipments. Australian media reported *China will prioritise coal imports from Mongolia, Indonesia and Russia. Import restrictions have left hundreds of millions of tonnes of Australian coal anchored off China's coast as trade tensions with Beijing deepen.* China would later regret its embargo decision on Australian coal as its citizens struggled in winter to adequately heat their homes and keep the lights. Australia coal ships were docked and unloaded. The imposition of a tariff against Australian barley exports and the boycotting of abattoirs came in effect. The wine industry was targeted with 'dumping' tariff imposts of 200%. Aussie timber exports, and the wheat and cotton industries with a net worth of more than a billion dollars, came under sustained economic attack by the Chinese Communist Party. Worse was to come with nationwide cyber-attacks on every arm of government from the federal to the local level; on industry, hospitals, educational institutions, the power grid, water and other major infrastructure targets.

Before the world was made fully aware of the bat-derived ravages of the Coronavirus, China went on a worldwide spree buying up medical supplies, including 90 tons of facemasks and other personal protection equipment (PPE) from Australia, knowing that the virus would spread to other countries. Chinese companies in Australia helped the CCP by gathering and dispatching PPE by cargo plane. This was an unpardonable act compounded by the World Health Organisation supporting China. In June 2021, Former American Secretary of State Mike Pompeo, called out

China's carelessness in spreading the Coronavirus and commented on the WHO's toadying attitude to China. *The World Health Organisation is an institution that utterly failed in the one job that it had, preventing a pandemic. At the moment of crisis, at the crunch point, they sided with Xi Jinping and the Chinese Communist Party and not with the world.*

There can be little doubt, the Coronavirus pandemic originated in Wuhan China and the CCP engaged in a realpolitik strategy to sow chaos and distraction worldwide, and that the strategy was to disrupt foreign economies. It is surely no mere coincidence that China immediately closed down all domestic travel, while allowing international travel to continue around the world. They even tried to bully Australia to accept flights from China when the Prime Minister decided to stop international flights. The CCP made a cold hearted, calculated decision to spread the virus outside China. Under cover of the pandemic induced panic China's belligerence against Hongkong and elsewhere escalated. The CCP covered up the origins and spread of the virus in China then allowed it to leave the country to spread worldwide. China profited from the 4 million plus human lives lost, and the devastating economic and health chaos caused in many countries around the world.

China refuses to acknowledge culpability, or give unfettered access to Wuhan laboratory data, most of which is now probably destroyed. The mainstream media refuses to thoroughly investigate the origin of the deadly virus. Nevertheless, the Coronavirus pandemic and the CCP's retaliation against Australia for calling for a transparent enquiry has woken the world up to China's global manoeuvrings and manipulations. China will continue to politically bluster and threaten the world economically and militarily. However, the genie is out of the bottle and everybody knows it.

China is using global issues such as climate change, the west's obsession with gender, racism and political correctness, to play a diplomatic and espionage long game of economic, political and military bullying to achieve its master plan of world dominance. According to an October 2021 Newspoll, *75% of Australians believe an increasingly belligerent China poses a significant threat to Australia's national security.* In May 2021, Prime Minister Scott Morrison took up the political cudgel, rejecting China's multi-pronged bullying of Australia. The PM defended our Aussie freedom to act as we please, without allowing a browbeating foreign country that oppresses minorities and its own people to interfere with our national sovereignty. *What we're doing is ensuring that we maintain our ground as a country; that we stand up for Australia and our values and how we want to live our lives.* It was a strong declaration of Australia's democratic resolve not to bow to Chinese Communist Party coercion and tyranny. At the same time Australia is bringing back manufacturing industries, finding new export customers to move away from China and signing trade deals with European and Asian countries.

It's as Simple as ABC — Australia Before China!

20

Quiet Australians and the Politically Correct Times in which We Live

Political Correctness is a way of controlling people as a means to power. If you can control what people say you can control what people think. Those with authoritarian instincts use political correctness as a way of shutting people up. Whether it's the Chinese Communist Party or a group of people cyber-lynching you on Twitter it's essentially the same means to power.

Senator Andrew Hastie

From the 1950s to the new millennium, the times would change dramatically and we would change with them, sometimes for the better and sometimes not. We would embrace a view of ourselves that was more imaginary than real. A view we are told where truth is relative and there is no longer just one truth but many and the differences do not matter. Our history is now broader in focus and multicultural, which has brought its own specific challenges and a redefinition of what it means to be an Australian. We are currently in the process of exchanging one national myth for another.

The old Aussie clichés and stereotypes no longer adequately describe the national psyche, though as a nation we are loath to let go of the past entirely. Australia Day is under attack as an outmoded celebration of oppressive colonialism. The April 2020, 250th Anniversary of Captain James Cook's landing at Kurnell Beach on the east coast of Australia on 29 April 1770, was portrayed by activists as the beginning of European tyranny.

History today is framed in terms of rigid political correctness, a constraint on what can be said and a revamped vision of the past demanding 'Sorry Days' for perceived historical injustice. National unity is something we give lip service; while being acutely aware of ethnic, religious and cultural divisions below the surface. The modern-day myth of white privilege is a political and cultural trope used by the Socialist/Green/Woke partnership, to declare Australia an irredeemably and deeply racist country. This is a false and exaggerated misrepresentation of Australia's past and present. It reduces race relations to a discriminatory power struggle where Aborigines are always seen as the losers.

oooOOOooo

Australia no longer calls itself a Christian country governed by Christian values. In the 21st century 52% of Australians identify themselves as Christians, 30% say they are not religious and non-Christian religions stand at 8%. (10% expressed no view on the matter.) This from a solid Christian base in 1911 with 96% of Australians embracing Christianity. The Catholic and Protestant divide of days gone by no longer partitions the nation in the way that it did. In addition to Judaism, Buddhism and Islam, there is a proliferation of religions thriving in Australia today. Christianity has been relegated to an inferior position of community importance. Christianity is the spiritual and moral core of western civilisation. As a nation Australia owes its compassionate and caring outlook to the biblical teachings of Jesus Christ. Christians need to stand up and defend their cherished religious beliefs, not simply buckle under to woke attacks from within and without their own ranks.

Sydney's Catholic Archbishop Anthony Fisher speaks of *Christianity under attack and of powerful interests* (seeking) *to marginalise religious believers and beliefs, especially Christian ones, and exclude them from public life.* On the broader issues of historical revisionism and the woke worldview the Archbishop writes *those without a sense of history are not only doomed to repeat the worst of the past. They live in the present rootless and with no well-founded identity.* The woke fallacy is bereft of existential meaning and universal significance.

Christianity is standing in the way of the new woke world order. Christians feel themselves under siege from an intolerant and divisive ideology that seeks the ruin and destruction of the Christian way of life. In the United Kingdom, *the police told a Christian café owner in Harrogate to stop displaying Bible verses on a TV screen because it's 'offensive and a crime'. The owner said he was shocked when officers from Lancashire police visited his café and ordered him to stop displaying the Bible text. 'It felt like an interrogation and they told me I was in breach of public order by displaying material that could be deemed offensive'.*

During the months of Coronavirus lockdown, the freedom to assemble for prayer and religious worship was one of the last restrictions to be removed as community transmission was brought under control. Senator Matt Canavan voiced the frustration and anger of many Aussie Christians when he said *if you can have 50,000 people in a stadium* (to watch a football match)*, why can't we allow people to go to church and worship their God and religion? Of all the freedoms that have been restricted during this time* (of pandemic) *I think freedom of religion should have been the first to be relaxed, not the last. It's one of the most important freedoms we have.*

Christians have shown commendable forbearance and dignity in the face of sustained and bitter assault on their right to free speech and religious belief. However, turning the other cheek has only enraged the political left who rant and rave against Christians at every opportunity. *We don't do God anymore!* scream activists. The Christian-hating message resounds: *Religious people don't have the right to preach their hateful bigotry!* The aim is to undermine the Christian message of charitable goodwill and demonise those who practise it.

oooOOOooo

There is a frustration among white Australians they are being denied the right to celebrate white identity. When Senator Pauline Hanson put forward a motion in the federal parliament in September 2018 stating *It's OK to be white,* all political parties voted against the proposal describing it as *demeaning and racist*. Many Aussies felt betrayed by the parliamentary putdown. Why it was asked is it a politically incorrect crime to be a white Australian?

Senator Mark Latham says woke social justice arguments are *primitive, anti-intellectual and driven by what people look like. I grew up on a public housing estate. We didn't own a house; we didn't own a car and everything I've done in life I've worked my guts out for. Any success and failure I've got in life is immaterial to my skin colour and immaterial to my gender. Nobody on the Green Valley housing estate said 'Mate, here is your ticket for white privilege in life'.*

Professor Geoffrey Blainey warned in the 1980s that a fervent form of multiculturalism and the new preference for Asian rather than European migrants could usher in racial tensions and a cultural divisiveness which would threaten the social and political fabric of Australian society. *When Anglo Celtic Australians,* he wrote, *show the same ethnic preference as minorities they are denounced as racists.* In the 1991 book, *Eye on Australia: Speeches and Essays of Geoffrey Blainey* Schwartz Books, Blainey criticised multiculturalists for holding an aggrieved view that *Australia was a desert between 1788 and 1950 because it was populated largely by people from the British Isles and because it seemed to have a cultural unity, a homogeneity which is the very antithesis of multiculturalism.* Blainey was pilloried in the media and scandalously driven from his position in academia for daring to state publicly what has increasingly come to pass.

The UK's Chief Rabbi, the late Lord Jonathan Sacks, described multiculturalism as a *disastrous policy, misconceived and profoundly damaging to the social fabric of every society into which it was introduced. The first people to try multiculturalism, the Dutch, were also the first people to regret it. The Dutch favoured tolerance and opposed multiculturalism. When asked what the difference was, they replied that tolerance ignores differences; multiculturalism makes an issue of them at every point. In a relativist culture, there is no moral consensus, only a clash of conflicting views in which the loudest voice wins. Multiculturalism was meant to promote tolerance, but gave rise to new and dire forms of intolerance.*

In discussing the distinction between assimilation into an integrated community and multicultural pluralism emphasising ethnic and cultural diversity. Associate Professor and Sydney University Sociologist Salvatore Babones writes *Australia has a greater proportion of foreign-born citizens than any other country in the developed world* (and) *faces the challenge of integrating immigrants on an unprecedented scale. Assimilation and multiculturalism are two fundamentally opposed approaches to integration. Assimilation aims at the forging of a single shared civic community, while multiculturalism assumes movement towards a multinational state. Democracy depends on assimilation. Australia should, of course, allow its citizens to embrace whatever cultures they choose, but should not question the unity of its own civic community, by officially promoting the idea that immigrants are expected to exempt themselves from it.*

Aussie short story writer and poet Eugene Alexander Donnini rejects the claim that western countries are inherently racist and incapable of accommodating a wide range of cultural and religious differences. *There is nothing stopping any cultural community living in a civic western nation from practising the traditions of their culture and religion, as long as such practices do not interfere with the rights, freedom and safety of fellow citizens which is guaranteed under the law fundamentally derived from enlightenment values. The freedom they enjoy comes with a responsibility to recognise the freedom and rights of others in their community, regardless of religion, culture or skin colour.*

Donnini defends the west and western civilisation as the principal drivers of today's material prosperity. *The arts and sciences of the west have flourished, resulting in the greatest scientific advancements and inventions in human history. The abolition of diseases, poverty and slavery, the creation of the internet, putting human beings on the moon, sound infrastructure construction and technology, air travel, the wonders of nanotechnology and quantum physics the list goes on. Why do you think people migrate to the west, mostly from anti-democratic (Marxist) and other (Islamic) closed societies? It is because the west, with all its imperfections, is free, creative and prosperous.*

oooOOOooo

Everybody must walk on egg shells and curb their tongues, unless of course they happen to belong to a privileged minority group that revels in identity and gender politics. In 1995 the Keating Labor Government introduced an amendment to the Racial Discrimination Act (1975) known as Section 18C. The amendment has serious freedom of speech implications which are still being challenged today. The expansive language of the amendment is capable of such broad interpretation as to be wellnigh meaningless. Even an unkind word can be labelled as hate speech and declared unlawful. Part of the amendment reads, *the act is breached if it is reasonably likely, in all circumstances, to offend, insult, humiliate or intimidate another person or a group of people.* In other words, offence of some kind by anybody in any situation can be subject to legal penalty. Section 18C is bullying coercive legislation which may have seemed a good idea at the time but has proven to be oppressive and acrimonious in practice.

Section 18C is a regressive, discriminatory and stifling law. It allows woke bullies to parade and posture as social justice warriors. Everything they oppose or dislike is labelled as offensive and insulting. People should be allowed to openly speak their minds on every subject without courtroom litigation hanging over their heads. Penalties should of course apply to those who promote violence, disorder and disharmony. Offence, insult and humiliation is in the eye of the beholder and is not a good measure to assess social or any other kind of justice.

The abuse of Section 18C makes the case better than anything else that Australia needs a Bill of Rights. The right to free speech, freedom of assembly and freedom of religious worship etc., should be formally codified against infringement and curtailment. The American Bill of Rights (1789) is discussed in the following terms. *The Bill of Rights spells out Americans' rights in relation to their government. It guarantees civil rights and liberties to the individual like freedom of speech, press, and religion. It sets rules for the due process of law and reserves all powers not delegated to the federal government to the people or the states.* Australia needs a Bill of Rights that limits government infringement, woke bullying and spurious litigation. A Bill of Rights that enshrines in law the inalienable rights of the individual. Nothing is more important and necessary to the democratic health of a nation.

oooOOOooo

In December 2021, a small group of people gathered outside ABC headquarters in Melbourne protesting against the ABC's biased news reporting. They shouted through locked glass doors *Tell the Truth! Tell the Truth!* For decades older Australians revered and listened to ABC radio and watched ABC television for instructive programming and even-handed news broadcasts. Today many Australians still watch and listen to ABC programs. However, they no longer trust the national broadcaster to be objective in its reporting. As one disgruntled Aussie put it *the ABC used to be the gold standard of news and television in Australia. Now it is no more than a propaganda machine for turning out the most ridiculous left-wing garbage — our ABC has become their ABC.*

Johannes Leak The Australian 15 June, 2020

Queensland journalist Peter Gleeson says *I grew up with the ABC and back then it was very much our ABC. The ABC is letting down average Australians, it produces leftist rubbish, it's as simple as that. Its shameless extension of the Labor Party and the Greens is there for everybody to see. The ABC starts its journalism from a single-minded agenda, what is best for the left. It then creates the content required to satisfy that demand. The ABC has no shame about their bias it's part of their DNA.*

The ABC prides itself on being a 'Conservative Free Zone' shutting down Aussie individualism, free speech and defence of traditional values in its partisan programming promoting a Socialist/Green/Woke agenda. In his memoir *More to Life than Politics* Connor Court (2019), Senator Richard Alston, Minister for Communications in the Howard Government, wrote of a partisan bias of monumental proportions, describing the ABC as a *hotbed of the narrow leftist thinking of inner-city elites*. Senator Alston went on to say *the ABC Broadcasting Act is quite explicit, stating the national broadcaster has the statutory duty to gather and present news and information that is accurate 'according to the recognised standards of objective journalism'. Whenever the subject of ABC bias arises, everyone defaults to the charter. But the charter is so vague and open-ended as to be virtually meaningless. The ABC seems to take its cue from what Humpty Dumpty famously said to Alice: 'When I use a word, it means just what I choose it to mean, neither more nor less'.*

Maurice Newman who served as ABC Chairman from 2007 to 2012, decries the left-wing bias and political partisanship of today's ABC. Newman criticises the ABC for embracing PC wokeness and engaging in cancel culture vitriol. *The ABC is captured by an ideology and everything they do is biased in favour of promoting that ideology. It's a propaganda machine for the green left. They don't bother to do fact checking. It's not about journalism anymore, it's about advocacy.* Michael Kroger, an ABC Director and Board Member for 5 years (1998-2003), wrote an article in the *Australian* newspaper on 26 November 2020, criticising the ABC's *constant narrative of denigrating our past, criticising our present and demonising our future.* Kroger admonished the ABC for its skewed left-wing bias and woke belittling of Australian society. *The ABC's news and current affairs division presents a grand narrative of the world as a dark place becoming darker by the day. It constantly highlights Australia's role in our diminishing world and presents us with a frightening future. In the eyes of the ABC, we are led by heartless politicians who refuse to open our borders to unlimited immigration. This is presented as a cultural failing of Australians who by extension are immensely selfish and obviously racist.*

It is not just displeased ABC viewers and listeners who disapprove of the ABC's biased news reporting. *I'm an old school lefty from way back. Voted Labor all my life. I worked for the ABC in the Parliamentary Press Gallery for 6 years in the 90's, but I simply can't watch any of the ABC news and current affairs programs anymore as they're completely agenda driven. The quality of journalism has regressed to a standard that is simply unacceptable.*

A former ABC newsreader describes left-wing prejudice in operation. *I worked at the ABC in the 80's. I was a radio newsreader on a metropolitan station, and, as such, I had no editorial control, I had to read what was served up. I asked the news editor why we went to great lengths to convey the Left's point of view, yet never presented the LNP or Conservative side of the stories. He replied 'They're f***en Tories. Who cares what they think?'*

oooOOOooo

1950s Australians and the society at large would not have been comfortable with or accepted today's profane and secularist Australia. There was internal coherence and stability of national purpose. Communal standards were maintained. Laws were respected and obeyed. Christianity was a strong moral anchor in spiritual life. Doors were left unlocked. Children, women and the elderly went about their daily business without worry or hindrance. There was crime, disturbance and wrongdoing at times; but people felt safe in their homes and on the streets in a way they simply do not today.

Inner-city Melbourne women have taken to walking in groups after dark for protection against predators. One woman said *it's made me really fearful of even walking home from the train station after dark. I hold my keys between my knuckles, I text my housemates when I'm on my way and when I expect to be home. It's about safety and feeling safe to live and walk around and not be scared to listen to music or not be scared to walk in a park if there's only one street lamp. It's sad, but it's a reality.* Another woman welcomed the group chaperone idea. *I thought it was great, that I wasn't the only one thinking the same.* What a sorry state of affairs when Aussie women need group protection in streets around their homes.

In the 1950s victims of crime had a confidence in appropriate sentencing and punishment for lawbreaking that no longer exists today. The rule of law has been diminished by judges ordering lenient bail conditions and dispensing soft sentences. Senator Pauline Hanson expressed the view of many Aussies, when she said *people are fed up with bleeding heart judges that are not listening to the public expectation of what they hand out in sentencing.* The rights of criminals ride roughshod over those of victims and their families. Today's deterrents deter no one, least of all criminals. Advocacy for reform and concern for the entitlements of offenders are front and centre in legal proceedings. A sentence of life rarely means life and even the worst criminal offenders look forward to early release and a return to the community. For convicted criminals and their lawyers, it is the parole period and not the length of sentence they hear in the judge's sentencing address.

A case in point is Daniel Morcombe's paedophile killer Brett Cowan who from inside his prison cell sneers at the legal system, tormenting his victim's family by appealing his sentence and endlessly seeking ways to create disarray in the legal process in his favour. In an edited version of the Morcombe family's Victim's Impact Statement, Bruce Morcombe spoke to Cowan face to face.

I have sat watching you in court for close to 40 days, listening to you describe and watching you with a smirk on your face, tell how you threw Daniel's lifeless body down an embankment and a week later returned and crushed his skull with a shovel 'chop, chop, chop, chop, chop', you coldly explained in an emotionless, matter of fact way. We now have to live out our days with the unimaginable image of wild dogs devouring our much-loved son's remains. How you sit here day after day, almost frozen in the one position, is chilling. Throughout this time, you have been completely devoid of any remorse for what you did to Daniel. I am haunted by thoughts of how long Daniel was held captive and what other unspeakable things you did. Sitting in the same room as you revolts me. Our family's first sleepless night without Dan haunts me even today. That feeling of helplessness and unimaginable pain never leaves you.

For the bereaved Morcombe family, the pain and the suffering of losing a murdered loved one never goes away. To fill the emotional chasm, they have become tireless campaigners for children and the rights of victims; knowing they will be called upon time and again, to oppose the legal manoeuvrings and sought-after access to prison privileges and later parole applications of the paedophile killer who brutally murdered their son. The Morcombe's world is forever turned upside down.

oooOOOooo

For young Australians the instilling of pioneer guilt and self-hatred begins in the school classroom. They are taught that European settlement in Australia was divisive, destructive and genocidal. Nothing good came from the British arrival in Australia, which is characterised as imperialist and a great catastrophe. Pioneers are racist caricatures, land thieves, killers of Aborigines and dirt-poor farmers who resort to crime and support 'hero' criminals like Ned Kelly. A larger historical narrative of Australians working together with a grand national purpose is blinkered, held hostage by repressive political correctness and victimhood studies that distort and misrepresent. Yet despite this ideology driven false view of Australia's past, statistics reveal a patriotism and confident pride among young people in the nation's achievements.

An Australian Institute of Public Affairs survey conducted in January 2020 revealed that 71% of Aussies believe Australia has a proud history and support Australia Day being celebrated on 26 January. The survey further disclosed that 68% believe Australia has become too politically correct. 83% of those surveyed said Australia Day should be an opportunity to respect the contribution that everyone has made and continues to make. Even among Millennials, 57% of 18 to 24 year olds agreed that Australia Day should not be changed from January 26 and 85% said they were proud to be Australian. A survey conducted by the left-wing *Guardian* newspaper reported that only 35% of Indigenous Australians wanted to change the date of Australia Day, while 70% of all Australians were opposed to any date change.

Spokesman for the IPA, Evan Mulholland, said *what we're finding is that the younger generation are actually really patriotic. We're having record numbers of attendance at things like Anzac Day parades, because people are proud to be Australians. 71% are proud of our history. People acknowledge our shared history and the tragedies of the past, but also celebrate what is great about the British institutions that have made*

Australia great and what we have to celebrate about the future. Quiet Australians, young and old, Indigenous and non-Indigenous deserve to be listened to in the noisy cacophony of those who seek racial division and tribal separation.

At the time of the 18th Century Enlightenment, the French Philosopher Voltaire wrote *we should be considerate to the living; to the dead we owe only the truth.* The truth starts with acknowledging the past honestly and accurately, the good and the bad, by recognising that the activist minority do not represent the viewpoint of Quiet Australians or speak for the majority of Indigenous, migrant and LGBTIQ+ Australians. Why shouldn't there be complex diversity and a variety of differing opinion among these groups? Wide ranging opinion and open debate is the essence of democracy. Only the left and those advocating perpetual victimhood think otherwise.

There is common ground to be found among all Australians outside the slogan shouting and cultural negativity, pursued by those seeking to profit from inciting national discord, mass generated fear and chaos. The indomitable spirit of our bush pioneers, the undaunted courage of the Anzacs, the mateship and resilience of everyday Aussies who coped with wartime loss and the hardships of the Great Depression should be remembered and celebrated. These sturdy men and women were patriotic Australians first and foremost. To erase their sacrifice and heroism, is to rewrite the past from the point of view of a fainthearted present by those who collectively have sacrificed very little.

Conclusion

People used to be equal; now some are considered more equal than others. Thought policing a person's every word and deed offends me more than anything else. We should be allowed to live our lives with freedom, dignity and democracy without government or any other kind of interference.

A Quiet Australian 2021

We are living in dangerous times when the very foundation of western civilisation, its deep-seated Judeo-Christian legacy and the productive capitalist enterprise are under sustained attack. Globalists are using Coronavirus lockdowns and the many restrictions placed on personal freedom and liberty to further their climate change control of the world. The young are indoctrinated into a cult preaching imminent world catastrophe, hatred of the past and scorn for the present. Multiculturism pretends to be benevolent and a non-discriminatory way forward. A nation is defined by the keystone stories it tells itself. If those stories are focused on the spreading of division, the stoking of victimhood resentment and the biology of skin colour then the facade of national cohesiveness is shattered.

Regrettably this is where we are in Australia today, living under the Coronavirus tyranny of politicians, bureaucrats and so called health experts. Menzies Research Centre Director Nick Cater deplores federal and state governments ruling by emergency health decree. *The instinct to order society from the top, with coercion if necessary, rather than trust citizens to establish social order by consent, grows stronger. If we have learned nothing else from this pandemic, we have surely learned that.* Our basic freedoms as liberty loving Australians are being eroded and taken away by intimidating political correctness and hair-trigger medical advice that restricts and diminishes rather than enhances the Aussie national character. If we let covid fear rule our lives and meekly obey those who tell us they must be obeyed, then as the old rural proverb goes *if you act like sheep, you get eaten by wolves*.

During the Coronavirus pandemic the authoritarian behaviour of state premiers, chief medical officers and an assortment of unelected government bureaucrats has shown how fragile the previously unifying concept of Australian Federation has become. Premiers said they made decisions based on the science and medical advice but rarely produced that advice for public scrutiny. In study after study the best science and medical advice from overseas has shown that the wearing of masks is of questionable value and lockdowns ineffective in eradicating Coronavirus.

Johannes Leak The Australian 26 July, 2021

Yet this was the blanket eradication strategy pursued in every state of Australia before vaccination altered the picture. There was no proportionality, no measured or targeted response. Chief medical officers fronted the media daily dispensing a one size fits all set of commands. Premiers acted as border closure dictators and mask tyrants. The delta and omicron variants followed an ever-expanding Greek alphabet classification of new variants said to be on the way. The police became Stasi enforcers for each premier's draconian mask mandates, social distancing decrees and a revolving door of other freedom denying measures. The federal government paid for everything but was not in control.

In July 2021, a public pushback came when thousands of Aussies shouting 'Freedom!' took to the streets in capital cities, protesting against yet another round of blanket community lockdowns. New South Wales Police Commissioner Mick Fuller called the stand-up and take your freedom back protestors *a bunch of anarchists*. The media joined in laughably describing what was happening as *a right-wing QAnon conspiracy*. New South Wales Shadow Police Minister Walt Secord added to the media frenzy, when he called protestors *far-right conspiracy theorists and anti-vaxxers* (who) *crawl back under the rocks where they live*. A stressed-out woman protestor complained. *I feel like we're being controlled and brainwashed by what they're feeding to us through our TVs*. A social media post denounced the police for encouraging people to *dob in a protester. Not a rapist. Not a burglar. Not a paedophile. Not a car thief. But dob in a protester! How shameful for us all!* Crime-Stoppers received over 15,000 phone calls as the street protests were happening.

Dan Andrews, who claims he cannot 'recall the creeping assumption' of ministerial responsibility behind the disastrous hotel quarantine shambles, has turned Victoria into a police state where neighbours report each other. On the 3 October 2020 the Melbourne *Age* reported *Victorians are dobbing on their neighbours in record numbers with hundreds of thousands of calls made to police to report covid breaches since the start of the pandemic. Data released by Victoria Police shows that at the height of the first wave of the pandemic, the police assistance line received about 100,000 calls during the month of April, 66% more than during an average month. Nearly 4 in 10 were people dobbing in other Victorians for breaching Coronavirus restrictions*. The compliant dobbing in was reminiscent of 'good Germans' informing on neighbours during the second world war.

While there are those who obediently and, in some cases, gleefully followed big brother direction, there were many who deplored the curtailment of their liberty and dob in overreach of bullying government sanctions. On the 21st of August 2021 despite the threat of arrest and a $5,000 fine, thousands of anti-lockdown Melbournians marched through the CBD chanting *Freedom! Sack Dan Andrews!* A young woman clutching her dog to her chest told reporters *Its inhumane! It's unconstitutional and it's unfair!* Another protestor said *What brought me out today? We're all in lockup, we're all at breaking point!*

Johannes Leak The Australian 26 July, 2021

A day later, 2,000 unmasked people including a man riding a horse, congregated in the coastal town of Coolangatta on the Queensland/New South Wales border protesting lockdowns and border closure. Protestor Mark Westley said *It's a direct attack on my freedom of liberty and freedom to move* (about). *It's affecting people's businesses and social lives. This will be the break-up of the Commonwealth of Australia, it will be the fragmentation of Australia into disparate, fighting, disputing groups and the end of democracy as we know it.* New South Wales Police Superintendent David Roptel response was to state *further inquiries will be made to identify those who were in attendance at today's protest and appropriate action will be taken.*

In Victoria dissent emerged from within the ranks of Victoria Police that exposed dissatisfaction with the Andrews Government's harsh 'tackle to the ground' enforcement policy of its Covid-19 health orders. During a media interview in October 2021, Acting Senior Sergeant Krystle Mitchell with 16 years' service as a Victorian police officer, dramatically resigned from Victoria Police. *All of my friends who are police officers working on the frontline are suffering everyday enforcing CMO* (health order) *directions that certainly a great majority don't believe in and don't want to infliction* (on the public). Knowing that she would be subjected to a Victoria Police Professional Standards investigation, Krystle went on to say *I will be resigning from Victoria Police effective from the end of this interview, because the consequences of me coming out publicly would be dismissal. I'm quitting because I can't remedy in my soul anymore, the way in which my organisation that I love to work for, is causing damage to the reputation of Victoria Police and the damage it is causing to the community.*

Former Prime Minister Tony Abbott commented on a crowd of Victorian protestors who marched to Melbourne's Shrine of Remembrance. *I saw a lot of people who maybe were a little misguided, maybe were a little over the top, but I saw a lot of people there who are sick and tired of restrictions, which, frankly, are now becoming absolutely unreasonable. Then you had the Victorian Police lined up like stormtroopers, eventually charging them with rubber bullets and tear gas. Obviously, people shouldn't break the law, but you've got people there at the Shrine of Remembrance with flags, with placards, to the best of my observation they were simply there to make a point. They weren't being violent, they weren't being vandalistic, they weren't being destructive.*

Real damage was being done to the lives of ordinary people and they were sick and tired of hearing the political and media spin. On 3 September 2021, the *Daily Mail* reported on *a man living out of his car after losing his home during the pandemic* (who) *called into the ABC Drive* (show) *giving his name only as Mark the Victorian.* (Mark delivered) *an emotion-charged tirade begging the broadcaster to stop using the phrase 'we're all in this together'. 'I keep hearing on the ABC we're all in this together, we're not. We're not in this together. The only time I want to hear that is when a politician or member of the media* says *'I'll give half my salary to someone who just lost their house'*, but we're never going to hear that are we?' We've got people losing their jobs, but we don't hear about the houses they're losing, the rentals or mortgages and marriages. And then we get the ABC and I'm quite sure you guys aren't losing any money. Of course, you're not, and you're earning big dollars. It's an insult to hear 'we're all in this together'. There's enough stress, I live in my bloody car now. I live in my frigging car and I've lost everything!' The ABC switchboard received messages offering Mark support and money saying: *He is 100% correct.*

The Morrison Government's national cabinet was not a constitutional or consensus national cabinet binding state premiers to an agreed-upon course of action. Tony Abbott called national cabinet a 'dog's breakfast' of competing agendas and political one-upmanship. Premiers attended talkfest meetings, mouthed covid platitudes and returned to their states where they did as they pleased. The unity of the nation, our federation and our identity as sensible Australians was being torn apart by autocratic premiers seeking only political and re-election advantage. As vaccination levels reached 70% and 80% in the various states, Coronavirus lockdown tyranny began to abate but the threat of future lockdowns remained ever present.

In November 2021, despite condemnation from the parliamentary opposition, the state's judiciary and a growing concern expressed by many Victorians. Dan Andrews rushed through the Victorian Parliament new pandemic emergency legislation, which was draconian and anti-democratic, granting the premier unprecedented power to control people's lives. Tens of thousands of Melbournians (the mainstream media again fudged the numbers reporting only a *few thousand protestors*) fed up with lockdowns and ongoing government restrictions took to the streets in angry Freedom protests. An exasperated father opposed to vaccination mandates carried a picket sign which read: *Severe Reaction to my First Dose. My Kids, My Choice not Yours Andrews. You Disgust Me!* People were outraged and lashed out on social media. *Victoria under Andrews and his new found power (as if he needed more!) will be hell on earth.* Crowds numbering well in excess of 100,000 gathered together in a series of rolling protests, which quickly escalated into a public movement to get rid of the Andrews Government. *I believe these politicians have underestimated the True Aussie Spirit!*

In the regional Victorian City of Ballarat on 5 December 2021, upwards of a 1,000 people marched in the street waving Southern Cross and Australian flags chanting *Shame on you Dan Andrews! Sack Dan Andrews!* At the Bakery Hill memorial site where in 1854 the Eureka Stockade Goldminer's Rebellion took place and the Southern Cross flag of stars was raised for the first time in opposition to harsh Victorian Government regulation. The site of a bloody confrontation that resulted in the deaths of 22 miners and 6 soldiers. Before the battle began miner's leader Peter Lalor *knelt down, head uncovered, and with his right hand pointing to the standard* (flag), *exclaimed in a measured tone: 'We swear by the Southern Cross to stand truly by each other to defend our rights and liberties'.* Ballarat's modern-day protestors opposed to Dan Andrews bullying style of government swore the same Eureka oath as their march commenced. In 1854 the colonial grievance centred on exorbitant miner's license fees. In 2021 the complaint was against intrusive QR codes and lockdown detention pandemic measures. Henry Lawson wrote an inspiring poem in 1887 titled 'Flag of the Southern Cross' celebrating the Eureka fighting spirit. *Fling out the flag of the Southern Cross! Prove ourselves worthy of the land we inherit now.*

Give up your taken for granted freedoms to a demanding government and those who promise utopian pipedreams and you will never fully get them back. President Ronald Reagan famously said *freedom is never more than one generation away from extinction. We didn't pass it to our children in the bloodstream. It must be fought for, protected, and handed on for them to do the same, or one day we will spend our sunset years telling our children and our children's children what it was once like in the United States where men were free.* African/American political pundit David Webb went one step further admonishing, *you may vote your way into communism. But your grandkids will have to shoot their way out!*

oooOOOooo

Many older Australians, those Prime Minister Scott Morrison calls the Quiet Australians, no longer recognise the Australia of their youth and feel besieged in a national paradigm not of their making. They feel culturally and politically bullied by minority groups. They do not trust politicians, the media, the justice system, banks or big companies to do the right thing. They deplore the fact that 86% of the Australian mining industry is in the hands of overseas interests; 11% of Australia's prime agricultural land is in foreign ownership; 29.7% of Northern Territory investment is controlled by offshore investors and 70% of Australia's wind farms are owned by foreign consortiums. They lament the fact that our precious water rights are traded for cash by foreign investors, monopoly farmers and city-based entrepreneurs. Australia is awash with foreign influence and the allure of foreign money.

The shabby treatment of Aussie farmers they see as a national disgrace. Once a jewel in the agricultural crown, two thirds of the nation's dairy industry is owned and controlled by foreign companies. The dwindling population of dairy farmers is squeezed so hard by milk industry middlemen and supermarket chains, that many have been forced to walk off farms pioneered by their family more than a hundred years ago. Some farmers did not live to do this. Sadly, they took their lives rather than face humiliation and defeat. The pioneer dream of an independent and prospering farming class clearly is no longer the cherished national ideal. The city rules supreme and the regions suffer. In the eyes of many Aussies the country is at a pivotal social, economic and cultural crossroad and the future looks uninviting.

More than ever before, we need an honest and informed public debate, not a politicised diatribe endlessly focused on skin colour, gender identity and a host of other judgmental ideas. On being chosen as the Northern Territory's Country Liberal Party Senate candidate in June 2021, Jacinta Price said *Australians want to bring back common sense. We don't want to be divided into different boxes. We want to be recognised as Australians, to support one another for a better country. Our Australian values are being eroded away by this woke nonsense we're faced with, cancel culture, all those sorts of things. We need to reinstate our Australian values for the benefit of all of us and they're the things I want to fight for while I'm in Canberra. To recognise that we're Australians and we shouldn't be dividing ourselves by the colour of our skin or anything else.*

We live under an oppressive regime of woke supremacy and woke privilege, where words and images are weaponised in an irrational and absurd way that ultimately robs them of unifying meaning and efficacy. The latest insanity is to replace the time-honoured word 'Mother' with 'Birthing Person'. Sillier still is the virtue signalling idiocy of the United States Congress in voting to end the congressional prayer with 'Awoman' instead of 'Amen'. In Victoria there is an anti-Christian campaign to abolish the recitation of the Lord's Prayer in state parliament. At the time of the August 2021 National Census, social media was awash with the woke Twitterati calling on people to tick the 'No Religion' box. We all know how ridiculous wokeness is and yet we allow the craziness to go on uncontested. Culturally we have hit rock bottom, when *for God's sake, you've got people fighting to get the monkey taken off the Kellogg's Coco Pops box. The reality is we're fighting too many woke battles that aren't really there!*

oooOOOooo

The majority of Quiet Australians have had enough of the daily hammer blows of political correctness and government control, that dictate what they should think, how they should feel and in what prescribed manner they should live their lives. Before the uncompromising era of political correctness and the restrictive tyranny of Section 18C of the Racial Discrimination Act took hold, decrying and diminishing the right of free speech and the older notion of Australian identity, people were not afraid to openly speak their mind and express an opinion that reflected badly on those in power or their neighbours down the street. It was their inalienable democratic right, courageously defended and selflessly fought and died for by previous generations of Australians.

Unfortunately for many Aussies this is no longer the case. Fear of retaliation from cancel culture has made them wary of exposing themselves to ridicule and condemnation. They fear losing their job, their reputation and their social standing in the community. Nobody wants to be called hateful names and singled out as a pariah. Nobody wants to engage in endless fights over words and past events. Facts don't matter nor apparently does every life matter. The merits of rational argument no longer govern reasoned and informed public debate. Slogan shouting and breast-beating designed to stifle and silence contrary opinion rules the public square.

In coarse Aussie vernacular, the majority feeling about these things can be summed up in the following words — *F*** Off! Let us make the* *decision as to how we should live and conduct our lives. Let us be the arbiters of what we think and say without hindrance, fear or favour from the state or anybody else. We are tired of the constant undermining of our free speech, of the belittling of our history as nothing but racist, evil and a product of white supremacy. Of the unfair muzzling of words and opinions that 'offend' those who would tear everything down, rewrite the past and take us towards a future of group think conformity. Why should we take the knee or be made to feel contrite for the things we and our families personally had no part of? Why should our flag and country be so disrespected? Our children lied to in school on so many important issues, and why should people of the Christian faith be mocked and trolled to the point of persecution? We should celebrate the centuries of achievement of western civilisation not act like petulant children in tearing it down. Who cares if somebody gets offended over everyday words? That's their problem and they should deal with it. Time to stop this divisive nonsense and acknowledge Australia and all of its people past and present as the envy of the world.*

In a public speech delivered at a Jewish charity dinner in April 2021, Prime Minister Scott Morrison voiced the sentiments of many Quiet Australians daily dealing with the ravages of identity politics, cancel culture and social media censorship. *Throughout history, we've seen what happens when people are defined solely by the group they belong to, or an attribute they have, or an identity they possess. The Jewish community understands that better than any in the world. You are more than your gender, you are more than your race, you are more than your sexuality, you are more than your ethnicity, you are more than your religion, your language group, your age. When we reduce ourselves to a collection of attributes, or divide ourselves, we can lose sight of who we actually are as individual human beings in all our complexity, in all our wholeness and in all our wonder. Seeing the inherent dignity of all human beings is the foundation of morality. If you see the dignity and worth of another person, another human being, the beating heart in front of you, you're less likely to disrespect them, insult or show contempt or hatred for them, or seek to cancel them, as is becoming the fashion these days.*

oooOOOooo

The 1950s was not a golden age nor was it a shining beacon of a perfect society. It was however a committed time of law and order, respect for the individual, freedom of speech within the margins of moral decency and national unity for all. Growing up on a Gippsland farm during the 1950s, there was childhood naivety and a straightforward innocence towards the world lost to the modern generation of Aussie kids. Bush children celebrated nature free of dire thoughts of climate catastrophe and species extinction. The climate was the climate, changeable and cyclical. Teachers did not indoctrinate their students in identity, gender or any other kind of politics. The Pioneers and the nation were respected. Children and adults knelt before God and saluted the flag. Eco anxiety, gender dysphoria, racial shaming, cancel culture and virtue signalling were not in the community lexicon. Children felt safe and experienced life with genuine optimism, strong parental guidance and a solid moral upbringing. For children who lived it without personal tragedy and heartbreak. It was the best of times, playful and carefree.

In his 1977 classic song 'And Now I'm Easy' Eric Bogle captures the raw essence, the struggle and the stoicism of farming life in 20th century Australia. Reminiscent of the pioneers, Bogle's words are a powerful testimony to the Aussie spirit of perseverance, endurance and hardiness. What follows is an abridged version of his famous bush ballad.

> *For nearly sixty years, I've been a Cockie of droughts and fires and floods I've lived through plenty. This country's dust and mud have seen my tears and blood but it's nearly over now, and now I'm easy. I married a fine girl when I was twenty, but she died in giving birth when she was thirty. She left me with two sons and a daughter on a bone-dry farm whose soil cried out for water. My daughter married young and went her own way. My sons lie buried by the Burma Railway. On this land I've made me home, I've carried on alone but it's nearly over now, and now I'm easy.*

Our pioneers have a remarkable story to tell: a sadly neglected story of decent, law-abiding and freedom loving people striving for a better life and a prosperous future for their families; a rewarding story of second and third generation descendants fiercely proud of their ancestors and their hard-won achievements. It is a true-life story of personal struggle and collective accomplishment suppressed in schools, universities and the national consciousness: an inspirational story that young people and migrant/refugee Australians need to hear without the rancour of woke politics and a contrived rewriting of the past blaring in their ears. Why shouldn't Australia's pioneers be acknowledged and commemorated? If not for their blood, sweat and tears in building the nation Australia would be a vastly different place than it is today.

Afterword

While this book was going through the publishing process the May 2022 Federal Election was held. The electoral defeat of the Morrison Government came about because of Scott Morrison's personal unpopularity as Prime Minister. More importantly it was an electoral response to a governing party that had lost its way. The Liberal Party was no longer seen to reflect the longstanding beliefs and traditional values of its Quiet Australian base. In trying to be all things to all people net zero, woke and fashionably 'progressive' the Liberal Party squandered the confidence and trust of aspirational hardworking Aussies. The political and moral lesson to be learned is clear. — If you stand for everything then ultimately you stand for nothing.

Australia now has a woke, climate obsessed Albanese Labor Government committed to big government spending, the implementation of green policies and a collectivist agenda. Albanese has not ruled out reinstating lockdowns and people smugglers are already testing Labor's border protection resolve. Next to the Andrews Government in Victoria; it is Australia's most radical left-wing government, power sharing with the Greens and Teal Independents, that in the next 3 years will undermine the economy, interfere with mining and fossil fuel exports, further degrade the nation's power grid and seriously compromise national security. The Labor Party is no longer true to its working class roots, instead it hankers after a woke/green inner-city constituency. The regions and the country in general will suffer a deep-rooted decline as Labor pursues its Socialist/Green/Woke vision. In America there is an overwhelming sense of buyer's remorse at the disastrously inept, economy destroying and ideologically driven Biden administration. Will Aussies feel the same community discontent and buyer's remorse in the crucial months and years to come?

Bibliography of Recent Books

Adamo, Christopher, *Rules for Defeating Radicals: Countering the Alinsky Strategy in Politics and Culture* Adamo (2019).

Alston, Richard, *More to Life than Politics* Connor Court (2019).

Bendle, Mervyn, *Anzac and its Enemies: The History War Against Australia's National Identity* Quadrant Press (2015).

Blainey, Geoffrey, *The Story of Australia's People: The Rise and Fall of Ancient Australia* Viking Press (2015).

Bunker, Bruce, *The Mythology of Global Warming: Climate Change Fiction VS. Scientific Fact* Moonshine Cove Publishing (2018).

Darmangeat, Christophe, *Justice and Warfare in Aboriginal Australia* Lexington Books (2020).

Dershowitz, Alan, *Cancel Culture: The Latest Attack on Free Speech and Due Process* Hot Books (2021).

Donnelly, Kevin, (ed), *Cancel Culture and the Left's Long March* Wilkinson Publishing (2021).

Andrew, Doyle, *Free Speech and Why It Matters* Little, Brown Book Group (2021).

Franklin, James, Nolan, Gerald, Gilchrist, Michael, *The Real Archbishop Mannix: From the Sources* Connor Court (2015).

Friedman, Jonathan, *PC Worlds: Political Correctness and Rising Elites at the end of Hegemony* Berghahn Books (2019).

Forrester, Joshua, Zimmermann, Augusto, (eds), *Fundamental Rights in the Age of Covid-19* Connor Court (2020).

Foster, Gigi, Frijters, Paul, Baker, Michael, *The Great Covid Panic: What Happened, Why, And What To Do Next* Brownstone Institute (2021).

Gergis, Joelle, *Sunburnt Country: The History and Future of Climate Change* Melbourne University Press (2018).

Hamilton, Clive, Ohlberg, Mareike, *Hidden Hand: Exposing How The Chinese Communist Party Is Reshaping The World* Hardie Grant Books (2020).

Hasluck, Nicholas, *Bench and Book* Australian Scholarly Publishing (2021).

Hawley, Josh, *The Tyranny of Big Tech* Regnery Publishing (2021).

Koonin, Steven, *Unsettled: What Climate Science Tells Us, What It Doesn't, and Why It Matters* BenBella Books (2021).

Levin, Mark, *American Marxism* Threshold Editions (2021).

Lopez, Mark, *School Sucks: A Report on the State of Education in the Politically Correct Era* Connor Court (2020).

Lomborg, Bjorn, *False Alarm: How Climate Change Panic Costs Us Trillions, Hurts the Poor, and Fails to Fix the Planet* Basic Books (2020).

Marlow, Alex, *Breaking The News: Exposing the Establishment Media's Hidden Deals and Secret Corruption* Threshold Editions (2021).

Markson, Sharri, *What Really Happened in Wuhan: A Virus Like No Other, Countless Infections, Millions of Deaths* HarperCollins (2021).

Marohasy, Jennifer, (ed) *Climate Change: The Facts 2020* Australian Scholarly Publishing (2020).

Mering, Noelle, *Awake not Woke; A Christian Response to the Cult of Progressive Ideology* TAN Books (2021).

Morano, Marc, *Green Fraud: Why the Green New Deal is Even Worse Than You Think* Regnery Publishing (2021) and *The Great Reset: Global Elites and the Permanent Lockdown* Simon and Schuster (2022).

Morgan, Patrick, The *Settling of Gippsland: A Regional History* Gippsland Municipalities Association (1997) and *Shadow and Shine: An Anthology of Gippsland Literature* Center for Gippsland Studies (1988).

Morgan, Piers, *Wake Up: Why the 'liberal' war on free speech is even more dangerous than Covid-19* HarperCollins (2020).

Moore, Patrick, *Fake Invisible Catastrophes and Threats of Doom* Independently published (2021).

Murray, Douglas, *The Madness of Crowds: Gender, Race and Identity* Bloomsbury Publishing (2019).

Murray, Douglas, *The War on the West* Broadside Books UK (2022).

Ngo, Andy, *Unmasked: Inside Antifa's Radical Plan to Destroy Democracy* Center Street (2021).

O'Brien, Peter, *Bitter Harvest: The illusion of Aboriginal agriculture in Bruce Pascoe's Dark Emu* Quadrant Press (2020).

O'Neill, Brendan, *Anti Woke: Selected Essays by Brendan O'Neill* Connor Court (2018).

Pawle, Fred, *Die Laughing: The Biography of Bill Leak* Australian Scholarly Publishing (2021).

Plimer, Ian, *The Climate Change Delusion and the Great Electricity Ripoff*, Connor Court (2017) and *Green Murder* Connor Court (2021).

Pluckrose, Helen, Lindsay, James, *Cynical Theories: How Activist Scholarship Made Everything About Race, Gender and Identity — And Why This Harms Everybody* Pitchstone Publishing (2020).

Ramaswamy, Vivek, *Woke Inc: Inside the Corporate Social Justice Scam* Swift Press (2021).

Ridd, Peter, *Reef Heresy? Science, Research and the Great Barrier Reef* Connor Court (2020).

Saad, Gad, *The Parasitic Mind: How Infectious Ideas Are Killing Common Sense* Regnery Publishing (2020).

Schellenberger, Michael, *Apocalypse Never: Why Environmental Alarmism Hurts Us All* HarperCollins (2020).

Shelton, Lyle, *'I Kid You Not': Notes from 20 Years in the Trenches of the Culture Wars* Connor Court (2020).

Soh, Debra, *The End of Gender: Debunking the Myths about Sex and Identity in Our Society* Threshold Editions (2020).

Sutton, Peter, Walshe, Keryn, *Farmers or Hunters-gatherers? The Dark Emu Debate* Melbourne University Press (2021).

Thrupp, Jake, (ed), *Australia Tomorrow* Connor Court (2021).

Thomas, Tony, *Foot Soldier In The Culture Wars* Connor Court (2020).

Wrightstone, George, *Inconvenient Facts: The science Al Gore doesn't want you to know* Silver Crown Productions (2017).

INDEX

Aesop 258.

Abbot, Tony 370.

Ackerman, Piers 271-272.

Adams, John 256.

Allen, John 157.

Albanese, Anthony 321, 378.

Alston, Richard 361.

Anderson, John 258

Andrews, Dan 241, 345, 347, 368-369, 371-372.

Antic, Alex 322.

Babbage, Ross 347-348.

Babones, Salvatore 358.

Baio, Scott 233.

Baird, Julia 256.

Baker, Kevin 254.

Ballsbridge, Dublin 91-92.

Bandt, Adam 318.

Barunga, Albert 192-193.

Barton, Emily 118-119.

Bates, Daisy 162, 191, 193.

Bean, William 188.

Bendle, Mervyn 143-144.

Beveridge, Andrew 159-160.

Biles, David 279.

Black, Jeremy 251.

Blainey Geoffrey 10, 153, 156-157, 263-264, 357.

Bogle, Eric 130, 133, 376.

Bolton, Robert 349.

Bradley, William 151.

Bridges, Archie 34.

Bromfield 190-191.

Brothers Robert 185.

Bruce, Mary Grant 47.

Buckley, William Francis 295.

Burns, Raymond 230-231.

Butler, Duncan 139.

Byrne/York Ellen 91.

Byrne, Hugh 91-92.

Byrne, Joe 39.

Byrne, Michael 120.

Byrne/Murray, Theresa 119, 120-129.

Byrne, Winifred 120-121.

Byrne, William 120-121.

Canavan, Matt 316, 321, 356.

Carr, Thomas 109.

Cashman, Josephine 266.

Casterton 116, 120-126, 128, 174.

Cater, Nick 366.

Champion, Rafe 313-314.

Christopherson, Don 160.

Clapham, Suzi 221.

Clarke, Jenna 322.

Clarke, Jidah 197.

Cleese, John 252.

Colangelo, Emelio 288.

Collins, William 148.

Cook, James 143, 216, 328, 355.

Cook, Tom Wills 202.

Crawford, Alex 163-165.

Crosbie, Clara Harriet 54.

Crowley, Peter 188.

Cullin la Ringo 199-202.

d'Abrera, Bella 215.
Dalziell, Anastasia 43-44.
Daniels, Bushy 39, 126-129.
Darmangeat, Christophe 145-146.
Darwin 134, 342, 345, 346.
Dawes, William 328-329.
Dawson, James 158.
Dean, Rowan 249, 304, 319.
Deeming, Moira 229-230.
Dennis, C J 40.
Deves, Katherine 239.
Dexter, Caroline 187.
Dexter, William 189.
Dillon, Anthony 266, 268, 279.
Dinning/Wallace Mary 117-118.
Docker, Fredrick George 159.
Docker, Joseph 158-159.
Donnini, Eugene Alexander 358.
Donavon Teaching Assistant 28, 31.
Doran, Ann 38-39.
Doyle, Andrew 247.
Dow, John Lamont 45.
Dreher, Rod 243-244.
Dunrobin 122-124, 125, 126.
Dutton, Charles 200.
Dutton, Peter 238, 342, 350.
Eddington, John 158.
Elkin, Adolphus Peter 148.
Elliot, William 198-199.
Emerson, Craig 293.
Emerson, Earnest 45.
Evans, George Essex 119.
Eyre Edward John 149.

Faithfull Creek 206-208.
Faithfull, George 208-209.
Fels, Marie Hansen 142, 149-150, 186.
Feutrill, Edward 34.
Fielding School Teacher 27-29,31 105.
Finkel, Alan 308.
Fisher, Anthony 355-356.
Fitzgerald, John 347.
Fitzgibbon, Joel 317.
Flannery, Tim 301.
Fletcher, Michael Shawn 334.
Floyd, George 276-277.
Flyn, Cal 188.
Fowles, Henry 132-133.
Franklin, Benjamin 259.
Franks, Charles 166.
Franks, Tommy 347.
Fraser, David 203-204.
Fraser, John 203-204.
Fraser, Martha 202
Fraser, Sylvester 204-205
Fraser, William 204.
Fryhofer, Sandra Adamson 236.
George, Jennie 317-318.
Georgiadis, Maria 291.
Geraldton 343.
Gergis, Joelle 329.
Gervais, Ricky 252.
Gibber, Jemmy 184-185.
Gibson, William 77-82.
Gippsland 11, 16-18, 21, 31-37, 41-49, 52-53, 61-63, 67-72, 74, 77-78, 82-83, 85, 89, 92-93, 95-96, 137-138, 167, 179-189, 288, 307, 327, 331, 337-338, 376.

Gleeson, Peter 360-361.
Goldberg, Bernard 320.
Graham/Dinning Mary 117-118.
Grant, Stan 154.
Grant, Thomas 168.
Green, George 38-39.
Green, Michael 311.
Greenhill, Mark 257.
Grieve-Williams, Victoria 264.
Gore, Al 300-301.
Grover, Jolene 234.
Gundagai 24, 335-337.
Guterres, António 306.
Hankins, William 292.
Hanson, Pauline 283, 344, 356, 363.
Hare, Francis Augustus 63, 80.
Hasluck, Paul 264.
Hassell, Cleve 157.
Hastie, Andrew 354.
Henderson, Mark 272.
Hoddinott, William 183-184.
Hoddinott, Uriah 183.
Holthouse, Hector 193.
Honeysuckle, Creek 206.
Hornet, Bank 202-205.
Hourigan, John 34-36.
Howard, John 9, 11-12, 153, 220.
Alfred, Howitt 149, 186, 261.
Howitt, William, 330.
Hudson, Frank 60.
Hughes, Robert 148-149.
Hurlston, Dean 257.
Isaacs, Frederick 176.
Jensen, Herbert Christian 65-66.
Johnstone, William 44.

Jolley, Liz 252.
Jones, Colleen 287.
Joyce, Barnaby 311.
Jurskis, Vic 334-335.
Kelly, Ellen 116, 117, 118.
Kelly, Ned 39, 45, 63, 65, 68, 70, 80-81, 94, 102, 116, 195, 364.
Kerkhove, Raymond 167.
Kerr, Jim 137.
Kidman, Sydney 343.
Kirby, James 159-160.
Kitching, Kimberley 342.
Korumburra 18, 23-24, 26, 27, 28, 32, 33, 39, 41, 50-51, 55, 61-67, 69-70, 93, 96, 97, 105, 107, 109, 110, 125, 130-132, 136-138, 140, 288.
Kroger, Michael 361.
Kurti, Peter 250.
Lambie, Jacqui 344.
Latham, Mark 221, 240, 251, 345, 357.
Leak, Bill 9, 252-253.
Leak, Johannes 9.
Lalor, Peter 372.
Lomborg, Bjorn 307-308.
Lawson, Henry 9, 29, 36, 48, 50, 84-85, 89, 98, 116, 257, 282, 325, 326, 372.
Lindsay, James 245.
Linzen, Richard 324.
Little, Rod 270.
Littman, Lisa 239.
Longfellow, Henry Wadsworth 45.
Lopez, Mark 230.
McArthur, Beverley 246.
McGlade, Hannah 267.
McGrath, James 250.
McMillan, Ewen 181.
McMillan, Angus 180-184, 187-189, 335.

Macalister, Lachlan 181, 182.
Macalister, Max Milton 182-183, 191.
Macalister, Ranald 182-183.
MacKay, George 194.
MacPherson, Ellen 163.
Makeham, Sam 132.
Maple, Henry 68-69.
Masson, Michael 315.
Mannix, Daniel 89-91, 99-104.
Marohasy, Jennifer 285, 305.
Maxwell, James 73, 77.
Maxwell, John 72-77.
Maxwell, Hugh 71-75, 77.
Meagher, Edward 137.
Melton, Charles 176.
Mencken, Henry Lewis 259, 324.
Meyrick, Henry 179-180.
Mills, Thomas 85-87.
Mitchell, Krystle 370.
Mitchell, Neil 342.
Mollison, Alexander 194-195, 207.
Moody, George 160.
Morant, Harry Breaker 162.
Morcombe, Bruce 363-364.
Morgan, Patrick 9, 41, 47, 155, 180.
Moore, Patrick 302-303.
Morrison, Scott 265, 293, 310, 320-322, 378.
Morrissey, Cecil (Snowy) 19, 22, 24-27, 32, 36-37, 40, 46, 107-108, 139-140.
Morrissey, Ethel Gladys 38.
Morrissey, James (Snakes) 36-37.
Morrissey/Murray Magdalene, Theresa (Madge) 21-22, 31, 33, 36, 38-40, 56, 89, 93-94, 98, 102, 107, 110, 115, 121, 124-127, 138-140.
Morrissey, Paul 244.
Mulholland, Evan 364-365.

Mundine, Warren 10, 227, 257-258.
Murray, Dermot 136.
Murray, Douglas 244.
Murray, James 121-125.
Murray, William 136.
Nakamura, Mototaka 303-304.
Nelson, Brendan 213.
Newcastle 208, 342-343.
Newman, Maurice 242, 361.
Nicolson, Charles Hope 63, 80.
Nova, Joanne 327.
O'Brien, John 29, 88, 295-296.
O'Brien, Peter 268-269.
O'Neill, Brendan 248, 276.
O'Sullivan, Matt 232.
Obama, Barrack 301.
Orton, Joseph 160.
Orwell, George 212, 250.
Packham, David 334.
Pam, H 131-132.
Parshley, Lois 309.
Pascoe, Bruce 144, 159-160, 178, 227, 268.
Paterson, Andrew Barton 4, 9, 18, 29-30, 61, 71, 83, 105, 118, 154,
Pavlou, Drew 348-349.
Pearson, Noel 260, 273.
Peck, Harry 84.
Pell, George 114.
Perrottet, Dominic 238.
Phillips, Alexandra 276.
Plimer, Ian 298, 305, 317, 321-322, 324.
Polding, John Bede 161.
Pompeo, Mike 351-352.
Port Fairy 158, 163, 173, 174, 175, 203.
Port Macquarie 166, 167, 208.
Praed, Rosa Campbell 176.

Index

Pye, Albert 134-136.
Pye, Mary 135.
Quinn, Roderic 41.
Price Jacinta 10, 215, 274-275, 279-281, 298, 373.
Radovik, Antonio 63-64.
Rawson, Samuel 167, 186-187.
Reece, Bob 157.
Reagan, Ronald 372.
Reid, David 208.
Reynolds, Henry 153-154.
Ridd, Peter 216.
Robinson, George Augustus 143, 185.
Rosner, Gideon 349.
Ross, Alex 262.
Roth, Edmund 192.
Rowling, J K 253.
Rufo, Christopher 248-249.
Sacks, Jonathan 357.
Schmidt, Gavin 304.
Schellenberger, Michael 301-302.
Schulze, Louis Gustave 147.
Scott, Dallas 267-268.
Scott, Robert 208.
Seaview 18, 36, 50, 110, 112.
Seibt, Namoi 302.
Semmler, Clement 118-119.
Sheed, Suzanne 288.
Sheldon, Geoff 272.
Shepparton 287-288.
Sheridan, Greg 312, 316.
Smith, George 176.
Smith, Kirralie 235.
Smith, Robert Brough 191-192.
Smith, William 189-190.
Stanner, William 261.
Steelman, Dick 17.
Strehlow, Ted 146.
Strzelecki, Paul 42, 180.
Strzelecki Ranges 18, 22, 27, 42, 48, 50, 56, 70, 126.
Switzer, Tom 215.
Tambo Crossing 71-73, 75, 76.
Taplin, George 146, 148.
Tench, Watkins 147-148.
Thomas, Tony 186, 228.
Thomas, William 185, 186.
Thunberg, Greta 227, 256, 300, 302, 305, 306.
Todhunter, Colin 319.
Tuckfield, Francis 161, 162.
Tudge, Alan 217, 225, 285.
Vincent, Jacob 195.
Vincent, Mary 195.
Voltaire, Francois Marie 249, 365.
Ward, Arthur 151.
Ward, Roz 234.
Walton, Daniel 310.
Warragal Creek 183-184.
Warragul 18, 27, 44, 53, 61, 65-68, 71, 77, 79-82, 110.
Weaver, J 205-206.
Western District Victoria 169-174.
Wilkie, Joann 238.
Williams, Alan 209.
Wills, Horatio 200, 201.
Wills, Tom 201-202.
Windschuttle, Keith 262-263.
Wilson, Edward 161-162.
Wiseman, William 205.
Yeats, William Butler 92-93, 94, 95, 97.
Young, William 197-198.
Zimmermann, Augusto 267.

www.ingramcontent.com/pod-product-compliance
Lightning Source LLC
Chambersburg PA
CBHW071358300426
44114CB00016B/2100